Lieut.-Col. J. H. CANNAN, C.B., C.M.G., D.S.O.
C. de G. (Belgian), 1914-1918.
Maj.-Gen., Q.M.G., A.I.F., 1939-45.

History

of the

15th Battalion

Australian Imperial Forces

WAR 1914-1918

by

LIEUT. T. P. CHATAWAY

Revised and Edited
by
LT.-COL. PAUL GOLDENSTEDT

The Naval & Military Press Ltd

Published by
The Naval & Military Press Ltd
5 Riverside, Brambleside, Bellbrook
Industrial Estate, Uckfield, East Sussex,
TN22 1QQ England
Tel: +44 (0) 1825 749494
Fax: +44 (0) 1825 765701
www.naval-military-press.com
www.military-genealogy.com
www.militarymaproom.com

In reprinting in facsimile from the original, any imperfections are inevitably reproduced and the quality may fall short of modern type and cartographic standards.

FOREWORD

By

Major-General J. H. CANNAN, C.B., C.M.G., D.S.O., V.D.
Quarter-Master General, Australian Military Forces,
World War II.

The production of the history of the 15th Battalion A.I.F. is long overdue.

Though delayed, its production had to be, in order that a history should be on record of one of the finest Infantry Battalions that ever engaged an enemy.

There was no long tradition or background to this battalion.

It emerged out of the willing response from thousands of Australians prepared to serve Overseas in defence of the Commonwealth and the British Empire.

When moving in ships to Gallipoli on April 25, 1915, many wondered how the battalion would perform, for, like the other units of the A.I.F., the Battalion had no battle honours, although some few of its members had fought in South Africa and in India.

When members of the 15th heard the officers, petty officers, and sailors of the landing destroyers speaking so highly of the bravery and fighting qualities of the men of the earlier battalions who had gone ashore, all ranks were determined to put up a similar good performance.

The battles and exploits of the 15th A.I.F. Battalion told in this history give a modest indication of how well they acted up to the best standards set by its sister units.

Read the chapters on Quinn's Post, Pope's, Hill 971 and Suvla Bay dealing with the Gallipoli operations, and you will feel honoured and proud to have had some association or contact with the 15th Battalion.

Its training in Egypt following the evacuation of Gallipoli and the forming from its ranks of a sister battalion, the 47th, was a test of physical fitness and true discipline. It resulted in the creation of two splendid fighting units.

Then came the real test of an efficient infantry battalion with the fighting that followed in France and Belgium.

Study these pages of the history dealing with Armentieres, Pozieres, Bullecourt, Messines, Paschendaele, the Somme of 1918 to stop the German break through, Hamel, August, 1918, and the operations south of the Somme onwards to victory, and you will find some of the finest and most heroic passages in the history of warfare.

With casualties amounting to 1,195 killed and 2,487 wounded, and a record of never any large numbers of prisoners having been lost to the enemy, a true picture of the fighting qualities of the 15th Battalion is revealed.

I had the honour to command and train the Battalion from its inception in September, 1914.

When I saw and got to know the types that were volunteering for service I was confident of the success of the unit wherever its service would lead it.

When I left the Battalion in August, 1916 to command the 11th Australian Infantry Brigade, it had, by its performances in battle, taken its place with the best fighting battalions of the A.I.F., and that, incidentally, meant with the best infantry battalions of either Allies or enemies.

The command passed to a most able and gallant leader in Lieut.-Colonel Terry MacSharry.

It was with pleasure that I found the battalions of my 11th Brigade fighting on the immediate left of the 15th Battalion at Hamel in July, 1918.

When you read the pages of the history of the 15th, throw your minds back to the days of Peace prior to 1914, and just draw a picture of the contrast. How was it that these volunteers reared and schooled in their peaceful homes in Australia went forth to battle and succeeded so magnificently? The vivid pages telling of the Battalion's exploits will answer the question.

Read again, and carefully, this history, and you will feel a pride and a satisfaction and a realisation that this 15th Battalion was indeed a unit something above the normal standards of a fighting unit such as have been encountered in any world war.

Keep this history ever with you, for in its pages the members of the 15th Battalion come to life, and are vividly before you, and their victories are quietly, soberly and feelingly enjoyed.

ACKNOWLEDGMENTS

I wish to acknowledge with thanks the help given me by Lieut.-Col. J. H. Treloar, M.B.E., and the Staff of the National War Memorial for their unfailing courtesy and practical assistance throughout the whole compilation of this History, during which they made available to me excerpts from the 4th Brigade War Diaries, and photostats of records which would otherwise have been unobtainable by me; to the late Lieut.-General Sir C. B. B. White for the information he so kindly supplied relative to the first three days on Gallipoli; to Major-General (Senator) C. H. Brand for the perusal of the M.S., suggestions given for improvement for same, and data supplied relative to the commencement of the canteen service; to Major-General J. H. Cannan, for correction of certain facts in the Gallipoli Campaign, and for perusal and advice proffered on all chapters until the reliquishment of his command of the Battalion; to Major Burford Sampson for his indefatigable aid in securing data, perusal of the M.S. and encouragement; and to the large number of ex-members of the Battalion and their relatives in Tasmania, New South Wales and Queensland, who have so kindly forwarded private correspondence, photographs and data relative to men who have crossed the Great Beyond. Acknowledgements are also due to Captain C. E. W. Bean for matter obtained from "The Story of Anzac" and the "A.I.F. in France", also to Lieut. the Hon. Staniforth Smith's "Australian Campaigns in the Great War", L. Broinowski's "Tasmania's War Record, 1914-1918", Newton Wanliss' "History of the Fourteenth Battalion", Captain G. Longmore's "The Old Sixteenth", T. A. White's "The Fighting Thirteenth" and Sir Philip Gibbs' "From Bapaume to Paschendaele, 1917."

Thanks are also extended to the magnificent assistance rendered by the Angels Remembrance, 15th Battalion, Club, without the help of which it would not have been possible to publish this history. The Committee of the Club has laboured ever since it was first formed in 1935 to put the story of the Battalion's fighting on Gallipoli and in France on permanent record. Incidentally, for the benefit of outside readers of the history, the name of the Club was derived from the Battalion's code word in France—"ARC". At the annual Anzac Day march, the Battalion has been led by the President ever since the Club was first formed.

T. P. CHATAWAY.

CONTENTS

Chapter.		Page.
	Foreword—Major-General J. H. Cannan	
	Acknowledgments	
	Introduction	
I	The Landing on Gallipoli	13
II	Quinn's Post	25
III	The Turkish Attack on May 19	51
IV	The Heights of Abdel Rahman Bair	67
V	Lemnos Island, The Evacuation and Back to Egypt	96
VI	And This is France	109
VII	Pozieres and Mouquet Farm	115
VIII	St. Eloi and Boorlartbeek	137
IX	Gueudecourt and Lagnicourt	146
X	Bullecourt	161
XI	Messines and Polygon Wood	177
XII	Templeux-La-Fosse and Winter	195
XIII	The Big Push	202
XIV	The Battle of Hamel	211
XV	The Battle of August 8, 1918	218
XVI	Lihu Farm and Jeancourt	225
XVII	Victory and Home	234
XVIII	Postscript	239
	Nominal Roll	243
	Supplementary Roll	293
	Honours and Awards	295
	Deceased Roll	303

INTRODUCTION

The outbreak of war on 3rd September, 1939, necessitated the publication of this history as soon as possible. In view of this fact certain plans originally drafted for the form the history was to take had to be radically changed. It was originally intended to deal exhaustively with the formation of the unit in Australia and its life and training upon the sands of Egypt. All this, however, has been erased and the following brief facts regarding the 15th Battalion's earliest days are given.

The 15th Battalion came into being owing to the large number of recruits offering their services to the Empire during the months of September and October, 1914. The 1st Australian Division was already formed, and in October it sailed for Egypt, there to undergo further training. In all the States of Australia the surplus men remaining in camp were immediately formed into units, and a new Brigade —the 4th Australian Infantry Brigade—was formed. This Brigade ultimately became part of the New Zealand and Australian Infantry Division under the command of Major-General A. Godley.

There are many claimants as to who was the first man enlisted in the 15th Battalion. Among them is Private J. N. Nicholson, of "B" Company, who states that he was placed in a row of empty tents and was there, as far as he can recall, for some days before a body of men marched in and took possession of them. Nicholson claims the honour with Private C. H. Burslem, as both were enlisted on September 9. Private L. C. E. Roppleman of Tasmania, however, is shown as having enlisted on September 5.

Sergeant R. Hunter, of "C" Company, who joined on September 17, claims that there was no 15th Battalion until the Maryborough, Gympie and Toowoomba lads were transferred from the Show Grounds to Enoggera Camp upon the departure of the 9th Battalion for Melbourne, where they joined up with the 3rd Brigade. This seems to be borne out by the fact that no less than 10 officers were appointed to the 15th Battalion on the one day—September 23, 1914. These officers were Captains Cyril Corser, D. H. Cannan, Lieutenants H. Kessel, N. T. Svensen, C. E. Snartt, L. N. Collin, L. G. Casey, T. Robertson and F. Moran. Four days

later Lieutenant-Colonel J. H. Cannan was appointed to command the unit, and the following day Major H. R. Carter was appointed second-in-command. It is therefore safe to assume that the 15th Battalion—or at least the six original Queensland Companies—actually came into existence on September 23, 1914, and all members of the Battalion in the camp at that date can share in the formation of it.

The two Tasmanian companies of the original Battalion were formed in Tasmania in October, 1914, and were the first Tasmanian men to go into the new camp site at Claremont. These two companies, "G" and "H", were commanded by Major Eccles Snowden and Captain H. C. Davies. To each of these companies were attached two junior officers. 2/Lieutenants N. Dickson and A. H. Hinman to "G" Company and Lieutenants J. A. Good and A. Douglas to "H" Company. The two "G" Company officers both lost their lives on Gallipoli Peninsula, Lieutenant Dickson having the dubious honour of being the first officer to be killed on service with the unit. The two "H" Company officers both returned to Australia but have since died in Tasmania. "G" and "H" Companies remained in Tasmania until the month of November when they sailed for Melbourne, and at Broadmeadows Camp joined up with the six Queensland Companies and as a Battalion helped form the 4th Brigade.

On November 22 the six Queensland Companies left by rail for Broadmeadows Camp near Melbourne. The officers commanding the unit were Lt.-Col. J. H. Cannan, in command, with Major H. R. Carter second-in-command. Captain W. O. Willis, Adjutant; Lieut. F. W. Craig, Hon. Quartermaster; 2/Lieutenant B. G. Matthews, Transport Officer; 2/Lieutenant N. O'Brien, Signalling Officer; Captain G. F. Luther, Medical Officer; Captain T. Power, Chaplain; Lieutenant H. Kessels, Machine-gun Officer. The Company Commanders were Captain J. F. Walsh, "A" Coy., with Lieutenant N. T. Svensen and 2/Lieutenant H. P. Armstrong in charge of the platoons; "B" Coy., Captain J. F. Richardson and 2/Lieutenants C. E. Snartt and J. Hill; "C" Coy., Captain C. F. Corser and 2/Lieutenants L. N. Collin and D. S. Freeman; "D" Coy., Captain D. H. Cannan and 2/Lieutenants S. W. Harry and L. G. Casey; "E" Coy., Captain H. Quinn and 2/Lieutenant T. Robertson; "F" Coy., Lieutenant F. Moran in command and Lieutenant L. J. Waters and 2/Lieutenant G. F. Dickinson.

During the stay in Broadmeadows Camp the first officer promotion from the ranks took place. This was Sergeant F. L. Armstrong, a South African veteran. The 1st Reinforce-

ments also joined the Battalion at Broadmeadows under the command of 2/Lieutenant Platt. They numbered about 110 strong and had for their senior N.C.O., C. S. M. Luxmoore, who afterwards obtained his commission on Gallipoli.

In the Brigade Competitions instituted by Colonel John Monash, a platoon of "F" Company under the command of Sergeant Mick Gray won the platoon event. The splendid work put in by Gray to ensure this victory placed him in the running for the vacancy in commissioned rank which was ultimately gained by Sergeant Armstrong. Gray was, unfortunately, rushed to hospital to be operated upon for acute appendicitis and upon his recovery was discharged from the army. It was many months before he again managed to enlist.

On Thursday, December 17, 1914, the 4th Brigade marched through the streets of Melbourne, receiving a remarkable ovation from the huge crowd which lined every vantage point to watch them go by. The salute was taken by His Excellency the Governor-General, Sir Ronald Craufurd Munro Ferguson, on the steps of Parliament House, Spring Street, then the seat of the Federal Government in Australia.

In the early morning of December 22, the 15th Battalion embarked upon S. S. "Ceramic" (A.40) at Railway Pier, Port Melbourne. About the same time the first reinforcements to the Battalion boarded the "Berrima". On the "Ceramic" were the 15th and 16th Battalions under the commands of Lieut.-Colonels J. H. Cannan and H. Pope; the Divisional Ammunition Park under the command of Lieut.-Colonel Tunbridge, and the Divisional Supply Column under Lieut.-Colonel Moon. On the "Berrima" were the 1st Reinforcements for the Brigade and the officers and ratings of the Australian Submarine AE2. It might be recalled that the sister ship to the AE2, the AE1, disappeared off the coast of New Guinea shortly before the outbreak of war. The life of AE2, however, was also of short duration for it was one of the first British submarines to enter the Dardanelles and it was in those waters it met its end, the majority of its crew being taken prisoner by the Turks.

Life on the "Ceramic" was spared from complete boredom by sports of all descriptions. Among the members of the 15th boxing proved the most popular. Two of the best performers in this respect were Sergeant "Scotty" Melia and Private Gordon Smith. A newspaper called the "Honk" was also produced by two members of the D.A.P., Private P. L. Harris, afterwards editor of "Aussie", who was editor, and

Private G. H. Vincent who was styled "The Printer". The first issue was published on the 4th January, 1915. In one issue, the 16th Battalion boasted of their officers and N.C.O's. running the ship, for practically every post from O.C. Troops to Orderly-room Sergeant was held by a member of that Battalion. To this boast the 15th Battalion replied in the issue following:

"Your recent claim to run the ship
Does not our hearts with envy fill.
In fact, when we complete the trip,
We'll let you do the running still."

All ranks were vaccinated during the last days of 1914. The sea was still as a mill pond and the heat daily increased, adding to the discomforts of vaccination. The first death occurred at Aden when the ship arrived on January 20, 1915, when Private C. Robinson, 16th Battalion, a South Australian member, died from pneumonia following on measles. He was buried in Aden Cemetery with military honours the day following. The second death occurred shortly after the ship left Aden on January 23, when Private P. E. Carleton, 15th Battalion, died from pneumonia. He was buried at sea with due ceremony. On January 27 another member of the 15th Battalion died, this time from sunstroke.

Suez was reached in the early morning of January 28, and the first news of the Australians being in action at Kantara, on the Suez Canal, was received. All precautions and defensive arrangements for the safety of the ship and men during the passage up the Canal were taken. At 9 a.m. on the 29th the Canal was entered. At the entrance, three British warships, the "Ocean", the "Himalaya" and the "Minerva", were anchored, and two allied vessels, one French and one Russian.

The ship left Port Said on January 31 and at 8.30 a.m. on February 1 she sailed into Alexandria Harbour. On February 3 the Battalion disembarked and was immediately entrained for Zeitoun, arriving there after nightfall. From Zeitoun to the camp site on the sands outside of Heliopolis was about two miles. This distance was marched at a reasonably slow pace, for the men had not yet got their land legs. Upon arrival in camp the unit quickly settled down and desert life became as familiar to many of the men as the plains had hitherto been. The New Zealand troops forming the major portion of the New Zealand and Australian Division were encamped at Zeitoun, where Major-General Sir Alexander Godley had his headquarters. Adjoining the 4th Brigade lines were those of the 2nd Light Horse (Queensland) Regiment and the troops intermixed after parades were finished.

Immediately upon settling down the new formation for battalions came into force. The original eight companies were formed into four, known as "A", "B", "C" and "D". The two Tasmanian companies "G" and "H" became "D" Company under command of Major Eccles Snowden with Captain Davies second-in-command. "A" Company was made up from "A" and "D" with Captain J. F. Walsh in command and Captain Herman Cannan his second. "B" Company from "B" and "F" with Captain J. F. Richardson commanding and Captain F. Moran second, Captain Moran having but recently been promoted to the senior rank. "C" Company from original "C" and "E" with the "E" Company Commander in charge and Captain C. Corser second-in-command. With this new formation the 1st Reinforcements company was distributed among the three new Queensland companies, and a batch of Tasmanian reinforcements arriving shortly afterwards under the command of 2/Lieutenant B. Sampson, was allotted to "D", and their officer, along with the Queensland officer, Lieutenant Platt, held in reserve. At the same time the ranks of all N.C.O's., which had been temporary only from the date of appointment, were made substantive.

An extensive period of training then set in. It included field days in the desert and route marches of increasing lengths.

On March 22 a Divisional Parade took place at Zeitoun before the High Commissioner, Sir Henry McMahon, General Sir Ian Hamilton and General Sir William Birdwood. On April 2 occurred the riot in Cairo of which so much has been written. This outburst resulted in the Brigade's members being confined to camp until further notice, though it is doubtful whether more than a few of its members took part in the riot.

About 9 p.m. on April 10 the Battalion marched to Zeitoun and entrained for Alexandria where on the following morning "A" and "C" companies embarked on the "Seeang Bee" and "B" and "D" companies, with Headquarters, on the "Australind". The Great Adventure had commenced.

CHAPTER 1.

THE LANDING ON GALLIPOLI

The "Australind" with Headquarters Staff and "B" and "D" Companies of the 15th Battalion on board weighed anchor at 6 a.m. on April 24 and put out to sea. After leaving Mudros Harbour she cruised slowly until within twelve miles of the entrance to the Dardanelles, and there "laid to" with other transports until Sunday morning.

Early after midnight on April 25, together with cruisers, torpedo boats and transports she steamed full-speed ahead for the southernmost tip of the Peninsula. Immediately the convoy reached the entrance to the Dardanelles the ships of the fleet opened a fierce bombardment of the Turkish positions. On the "Australind" were a number of pontoons which were to be utilised in the landing of the English troops at Cape Helles. Arriving off Helles the men upon the "Australind" watched with interest the beaching of the "River Clyde" and the landing of the 29th English Division. Nearby, the flagship of the fleet, the "Queen Elizabeth", hurled shells into the Turkish forts, while the Russian vessel, "Askold", nicknamed by the men the "Packet of Woodbines" owing to it having five funnels, blazed away on the right.

At 11.45 a.m. the "Australind" left the entrance, and steaming up the coast took up her position opposite what is now called Anzac Cove.

Upon the "Australind" were the Battalion's Commanding Officer, Lt.-Col. J. H. Cannan, the Adjutant, Captain W. O. Willis (A & I Staff), its Machine Gun Section under Lieutenant H. Kessels, and its Signalling Section under Lieutenant N. O. O'Brien. There were also "B" and "D" companies commanded by Captain J. F. Richardson and Major Eccles Snowden respectively, while the seconds-in-command to each company were Captains Frank Moran and H. C. Davies.

When the "Australind" was lying off Cape Helles the "Seeang Bee", with the other half of the 15th Battalion—"A" and "C" companies—one company of the 13th Battalion commanded by Captain Hunt, one of the 16th Battalion commanded by Captain Jack Miller, and 150 New Zealand Infantry Brigade reinforcements, put to sea. The Commanders of the two 15th Battalion companies were: "A" company, Captain Jack Walsh and Captain Herman Cannan; and "C"

company, Captain Hugh Quinn and Captain Cyril Corser. The O.C. of the ship was Major Bert Carter, second in command of the Battalion.

The division of the Battalion into two parts made the task of the Commanding Officer incredibly difficult, but it had this merit, that no ship sunk by an enemy submarine or mine, or landing party annihilated when going ashore in the pontoons or cutters, would completely wipe the Battalion out.

The "Seeang Bee's" trip was uneventful, other than the incident of a torpedo boat's kindly crew passing crisp newly-baked French loaves of bread up the side of the vessel. On the Peninsula, before bread became a daily ration, the memory of those crisp brown loaves was awakened when munching at the sixpenny bit iron ration biscuits to quieten the pangs of hunger.

It is rather an astonishing fact that the division of the Battalion should have placed half the unit on what was known as the best "tucker boat in the fleet"—the "Seeang Bee", and the other half upon the "Australind", with the reputation of being the worst. So bad was the food upon the "Australind" that many of the men of "D" company contracted dysentery before landing.

To the majority of our men nothing seemed capable of astonishing them. When we entered the Suez Canal, after our long and tedious sea voyage from Australia, their complete indifference to this mighty engineering feat was astounding. "Why it's not a decent irrigation channel", one man declared in disgust, as he manhandled sandbags to barricade the decks against stray shots from the Turks in the vicinity of the waterway. The Pyramids of Egypt were to some of the men only a heap of stones, while the famous Citadel would have made an excellent top-piece to a bridal cake if done in icing. Off the Peninsula, this apparent indifference outwardly existed. A few of the men took a marked interest in the exploding shells upon the highlands, also in the "River Clyde" with her dropped side, and the "Queen Elizabeth" owing to the size of her shells, but even that interest seemed at times forced. Death stalking the smoke covered ridges, where men were desperately clinging to every vantage point gained, and wounded leaving the shore in boatloads on their way to the only hospital ship and the transports already taking the overflow from it, did not stir them from their habitual air of indifference.

Many took to card playing, as if the spectacle before their eyes was but an imaginative effort of an individual's

brain and not the reality of two nations at war. About them, the smaller craft flitted and chugged. A few men who did take an interest in the general activity, yelled questions to the passing ships—questions that were rarely answered for the voices were lost in the general volume of sound.

To the gamblers, deeply absorbed in their games, war was non-existent. During the long hours of the night, when "C" company awaited the order to go ashore, time whiled away playing cards was probably put to good use, for minds concentrated solely upon poker or in some cases euchre, were at peace. The continuous roar of the heavy guns and the rattle of rifle and machine-gun fire from far up in the hills, could not deprive the players of that oblivion to all but the game before them; nor, could you, from the set faces of the players note any emotion except a fierce glint of pleasure in the eyes of the man who pulled off a palpable bluff, or displaying a full hand, scooped a jack-high pool.

One game of cards invented by Private Harry Byrne, of "C" company (whose fearlessness led to his death at Quinn's on May 9), was of the class to set the bravest of hearts quivering. This game was picking the first man to be killed once the platoon was ashore. It was grim humour, and all eyes watched anxiously as the pack was ostentatiously shuffled, and the cards dealt one by one to a group of players. The first man to receive the Nine of Diamonds—that much abused card with the ominous name of the "Curse of Scotland"—would be the first to lose his life. Card after card fell, then a sigh of relief burst from the greatest part of the players as the fatal piece of pasteboard fell to the lot of young Percy Toft, one of the midgets in the Battalion. That the "Curse" was harmless as a Gypsy's forecast of evil, time showed. He went right through the war.

All minds, however, were not so easily diverted from the chances of death awaiting them. On Lemnos Island a story had been circulated by a naval rating in connection with the landing of some Marines during the first bombardment of the Peninsula by the fleet in the month of February. Men had been sent forward after the bombardment to dismantle the forts. Two landings were made, and according to this seaman, the second landing party recovered the bodies of three men, who had been captured by the Turks, from the first landing party and subjected to death by crucifixion. The very horror of this story, combined as it was with the further information that the Turk made a habit of hamstringing every wounded man who fell into his hands, so as to render such men unfit for further service when healed,

drew our men closer than ever together. Solemn vows were made that should a man lie wounded and a retirement ordered, his friend or the man nearest him would despatch the sufferer.

There are two unauthenticated instances of this happening within the ranks of the 15th Battalion. The first occurred during the hectic retirement from the Turk trenches captured in front of Quinn's Post on the morning of May 10. A fatally wounded man pleaded to be despatched before the enemy re-occupied the line. As his hours were numbered his wish was complied with. The other case occurred during the tragic retirement after the failure to capture Abdel Rahman Bair on August 8. In this case a badly wounded man, crawling slowly towards safety discovered a friend of his past aid. He risked attracting the searching Turks' attention and fired the shot to end the man's life.

While "C" company was indulging in cards or sleeping, or in watching from the ship's rail for vessels coming alongside the transport with wounded aboard, "A" company was engaged somewhere far up in the hills in the foremost part of the fighting line. This company had disembarked about 4 p.m. when H.M.T.B. destroyer "Beagle" pulled alongside the "Seeang Bee" and took off Captain J. Walsh's company and that of Captain J. Miller's of the 16th Battalion. In the short distance to the coast, the destroyer came under heavy shrapnel fire and some of the ship's crew were hit, but curiously enough not one member of the infantry. There were five ship's boats attached to the "Beagle", and when the water became too shallow for the destroyer to get any closer to the land, the troops were transferred to these boats and rowed the rest of the way to the shore.

The landing troops were up to full equipment, with two white bags of emergency rations (iron), an extra 200 rounds of ammunition, wearing caps instead of their broad brim felt hats, while upon the top of the pack was carried a small bundle of firewood. The order to wear caps came after the vessels had left Mudros Harbour. The reason given for the wearing of this headgear was that the men would not be so conspicuous to the enemy as they would in their slouch hats.

The five boats held in all about 80 men or two platoons. No. 2 Platoon under the 1st Tasmanian Reinforcement Officer, 2/Lieutenant Burford Sampson, and No. 4 under Lieutenant Leo Casey, together with the company-commander Captain Walsh, the C.Q.M.S., W. A. Brooks, and the Battalion Armourer-Sergeant R. B. McIntosh, were the

first to go ashore. To some among these lies the honour of being the first men of the 15th Battalion to set foot upon Gallipoli Peninsula. Sergeant N. R. Mighell, No. 2 Platoon's sergeant, was left aboard the destroyer, while in the boats were men from Nos. 1 and 3 Platoons, one of whom was Private Jack Fleet. The men left aboard the destroyer were under the commands of Lieutenants N. T. Svensen and Sam Harry. It was from the party in the boats the first casualty in the 15th came, Cecil Rush of No. 4 Platoon, being hit on the head with a shrapnel pellet just as the boat reached the shore. When the two platoons of "A" company went ashore they were met by Colonel W. G. Braithwaite, a Staff Officer of the N.Z. and Australian Division, who exclaimed to Captain Walsh: "For God's sake hurry, Sir. They are giving way on the left!" Walsh, whose coolness and ability for leadership were very soon displayed, was not moving off without a guide. He gave orders to seek shelter beneath an overhanging bank until he found someone from whom to obtain definite instructions. While Walsh was searching for an informant, Casey and Sampson's men collected some picks and shovels and a case of ammunition so as to be ready for any emergency.

A few minutes after Colonel Pope arrived upon the scene with his 16th Battalion, and meeting Walsh said, "We're off to the firing line. Tack yourself on to me." Walsh did so, and the column of men trailed along the beach, and turned up Shrapnel Gully until they came to what was afterwards known as Monash Valley. At this point the 15th men shed their packs, and were drafted into a section of the line now called Courteney's Post. It was then just on sunset. Pope's men meanwhile continued up Monash Valley to the higher ground which afterwards bore his name.

When Walsh and his men entered Courteney's it was not in the true sense of the word a post at all. There was a short section of trench that had evidently been built by the Turks during their retirement, for its depth was scarcely three feet and it was not quite twenty yards in length. The position was commanded by Captain Chester of the 3rd Battalion, who had with him several other officers including Lieutenant Huegh, afterwards killed, of the 1st Battalion. Its personnel consisted of men from the 1st, 2nd, 3rd, 4th, and 12th Battalions. On the right flank were some men under the command of Major Lamb, practically all of whom were 3rd Battalion. Orders were received from time to time by Walsh from Lamb, but owing to the distance separating the two men, Walsh was compelled to act at most

times on his own initiative. The picks and shovels brought from the beach proved of exceptional help. Casey's No. 4 Platoon was ordered in on the left and Sampson's No. 2 on the right, enclosing in much of what to-day is known as Steele's Post.

Captain Walsh's genius for soldiering asserted itself the moment he took control of his sector of the line. He not only commanded the mixed assortment of men from the various units he found there, but some New Zealanders also who found their way to the place. Scrubby undergrowth grew profusely about the position and to its left front ran a gully, known later as Mule Gully. The men were set to work digging a system of trenches, and volunteers were called to form a screen well out in front for the purpose of giving plenty of warning of any attempt by the enemy to approach the line under construction. Two of the first men to volunteer were Sergeant Tom Dann and Private Fred Hanley, and throughout the whole of the Gallipoli campaign these men were ever to the fore when things were at their worst. They both had an incurable habit of volunteering for anything that spelt danger. Sufficient volunteers having been obtained, 2/Lieutenant Sampson was placed in command of the screen and immediately took his men out and placed them in position. This screen remained out throughout the night. Several attempts were made by the Turk to penetrate it but on each occasion they proved fruitless.

It was during this first night that the sound of digging was heard on the left flank and slightly forward of the position Walsh was occupying. Upon receiving this report from Sampson he ordered him to find out who the men were. Sampson took with him Sergeant Ray Tickner and cautiously the two made their way across the gully until on the ridge they discovered a digging party. The party naturally took the two men for Turks and opened fire upon them, luckily failing to cause any casualties. Upon making themselves known to the digging party they discovered it was commanded by Captain Jacobs, of the 1st Battalion, and a New Zealand officer. With these two officers were a a few New Zealanders and Australians. They were digging-in on the side of the ridge with their entrenching tools in the spot afterwards too well known to the 15th Battalion as Quinn's Post.

The New Zealand officer accompanied Sampson and Tickner back to Walsh and endeavoured to influence him to give some men for the construction of the post. Walsh

promised to speed all the work up upon the left flank in an endeavour to get as close as possible to Jacob's position by morning. While Walsh was busy with two platoons in Courteney's the other two platoons of "A" company had landed, reaching shore about 6 p.m. There had been a slight delay in their going ashore but no time was lost in marching them up Shrapnel Gully to the Pope's Hill position, and upon arriving there they were immediately told to return to the beach and marched straight back the way they came. At nightfall they were sent on to the right flank, where within sound of the waves they immediately started digging a line of trenches. When daylight came Lieutenant Harry and his Sergeant, Bill Mundell, indulged in the choicest of language, for their instructor of the night before had for some inexplicable reason ordered them to build trenches facing the sea.

About 6.30 p.m. "D" company went aboard a destroyer and after steaming about for a short time was finally put ashore about dusk. The officers landing with "D" were Major Eccles Snowden, his second-in-command Captain H. C. Davies, and Lieutenants J. Good, A. Douglas, N. Dickson and A. G. Hinman in charge of the four platoons. Many of the "D" company men were ill with dysentery and for this reason the company could not be worked too strenuously to commence with, so they employed themselves collecting ammunition until almost midnight, when orders were received for the company to reinforce the Third Brigade under General MacLagen on the position known as Razorback.

One thousand rounds of extra ammunition was supplied to every two men, immediately following which they marched up Shrapnel Gully to the point where they scaled the side of the gully gaining the high ground of this narrow feature. There they were met by an officer who told them the Turks were massing for an attack down in the gully to their immediate front. As the company had not the slightest idea where the front line was inquiries were made from men lying about in shallow funk holes as to their true position. To their astonishment they were told they were actually standing upon the front line. The disintegration of the company as a whole then took place. A Third Brigade officer called for a sergeant and twenty men to reinforce his right flank. Sergeant J. J. Corrigan and twenty men were sent along. The other platoons were drafted here and there and everywhere and it was not until the Monday afternoon, when General Bridges appeared upon the scene and ordered an advance, that many of "D" company saw familiar faces again.

Corrigan and his men moved forward with the unit they were attached to and after the charge found that No. 16 platoon, Lieutenant Hinman's, was visible to them on their right flank.

In the meantime, during the Sunday evening, Colonel Cannan and his headquarters staff had landed and established their position at the head of Shrapnel Gully, almost directly behind Courteney's and Steele's Posts. While "D" company was on the beach "B" company, under Captains Richardson and Moran, landed at 8 p.m., two destroyers bringing them in and transferring them into lighters. The platoons were in command of Lieutenants C. E. Snartt, G. F. Dickinson, L. J. Waters, and Sergeant Maurice Little. Owing to the Transport Officer, Lieutenant B. G. Walsh, being left behind sick in Egypt, Lieutenant Jack Hill, who commanded the platoon, was detailed to look after the Transport. Hill's platoon was the only platoon in the Battalion which landed without an officer.

Lieutenant B. G. Matthews did not return to the unit, and was transferred to Colonel V. C. M. Sellheim's staff in Cairo and afterwards in Horseferry Road, London.

Upon reaching the beach, "B" company was sent up Shrapnel Gully, and climbing up the high country to the right, an order was given to fix bayonets and clear the ridges of the enemy. This first charge of "B" company's was a bloodless one for the Turks had already evacuated the position. They were then set to work digging a supporting line directly behind the front line. During the construction of this they came under heavy rifle fire and a number of casualties resulted. When "B" company moved forward to the position they were now occupying—the right flank of the line extending along the Razorback—a platoon was left on the beach near Fisherman's Hut, and told to dig in and make shelters in the cliff for the night. This platoon remained there until daylight, when it moved out from the cliff down to the beach. They had barely stepped clear of their possies when Turkish batteries opened out and their shells blew the tin and other material used in making the shelters, skywards. One youngster, Private H. A. Bennett, was so affected when he saw his bedroom going up into the air that he fainted. He quickly recovered, however, and afterwards proved himself one of the gamest men in the company.

Upon leaving the beach they went past Fisherman's Hut, carrying full equipment and a box of ammunition to each two men. During this journey the Turk shrapnel pelted them continuously and caused a number of casualties. The

first man to be wounded was Private "Wally" Rose, who glancing back at a bursting shell, received a shrapnel pellet in the right temple. The pellet passed through his head and he spat it out of his mouth. Some Royal Army Medical men, who were nearby at the time, realised the seriousness of Rose's wound and compressing the temple artery, which had been severed, stopped the flow of blood and saved his life. Private M. J. Bailey was another man hit on this march, receiving part of the casing of a shrapnel in his nether quarters. Private M. J. Bailey returned to the unit and served continuously until the last battle in France, when along with some of the original men, including Corporal Gordon Smith, he met his death.

Before going any further with "A", "B" and "D" companies it is necessary to trace the doings of "C" company from early Monday morning. At 10 a.m. H.M.S. Destroyer "Usk" came alongside the "Seeang Bee" and took off the greater part of the company. Much shelling took place while the destroyer and its three hundred men approached the shore. One shell, bursting above the ship, injured some of the sailors but the infantry escaped hurt. After transferring to the pontoons there was further shelling, and a pellet from one burst hit Private W. Spiers on his collar badge in such a manner that the Rising Sun badge closed around the leaden ball holding it securely in a setting which could scarcely be improved upon by a jeweller. Spiers carried this memento with him until the end of the war, and peculiarly enough, it was the only occasion that his life seemed to be really threatened, for he served throughout unscathed.

Upon getting ashore the company was met by the Battalion Quartermaster, Lieutenant Fred Craig, who had landed the night before with Colonel Cannan and his headquarters staff. An extra bandolier of cartridges was handed out to every man, making in all 350 rounds per man. After a hasty meal, the company moved forward in file up Shrapnel Gully to a point behind Courtney's Post, where Headquarters now was. Streams of wounded filed past them on their way up and intermittent shell fire was encountered. Following behind "C" company came the platoon of "B" that had been left upon the beach all night. When the column arrived near to Battalion Headquarters it was halted, and Captain Hugh Quinn went to Colonel Cannan for instructions. Quinn had barely gone when Colonel C. B. B. White ordered Captain Corser to take the men up on to the high country.

Corser acted immediately and two platoons, Nos. 11 and 12, under the commands of Lieutenants D. S. Freeman and Leslie Collin, moved on past an Indian mountain battery that was firing shots at frequent intervals toward the Turk position. It was while climbing this steep hillside that the first casualty in "C" company occurred. A young chap, Private J. W. Henderson, who shared with Private G. S. Rogers the honour of being the youngest man in "C" company, both being 18 years of age, had his ear drums broken when he passed in front of the mountain battery just as it fired. Captain Corser, who was seriously ill just before leaving Egypt for Gallipoli, was still far from well and had to be aided up the steepest parts. At the top of the rise the men kept under cover waiting for the order to advance. Freeman's platoon occupied the right flank and Collin's the left.

While the "C" company's platoons were awaiting their order to advance, the whole line upon the Razorback was also preparing to go forward a distance of some four hundred yards. This general move forward, which embraced both "B" and "D" companies, some men from the 9th Battalion and the greater portion of the 3rd Brigade, took place at 4 p.m. "B" company in the charge took its objective with ease, which proved to be a line of very shallow trenches. In this advance Captain Richardson was wounded, and the command fell to Captain Frank Moran. Besides Richardson wounded, Private Dave Gillies received two wounds from shrapnel fire, and during the deepening of the position won a regular string of casualties occurred.

"D" company was occupying shallow trenches stretched across a ridge in fairly open country with a slight hollow immediately in front and facing another ridge covered with scrub though not supposed to be occupied by the enemy. This company was subjected to an enfilading fire from shrapnel throughout the day. About 5 p.m. General Bridges instructed the men to move forward and occupy the next ridge. Lieutenant N. Dickson, who had with him Sergeants J. J. Corrigan, G. S. Williams, W. Ellis and Privates F. G. Gale and L. C. F. Lenders, immediately rose to carry out the order when he fell mortally wounded. Deprived of their officer, but still under the command of an officer belonging to the 2nd Brigade, the men moved forward and occupied the position allotted to them without much difficulty.

Sergeant W. Ellis, who was with Lieutenant Dickson at the time, writes:—
"During the afternoon we came under shrapnel fire which did no harm, and at about 5 p.m. a Staff Officer rushed up and instructed

us to advance and occupy the next ridge. Lieutenant Dickson, who had been lying next to me all day, rose on his knees to put his equipment on, and immediately fell forward on his face saying, 'I'm done, Sergeant'. I crawled to him, but could see no sign of a wound, and he was in such agony that he was unable to tell me where he was hit. The line then had not moved and I sang out and asked the officer in charge if I could carry Dickson down, and he answered yes. I called Private Gale and we laid down on either side of Dickson, who was lying forward on his face, and we got him up and carried him back, being heavily fired at from the left flank. As soon as we got under a bit of cover, we examined Dickson to see what had happened to him, and found a small puncture in his stomach evidently caused by a rifle bullet. As we could do nothing for him we carried him further down the gully and handed him over to an M.O. . . . . . I might say that on our way back to the line, we met some troops coming back in some disorder, and Private Gale was wounded in the arm by a shrapnel pellet which severed an artery. I fixed him up with his first field dressing and with assistance took him back to the same doctor who attended Dickson."

With the "C" company men a complete misunderstanding occurred. A Staff Officer appeared on the high ground and is alleged to have instructed Freeman to advance immediately. Another Staff Officer is stated to have countermanded the order for advance and informed the waiting men that they were to stay in the position they occupied as supports for the front line. Whatever was the real intention of those in command will never be known. Lieutenant Freeman took it upon his own shoulders to order his platoon into action and jumping out, the platoon, working in sections, began to cross the flat country lying between the front line and the gully. They immediately came under heavy machine gun and shrapnel fire. Lieutenant Collin, who had heard the countermanding order, had passed down the line to discover what was intended, and during his absence Sergeant-Major A. Marshall, seeing Freeman's platoon moving in front of him, gave orders for No. 12 Platoon to advance in sections, thus conforming with the general plan. No. 12 hopped out under this N.C.O's. command, and in turn was subjected to a heavy fire. The two platoons advanced with machine-like precision against a hail of lead until in short dashes they arrived within a few yards of the line recently captured. There they lay subjected to the full blast of concentrated fire, unable to get into the front line because it was already overcrowded, and without any orders to retire under cover.

It was not known until afterwards that some of the men in No. 11 Platoon, learning of the countermanding order after the advance began, started to retire in compliance with it, but some of the platoon advanced still farther, and two of them, Private Percy Toft and Sergeant Bob Hunter, of No. 12 Platoon, who had been the connecting link between the two platoons, entered the front line. In front of No. 12 Platoon, the men of which were ignorant of what was hap-

pening, the men in the line kept urging them to go back, as there was no room in the trench for them. The shortening of the enemy's range at this stage began to cause casualties, when suddenly Lieutenant Freeman arrived on the scene, wandering across the area as if there wasn't a Turk within a thousand miles. This intrepid officer calmly stood in the line of men stretched out across the open, until Marshall in a rage urged him to get down and not give the Turks the range. Freeman would not, but started to walk along the line telling the men to retire. With his departure the platoon, working in sections, made the journey back to the gully with the loss of but a few men.

In "The Story of Anzac", the Official Historian, Dr. C. E. W. Bean, says: "Some of the 15th were found retiring, not in panic, but apparently on some order. The 9th and 10th went in with them and formed the line in front."

Back in the gully the men began to sort themselves out. Some twenty members of No. 12 Platoon came under the command of Lieutenant Frank Armstrong, of No. 9 Platoon. Lieutenant Collin took command of all the men around him, and Lieutenant Freeman wandered about the open for some time after the retirement collecting most of his own platoon and a few men belonging to other platoons. The men didn't care a rap whom they served under so long as they were at an officer's call, so some semblance of order was regained. The casualties in this mix-up are not known, but they were considerable. One of "C" company's wounded was the well-known Private "Tiger" Henry.

The transportation of the wounded to the beach was in itself a nightmare, even when stretchers were available to carry the men, but when as in the case of Sergeant Little's platoon, the men were detailed off to carry wounded by means of an oil sheet the task was a tremendous one. The wounded lay everywhere and as it was essential to get them out of the exposed area as swiftly as possible, oil sheets had to be used. The case of two men's journey—Privates Ralf Reid and Wally Mant—will give some idea of the difficulties associated with carrying of a helpless man upon an oil sheet. Reid and Mant were given a very badly wounded man, and starting on their journey, sliding and slipping down the steep hillside, their hands continually cramping from the insecure hold upon the corners of the sheet, the heavy shrapnel fire continuously bursting above them, and the persistent urge to halt—if only for a few seconds so as to ease the cramp in their hands—made the journey one long agony. The two men had not even the satisfaction of afterwards knowing that the man lived, for he died a few moments after they

arrived upon the beach. No praise can be too great for the work of the regimental doctors and their medical staff, including the company stretcher-bearers, on this afternoon. Doctors Luther (15th) and Butler (9th) were both, at various times, in the front line attending the wounded, but it was the remarkable coolness of these two men wandering across the open and succouring the wounded lying exposed to the enemy's fire that awoke within the men a feeling of admiration and instilled a confidence into the fighting men that whatever befell them, aid would always be at hand.

During the Monday night, "B" and "D" Companies dug frantically so as to have as much cover as they could by daybreak on Tuesday morning. It was during the early part of the night a cry was heard continually coming from in front of "D" Company's position. So insistent became this call for help that a patrol was ordered out under Lance-Corporal J. Brooks. The men in the trench were rather dubious about cries such as these, for during the early night a voice had spoken to the men in the trench asking them in the best English to surrender. In one section held by "B" Company, it was stated some Turks approaching the position of the trench, and quite unaware that the company was there, stopped when halted by the English command, and turned and addressed the men in English. German officers had also been noticed during the day speaking to the Turks, and some of these officers are said to have daringly approached the line and called out in English to the lads holding it. So the sound of an English voice from No Man's Land was not an uncommon one. Brooks brought in a member of the 9th Battalion who had been lying wounded between the two forces since the Sunday.

Throughout the night of April 26, in other parts of the line, and in the vacant spaces directly behind the front line, badly wounded men were discovered. Behind the 3rd Brigade lines on the Razorback, in a small hollow in the ground, were a considerable number of the fallen whom the burial parties had not been able to reach. Among these a badly wounded man lay. This man's companion, who was in the front line immediately forward of this position, had constructed a rude shelter out of the bodies lying around, to shade his mate from the heat of the day. Two members of "C" Company, 15th Battalion, discovered the wounded man and, making a stretcher from their rifles and puttees, took him to the nearest dressing station. In front of Courtney's post where "A" Company men were scattered among a collection of various units, two men were rescued some two hundred yards

in front of the position. This rescue was effected by Private Joe Westaway and another man whose name has been forgotten. Westaway, who was a big man, and the other who was very small, started off in the direction of the cries, and the first wounded man they found was some six feet in height and heavily built at that. This chap coolly suggested that the two men should leave him where he was and rescue the other man instead. So they left the big man and walked on to the other chap who was of medium build. Westaway loaded his companion up with the smaller man and then went over to the big chap and carried him in.

During the late hours of Monday, April 26, to No. 10 Platoon under Lieut. Tom. Robertson which did not participate in the fighting upon the Razorback, but was in support to the troops holding the line behind Johnston's Jolly, came disaster. An officer, now believed to have been a German in the guise of an English Engineer Major, approached Lieut. Robertson, and asked him if he belonged to the 15th Battalion. Upon receiving an assurance that Robertson did, he then exclaimed: "Colonel Cannan said you were to go with me!" Suspecting nothing, Robertson detailed the number of men the "Major" required for the party and, leaving Sergeant S. L. Stormonth in charge of the remainder of the platoon, followed the stranger.

With no knowledge of the country, the party quite unsuspectingly passed through the front line into No Man's Land, and being shown a position were told to dig a line of trenches. The "Major" then left them and the lads, setting to work with a will, were down a little more than four feet by daylight. Some time after daylight, a Turk officer walked over to the trench and pointed out to the occupants that they were surrounded on three sides and had better surrender. Robertson said: "No!" and firing his revolver into the Turk, gave the order for his men to get back as quickly as possible. When the men started their run back they found nearly two hundred yards of country ahead of them. The enemy's machine guns opened fire, and seven men only managed to reach the Australian line. Robertson's tall form was last seen to dodge behind a clump of bush, where he stopped and turned as if to see how his men were faring. The seven men who survived the trap were Corporal W. H. Nicholls, Privates Stan Cousens, H. Cooper, A. J. Small, R. T. Owens, H. L. L. Smith (who was badly wounded), and F. J. Merrell, who had an astonishing escape from death. Merrell had a bandolier slung across his back, and when half-way home a machine-gun bullet struck the bandolier, and cartridge after cartridge exploded, luckily inflicting only slight

injuries. Two of these men, Corporal Nicholls (who was afterwards killed in France), and Private Jack Merrell, were to receive their commissions at a later date.

H. L. L. Smith, who was shockingly wounded in this retirement, with a bullet in each thigh, a smashed shoulder and a bullet through the lungs, forwards the following version of what happened. The other version was supplied by Stormonth, who stated he was with Robertson when the order arrived, and the other details were supplied to him by Nicholls and others, after the incident:—

> "About dusk on the night of 26/4/15, Mr. Robertson and 28 volunteers were asked to go out on outpost duty, and were taken out to the position by a Staff Officer—a big, stoutly built, florid, light-haired man. When just in front of our lines I overhead Mr. Robertson ask: 'Is this an order from H.Q.?' and the Staff Officer replied, 'Yes,' and then proceeded to take us out. We went out to the S.E. edge of Johnstone's Jolly, overlooking Legge Valley, and dug a shallow circular trench around a small rocky knoll, just over the edge of the Jolly. I should say from memory, about eight feet below the level of the Jolly. We stayed there that night, and waited till daylight, when we were supposed to be relieved, but no one came. In the meantime we had been exchanging shots with Turks on our left front, and had been getting the best of it. The Turks then opened up with a couple of machine-guns from about opposite to us, and this kept our heads down, but did not stop some of the men from the back of the knoll spotting a company of Turks advancing up Legge Valley on our left. Still covered by intense machine-gun fire, the enemy advanced until opposite and just below us, and spread out in a half-moon shape, when the machine-gun fire stopped. A Turkish officer jumped up level with us and called upon Mr. Robertson to surrender. Now, while keeping low under the intense machine-fire, Mr. Robertson had summed up the position, and he told us we were in a tight corner, and that when the machine-guns stopped, to fire three rounds rapid at the enemy and then bolt for our lines. If any man dropped two men were to pick him up and take him to safety. When the Turk officer called upon Mr. Robertson to surrender, he said: 'Surrender be damned,' and shot the Turk officer with his revolver. Then hell broke loose, and as we had to climb up the slope we were exposed to the enemy machine guns as well as rifle fire. We temporarily checked the enemy when we opened fire, but not for long, and most of us were either killed or wounded. I do not think Mr. Robertson ever left the trench alive, but whatever happened he certainly did not get anywhere near the line."

Anyone who recalls the front line to the right of Courtney's Ridge on the Monday night will remember the ridiculous orders that were continually passing from mouth to mouth throughout the whole line. Such messages as the British force at the southernmost point of the peninsula had gained considerable ground and was actually to our front, or the message that this force was about to attack and so that no accident should occur, all magazines were to be emptied and bayonets alone fixed, and whatever we did we were not to fire under any consideration, and the many other orders which, unfortunately in some instances, were obeyed. It was not, however, until about 2 a.m. that an order which at last appeared authentic came along the line. This order

read: "No orders to be taken notice of except those actually written by the officer commanding." About 4 o'clock rumour had it an interpreter was caught speaking to the enemy and he was to be tried and shot at daylight. Whether this was true or not we did not learn, but the continuance of the stream of orders ceased about this time.

Monday night had been a scene of activity throughout the whole front. On Courtney's and Steele's Post sectors attacks had been launched by the Turks, none of which seriously menaced our men, but on the Razorback information had leaked through that the Turks intended attacking in force at daylight. The "C" Company men, under Lieutenant Frank Armstrong, had been utilised constructing saps towards the front line from the head of the Gully. These men were down some four feet or more by daylight, but in places the trench was so shallow that it afforded no cover whatsoever. With the break of day, this party came under heavy enfilading shrapnel fire, and Armstrong had the perilous job of conducting his men from the position they were in back to the Gully with its shelter in the overhanging banks. After the loss of some eight men this was done. But, with the front line men, daylight found them in shallow trenches and subject to a partial enfilading fire from shrapnel and machine-guns. It was evident that the Turks did not know exactly where the earthworks were. Small scrubby trees were plentiful, but on "B" Company's left front was a clearing about a quarter of an acre in size. Across the Gully on this front the country rose again to another height, and in this area was the Turk. During the day the whole peninsula was subjected to an intense bombardment, consisting mainly of shrapnel, though high explosive was used by the two Naval vessels, "Goeben" and "Breslau," which were participating in the battle from the Asiatic side of the Peninsula and whose shells, coming from a long distance, were easily distinguishable from those of the guns nearer to hand. In Shrapnel Gully shells burst continuously. Just on sunset the expected attack took place upon the whole front. Bugles commenced blowing and, with the evident intention of deceiving our men, the Turkish buglers played the various calls of the British Army—most of them quite incorrectly—and, to the astounded troops listening to the musicians, such a call as "Come To The Cookhouse Door" was mixed up with the "Reveille" and the "Charge."

Captain Frank Moran, who throughout this day had displayed such courage and shown such consideration for his men that he became widely known as "the little mother,"

warned his men not to fire until the Turks were close to them. So well did the men under his command obey his orders that a Turk actually stood upon the parapet exclaiming, "Me Injun'" before he gave the order for battle. Into the dense mass of Turks the men opened fire. Machine-guns joined in and the guns of H.M.S. "Orion," standing close in under the lee of the land, opened fire with shrapnel at close range. The attack faded away along the whole front, and when calculations were afterwards made it was estimated that over 3,000 Turks were lost in the engagement.

It was during this Tuesday (April 27), when the bombardment of the Peninsula was at its height, that Captain Jack Walsh met his death. Tireless and cool under the most trying circumstances, he gave inspiration and initiative to all with whom he came into contact. On this afternoon, with field glasses to his eyes and in the company of Lieutenant Sampson, he was attempting to locate an enemy machine-gun that was causing a number of casualties among his men, when a sniper's bullet passed through the right lens and penetrated his brain. Captain Walsh was promoted to Major a short time before his death, and was one of the gallant leaders who, falling early in the fight, has received practically no recognition for his work. There was not a member of his company who did not feel that his name should have been perpetuated in the Post he had done so much to construct. Although his active service life was but a few days, the men who served under him vividly recall him to their minds as one of the finest company commanders the 15th Battalion ever had. He was a combative leader, and contained in his rather slim form that essential driving force that compels men to give of their utmost, even when at the last stage of physical and mental exhaustion.

It was after the death of Walsh that some 16th Battalion men, commanded by Major V. F. B. Carter and Lieutenant Mountain, came to the post. Unfortunately, both of these officers were killed within twenty-four hours and were buried in the same grave as Major Walsh, Private Paddy Byrne and another 15th Battalion man, Sampson, reading the burial service over the grave. Before leaving the post, it is necessary to make reference to two of the men who did considerable work during its construction—the two Byrnes. They were both Englishmen but, not as many thought, brothers, Paddy Byrne had proved himself as a daring and resourceful soldier, besides being a willing and energetic worker during the entrenching. H. H. Byrne, better known as "Nosey," who died from his wounds on May 4, was the Sandow of the company. Byrne carted nine boxes of ammunition up from

the beach to Courtney's on the Tuesday night. No mean feat this when the distance was practically a mile and the weight of each box 80 lb.

Amongst other men in this post were the two Danns—Sergeants Tom and Frank. Tom received his commission at a later stage with the Battalion. He was wounded three times on the Peninsula when with the 15th, and twice in Flanders when serving with another unit. Frank was wounded on the Peninsula and finally lost his life with the unit at Pozieres. Another member of the post was old grumbling Fred Stacey, a South African and Matabele war veteran, whose continual grumbling quickly became a source of amusement to his friends. Then there was Lance-Corporal Keith Watson, who afterwards lost his life on Pope's Hill; Roy Tickner, who received his commission and lost his life with another unit in France; A. T. Wertheimer, who also obtained a commission and lost his life with the 12th Battalion on Broodseinde Ridge; Jack Fleet, a D.C.M. and French Medal Militaire winner; the tall Belgian, F. G. J. M. Dubios, who lost his life in August; Paddy Lennan, who gave his life for his friends at Gueudecourt in France; Corporal Vidgen commissioned at a later date and killed in August; J. P. N. Price, the inveterate sniper, who bagged many a Turk until a Turk bagged him; and the well-known Lance-Corporal "Scotty" Wright, who, with Staff-Sergeant-Major Corbett, received the first D.C.M. in the Battalion. All these men worked like Trojans and, when relieved on the Thursday by the Royal Marines Light Infantry, left the trenches they had built some five feet deep, with firesteps and rude shelters—a position which in time became almost impregnable.

On Wednesday, April 28th, an effort was made to bring all the stray men from the various units back under their proper commands. Slips of paper were sent along the front lines, and to them the names of first one unit, then another, were applied until the exact number of each battalion was known. Word was then passed along for the different units to filter out of the system of trenches to stated collecting points. The men of the Razorback were to gather on the beach and, to some of "A" Company at Courtney's and Steele's Posts similar instructions were sent. The "A" Company men who did journey to the beach were immediately chased back to the line by the beach officers, who would not listen to what the men said. "C" Company came out under their own leaders and remained on the beach for the night. "B" Company also filtered out along with "D." Privates P. Toft and S. M. Bentzon, of "C" Company, failed to locate "C" upon the beach and passed up the Gully to Pope's Hill

OFFICERS OF THE ORIGINAL 15th BATTALION.

STANDING: Capt. J. Richardson, Lt. Matthews, Capt. D. H. Cannan, Lt. L. R. Collins, Lt. L. G. Casey, Lt. T. Robertson, Capt. J. N. Walsh, Capt. Hughie Quinn, Lt. Platt, Lt. C. E. Snartt.
SECOND ROW (Sitting): Lt. Kessell, Major H. R. Carter, Lt.-Col. J. H. Cannan, Capt. Guy Luther, Capt. Cyril Corser, Capt. F. W. Craig, Lt. Griffiths.
FRONT ROW: Lt. J. Hill, Lt. Svenson, Capt. F. Moran, Lt. Sammy Harry, Lt. F. L. Armstrong, Lt. G. F. Dickinson, Lt. L. G. Freeman.
MISSING FROM THIS PHOTOGRAPH: Lt. Waters, Lt. Hill (Duntroon), Billy Willis (Adjutant A. and I. Staff), Major Snowden, Capt. Davies, Lts. Douglass, Goode, Dickson and Newman (all from Tasmania).

F. COY., 15th BATTALION.

WINNERS 4th BDE. CHAMPIONSHIP SECTION DRILL.

STANDING: Capt. F. Moran, Col./Sgt. Weston, Corp. Cummins, Ptes. D. Gillies, A. D. Brown, G. Hawkes, W. Hardaker, Sgt. Gray, Pte. R. McAndrews, A. B. Shrubb, L/Corp. Sidney, Lts. Waters and Dickinson.

KNEELING: Ptes. Jones, Avery, E. Hanman, Bardon, R. Cott, L. Morris.

SITTING: Ptes. J. M'Intyre, Loftus, Robertson, Greenwood, H. Taylor, Harrison, V. Watkinson.

with "D" Company. Two members of "D" Company whose work upon the Razorback is worthy of mention were Bugler H. G. Richards and Private (afterwards Sergeant) E. C. Williams. Richards had proved himself the Gunga Din of "D" Company and throughout the Monday night, all Tuesday and most of Wednesday had run the gauntlet of enemy fire over and over again getting ammunition, water and food for the men in the line. This was no mean feat when it is realised that most of the country Richards covered was being swept continually by machine-gun and shrapnel fire. Williams was wounded by a bullet hitting him right on the bald patch in his head. On the Wednesday he was wounded again with a shrapnel pellet in the arm. With his head bandaged and his arm in a sling, he still carried on until he got a third wound a week later at Quinn's Post which finally put him out of action. The last wound was also in the head.

When Lieutenants Casey and Sampson took their platoons out of Courtney's to join up with the rest of the Battalion, to the astonishment of No. 2 Platoon, they were ordered to line a ridge east of Colonel Monash's headquarters to protect the Colonel and his staff from a suspected Turk attack through the portion of the line known as Bloody Angle, next to Quinn's.

The Battalion, less Captain Hugh Quinn's "C" Company, and one platoon of "B" Company under the command of Lieutenant Dickinson, took over the front line on Pope's Hill and Russell's Top on May 1. That night it was learnt an attack would be launched upon the Turk position on the following day, Sunday. In all attacks made by the Australian troops upon Gallipoli Peninsula, one factor alone was essential for success—surprise. Once that element was lost it was a waste of good lives. No example is more striking than that of "D" Company's charge from Russell's Top, unless it be the Hill 60 fiasco at the end of August or the disastrous Bullecourt slaughter in France in 1917.

In this attack, the first to be made from the 4th Brigade's lines, which then included Russell's Top, Pope's Hill, Quinn's Post, Courtney's and Steele's Posts, scenes of the fiercest fighting during the first month of Gallipoli, only "D" Company of the 15th Battalion was engaged. Between Pope's Hill and Quinn's Post ran a gully—a branch of Monash Valley—and into the fork of this ran a spur of Dead Man's Ridge, upon which the enemy was situated. The plan of attack was that the entire line should be pushed outwards so as to control this spur, thus depriving the Turk of his view into Monash Valley and Shrapnel Gully. This would allow

movement up and down the gullies, free from the incessant sniping which continued throughout the greater part of the day. The three battalions which were to take part in the charge were the 16th under Colonel Pope, upon the right of the advance, the 13th under Colonel Burnage, in the centre, and the Otago Battalion under Colonel Moore, upon the left flank. "D" Company of the 15th Battalion was attached to the Otago Battalion. The charge was timed for 7 p.m.

Before the charge took place the Battalion suffered quite a number of casualties while merely holding the line. Among the first to fall was Major Eccles Snowden. This left Captain H. C. Davies in command. Captain Frank Moran, of "B" Company, was hit in the knee by a sniper's bullet. Despite this wound he carried on and, though in considerable pain, he hobbled the length of his trench munching a biscuit and instructing his men to keep their heads down. Another "B" Company officer, Lieutenant Snartt, became a casualty shortly after Moran.

Among the others who were hit was Bentzon, of "C" Company, who got a bullet in the brain. Bentzon was a good linguist and spoke French like a native. He had lived in France for years and would have been invaluable to us on the Western Front.

When the Otago Battalion, which had been seriously delayed, got into position for the charge, the 13th and 16th Battalions had secured their objectives. As it was now too late to do otherwise than attempt to connect up with the left of the 13th Battalion the order was given for the New Zealanders to go over immediately. All the elements of surprise had long since been lost, for the cannonade accompanying the fight the 16th and 13th were waging, was sufficient to awaken the dead. It was then almost 8 p.m. The Otago men, who were in full kit, found difficulty in getting out of the trench, and the men of the 15th gave them a leg over. When the first New Zealand platoon stood upon the parapet, the Turks opened out with machine gun and rifle fire and many of the attackers fell back into the trench. The rest disappeared towards the Turkish line. Then platoon after platoon leapt out and with each successive wave the intensity of the enemy's fire increased to such an extent that by the time No. 12 platoon topped the parapet there was a continuous hail of lead. The trench was choked full of dead and dying men and it was almost impossible to move.

During the whole time Captain Davies sat unconcernedly upon the parapet, exposed to the full blast of the

Turkish fire, and yet was not even scratched. But, when "D" Company was given the order to charge, he rose to his feet, gave the order, and immediately fell back into the trench with a bullet through his ankle. That finished his service with the 15th.

Lieutenant A. B. Fenton, writing of this engagement, says:

"In front of the trenches at Pope's Hill there was a gradual slope up to a fairly high ridge covered with bushes. We got orders to stand up in the trench so that a New Zealand Battalion could step onto our backs and pass over the trench. They were going to attack the ridge in front.

"After the New Zealanders had crossed over and gone on, Lieutenant Good came along the top of the trench and said: 'Come on, you men.' We all climbed out and followed him, but what with the darkness and the bushes we got scattered. I came across Lieutenant Douglas wounded in the neck, and took off his equipment and bandaged his wound. At that moment Sergeant Corrigan came on the scene. Douglas said, 'You take charge now, Corrigan.' Douglas went back and was hit in the hand on the way down. After Douglas had gone, a number of us gathered around Corrigan, but no one, not even he (Corrigan), knew what we were there for. We were all more or less arguing when a voice in the darkness said, 'Do you want someone to lead you?' Corrigan asked 'Who are you?' He got the reply: 'Jock McCarthy, of the Otagos.' Someone vouching for the truthfulness of the statement, some twenty or more of us followed him up to the top of the ridge. When he called out 'Charge!' we all let out a blood-curdling yell, and the Turk poured a withering fire into us. We were right on their trenches. Men all around me fell, including Corrigan, and, thinking they had all gone west, I went back to our old trench.

"On arrival there I found the trench full of men, and from the top of the trench I called out: 'Is there an officer here?' A voice answered, 'Yes.' I told him that out on the ridge were a lot of men, without either officer or an N.C.O. and no one knew what to do. He then said: 'I'm a machine-gun officer and I don't know what's to be done.' He rather nettled me by asking: 'What did you come back for? Why didn't you stay with the others?' I replied: 'If you think I ran away come with me and I'll show you where to put your machine-gun.' He asked: 'Where?' And was told in the b . . . Turks' trench. Someone then said: 'If you will lead us out we will go with you.' So, getting the 40 or 50 New Zealand and 15th Battalion men together, we got out of the trench and went back to the ridge.

"In the meantime a company of the 13th Battalion had also got on to the ridge. I explained to the 13th officer who we were and asked for orders. He gave instructions to extend the left flank and dig in, which we did. Greatly to my delight and relief, Corrigan came along. He had not been hit as I thought, but when the Turks opened fire he had thrown himself down.

"By daylight we had dug a fairly good line of trenches on the crest of the ridge, but during the day the Turks began to come along a deep gully on our left flank which was in the air, and started to move in behind us. Despite a number of messages which Corrigan sent back for something to be done to help us, no notice was taken, and, during the afternoon, we all got out of it. That night the Turks occupied our trenches and looked right down on our position at Pope's."

The failure to link up the left flank compelled the retirement a day later of the 16th and 13th Battalions and a number of R.M.L.I. from the precarious positions they had

secured and held on to only after the most desperate fight. The retirement of the R.M.L.I., however, was a bit premature. There were in this unit a number of exceptionally young lads who, immediately upon the beginning of their retirement, became a bit flustered. The 15th Battalion, holding the Pope's Hill line, however, stuck it out. It was during the course of this retirement that Captain Willis and other officers, together with Colonel Cannan, passed through the trenches encouraging the men to remain firm. During this operation, Captain Willis was hit through the neck and killed. Lieutenant Kessel, who had passed through with Willis, went to the machine post commanded by Staff-Sergeant Corbett and had barely reached the post when he got the wound from which he died later on in Egypt. It is impossible to pass over the operations from Pope's Hill without making reference to the stretcher-bearers. Doctor Luther, who was as hardworked in those early days as any member in the unit, found time to scribble a few lines in a little diary found upon his body after his death. "The bearers were wonderful and did the work of a hundred men," he recorded. It was estimated that over 250 cases were handled by the 15th stretcher-bearers during the fighting. Among the bearers were Jack Hynes, Corporal Keith Murray, J. E. Hammans. G. E. Gower, W. F. Stevenson, W. P. Darby and Moles, Rubonison and McKenzie. Luther knew the strain his men had been under and, when the Battalion was relieved from the front line and was bivouacking in Rest Valley, he gave them permission on May 4 to go down to the beach for a swim. On their return from the swim two shrapnel shells burst among them and two of the bearers were wounded and there were 14 casualties among a number of men nearby.

On May 4 two reinforcement officers with 50 other ranks reported for duty. The officers were Lieutenants E. G. Wareham and H. C. Herne. Lieutenant Sam Harry was appointed Acting Captain and Adjutant at this time in lieu of Captain Willis (killed). Among other "A" Company casualties was a young Victorian, Lance-Corporal C. Kauffman. Privates W. F. Perkins and L. W. Mazlin were among those who also gave their lives. Lance-Corporal Keith Watson, one of the most popular young fellows in "A" Company, also got a wound which resulted in his death. Others wounded included Privates E. W. Tilley, M. Hewitz, Frank Dann, J. R. ("Scotty") Taylor, D. Robertson, W. Archibald, F. A. Bruce, G. Brindell and G. H. Busby. Sergeant Fred Hanley, writing of the death of Watson, says: "This young chap was standing in the trench talking to Lieutenant B. Sampson. 'Nosey' Byrne and I were sitting behind the parades. I heard the young

chap say to Sampson: 'When this war is over I am going to China. I have an uncle there.' He had just said that when he was hit. They passed him over the parades and 'Nosey' took him in his arms and ran with him to Dr. Luther. He died on the way, for the jugular vein was severed." Byrne, who was hit the day after Watson's death, was struck in the hip. He died from the wound shortly afterwards. It was not until May 5 that the Battalion was to operate again as a complete unit. The losses in the charge from Pope's Hill had practically wiped out "D" Company, there being but two officers left—Lieuts. J. A. Good and A. G. Hinman. "A" Company still had three officers—Lieuts. Casey, Svensen and 2nd Lieut. B. Sampson. "B" Company was in the worst state. Included in its losses were Captain Richardson (wounded), Captain Moran (wounded), Lieutenant Waters (killed), and Lieutenants Snartt and Dickinson (wounded)—the last-named being wounded in the interim at Quinn's Post. This company's one original officer, Lieutenant J. Hill, had not landed, being aboard the "Australind" in charge of the unit's transport. "C" Company lost two officers killed—Lieutenants Freeman and Robertson—and the second in command, Captain Cyril Corser, was wounded. Pope's Hill had proved rather disastrous to the little coterie of Englishmen in "A" Company, who circled around the ex-lecturer of an English University, Private A. B. Blagden. Blagden was a very popular man of considerable knowledge. He was the first of these men to be wounded and afterwards, on his return to the unit, he accepted in Egypt a commission in an English regiment. Private A. B. Roberts, another member of this group, was the son of a Welsh clergyman and had been associated in a minor capacity at one stage of his career with the New York Stock Exchange. He lost his life at Pozieres in 1916. Private A. C. Hammond was a son of an English clergyman and was wounded the day after his two friends were hit.

In the official History of Australia in the Great War, Vol. 1, "The Story of Anzac," by C. E. W. Bean, the strength of the Brigade is recorded by General Monash as follows:—

	Officers	Other Ranks
13th Battalion	9	500
14th Battalion	15	620
15th Battalion	8	350
16th Battalion	9	300
4th Brigade	41	1770

The above figures for the 15th Battalion did not include Headquarters Staff, consisting of Lieut.-Colonel J. M. Cannan, Lieut. F. Craig (Q.M.), and Lieut. N. O'Brien, Sig. Officer. Besides Lieut. J. Hill aboard the "Australind" there were also aboard the ships off the coast Captain H. Cannan of "A" Company and Lieut. Platt, 1st Reinforcements.

* * * *

CHAPTER II

QUINN'S POST

On the Wednesday night, April 28, "C" Company, as previously mentioned, remained on the beach. They were busily sorting themselves out and obtaining something to eat, when orders came for a fighting patrol to move along the sea-front to the left of the New Zealanders—a position which was afterwards known as No. 3 Outpost. This order deprived the Company of all sleep, and Captain Corser, about 11.30 p.m., led his men to the position that had to be entrenched and guarded throughout the night. It was suspected by the New Zealanders that the Turks would attempt to sneak along the beach and roll up their flank.

The patrol passed Fisherman's Hut and moved to the spot where so many Australians were put out of action on the first day by small parties of Turks secreted in the scrubby high-country on that flank. The first sign of life met was a fishing boat belonging to a Greek lying snugly at anchor. This vessel Lieutenant Collin ordered to be boarded and searched. Privates Ross Hayes, C. Quinn, Teddy Bryans, J. Coogan and J. White, of No. 2 Platoon, boarded the vessel and, after a thorough search, discovered a Greek fisherman hiding under a tarpaulin. The man was a trader from Lemnos Island seeking to sell his wares to the Australian troops. Later on, these traders were compelled to leave the Peninsula after dark, and at a later stage still they were forbidden to trade altogether.

The second effort to get into touch with the enemy was entrusted to Sergeant Bob Hunter who, with a number of men, was detailed by Captain Corser to man a punt discovered on the beach, and proceed as far along the coast as was deemed wise, so that the enemy would disclose himself by opening fire upon the boat. Hunter took with him Privates C. Quinn, R. Hayes, Wetherall and Ben White, a man six feet six in height and the tallest soldier serving in the Unit.

Private Charlie Quinn was a well-known Collingwood (Victoria) swimming champion. He, along with the other men, composed most of the boat crew used by Colonel Cannan for forwarding despatches to Brigade while stationary in Lemnos Harbour. Luckily for the men in the punt, this **decoy business did not entice the Turks to bite, although**

movement could be clearly heard in the brush and scrub. In the early hours of the morning, Corser brought his men back to their starting-off position, and there they stood to arms awaiting dawn. With the break of day, "C" Company was ordered to take over the position then held by the 14th Battalion under Major Rankin—Quinn's Post. During their night on the beach they had one casualty—a young chap wounded in the lung. Before mid-day they passed up Shrapnel Gully into Monash Valley and took over.

The trenches at this time were extremely shallow and consisted of a number of disconnected pits. The longest section of trench was barely fifteen yards. All the approaches to these positions were under snipers' fire, a state of affairs that existed for at least a week or more after taking possession. Lieutenant Leslie Collin, with No. 12 Platoon, took over the centre of the Post; Lieutenant Freeman, with No. 11, the right sector facing across Courtney's and Lieutenant Frank Armstrong, with No. 9 Platoon, the left sector. One platoon of "B" Company under Lieutenant G. Dickinson took over to the left of Armstrong again, and the remnants of Lieutenant Tom Robertson's No. 10 Platoon under Sergeant Stormonth and Corporal "Taffy" Nicholls entered the Post to the extreme right of Freeman. The country between this section of the Post and the extreme left of Courtney's Ridge was unoccupied and the various units holding the line invariably lined this ridge at night time to avoid a surprise move through our lines, withdrawing their men at daylight.

The men in the Post found it was impossible to do anything during daylight owing to the activity of snipers. Many men had lost their lives through being unaware of the proximity of the Turkish line, and owing to the fact that the trenches could be enfiladed from the higher country on the left. To move up and down the short sections of trenches, as the officers and non-commissioned officers were compelled to do, was fraught with constant danger. At the furthermost point in the line, where a sudden turn changed the alignment to almost due west, practically at right angles to Courtney's Post, which looked east, enfilade fire from snipers did not cease throughout daylight, and in the other arm of the Post, running north into the higher country where Dead Man's Ridge and Baby 700 were, many lives were lost.

Among the very first men to lose their lives in the centre sector of Quinn's was Private John McLeod, a member of the Bagpipe Band. So severe was the sniping on the first day that all movement in the trenches ceased and the men sat with their backs to the parapet. In the afternoon the snipers

Major H. QUINN.
Killed in Action.

C.S.M. A. SKINNER,
D.C.M., M.M., 1914-18.
Capt. 2/15 Bn. A.I.F., 1939-45.

Sgt. R. A. HUNTER, M.M.
Capt. C.M.F., 1939-45.

Sgt. F. HANLEY.

Major J. F. WALSH.
Killed in Action.

Lieut. D. M. GILLIES.
Killed in Action.

Sgt. J. CRAVEN, D.C.M.
Later Capt. 14 Bn., 1914-18
Brig 7th and 11th Bdes. C M F.,
1939-45

Capt. S. L. STORMOUTH.

left the trench alone and concentrated more around headquarters, where runners and officers were continually entering. During that afternoon eleven men were hit at this spot. Among those killed were Sergeant Spritch and Privates Ballard and Tom Jones. One of the Coogan brothers, Tom, was wounded.

The moment night came most of the men in the Post set to work digging and those not digging kept up continuous rounds of rapid fire to keep the enemy quiet. At the angle to the trench line sandbags were erected to destroy the vision of snipers, while behind the front line a strong sandbag defence was erected. Behind this sandbag barrier, what supports the Post had, usually found shelter from observation and the enemy's machine-gun and rifle fire.

The nearness of the Turkish line to ours may be gauged from the fact that the New Zealand Battery on our left flank firing across the Post into the Turk trench throughout this afternoon frequently dropped shells into the position occupied by "B"' Company. It was during this time that Lieutenant Dickinson was wounded, the bullet passing through his face and causing all who saw the effects of it to doubt whether the young officer would live. Within twenty-four hours the "B" Company Platoon was withdrawn and it rejoined its own company upon Pope's Hill. "C" Company lengthened Armstrong's sector of the Post to take in the trenches occupied by the "B" Platoon, and a day later Sergeant Denis Taylor with a number of men of No. 11 Platoon took over from Lieutenant Armstrong just prior to the Turks launching a fierce attack.

On Friday morning, April 30, Lieutenant Freeman was killed. The Post had been rather quiet for an hour or more until suddenly a sniper commenced putting his shots right into the centre of Freeman's trench. About 8 a.m., a young Westralian actually stood upon the parados of Collin's trench and asked for his brother who was serving in the 15th Battalion. After this the annoyance caused by the sniper was too much for the impetuous Freeman, and leaping from his trench he ran across the high ground into the trench occupied by Lieutenant Collin. How he escaped being fired upon is a mystery. Once in the trench he soundly rated Collin's men for not putting the sniper out of action and seizing a rifle, nestled into the parapet and fired a shot. Declaring he had missed, he jerked the bolt back, nestled down again, and fired a second shot. Simultaneously with its report came the crack of a sniper's rifle and Freeman fell back dead in the trench.

It would be in place to record some of the characteristics of the officers who defended the Post during this hectic week. In strange contrast to Freeman was the youthful serious-faced Leslie Collin. Day and night this officer religiously carried out his duties without taking any undue risks as befitted a man carrying so much responsibility. He was a tower of strength to his tired and sleepy men, and imbued them with a sense of responsibility almost equal to his own. In "Tubby", Lieutenant Frank Armstrong, a South African veteran, was a man with all the dash of Freeman, but with just that amount of restraint which enabled him to control it until the right moment. He was a cheerful bird and cracked jokes incessantly. Then there was Captain Corser, second-in-command of the Company, who, like the subalterns, lived in the line with his men. He was a quiet softly-spoken fellow who always struck one as being exceedingly shy. The work of the Post during this week fell upon these three officers and the various non-commissioned officers in charge of the sections in the platoons. Among the N.C.O.'s. were Sergeants Hunter, Stormonth, Sparks, Taylor, and Corporals Crocker, Nicholls and Melia.

On the afternoon of Freeman's death, a fierce attack was launched by the Turks upon the position held by the Royal Marine Light Infantry, who but a short time before had relieved "A" Company on Courtney's Ridge. The Turks swarmed in large numbers into No Man's Land in full view of the defenders of Quinn's, who immediately brought a terrific rifle fire to bear upon them. The enemy's machine guns retaliated at once, and a fusillade of shots flew across the parapets at Quinn's, compelling the defenders to keep their heads down. The sandbag barrier previously mentioned as being constructed upon the first night held a number of reserves, and these men, sheltered from the fire of the machine guns, kept up a continuous fire into the Turkish ranks. So intense was this shooting that a body of the attacking forces was diverted to deal with them and a first-class duel ensued. The members behind the sandbag shelter were finally compelled to shoot only in turn, and the men in the front line gazing back at them watched in amazement man after man making his shot and risking certain death each time.

During this encounter the Turks entered the Royal Marines' front line, but they were driven out by a brilliant counter-charge. The tally of the various riflemen in the sandbag shelter was considerable, one man being credited with having scored seventy hits. The occupants of the

shelter, under the command of Sergeant Denis Taylor, were Privates Back, H. Byrne, "Bluey" Williams, "Darly" Smith, and George Stupart. Back was credited with 70 hits.

On Saturday afternoon, May 1, at about 4.30 p.m., a heavy attack was launched against the Post. Owing to the garrison having had very little sleep since the day they landed, the attack almost caught them napping. In the left sector, Sergeant Hunter awakened his men by putting his boot into their ribs, and the astounded men jumped to their feet to find the Turks charging down upon them. They were standing upon the parapet calling upon "Allah!" There had been nothing to prevent them entering the trench, for most of the defenders were lying down when they first came. Failure to do so lost them the day. The defenders pumped lead into them for all they were worth, while from Pope's Hill and from our rear, the machine-guns of the Brigade opened out with a terrific fire—the bullets actually licking the top of the parapet, compelling the attackers to go to earth. A few yards in front of the Turk trenches, standard-bearers could be seen trying to keep aloft the Turkish flag. With astounding gallantry the attackers came on again and again, only to wither away under the hail of defending lead. German officers could be clearly seen haranguing their men. As a final desperate effort to retrieve the day, the unwounded Turks—many of whom were hugging the ground so as to escape the intense fire—seized the bodies of their dead comrades, and, using them as cover, sought to crawl closer to our parapet, while others, worked up to the madness of fanatics, rose erect, holding the dead bodies in front of them as a shield, and charged once again.

So heavy was the fire, the defenders' rifles were red hot and very difficult to hold. When matters had reached this critical stage, word was passed along the line that Captain Corser would lead the garrison in a charge, hoping thus to relieve the pressure upon the Post, and at the same time, put the enemy to flight. But, the moment Corser mounted the parapet, and before the word "Charge" left his lips, he fell back into the trench with a bullet in the stomach. At this moment the Turks gave up and streaked back to their lines as best they could.

The losses in "C" Company were not heavy, but they were serious, for several of the best men in the Company lost their lives. Among those killed were Sergeant Denis Taylor and "Jack" Beverley, and among the wounded, our tallest man, Ben White, got a bullet in the shoulder, putting him out of action for all time.

During the period when the remainder of the Battalion

was resting after being relieved from Pope's Hill, "C" Company still held on to Quinn's Post. The company was not relieved until May 5. On this day, after the relief by the R.M.L.I., the men were sitting behind the parados awaiting orders, when suddenly the Turks launched another attack. This attack was the commencement of a bomb war that was to be continued with desperate intensity for many weeks afterwards. The Turk was armed with a spherical-shaped bomb, known by us all as the "cricket ball bomb." It had a time fuse arrangement, and when first used the fuses were slightly too long, which enabled a man, if he was smart enough, to pick up the bomb and hurl it back before it exploded.

In the midst of the hullabaloo this afternoon, General Godley suddenly arrived and, drawing his revolver, ordered the men of "C" Company to man the hill directly behind the right angle of the Post. This order should not have been given, for every member knew well the position was fully exposed to the enemy, and nothing could possibly live there. The men naturally hesitated to obey the order. Frantic requests were also being received from the front line for reinforcements for the English regiment, and the company split up, some entering the front line and some obeying the irate General's command. Those who went up the hill became casualties immediately. Those who entered the front line found nothing but chaos. The dead of the Royal Marines lay everywhere. The fighting was mad and furious. Bombs came over in shoals, and while the British troops holding the line were practically wiped out or wounded, and the few remaining had not the slightest idea how to deal with the situation, the reinforcing "C" Company men distributed themselves amongst the Marines, seized all the rifles they could lay hands on, and commenced to beat the Turks back. The bombs made the riflemen very uncomfortable, so a number of the men took it into their own hands to hurl the bombs out of the Post while their fellows kept up rapid fire.

In the right angle of the trench, Private W. L. James became the official bomb thrower, and in the north angle of the Post Corporal Crocker performed a similar duty. Where it was impossible to get the bombs in time, overcoats or sandbags were thrown over them, while in other places the deadly missile was kicked into a bay or a hole in the ground where it could explode without doing damage. James had a narrow escape from death with a short-fused bomb and from then on the trench was kept clear for him while he ran up and down catching them in the air and hurling them

over the parapet. Corporal Crocker, unfortunately, did not escape a short-fused one and died from the injuries he received.

The moment matters had settled down, most of the Australians were ordered from the Post, but a few remained there for the purpose of strengthening the Marines and initiating them into the mysteries of the position, Sergeants Hunter and Nichols, along with several privates, took up this duty, but the young Englishmen, most of whom appeared to be in their early 'teens, were quite incapable of dealing with such a situation, so that night a number of men from "A" and "C" Companies were sent into the Post.

It had been noticed by many of the men that the Turk carried his bombs by a hook attached to his belt. On this night a curious casualty occurred indirectly attributable to this fact. Private J. E. Nystrom, six feet of solid bone and muscle, was posted with other sentries and while gazing over No Man's Land allowed his imagination to stray upon the possibility of a bomb hooking up in his clothing. A fatigue party was at work in the trench and one of this party, diligently wielding a pick, drove it through the slack of Nystrom's pants, just at the most interesting part of his meditation. Nystrom stood for the moment transfixed with horror, and waited for the bomb to explode. When his startled brain functioned, he turned, and with one swift blow he knocked the unfortunate fellow with the pick senseless. Nystrom admitted that the impulse came solely from relief. Finding it impossible to bring the man round, stretcher-bearers were called and the prostrate form was carried down to Doctor Luther.

On May 6 half of the Battalion was in the Post, "C" Company occupying the right flank of the Angle and "A" Company the left. It was owing to the inclusion of "Ganger" Slack in "A" Company that the first hint of the enemy attempts to mine under the position came. Slack, an old miner, declared that he heard the enemy at work. During the night of the 6th and 7th, many men, once being informed that mining was taking place, began to hear things also, until soon the whole garrison vowed they could hear the sound of the picks.

Throughout May 7 snipers became very busy again and a number of casualties resulted. At this time periscopes had been in general use for almost a week, and enemy snipers indulged in much fancy shooting whenever they appeared above the parapet. The trenches, too, had all been deepened a little and it was daily becoming safer to move about.

Reinforcements totalling 52 other ranks arrived on this day under Lieutenant H. P. Armstrong—the original commander of No. 2 Platoon, who had been left in Egypt sick when the unit sailed. The total casualties in the Battalion up to this time were estimated at Officers 15, Other Ranks 250.

In the little flat as you came out of the sap leading into Bloody Angle there gradually came into being a cemetery. As the days passed, the number of graves seemed to increase in a most alarming manner. Originally, there were but two or three graves, among the first few being one grave belonging to the 14th Battalion in which no less than 39 men were buried. Another grave close to this one contained the body of a 4th Battalion man. But, after the 15th Battalion took over the cemetery, the number of crosses daily increased until when relieved from the line the men would gaze apprehensively at them, and it became almost a religious duty to scrutinise the crosses and find out whether a comrade of the Egyptian days had passed on. Many a cross was fashioned with more than mere care, and the name and unit of the man along with his regimental number were printed clearly with indelible pencil. Later on, names were painted on most of the crosses so that time and weather should not obliterate the record.

It was not an uncommon sight to see on one side of the pathway a man fashioning rude crosses, and on the other side a man collecting jam tins into which enthusiastic miners stuffed explosives and all manner of pieces of metal, so as to produce a weapon capable of competing with the Turk cricket bomb. The frightfully crude affairs made at first were a greater danger to the men using them than to the Turk. The first of these jam-tin contraptions used at the Post was on May 7th. There were very few made then, but Captain Quinn had managed to secure two, and with one of these, Lieutenant Maurice Little decided to experiment. The long fuse had to be cut and then ignited with a match or lighted candle. Little threw one of them from the Post that night, and if noise meant anything they were of considerable value.

Lieutenant Maurice Little lost his eyesight through the premature explosion of one of these bombs on May 29, and Lieutenant Joe Sparks lost his hand on May 19 from the same cause. Besides these two officers, a number of the rank and file suffered similar misfortunes. But cumbersome as these jam-tin bombs were, some of the men became experts in the handling of them, and it was said in "A" Com-

pany that Private Alan Marshall, the one-time Interstate cricketer from Queensland, could hurl a jam-tin bomb not less than sixty yards. Private A. Lahiff also was looked upon as one of the crack bombers in the Battalion. Marshall, unfortunately, was wounded early and died of sickness in Malta. On May 7th, Captain Herman Cannan, second-in-command of "A" Company, came ashore from the "Seeang Bee" and reported for duty. On May 9 Father Joseph Power, our Chaplain, also came ashore and joined the unit. These two officers, together with Lieutenant Jack Hill and Lieutenant Platt, and 68 Other Ranks, took part in the dummy landing made in the Gulf of Saros.

On May 8 the half of the Battalion resting relieved those defending Quinn's, and a change-over in the control of the Post took place, the second-in-command of the 15th Battalion, Major Bert Carter, taking charge.

On this date, Lieutenant Keith Anderson, with 48 other ranks, also reported for duty. Almost immediately this officer entered the Post in command of a "D" Company platoon, and on the morning of the 9th, the Turkish Asiatic batteries opened fire upon the trenches. The few shells that landed in the Post killed Anderson and two other men, and before the shelling ceased the Company's casualties totalled 30. It was the first sample of H.E. from big guns we had tasted, and in the close confines of the trenches they proved most destructive.

On the morning of the 9th the men of "C" Company, under the command of Lieutenant Wareham, were withdrawn from their trenches and moved into Monash Valley, where they bivouaced on the side of Pope's Hill. This was the first day Maconochie rations were issued to the men of the 15th, and they built little fires all over the side of the hill to heat the ration until orders came for the fires to be put out. Up to this time the troops had subsisted on bully beef and biscuits and a little jam and cheese. The Maconochie rations were a pleasant change owing to the inclusion of potatoes and beans. There was very little tea drinking owing to the necessity of each man having to make his own. In the afternoon came the news that there would be a charge from Quinn's that night. The plan of attack matters little to this history, but roughly, General Godley had ordered a reconnaissance of the Turk position in front of Bloody Angle, for the purpose of discovering how far the Turks had proceeded with their tunnelling under the Post. Included in the plan was an instruction that if the enemy's trenches could be held they were to be consolidated. Three small attacking parties were detailed. They were to sneak

out of Quinn's Post, crawl as close to the enemy's line as possible, then jump in upon him. Should this prove successful, the position was to be consolidated by the construction of three saps from our own line to the captured trench. These saps would serve two purposes: One enabling communication to be made to the captured position in daylight should it be held; and the other, that of allowing the attacking parties to regain their trenches under cover should they be driven out. The officers commanding the parties were: Lieutenant H. P. Armstrong, better known as "Daisy," Armstrong, 2/Lieutenant H. G. Smith, and 2/Lieutenant Fred Youden. 2/Lieutenant H. G. Smith had, along with Sergeants E. M. Little and A. E. G. Leitch, been promoted to commissioned rank but a few days before. Corporal F. C. Youden had obtained his rank on April 27. Prior to the charge, these N.C.O.'s were observed wearing stars which, in one case owing to the shortage of these insignias of rank, were marked in indelible pencil on the shoulders. On the morning after the charge, Staff-Sergeant-Major E. Corbett and Sergeant B. S. Atkinson assumed commissioned rank and, on the 14th, owing to the severe losses in officers during the attack, Warrant Officer G. King, Sergeants J. E. Sparkes, J. J. Corrigan, H. R. Kock, W. T. Mundell and Company Quartermaster J. C. Browne, were appointed 2/Lieutenants. Of the digging parties two were commanded by an "A" Company Sergeant—the centre digging party being under the command of Lieutenant Frank Armstrong, of "C" Company.

The signal for the attack was to be a burst of machine-gun fire from Pope's Hill. For the first and last time rum was issued to the Battalion before a charge. In this instance the officers commanding were following the established rule of the British Army. There was considerable delay at the commencement due to a suspicion that the Turks were wide awake, because of their unusual activity with rifle and machine-gun fire and the firing of a number of star shells. As these were the first seen upon the Peninsula, they caused slight consternation. The attacking parties consisted of 25 men under 2/Lieutenant Smith on the left flank, 25 men on the right flank under Lieutenant "Tom" Armstrong; and 30 men in the centre under 2/Lieutenant Youden. The centre men were drawn from Nos. 11 and 12 Platoons of "C" Company with the exception of Sergeant Bob Hunter who was lent to Youden for the night. The right-hand party under Armstrong was practically drawn from No. 2 Platoon though one N.C.O., Corporal F. R. Cawley, was drawn from No. 1 Platoon. The picking of the men necessary for this charge was left by Armstrong to Private G. Westaway who displayed

splendid judgment in the men he chose. Hunter, who had the picking of the centre party, chose practically every man from his home town of Maryborough. The left party was picked by Lieutenant Little and included besides its officer, Lieutenant Smith, an ex "A" Company N.C.O., Sergeant Sam Hawkins, and Corporal Broadbent.

The defence of the Post itself was in the hands of Lieutenants Leo Casey, Svenson, Maurice Little, Good and Bill Mundell. "D" Company supplied the carrying and one digging party. "C" Company supplied the centre digging party and two platoons, one under Lieutenant Wareham, and the other under Lieutenant Collin, were to be held in readiness to occupy the line the moment the position was captured. Each member of the assaulting party was supplied with two sandbags to be used in consolidating the trench when it was won. These they tied around their waists so as not to impede their progress when crawling.

At 10.45 p.m. the signal from Pope's Hill was given, and the men left the line. Lieutenant Youden was hit along with seven others the moment they got onto the parapet. With Youden were two runners, Toft and Richardson. Youden was aided by Richardson and the crawling continued, even though the party was under the impression the Turks had seen them. When within striking distance of the enemy line, they stopped. As Youden was quite silly from the effect of his head wound, Hunter leapt to his feet and gave the order to charge. With a yell, the men sprang upon the astounded Turks, who for a few moments put up a stubborn resistance then fled. Harry Byrne, whose rifle stock had been cut away by a bullet, landed between the fleeing Turks and a sap to which they were racing to effect their escape. Turk after Turk endeavoured to escape his vicious stabs and when he had despatched the last one, he jumped out of the trench and went searching further afield. That was the last ever seen of him. Richardson, Youden's runner, was found dead on the Turkish parapet shortly afterwards, evidently killed when on a trip to Headquarters. Bert Back was shot through the shoulder, but he was quite unwilling to leave the fighting.

Following close upon the assaulting party came Collin's men. They spread themselves throughout the trench and attempted to consolidate, which was an extremely difficult matter owing to the number of dead Turks buried in the original parapet. Youden, because of his wound, was by this time quite enfeebled so Toft took him back to the old line, and Lieutenant Frank Armstrong who had already got his

sapping party into No Man's Land, and was as miserable as could be because he was out of the fighting, took advantage of Youden's condition to immediately go forward and take his place in command. With Armstrong in the front line, 2/Lieutenant B. Sampson saw his chance to be in the fight and he immediately took command of Frank Armstrong's sapping party and the first opportunity he got he also entered the front line.

The line that was captured was perfectly straight with practically no earth on the original parados whatever. In the parapet were buried the dead. When Sampson moved forward to speak to Frank Armstrong, that officer was very dubious about his right flank and asked Sampson to discover what had happened. Sampson made his way along the trench system accompanied by his batmen and runner, Private Bass, and found it unoccupied except for two Turks who were too busy firing at our line to notice Sampson's approach. These two men he shot, and continuing on his way suddenly came upon some of "Tom" Armstrong's wounded, and from these he learnt that Armstrong and his party had penetrated too far. He then sent for the right digging party so as to have sufficient men to hold the trench. To dig in the trench was well nigh hopeless. Body after body was hauled out, and the work became so nauseating and horrible that many of the men stopped digging altogether.

While this work was going on, Sergeant Vincent of "C" Company arrived with an extra thirty men. Casualties were already taking place and the extra men rather overcrowded the trench. In the centre position a similar state of affairs existed.

From far down the gully the sound of shooting could be heard. This was Lieutenant "Daisy" Armstrong's party, which had passed over the front line, on through the stunted undergrowth and communication saps, and was busy raiding a Turk stronghold. With Lieutenant H. P. Armstrong in the gully were: Sergeant Franz Kock, Corporal R. Tickner, Corporal F. R. Crawley, Privates G. Westaway, W. Gordon, A. T. Wertheimer, J. F. Horrigan, J. Hertherington, J. E. Yates, Lance-Corporal A. Wright, Privates H. Moore, H. J. Myles, J. E. Nystrom, P. S. Hartigan, F. A. Hanley and a few others. With Sampson and a sapping party and Sergeant Vincent's thirty men occupying the right flank, "Daisy" Armstrong and his party down the gully and out of touch with the line altogether, Frank Armstrong commanding Youden's men, Leslie Collin's men to the left of Frank Armstrong's position

and crowding the trench almost to suffocating point, a block in the line between this position and the section the men on the left flank had captured, now known to have been caused by the enemy, and three saps being dug as rapidly as possible to the various positions, things were becoming somewhat confused.

In an effort to obtain more space in which his men might be able to work, Frank Armstrong sent five men, amongst whom were Corporal Basil Atkinson and Private "Bluey" Williams, to the right flank. Having walked along the trench system the whole way, they discovered Sampson trying to keep his men digging. It is almost certain at this hour in the battle there were no live Turks whatever between Frank Armstrong's position and that held by Sampson. In the trench were a number of dead Turks, and two lay upon the parapet more than two-thirds of the way across. It must have been after these men arrived that the Turks once again entered that sector by means of a communication trench entering at some point of it. The left flank was still in the air.

Up to this time men had been crossing and recrossing No Man's Land almost with impunity. Shadowy forms were seen flitting about, many of whom were sections of the various carrying parties detailed to keep up supplies to the three attacking parties. More and more men were drifting or were being drafted from the various digging parties into the front line. Sergeant Strachan, in charge of the left digging party, was wounded, and Lieutenant Hinman took charge only to fall dead from a stray bullet a few minutes afterwards. Shots from the Turkish line were now becoming frequent and in the position occupied by Frank Armstrong and Sampson casualties began to occur. Man after man was hit. In Armstrong's position Driver Scouller and Corporal Ferguson were killed. Byrne was missing, and Bock and Bryans were wounded. In Sampson's position a similar state of affairs existed. Upon Lieutenant Hinman's death Corporal "Dick" Goss took command of the left digging party. Here, digging had to be almost suspended owing to the heavy fire.

The men of Frank Armstrong's party, who were blazing away continuously at an enemy they could not see, and certainly could feel, began to run short of ammunition, and calling for volunteers, Armstrong despatched Private Alf. Elliott, an original drummer in the band, with another man whose name has been forgotten, to bring two cases up from the post. On arrival at the Post, Elliott received the two cases from Sergeant Allen of the 16th Battalion and, on his return journey, took Lieutenant Wareham with him. Elliott's

companion being wounded, Lieutenant Wareham carried the extra case over to the line. Passing along the trench to the extreme right of Armstrong's position held by Sergeant "Taffy" Nicholls, Wareham took charge. Here the Turks had reached to within five yards of the defenders. A Turk officer could be clearly seen waving a sword and urging his men on, and Wareham, taking a pot shot with his revolver, hit the man in the wrist. A few moments later, Wareham, who was very anxious to secure a prisoner, was shot dead at close range.

On the extreme left of Frank Armstrong's position, Lieutenant Leslie Collin, who had with him the greater part of No. 12 Platoon, including Sergeant Alex. Mashall, Sergeant R. Hunder, and Privates Duncan, C. Quinn, and R. Hayes, received orders to try and connect with Lieutenant Smith's party. Collin's men attempted to prevent him from going, but the quiet, boyish-faced officer was not to be swayed from what he thought was his duty. "Orders are orders," he told them, "and though I know it is death—I must obey them." He took with him one man, and neither was heard of again. It was evident by this time the few men belonging to Smith's party who had actually reached the Turkish trench were completely isolated and individually carrying on a form of round-the-corner-fighting. Lieutenant Good was therefore sent out to control the sapping party working through to Smith's position, thus relieving Goss of this responsibility. It was known early in the fight that Smith was fatally wounded, but it was not known that matters were in such a parlous state as was afterwards discovered. In the charge on the left flank the men had followed Smith's lead, but unfortunately, without any knowledge of what was intended by those in command. The same ignorance of what was required existed among Youden's and Collin's men in "C" Company, all of whom were under the impression that it was merely a raid.

Among the men of "B" Company were two non-commissioned officers who played a very big part in the holding of the left sector of the line. They were Sergeant Sam Hawkins and Corporal H. O. Broadbent. With these two men were Corporal Dal. Cummins, Privates J. Sexton, R. Reid, Mackay, Connel, Pshovolodsky, and a few others. The men with Broadbent and Hawkins had not the slightest idea of what was happening, or what was likely to. They merely fired at any flash to their front or flanks and were quite incapable of moving owing to the enemy being in the same trench as themselves, and not having the wherewithal in bombs to compel the Turks to keep at a reasonable distance.

Privates R. Reid and Connel were not of the attacking party. They were part of a "B" Company carrying party and had narrowly escaped death when approaching the section of line held by the Turks between the left and centre parties. Upon arrival at Broadbent's trench, they were immediately commandeered as reinforcements for the small garrison.

Hawkins and Broadbent were both wounded in the Post about a week later, both dying from their wounds. Pshovolodsky met his death quite early with a bullet between the eyes, fired by a Turk less than five yards away. This Turk was clearly seen at the moment he fired, owing to a white head dress which he wore. The shot was fired over the sandbag barricade erected on the party's left flank to prevent surprise in that direction from the Turks. Pshovolodsky's death necessitated one of the garrison being detailed to fire shots continuously over the top of the barricade to prevent a repetition. Lieutenant Smith lay mortally wounded a few paces from where Pshovolodsky fell. Several attempts had been made to get him out of the trench, but the fatal result of the last attempt when two men were killed, compelled the defenders to reluctantly abandon any hope of giving their officer a sporting chance of life.

It is doubtful whether Hawkins on the left flank and Broadbent on the right had the slightest idea of the lay of country. They held a very small part of the enemy's line and were too busy holding it to learn anything. Though the left flank had no strenuous opposition from the outset of their charge, the right flank under Lieutenant H. P. Armstrong had a much better passage. The instructions to the men were simplicity itself. Upon the signal by the machine gun on Pope's Hill, the men left the trench and lay down in the open. The word "Ceramic" was then passed along the line from right to left, and the last man to receive it stood to his feet, then the whole line rose and advanced upon their objective at the double. This party encountered no opposition whatsoever, for on their arrival at the first line they met but two sentries whom they bayoneted, then passed over the second line into the third line of defence, which many of the men, failing to notice, fell into. Up to this time there had not been a casualty. The third line was but waist deep, and still under the impression that nothing they had encountered could possibly be their objective, they continued on their way. The men on the left of the advance, found themselves entering a gully. The leader of the party, Joe Westaway, entered this gully closely followed by Hartigan and Handley and encountered two Turks whom he

despatched with the bayonet. Stumbling upon some telephone wires Westaway cut them. At that moment a Turk appeared upon the scene and Hartigan shot him. Hastening to this man's aid came another Turk and he was also shot. Up to this time the operation had been conducted in silence, but after the shooting, Armstrong and the men on the right flank were drawn over to the left and also entered the gully. The officer immediately gave orders for the gully to be searched, but owing to the narrowness of it, movement could only be made in single file. Private Harry Moore was the first man at the sharp bend, and peering around it, gave a yell. The enemy were on the south side of the gully and at Moore's yell the party raced to his assistance. So swiftly did they act that a line of men was thrown around the position, completely cutting off the enemy's retreat.

The position captured was a system of dugouts in front of which the bank had been cut away forming a large bay. Armstrong, seeing that the Turks could not get away, posted two men in the communication trench leading from the gully and up which any reinforcing Turks would have to come. He was in a quandary what to do with the Turks for he had no desire to have so many prisoners upon his hands, besides being apprehensive regarding the large numbers of Turks near at hand. Taking up his position upon the high bank overlooking the scene he at last made his decision and gave orders to close with the enemy, using only the bayonet. The Turks further up the communication trench, alarmed at the noise now taking place, jumped from their sheltered positions and streaked for safety across the skyline. Upon these the party opened fire at a range of some ten yards.

For the first time since the assault began a member of the party—Sergeant F. R. Koch—thought it might be advisable to let Colonel Cannan know what was happening. Armstrong concurred with Koch and despatched him to the Colonel. While Koch was absent, Miles and Hanley were posted as sentries further down the gully to guard against any surprise attack and a search of the position was made. The only Turk that attempted to draw near them during this time was shot by Miles. The only man in the party wounded was Gordon. When Sergeant Koch arrived back from Colonel Cannan matters assumed an entirely new complexion. The party had travelled too far, and were ordered back to the line where they had killed the two sentries—the one Sampson with the right digging party was consolidating. This retirement was effected easily, no opposition whatever being met

with. Private F. G. Green was thought to have been one of this party. He was reported missing.

When Lieutenant Armstrong returned from the gully with his men, Sampson left for the centre digging party again. While travelling across the open with Private H. "Darky" Kelly, who was carrying a pick, he stumbled upon a man secreted in a shell hole. Thinking it might be one of his own men doing a bit of shirking, he stooped over to speak to him when, to his surprise, the man sprang up and hit Sampson a glancing blow on the head with a shovel. Kelly acted immediately and swung his pick into the Turk's brain. This sudden attack from a Turk well behind the line told Sampson that the enemy once more occupied the line between the centre and right parties. He hurried over to Frank Armstrong to tell him so, but Frank had already received the news from Corporal Jack Craven[1] who having been detailed to get connection with the right flank had had a narrow escape from being killed, for the Turks between the two positions threw a shower of bombs at him and blew him out of the trench in which he was walking.

Jack Craven, writing of this incident, says:

"When sent to get in touch with the right flank I made my way down the hill in rear of then Turkish positions and seeing a light I ran into a Turkish shelter—full of Turks. I fired a couple of shots into the group and beat a hasty retreat with several chasing me. They threw several bombs at me—one of which blew me, slightly wounding me in the head, into an empty trench from which I again fired and sent them to ground. I then made my way back to Frank Armstrong and informed him that he was cut off from the right party."

Matters were becoming serious now, and as the firing from the Turks grew more intense, the centre and right digging parties began to have heavy casualties, and movement within the different systems became almost impossible. All the wounded who were not stretcher cases were drafted out of the line, while the transport of the stretcher cases in Frank Armstrong's sector was placed in the hands of Corporal Jack Craven, who, with the aid of bearers, cleared that section of the line of its badly wounded as swiftly as practicable. Lieut.-Colonel B. Sampson, writing of this says:

"Frank Armstrong's memory should be cherished for the reason that all through that hurly-burly and confusion, he, all that night, was cool, and was determined to get all the wounded back into our lines. It is well that he did so, for their fate next morning would have been certain."

---

[1] Craven went right through the War, and during the period between its conclusion and the beginning of World War II, he took a prominent part in Militia training, to ultimately command as Brigadier Craven, first the 11th, and then the 7th Brigades in the early years of hostilities. A breakdown in health prevented his going abroad, but he remained to command No. 2 L. of C. in Queensland, through which Australian, British, American and Dutch troops passed to the operational areas in the South-West Pacific.

The runners from the different sections were also experiencing trouble. Private Gordon, of "A" Company, had been hit twice but he still carried on. Toft of "C" Company, who was now attached to Frank Armstrong, had also been hit early in the night, but he was not stopped until near morning when he got a bullet in the back. Bass of "A" Company, who acted as batman and runner to Lieutenant Sampson, had a very arduous time but so far he had escaped injury. The "B" Company runners were not able to operate owing to the intense fire concentrated upon their parados, where to expose oneself for a moment meant death. The last trip Toft made to Battalion Headquarters coincided with a yell for reinforcements from the front line—not the first by any means. Time and time again these cries would start for no apparent reason whatsoever. It was held by many of the men in the centre sector (Frank Armstrong's position) that the cries for reinforcements were probably started by German officers in the section of trench between them and the left sector, as it was from this quarter that most of the cries originated. The men on the extreme left of Frank Armstrong's position thought that the cries were coming from Broadbent's party. The moment a cry started it was taken up immediately by members of the digging parties, who were always keen to pass any message whatever back to Headquarters so as to aid their friends.

The Colonel, hearing the cries, ordered Captain Margolin of the 16th Battalion and his men out. When Margolin arrived, he discovered the trench crammed with men, and finding Lieutenant Harwood, also of the 16th, and some thirty men were lying in No Man's Land he immediately withdrew. Toft got his wound when he had guided them to Lieutenant Frank Armstrong's position. It was after the failure of Lieutenant Leslie Collin to connect with the left flank, that the Adjutant, Captain Sam Harry, who, it is stated, had visited previously both the left and right flanks, approached the extreme left of Frank Armstrong's position where Sergeant Bob Hunter and men of No's 12 and 11 Platoons were holding out against the Turks behind a sandbag shelter. In company with Captain Harry was 2/Lieutenant Mundell. Upon leaving the trench the two officers were seen to veer to the right and warnings were yelled to them. Harry turned to the men and said they were going to Smith's position. As he was taking the very route on which Collin and Wareham had disappeared, the men in the trench were not surprised when a few moments later Mundell came back to say that Harry had been killed.

Capt. E. K. CARTER, M.C.

Capt. J. T. HYNES, D.S.O., M.M.
Cross of Kara George,
Serbian 2nd Class (With Swords).
M.I.D.

Lt. J. M. RAE, M.C., M.M.
M.I.D.

Lt. B. J. SHAW, M.M.
Killed in Action

Lt.-Col. T. P. McSHARRY,
C.M.G., D.S.O. and Bar, M.C.
4 times M.I.D.
Killed in Action.

Lt.-Col. B. SAMPSON, D.S.O.
Mentioned in Despatches.

**15th BATTALION, A.I.F., 1914-18, MEMORIAL,
ANZAC SQUARE, BRISBANE.**

There has been much mystery about the loss of these officers, but in the morning, after the Turks had recaptured their trench, they were seen to pull many bodies into the trench from the front of their parapet and after taking what might prove valuable, threw them out again. It is quite certain that those bodies not recovered during the armistice were buried by the enemy. Regarding this, Lieutenant-Colonel B. Sampson wrote: "Most of our dead left in the Turkish trenches were, when the Turks captured them, simply thrown out over the parapet, because I remember distinctly identifying some of the bodies through my periscope. Lieutenant Hinman we recognised because his glasses were still intact and quite a number of them were used during the armistice to fill up the communication trenches, so that even when dead their poor old bodies served a useful purpose."

About 3 a.m. or a little later, Corporal "Dick" Goss was ordered by Lieutenant Good to take a man and find out the length of trench occupied by the Turks between the left and centre sectors. Goss took with him Private A. R. Langdon, and more by good luck than anything else, struck the extreme right flank of the left party, where Broadbent and a few stalwarts held out. Leaving this position, they managed to reach Frank Armstrong's sector, in accomplishing which Langdon was wounded. From the data gathered, some idea was formed of the length of trench held by the enemy, and this information was passed on to Major Carter. Following upon the return of these men, Lance-Corporal Boden led forward a party of the 16th Battalion to show them where the trench occupied by the Turks lay. This party was under the command of Captain Townshend, 16th Battalion, who was a Queenslander, born in Mackay, and Lieutenant N. H. Burston, a Duntroon graduate. With them was Lieutenant Mark's platoon of the 13th Battalion, called from Pope's Hill only a few minutes before the charge took place. It was an astonishing charge. The men in Broadbent's sector thought they were surrounded by the Turks, and immediately opened fire until cries of, "You are firing on your own men!" rent the air. It was over in a minute, Townshend and Burston both being killed, Marks alone, with three men, reaching the parapet of the trench before being compelled to retire.

Sergeant Hunter, who with Youden had led the centre charge, was sent back to the old line by Frank Armstrong just about this time, and in the Post he met the Brigade Staff Officer, Captain Joss. Joss suggested that another attempt should be made to relieve the situation with a charge by the R.M.L.I., but this was not done.

It is hard for men who served with the unit in France to appreciate the difficulties in the way of linking up captured positions on Gallipoli. In France, working from both ends, the consolidating parties soon joined forces by the simple expedient of bombing their way along the trench. But it must be remembered that at this stage of the campaign on the Peninsula troops had had no previous experience of trench warfare, and they were not in possession of the weapons best suited for that type of fighting. Expedients such as men firing continuously on end into the wall of a trench so as to prevent bombers getting close enough to hurl their missiles were freely practised. Sandbag barriers to block the Turk's view and to minimise enfilade fire and impede his progress were also used. The men knew that once it was daylight their chances of retaining the positions they had won were remote so long as they remained a series of disconnected holes in the ground as it were. Much depended therefore on the men working on the saps, and when the centre sap linked up with the captured position and the right and left saps began to become within measurable distance of likewise linking up with the forward areas, the men took a more hopeful view of the situation. The feat of digging these saps probably had few equals up to that time in the history of warfare. Many lives were lost during their construction, and casualties were exceptionally heavy in a party of Marines who were working on the centre sap.

At dawn the men in the forward trenches were in a precarious position. They were being bombed by Turks hidden in the communication saps and support trenches. Heavy rifle and machine-gun fire enfiladed Frank and "Daisy" Armstrong's positions, and the former, using his own discretion, gave the order to retire. Down through the saps the men passed on their way home to the Post. When the last man was on his way to safety, Armstrong, with his two Sergeants, Sparks and Stormonth, took to the open country. On the left flank, where the sap was not completed, the little bunch of men with Broadbent in command also took to the open country, for they saw themselves in imminent danger of being wiped out. Of this gallant band, Private Archie Mackay fell dead as he topped the parados. Quentin Connel fell wounded, and the men scattered, as heavy fire poured into them from both flanks. Broadbent's party got back just as their excitable French-Canadian friend, Louis Melidine, fell dead with a bullet in the brain. On the right flank, "Daisy" Armstrong hesitated to see how his men were getting on and was killed instantly with a bullet in the head.

The exhausted men found no relief once they regained

their trenches for the Turkish counter-attack was at its height. Bombs were flying everywhere, but few actually entered the Post. From the left flank the rifle and machine-gun fire, sweeping down the trenches, took heavy toll of the defenders. Our guns were bursting shrapnel above the Turkish reserves, while the Brigade machine-guns raked them from end to end.

To prevent the Turks coming too far into Lieutenant Svenson's section, Svenson and Casey began building a sandbag barrier and both were wounded. Casey lay in the trench to all appearances dead. Yet the men there—part of the right digging party who had been working all night—attempted to patch up his numerous wounds. Finally, with the aid of other men, they got him out of the trench and down to Doctor Luther. It was said of Luther that he was at his best where the fighting was heaviest, and that no medical officer on the Peninsula could keep up with his high speed in cleansing and dressing of wounds. Through his hands passed the great majority of the men, and when it was not 15th men he had to deal with, he invariably turned round and aided the medical officers in other units. Once the casualties of the retirement had passed through his hands there was still plenty of work to do. The bombs falling in Casey's old position fell among a crowd of exhausted men. These men fought on, and as the morning passed, casualty after casualty left the trench. Private Jack Fleet was wounded at the outset with a machine-gun bullet that cut his neck. A muffler he was wearing at the time saved his life. He did not leave the trench, however, and, with Sergeant Lucas and "Tibby" Hutchinson and a few others, a continuous rifle fire was maintained over the parapet and the bombs falling into the Post were hurled back to the Turks. Lucas was wounded early with a bullet in the face. A bomb fell beneath Wood and inflicted serious injuries. "Nugget" Alexander, stooping to pick up a bomb, lost his life, and Lennan a few moments afterwards was wounded. Fleet and Denehey were now the only two left in that sector of the Post. These two kept racing up and down the sector of the trench, firing at different points in an endeavour to bluff the Turks into thinking that the trench was fully occupied.

Although quite a number of casualties occurred as a result of the practice of picking up bombs and hurling them back, the men were not deterred. They continued doing it until they left the Quinn's Post position. A few days after the death of Alexander, Bugler David Crosby, during a sharp

exchange with a party of Turks, was throwing bombs out of the trench, when he unfortunately collided with another member of "A" Company and, falling across a bomb, he was badly injured. His cries to be put out of his agony were reluctantly ignored by the men in the trench. Crosby, however, finally recovered from his wounds.

In "C" Company's sector, Frank Armstrong and his retiring men had passed right through the front line, whose sole occupant at the moment was Sergeant Hunter. As they passed to the back of the Post Armstrong learnt that the line was not guarded and immediately turned his men face about and marched back into it. After his arrival, while gazing over the parapet, he saw some of his wounded men out in front, and endeavouring to scramble over the parapet to their aid, fell back riddled with bullets. In "B" Company's sector on the left flank, Lieutenant Maurice Little was holding the Post with the remnants of Broadbent's force and the men who had been engaged on the sapping upon the left flank.

The official estimate of the losses in this engagement was Officers 14, and Men 193. In the 14 Officers, were included Captain Townshend and Lieutenant Burston of the 16th Battalion. Our own officers were: Killed, Captain and Adjutant Sam Harry, Lieutenants Frank and H. P. "Tom" Armstrong, L. N. Collin, A. G. Wareham, A. G. Hinman and 2/Lieutenant H. G. Smith. The four officers wounded were Lieutenant N. T. Svenson, 2/Lieutenant Leo Casey, 2/Lieutenants F. C. Youden and Burford Sampson. Sampson was wounded just before morning, being hit with a machine gun bullet in the shoulder while passing across No Man's Land to Frank Armstrong's position. Among the non-commissioned officers killed were: Sergeant G. E. Weston, Corporals "Scotty" Melia, R. MacDonald and R. Vincent. The last named was an actor and he enlisted under the name of Vincent, his correct name being Suckling. A number of men were reported missing. Some of them were afterwards discovered in hospital. The official figures and those estimated by the 15th Battalion medical staff do not agree. The first figures issued were over 300, but many of the men were wounded more than once and returned to the firing line after treatment.

The Battalion was not relieved until May 11, when Colonel Pope brought his 16th men back from a fatigue duty on the Beach to take over the Post. Although the 15th had suffered severely, the strength of the 16th at this time was only a little over 200. While the Battalion were bivouacking

in its old spot—Monash Valley—2/Lieutenant K. W. Crabbe, of the 14th Battalion put two trench mortars into position at the Post. A day later the 15th once again relieved the 16th and the companies occupied the same sectors as before. Of all the unpleasant jobs that men in the unit were asked to perform that of guarding the newly built saps at Quinn's was the worst. The sap on the left flank was particularly noted for its record of killed and wounded. At one point in the trench snipers accounted for Privates Mervyn Collins, Billy Cairns and Arthur Gill all in the one day and within half an hour, the first two named being killed outright. In the same neighbourhood Sergeant Sam Hawkins and Corporal Broadbent received the wounds that caused their deaths.

It was shortly after the wounding of these two N.C.O's. that the 2nd Light Horse relieved the defenders of Quinn's. This relief did not include all the 15th, for some of the N.C.O.'s and officers, including Sergeant Bob Hunter and Captain Burford Sampson, were left to teach the Light Horse the danger spots in certain localities. Besides these men with the Light Horse, a party of 30 men from "D" Company were on duty each night guarding the gap between Quinn's and Courtney's Posts. This party lined the ridge during the night and came down again just before daylight. They carried on until the 15th, when they were absorbed into a digging party in a support trench behind the Post, where, on the 17th, the N.C.O. in charge of them—Corporal "Dick" Goss—was wounded.

By this time the face of Quinn's—from the rear at any rate—had undergone many changes since the 15th originally took the Post over. Bomb-proof shelters were being erected, support trenches had been dug and terraces for the holding of large reserves, and resting places for men when off duty from shrapnel or sniper's bullets had been constructed. So rapidly was this work carried out, that a man wounded in the early part of May and returning to the unit a fortnight later would have found difficulty in recognising the place again. Consequently, it was becoming daily more safe to move about in.

On May 15 Captain Sampson, commanding No. 3 subsection at Quinn's was surprised to receive a visit from Generals Birdwood and Godley. These two officers wished to see for themselves the state of affairs in front of the Post where the Turkish dead heaped up against the parapets exuded a stench that at times was overpowering. Sampson warned the General of the risk he was taking, but borrowing that officer's last periscope, he put it above the parapet and

stared at the accumulation of bodies in front. So interested was he in the scene that, ignoring Sampson's warning not to expose the mirror too long above the trench, the expected finally happened. Crack! came the report of "Johnny's" rifle and the General dropped to the bottom of the trench, his hands over his eyes, muttering, "What a rascal!" In reply to Sampson's anxious inquiry as to whether he was badly hit, Birdwood replied, "No!" Blood was streaming down his face, but the wound turned out to be only a superficial one caused by splinters of glass. The periscope in question was a large box-shaped arrangement made from plywood, being one of four that Captain Walsh and the officers of "A" Company had made at their own expense by an Egyptian in Cairo at a cost of 100 piastres each.

When General Birdwood, in company with General Monash and a naval officer, were in Quinn's Post on May 12, Private A. Elliott, "C" Company, who had purloined some onions and potatoes from the Q.M. store and, with bully beef and biscuits, made an appetising stew for his comrades and, ladened with a kerosene tin full of the boiling mixture, met the staff in the front line just as "Johnny" Turk hurled a bomb into the trench. Not wishing to lose the stew, Elliott stood transfixed as the bomb exploded. Calmly placing the stew down, he removed his boots and, with a penknife, began to extract the pieces of bomb that had entered his feet. Birdwood asked him what he was trying to do and, discovering that the boy was operating upon himself, said, "That won't do, my man—you go to the beach." Elliott attempted to get to his feet to obey, but found he could not walk. He was taken down to Doctor Luther and was afterwards conveyed to the Casualty Station on the beach by Simpson and his donkey.

On the same day those men who constituted the remains of the centre attacking party of May 9—there were nine in all—were withdrawn from the line and taken down to the foot of Pope's Hill, where they were interrogated by General Birdwood and Colonel Monash on the fighting ability of the Turks. General Birdwood was very anxious to learn whether the Turks fought back when faced with the bayonet. Among the nine was the leader of the charge, Sergeant Bob Hunter, the imperturbable Ross Hayes, quicksilver Charlie Quinn, quiet Jack White, "Bluey" Williams—the man with the mop of scarlet hair—and Corporal Basil Atkinson. After their interview with the General, these men, together with the remains of No. 11 Platoon, were placed under the command of Hunter until a few days later Lieutenant Horne, better known to the battalion as "The Bagman," assumed command.

Up to this date the casualties among officers had been very high. There were: Killed 12, Missing (now known to have been killed) 2, Wounded 13. Among the wounded officers Lieutenant H. Kessell, our machine-gun officer, had died in Egypt, and Lieutenant Leo Casey did not recover from his injuries until after the war ended.

On Saturday, May 15th, at 1.45 a.m., the Light Horse attacked the Turkish trenches in front of Quinn's. In this case the assaulting parties were but two, consisting of 30 men each under the commands of Captain Birbeck and Lieutenant Ogilvy with two digging parties of 20 men each under Major Graham and Lieutenant Potts. The 15th's share of this attack consisted of the holding of the line and the supplying of guides and messengers to the attacking parties. Among the guides were Sergeant Ray Tickner and Privates N. H. Boyd and G. Kidd, all of whom had been in the attack on May 9th. The 15th men had entered the 2nd Light Horse's trenches on the evening of the 12th, and when zero hour approached they hoisted the attackers upon the parapet. As in the case of "D" Company's attack from Russell's Top, the unfortunate Light Horsemen did not get a running start. They were shot down upon the parapet so soon as they got up and fell back into the trench. A few of them did manage to get to the front line, but it was impossible for them to do anything when they got there. Captain Birbeck, who was in command of the right party, was wounded. Major Graham, in charge of the digging parties, leapt out of the trench and sought to rescue some of his men. He recovered a few before being killed. The casualties of the assaulting parties were: Killed 25, wounded 21. The guides lent by the Battalion were either killed or wounded, our casualties being: Killed 3, wounded 11, Boyd and Kidd were reported missing.

The day following, the commissariat department of the Australian Army was too generous. Instead of plum jam covered with flies, someone got the wonderful idea of sending a ham bone along the trench. Dirty fingers pulled at the meat, or hacked slices off with their jack knives until it was difficult to tell what it was, owing to the finger marks. When it arrived in "A" Company's trench, one greasy paw after another released it until it looked as if it had been rescued from a dog's storage plant. Then it passed to the last man in the trench, Old "Ganger" Slack, who, after seizing it with both hands, gnawed at it until satisfied, then hurled it over his head into the Turk's trench exclaiming, "Here you bastard—you can have it now." There was silence for a few moments, then "Johnny" started.

For a hectic hour he kept that gang of men running about dodging his bombs, while from their lips came a string of curses at "Ganger" for having disturbed a peaceful hour and probably ruined their digestion for all time.

At 11 a.m. on May 15, the Battalion was relieved again by the 16th and a troop of the 3rd Light Horse, and retired to billets once more in Monash Valley. They remained here for the next two days, and on May 18 re-entered the Post at midday. The afternoon passed away quietly, but just before midnight the Post was reinforced by two companies of the 16th Battalion, as it had been learned that the enemy intended attacking. Later in the night another company of the 16th and a squadron of Light Horse were brought into reserve. About midnight the enemy opened heavy fire upon the Post and a positive landslide of stones and earth from the kicking bullets fell into the trench.

♦ ♦ ♦ ♦

CHAPTER III.

THE TURKISH ATTACK ON MAY 19.

The Turkish attack on May 19, which was launched against the whole Anzac front, had its harbingers in the Quinn's Post area in the form of some forty 9.2 H.E. shells that were thrown into Monash Valley just after the Battalion had moved out to reoccupy the Post. The sole damage done was one man killed and three wounded, belonging to the 15th, and some thirty or more casualties among members of other nearby units. The wounded 15th men were in reality injured from the falling lumps of rock and earth.

The companies occupying the front line were "A," "B" and "C," the latter in between "A" on the right and "B" on the left. Part of "A" Company—Lieutenant Harold Koch's platoon—was on the extreme right of the Post with a field of fire across the Courtney's Post front. It is doubtful whether in a defensive action of this description the true facts as to when the Post came into action against the Turks will be known. In "C" Company's sector, where the men occupying it were without a commander, being commanded by Sergeant Bob Hunter and other non-commissioned officers, Hunter, who was half asleep at the feet of Private C. Quinn, was awakened by that soldier, who had spotted the Turks leaving their trenches. He leapt to his feet and gave the order for his men to fire. In the Bloody Angle sector of the Post held by Captain B. Sampson, with Lieutenants Leitch and Mundell's platoons, the enemy had approached the position by means of saps, and were not at that time visible to the men holding the line. Sergeant Tom Dann therefore suggested, when the Turks commenced bombing the trench, that the men should retire under the bombproof shelter—a few yards away in the support line—so as to be ready for an emergency. Remaining in the trench with Corporal F. Storey, the two men replied to the Turks' bombing, keeping them at a distance. To ensure more accuracy to their throwing, they frequently leapt upon the parapet and, lighting their bombs in full view of the foe, threw them among the attacking bombers. A little further along the trench, where the same difficulty as Dann was confronted with was occurring, Corporal F. Cawley and Private F. Hanley were likewise bombing the Turks, and it was from

this vantage point Dann learned that a number of Turks had crept closer in to the parapet, thus missing his bombs which were all going over their heads to their rear. On receipt of this information, Dann cut his fuses to two-second ones and rolled them over his parapet, freeing the trench from this new menace.

When the Turks left their trenches in numbers in front of this spot, a fierce rifle fire came from the men who had been secreted in the bombproof shelters, and the surprised Turks fell away before the onslaught of lead. So close was the fighting at this point that Sampson, Leitch and Mundell were emptying their revolvers into the mass of attackers. In Lieutenant Little's and Lieutenant Sparks' sectors—5 and 6—the enemy also penetrated to within a few feet, but were bombed out. Sparks discovered that the Turks had sapped from the old left-hand communication trench built on May 9 and, in endeavouring to bomb them out, one of our jam-tin contraptions burst in his hand and blew it off. Little, with the aid of Lance-Corporal Chippendale, had cleared the attackers from the front of his sector. In the right sector, commanded by Lieutenant Koch, near to the 14th Battalion, Privates J. Armstrong and Fleet were on sentry at the time when the attack was launched. They also opened fire, though at the commencement the enemy appeared to be moving parallel with their front, apparently more intent upon Courtney's Post than upon Quinn's. The German and Turkish officers leading the charge displayed the most outstanding bravery. With swords waving above their heads, and their followers calling upon "Allah," they stormed towards our line. As their foremost ranks dwindled beneath the heavy rifle and machine-gun fire, hundreds of men seemed to spring forward to take the places of those who fell.

The rifles of the defenders of the Post ran hot, and wounded men struggled up and down along the line of firing men, pouring oil upon the bolts and muzzles of their weapons. Down in the valley in front of Courtney's thousands of Turks could be seen ready to reinforce the men in the foremost positions. Into this dense mass of men H.M.S. "Triumph" opened fire, bursting her shells with remarkable accuracy. When the smoke cleared away not a man was to be seen. It was at this moment that the right flank of the Post was attacked. A yell from Armstrong, "The bastards are on top of us!" rent the air, and as if from the ground itself sprang into view line after line of Turks charging down upon the Post. Machine-guns playing across the front swept the attackers off their feet, but their numbers appeared endless, for more and yet more rushed forward to fill the gaps. As

one wave of the attacking troops got to within striking distance of the parapet, a sudden burst from a machine-gun put them out of action.

The enemy then turned his own machine guns upon the defenders. Playing along the parapet, he compelled them to keep their heads down and to utilise the old manner of firing, by raising their rifles over their heads and pulling the trigger. It was during this procedure that Turks entered a slight depression to the right front of the line. In this depression the enemy were practically invisible to the men in the trench while they were lying on the ground and the sector was completely surprised when a yell arose, "The Turks are in the trench!"

As it happened the enemy were met with rapid rifle fire at point blank range—less than five yards—and only three of the attackers gained the parapet. One fell dying into the trench and the other two died upon the raised earth. At no other point in the 15th line did a Turk, dead or alive, enter the trench. In the lull that followed before the second attack, which swiftly petered out, being rather a half-hearted affair, the men, jubilant over their victory, grew careless and disported themselves upon the parapet, exposing themselves in the most ridiculous manner by taking potshots at an enemy whom they no longer feared. This foolishness resulted in a number of casualties.

The total casualties were: Killed 12, Wounded 43. Among the wounded was that fine ex-South African soldier, Private Harry Dillon, who, despite a bullet wound in the shoulder, carried on throughout the battle until finally another bullet shattered his hand and he had to leave. Sergeant A. E. Musgrave was also wounded at the commencement of the fight but refused point blank to go to the doctor, and when he did get there refused to be evacuated until Doctor Luther took him to the Beach himself. The loss of Lieutenant Joe Sparks filled his platoon with deep regret for this newly-created officer was intensely popular with all ranks.

The respect of the Australian for the gallantry of the Turk no matter what individually he might think of him for his cruelty, is instanced in the following. When the charge had finally ceased, sniping by our men continued throughout the day. During the course of that day, Private Jimmy Armstrong, who was a splendid shot, had, with his companions, bagged a considerable number seeking to cross an open position so that they could reinforce their men in the front line. As man after man ran across this space, a

bullet greeted him from our trenches, and as the range was short many of the Turks bit the dust. To the astonishment of the men in the trench, after one of their number had fired and hit his man, Armstrong, who was watching closely, saw a young Turk calmly walk to the man who was hit, pick him up, and gaze long and steadily at the trench from where the shots were coming. It was a tense moment for the men in the trench, a moment broken by the voice of young Jimmy pathetically declaring, "Don't shoot—it might be his brother." In silence they watched the young Turk remove the injured man.

An armistice for the burial of the dead which lay about in large numbers during the days following the engagement was granted on May 24 after a series of lengthy conferences several days beforehand. When the first flags were hoisted matters moved quietly for a moment, then two men in the Post were hit—one being killed and the other wounded. Colonel Cannan immediately made a protest and it appeared that the shots were fired by men quite unaware that the armistice was in force. A demarcation line was observed by both sides, and beyond this line neither side ventured. With heads poking over the parapet and men shouting or smiling greetings to the enemy, a change rapidly came over the scene. Man after man ventured out until the space between the two trenches was full of troops. All the talk of treachery, and the rumours of Turk cruelty were forgotten by the Australians on this day. Signallers and medical men, headquarters staff and stretcher bearers, naval officers and machine gun and artillery officers all appeared upon the scene. Sketches were made of the opposing line, machine-gun positions were located and the saps that had cost so many lives were used as graves in which to bury the dead, thus doing away with this menace to the safety of the Post.

Several amusing incidents are recorded, especially that of Doctor Luther, who, in company with some Maryborough lads, was wandering around viewing the sights when one of them noticed some Turks working upon a section of the trench. He drew Luther's attention to this and the Doctor spoke to the Turk officer about it. A shout of laughter greeted the Turkish officer's manner of dealing with his men. Walking over to the delinquents, he dealt them vicious kicks in the seats of their pants, and drove them away from their earthworks. When Colonel Jim Cannan remarked to a number of "A" Company men who were accepting cigars from the Turks in exchange for gifts they offered, that the cigars were good and they had better ask the Turks for them

after the armistice was over, the suggestion that the Colonel should take that office upon himself raised a hearty laugh.

Directly opposite Corporal Jack Craven, who was holding the Red Cross aloft in front of Quinn's, was a Turk wearing the uniform of a Turkish N.C.O., and holding the Turkish Red Crescent. This Turk was obviously so superior that it was rumoured that he was a Turkish general or a German officer. Craven endeavoured to make conversation with him in broken Arabic and French, but the Turk, taking not the slightest notice scanned the lines continuously. It was not until after the war that it was learnt through Leman Von Sanders' book—"5 Years In Turkey"—that this soldier was Kemal Pasha, who twice frustrated the Anzacs at the landing and at Hill 971, and who was destined to become Dictator of Turkey after the War. Von Sanders mentions this incident as having occurred in front of Bombe Post, which was the Turkish Quinn's. It is also mentioned as a footnote in "The Story of Anzac," Vol. 2, and in Lowell Thomas' "The Grey Wolf."

At 12 noon on May 25th, the Battalion was relieved by 100 men of the 16th Battalion, 100 of the 10th Light Horse, and 60 of the 13th Battalion, and returned to their bivouac in Monash Valley. During the afternoon the Battalion once again moved up to Quinn's as support in anticipation of an attack being launched when the mine set beneath the sap from which most of the bombing of the Post was coming should be fired. The explosion was said to have been successful, and the Battalion returned to its camp about 6.30 p.m., as the enemy remained inactive. For the next three days the Battalion remained in bivouac and suffered a number of casualties from snipers.

On May 27, Colonel Cannan received an invitation to spend two days aboard H.M.T. "Arcadia" as the guest of the Commander-in-Chief, General Sir Ian Hamilton. On this day, Lieutenant Fred Youden and Lieutenant Harold Koch returned from hospital. With the additional reinforcements and details that also arrived, the strength of the Battalion at this period was: Officers 22, Other Ranks 520. Lieutenant Bill Mundell, who had contracted laryngitis, was evacuated ill to hospital, and Captain Herman Cannan was in the same hospital.

In the mix-up associated with the blowing-up of Quinn's Post on May 29, it is difficult to obtain a clear-cut narrative of the general sequences of events. The Post was held at the time of the explosion by the 13th Battalion under Colonel Burnage. The 15th was bivouacked at the foot of the hill under the command of Major Bert Carter.—Colonel Cannan

being still the guest of Sir Ian Hamilton. At this stage in the history of Quinn's Post there was a permanent commander of the Post, Colonel Chauvel, and a permanent adjutant, Lieutenant T. P. McSharry, 2nd Light Horse, who later on became more than well-known to the 15th. Warnings regarding the activities of Turkish miners had been frequently given by the infantrymen who had volunteered for the job of tunnelling to counteract the enemy's burrowing. But all these warnings were ignored. When "Ganger" Slack came off duty just before midnight on the 28th, he shrugged his shoulders with disgust, and declared emphatically the Turk mine would go up within a few hours. Slack had heard the charge being tamped into position and knew well what that portended. The frantic endeavours that had been made during the two previous days to stop the inroads of the Turk were now realised to have failed. Orders were therefore given for the men of the 15th to sleep with their boots on, as in the event of the Post going up it was their duty to regain any trenches lost.

In the shift after midnight were a number of 15th men working as miners. Among these were Privates H. Evans and J. Fleet. The sound of the Turks working could be clearly heard by these two men. After cleaning up from their night's work, they changed over with the new shift and made their way down the hill preparatory to getting some sleep, which they badly needed. Fleet, who, in his spare time was also a runner attached to Battalion Headquarters, "dossed" close to Headquarters so as to be handy to a call. He had barely laid his head down before the explosion took place. With one bound he was in Major Carter's Headquarters, received his orders and sped off to the various company commanders. Captain Sampson, who at this time was commanding "A" Company, owing to Captain Herman Cannan being on the sick list, was awake at the time of the explosion, and his company was "fallen in" before Major Carter's orders reached him.

Hastening with his men up the hill, and closely followed by "C" Company under the command of Sergeants Hunter and Stormonth, he arrived amid the general confusion then existing and sought out Lieutenant McSharry for orders. Carter also arrived at the Post with all speed, and ordered Nos. 11 and 12 Platoons of "C" Company into the short sector of trench to the left of the main sap, giving Hunter instructions that his men were not to be used except in an emergency. Stormonth was drafted over to the right flank connecting with the right of Lieutenant Perry's 13th Battalion platoon which was holding its own and forcing the

Turks into the very centre of the Post. When Sampson received the order from McSharry to retake the left arm of the angle and do precisely the same as Perry was doing, Colonel Burnage was giving Lieutenant Koch orders where he was to take his platoon. Sampson led his men directly across the rise into the trench on the left and at this moment a bomb landed, wounding Lieutenant Koch of the 15th and Colonel Burnage and Captain Marks of the 13th Battalion. Colonel Pope then took over Colonel Burnage's command. Koch's men, now leaderless, acted upon their own initiative and ran in the direction in which they had seen Colonel Burnage pointing. This group, slightly to the right of Sampson's men, met opposition the moment they touched the skyline, but owing to the luck that is sometimes present in warfare, missed the sweep of machine-gun fire that struck Sampson and his men to the left of them. This escape was due to a Turkish carrying party being between them and the gun that was firing. The carrying party, laden mainly with bombs, seeing Koch's men, immediately dropped their loads and commenced hurling the bombs at the platoon. For a few seconds the men fired rapidly at the enemy in the trench, quelling them for the moment, and then rushed in with the bayonet. Then a strange thing happened. Fleet, along with two other men, was lifted clean out of the trench and commenced rolling down the hill on to the bayonets of the men in the support line. Aided by their mates, the three men regained their feet and struggled up the slope back into the trench, apparently none the worse for their queer experience. This group of men included among them Sergeant Tom Williams and Privates Jack Hynes and Jimmy Armstrong, while a sergeant from "D" Company, whose name has been forgotten, was foremost in the attack. They hung on like grim death to the small sector of trench they had captured. At the same time Sampson, who had led his men to the left, met opposition from the Turk machine-gun, and after he had jumped into the front line that the Turks were occupying, found no men were with him. Jumping out again to find the reason, he discovered his first six men lying in a row, having been mown down by the gun. Hastily picking up his Corporal, Andy Hooper, who had been closest to him when the charge commenced, he called to the survivors and leapt back into the trench again, carrying Hooper with him. Hooper unfortunately was dead. With the rest of his men in the trench, he began to clean it up with jam-tin bombs. The result of the combined operations of the two platoons of "A" Company was that all that section of the Post was rapidly freed of the enemy, who were forced into the small

support bombproof shelter connected by three short saps to the front line. From this point Sampson could not venture any further owing to the shortage of bombs. They had used all they had brought with them and to move into the straight section of the front line connecting up with the larger bombproof shelter was merely suicide. At the same time as Sampson's two platoons commenced their charge, Lieutenant Leitch was ordered to charge to the right, but the moment his men showed above the skyline the enemy's machine-guns effectively stopped their advance, Leitch falling out of the battle with a shattered hand.

It is quite unnecessary in this history to delve into all the whys and wherefores of the many changes of plans that took place until the very moment the Post was cleared. It was a case of too many cooks. Generals, Colonels, Majors and Subalterns, besides N.C.O.'s and, in some cases privates, all knew how to handle the situation. The enemy were confined to one section of the trench only, and in the natural course of things would have been compelled to surrender, for their retirement across the open from the position they held was impracticable owing to the cross-fire that could be concentrated upon the position when day broke. But General Godley issued the command that the trenches must be cleared of the enemy at once. The two "C" Company platoons held in reserve Carter refused point blank to use unless Major Quinn conducted the operation in person. Upon McSharry agreeing to this, Quinn was sent for.

At this time "B" Company, under Captain Hill and Lieutenant Little, was awaiting the order to charge also, and upon the arrival of Major Quinn these two officers led their men—Hill to the left of the small bombproof and Little in between the two bombproofs. Hill's men, consisting solely of the Transport Section which had landed with him only a few days before, gave a cheer at the commencement of their charge, with the result they were greeted with a shower of bombs and many of them became casualties. Little's party, which included Sergeant Eric Simon of "A" Company and Sergeant Bob Hunter of "C" Company, besides Quinn, Hayes and other members of the same company, had gained the crest, but could not venture any further without risk of annihilation. Major Carter, standing just below Little's position, transferred to that officer a number of jam-tin bombs, and with these the party commenced clearing the sector in front. McSharry at this period gathered some men together and, gaining possession of some stick bombs, reinforced Little. Under the combined fire, the front line was finally cleared.

It was during the bombing of the fleeing Turks that a jam-tin burst in Little's hand, destroying his eyesight and blowing off his hand. Hunter immediately took control, but within a few minutes a shell from one of our batteries burst and he was badly wounded. Luther, who was close up on the fighting, immediately treated Hunter for a severed femoral artery and saved his life. Then Private Charlie Quinn was wounded. Simon had been doing excellent work throughout the fight, especially in stopping the sniping of Little's men from the loophole in the big bombproof, and he became a casualty also. In "A" Company sector, Fleet became suddenly weak and ill, and upon inspection it was found he was wounded and had to be taken from the trench. Sergeant McKenzie also became a casualty with a bullet in the jaw.

Colonel Chauvel had arrived upon the scene during the fighting and he gave the order for the front line to be manned once again. Major Quinn was given the command of the charge, but Quinn was in a very argumentative mood and though two companies to be used in the charge were ready to start, he refused to give the order. Finally McSharry, who had borne most of the responsibility throughout the whole affair, and to whom the most credit is due, took Quinn with him up the sap to show that officer just what was intended. At the junction of the sap and front line, Quinn was killed with a bullet in the brain. Major Hugh Quinn was twenty-seven years old at the time of his death. He was born in Charters Towers, North Queensland, and practised his profession in Townsville. In the North he was well known as an amateur heavyweight boxer. He had commanded "C" Company from its inception and was the first company commander in the Battalion to be killed in action. Quinn's Post, which bears his name, is now part of Australian history, allied for all time with the name of Anzac.

It was known at this time that the enemy was bottled up in the two bombproofs. McSharry was strongly opposed to charging over the top of the bombproofs, thus bringing his men into full view of the enemy and losing too many lives. But Colonel Chauvel demanded the charge. Colonel Pope made the final arrangements. The charge was to be made with the remaining men of Quinn's own company and Herring's company of the 13th Battalion. Again luck was with the Australians, for the Turks had decided to attack on the left of Quinn's and opened out with a fierce machine-gun barrage upon the Post in order to keep the defenders' heads down. The moment the barrage lifted the order was given to charge. The men sprang forward, raced up the slope, and

jumped into the trenches, meeting with no fire whatever, as the enemy was too afraid of hitting their own men charging towards us on the left. About 8 a.m. the enemy confined in the large bombproof surrendered. Captain J. Hill had cleared the tunnels of the smaller bombproof when he heard cries from the larger one, and risking treachery, entered it almost simultaneously with some of Herring's men, who approached from the other end.

The Australian losses were: Killed 33 and wounded 178. In the clean-up of the trenches 23 dead Turks were removed. Seventeen prisoners were taken. The loss to the 15th Battalion of officers in this engagement was— Killed: Major Hugh Quinn. Wounded: Captain Hill, Lieutenants H. R. Koch, E. G. Leitch, E. M. Little, and G. King. The last three mentioned officers did not again serve with the Battalion.

In the afternoon the Battalion left Quinn's Post and returned to bivouac, leaving behind them 275 men to help hold the line. On May 30th another 75 men were withdrawn from the Post and, at 1 p.m., a demonstration was made in the gully between Quinn's and Pope's Hill so as to attract the attention of the enemy while an attack was launched from Quinn's. At 6.30 p.m. the balance of the 15th Battalion was withdrawn from the Post and joined up with the unit. The Battalion remained in bivouac until May 31, upon which day Lieutenant C. Davy and 56 other ranks reported for duty. Upon this day also confirmation that the long-promised rest was about to eventuate came, when part of the unit was transferred to Rest Gully.

REST GULLY

On June 1 the Battalion bade farewell to Quinn's Post and made its way down Shrapnel Gully to its new home. The sudden change from the anxious life on Quinn's was very much appreciated by the men at the commencement of their rest. But as the day went by and the many duties multiplied until rest became non-existent, even the life of the trenches at Quinn's seemed a long holiday compared with what they were now undergoing. The Gully was situated directly below the Sphinx, and the one drawback mentioned in regard to it during the first few days of occupancy was that the spent bullets, fired by the enemy at the defenders on Walker's Ridge, often penetrated into the Gully.

Rest Gully had its attractions as well as its disadvantages. Some of these the troops found diverting though naturally their tastes did not all run in the same direction. Some found swimming a great sport. Even the prospect of being heavily shelled did not stand in the way of taking a dip in the sea.

The weather was becoming warm and the lice, according to one authority, multiplied faster than rabbits, and were more annoying than mosquitoes in a mangrove swamp. Up on the Sphinx a sentry was posted to keep a lookout for Anarfata Bill when he opened fire. The moment the flash of his guns was perceived a whistle would be blown and all the troops immediately took cover until his shell had exploded. Anarfata Bill was not the only attraction to the men on sentry, for the peaceful sight of a Turkish farmer tilling his land near the olive grove on the left flank interested many. This scene of rural peacefulness seemed quaint and unreal, but during the period in France similar scenes became almost of daily occurrence.

It is impossible to trace the disappearance and arrival of many men during the time spent in Rest Gully. The strength of the Battalion in officers and men was forever changing. On June 1 two elderly N.C.O.'s—Q.M.S. Lord and C.S.M. Hansen—were both admitted to hospital sick and being declared medically unfit, left the unit for all time. On June 2 three officers reported for duty with 7 details and 106 reinforcements. These officers were Captain Frank Moran, O.C. "B" Company, from details and Lieutenants Walter "Granny" Coombs and C.M. "Nigger" Johnston. The latter at the end of 1918, after a term on Brigade and in command of the 14th Battalion, assumed command of the 15th and took that unit into its last engagement in France and the War. On June 4, with the addition of another 40 details and reinforcements, the unit's strength had grown to 18 officers and 622 other ranks. On June 12 Captain Herman Cannan reported back from hospital, and on this date Sergeants S. L. Stormonth and D. M. Gillies were appointed Second Lieutenants. On June 21 there came to the 15th from the 2nd Light Horse, the man who was to lead the unit for so long throughout the heavy fighting in France, Lieutenant T. P. McSharry, who immediately assumed the duties of Adjutant. On June 22 Second Lieutenant W. F. Eather, who afterwards transferred to the 47th Battalion upon the forming of that unit at Tel-el-Kabir, joined up, and on June 26 Lieutenant G. F. Dickinson, whom no one expected to see with the unit again, returned. On June 27 the battalion had 25 officers and 670 other ranks. On July 9 and 10 Lieutenant W. T. Mundell and Major Eccles Snowden reported back from hospital, and Lieutenant F. J. Platt landed from the "Seeang Bee." On July 19 the Battalion strength had decreased to 24 officers and increased to 717 other ranks[1].

---

(1) The decrease is due to illness of officers of which records are scanty.

On Sunday, June 6, the first church service upon the Peninsula at which members of the 15th Battalion attended was held. The Anglican service was conducted by the Reverend Colonel Wray and the Reverend Captain Gillison, Chaplain of the 14th Battalion. As regards Captain Gillison, the 15th Battalion rather claimed connection with him—though a sad one. It was in Dr. Luther's dressing station on the right flank that Gillison's nephew died from his wounds on April 28, and upon the Chaplain joining the 14th Battalion on Gallipoli, he immediately made acquaintance with Luther and was conducted to the grave in Shrapnel Gully where the lad was buried. Luther and Gillison, both non-combatants, were killed within a few days of each other in August. The Roman Catholic service was conducted by the Right Rev. Chaplain Thomas Power, a man who endeared himself to all with whom he came into contact. Throughout the services stray bullets whistled overhead, but no one was hit. At the next service, held on June 13, the Turk did not depend upon stray bullets. During the day he bombarded the camping ground with shrapnel. The bombardment was heavy, but no casualties ensued except among the mules, six of which were killed. On neither day were the services unduly interrupted and it is a significant fact that the majority of the men thoroughly enjoyed them. In several diaries it is noted that the writers make the statement: "It is jolly good to be able to sing the old hymns again." This simple statement written on the spot speaks volumes for the true spirit in the hearts of so many of the men; men who, from the date of the Landing, had uttered all manner of curses against living conditions (mostly the lice), the food and "Johnny" the Turk.

A message from General Godley, officer commanding the New Zealand and Australian Division of which the 4th Brigade was a part, was read to the men of the Brigade at the church service on June 6. Its contents were as follows:—

> "Please convey to Colonels Monash and Cannan and all officers, N.C.O.'s and men of the 4th A.I.F. Brigade my high appreciation of the gallantry and determination of the troops who took part in the attack on the Turkish lines from Quinn's Post on the night of 9/10 May. The operation was necessary in order to relieve pressure on our forces in the South, and was completely successful. Not only was the enemy obliged to deploy all his supports and reserves in order to meet that attack, but large numbers of Turks were killed, and there is no question but that a severe blow was inflicted upon them. The whole of the rest of the Division is filled with admiration of the gallant conduct of their Australian comrades."

This belated praise for the work of the 15th upon the night of May 9/10 came about through the capture of a Turkish officer who kept a diary and unwittingly supplied the following information to our Corps Commander:—

"In an attack on May 10 the losses of two Turkish regiments alone amounted to 600 killed and 2,000 wounded."

The greater number of these casualties occurred no doubt during the Turk counter-attack when they reoccupied the trenches we had vacated, and during the continuance of the movement of their troops during broad daylight when our machine-gun and shrapnel fire played havoc in their ranks.

It was on this parade that the first two men to receive decorations in the 15th Battalion were named. They were 2nd/Lieutenant E. Corbett who, as Staff-Sergeant-Major in charge of the battalion machine-gunners after the wounding of Lieutenant H. Kessell on Pope's Hill, did excellent work during that engagement and at subsequent dates; and Private A. "Scotty" Wright of "A" Company, whose splendid work from the day of the Landing had at last been noticed. Both men received the Distinguished Conduct Medal[1].

The Australian troops, from their earliest days of training, had been trained to keep their lines and billets clean. Not that this was essential for, compared with troops of other countries, there is no doubt that the Australian stood supreme in the old adage: "Cleanliness is akin to Godliness." To help maintain the cleanliness of the camping ground there was an incinerator into which all refuse went. The report had been circulated among the Turks, evidently with the idea of making them fight harder than ever, that the Australians were cannibals. One day an unfortunate Turk was brought down into the Gully, and the first thing his panic-stricken eyes beheld was the smoking incinerator. With a howl of anguish and yells for help to Allah, he balked passing it like a stubborn mule.

On July 14 the two "A" Company Captains, Herman Cannan and Burford Sampson, set out for Steele's Post to visit

---

(1) In Sir Ian Hamilton's despatch for June 12, 1915, the following members of the 15th Battalion were mentioned: Staff-Sergeant-Major E. Corbett, Private A. Wright, Corporal L. Melia, Lance-Corporal J. Craven, Private H. Edelstin, Private W. L. James. All excepting L. Melia were awarded D.C.M.'s.

Corbett's and Wright's services with the Battalion were not to last much longer. On July 30 Corbett became ill and was sent to hospital, was transferred to the Permanent Supernumerary List of Officers and retained for duty in the A.I.F. Depots, England. Wright, about the same time, was mounting guard in Reserve Gully with Privates Jack Hynes and Yates. As the three men moved down the Gully to take up their duties a shrapnel shell burst above them and Wright was seriously injured. When "Scotty" Taylor and Fred Hanley ran to see what had happened they found Hynes holding the main artery of Wright's thigh which had been severed with a shrapnel pellet. Hynes' pipe, which he was holding between his teeth, was severed by a pellet and he still retained the mouthpiece between his teeth while he attended to Wright.

the grave of Major J. F. Walsh. On their way up to the Post they met Captain Ritchie, a N.Z. Medical Officer, who had been on the "Seeang Bee" with them, and Ritchie decided to accompany them. After inspecting the grave and making arrangements for a new cross to be placed above it, they met Captain Jack Yeoman of the 6th Battalion, who was known to Sampson. At the request of Yeoman, the three officers visited a newly constructed C.P. that looked down Mule Valley. While doing so, a Turkish H.E. shell of some 8-inch calibre landed among them. Ritchie was badly wounded and the two 15th officers were badly shaken. In Sampson's case both ear drums were ruptured, the hair burnt off the head, and pebbles and dirt driven into his legs. Fever set in that night and later he was evacuated.

As a health resort, Gallipoli Peninsula was an utter failure. From the day of the Landing diarrhoea had become a nightmare to the men. The flies, the continual odour of rotting bodies, along with the inadequate and mostly unpalatable food, and at intervals a marked shortage of water, all helped to aid this dread disease in undermining the health of the men. In this matter our medical staff was faced with a most difficult problem. Any man capable of standing erect, sick though he happened to be, could not be evacuated without seriously weakening the unit. Added to this, loyalty to their mates prevented the men leaving the Peninsula other than upon a stretcher. At this period of the campaign, June and July, Dr. Luther was in a dilemma and freely admitted it. What he had at his disposal he freely used to alleviate the distress. Tricks were played upon him by some of the men, as was perhaps natural. The old one of chewing cordite was tried by a young chap who was run down with dysentery and thought he might have a spell in the Beach hospital. His scheme failed, and Luther told him that if he ate a little more he would rest forever on Gallipoli's shores, so the youngster sought "Grumbling" Fred Stacey's aid. This the lad did with remarkable results. Completely cured within a week after taking Stacey's advice to eat soap, he found at the end of a fortnight that he had gained weight. The determination of some men not to be evacuated is worth recording. Particularly so is the case of Private Joe Coogan of "C" Company. Coogan was seriously ill. His friends tried to persuade him to go to the doctor, but he would have none of it. Time went on and he struggled through the August fighting till the unit left for its protracted holiday on Lemnos Island. The morning after the unit's arrival there Coogan's unconscious form was found in the latrine.

Dr. C. E. W. Bean, in his "Story of Anzac" (Volume 11),

has dealt fully with the general health of the troops. On page 377 he gives reasons for the increase in sickness which were agreed upon by the four regimental Medical Officers of the 4th Brigade. They are as follows:—

1. The men's health was below normal and was getting worse.
2. No further steps could be suggested towards improving sanitation or hygiene.
3. The principal symptoms were—gastric derangements, bronchial affections, rapid pulse, loss of weight, heart dilation.
4. The predisposing causes were—irregularity of rest and meals, restricted dietary (as regards variety), hot weather, flies, dust.

This information was obtained on July 29. The historian goes on to refer to Colonel Monash's view that the position was not very serious. That the condition of the troops could be anything other than serious is very difficult to understand. But an operation was contemplated, the result of which, the Brigadier thought, would be that "the condition of the troops would markedly improve." This operation which was to be so health-restoring was to prove the most difficult operation undertaken upon Gallipoli Peninsula. It seemed more reasonable, as the men were to be asked to perform miracles, to husband their strength instead of utilising it upon every conceivable task it was possible to imagine.

The worst feature of the strain on the failing strength of the men was the amount of digging they were called upon to do. So long as a man who participated in destroying the Gallipoli landscape lives he is not likely to forget the days when he "rested" in "Rest Gully." The work was not only arduous — it was dangerous. There were frequent casualties and the intense nerve strain that the supposed rest was expected to relieve was not in any way diminished, if anything—it increased. The duties included both day and night work, and when towards the end of July stores and ammunition were unloaded under shell fire the joys of soldiering had reached their greatest heights. The saps and communication trenches dug included those which were to be used during the August offensive. One near to the beach belonged to that category of sap where each shovelful displaced caused an avalanche of sand to fall into the hole just made.

The most trying part of the day came after the dismissal of the various fatigue parties, for it was then that the men cooked their food. The ration was composed almost entirely of bully beef, hard biscuits, cheese, jam, sugar, tea and some bacon, while bread, when on issue, was at the rate of six men to a loaf. The cheese and bacon can well be visualised after the day's heat, for there were no such things as ice chests. Having to cook their own

food after a heavy day's or night's work did not tend to make the unsightly ingredients any the more palatable. If the cooking arrangements had been conducted in a similar manner to those in France, no doubt a marked improvement in the men's health would have been noticeable; for though many were amateur cooks, the great majority would have been despoilers of even the most cleanly and attractive of viands.

On the night of August 2 the first attempt was made at a concert to counteract the mental fatigue of the men. The life and soul of this performance was Hon. Lieutenant Fred Crane, an old Hobart harrier, who had acted in the capacity of bandmaster to the battalion since the days of Broadmeadows Camp. Crane was the moving spirit of the evening, and his sparkling humour was just the tonic his war-weary comrades required. The climax to the performance was reached when three hearty cheers were given to Crane for the pleasant evening, and Johnny the Turk, hearing the cheering, thought our men intended to attack from Walker's Ridge and opened up a heavy machine-gun and rifle fire upon these trenches. This was essentially Crane's last public appearance with the unit.

◆ ◆ ◆ ◆

CHAPTER IV.

THE HEIGHTS OF ABDEL RAHMAN BAIR.

In dealing with the attack by the 4th Brigade upon the heights of Abdel Rahman Bair—better known as Hill 971— a number of salient points, all of which helped materially in the failure of the project, must be borne in mind. They can be summarised as follows:—

1. The delay in starting caused through the congestion of troops crossing the Brigade's line of route.
2. The absence of sufficient guides thoroughly conversant with the country.
3. The weakness of the original men of the units through continuance of diarrhoea or dysentery.
4. The difficulty of cohesive action owing to the operations being conducted at night.
5. The mistake in locality.
6. The failure of General Sir Frederick W. Stopford's landing force at Suvla Bay to take full advantage of their success and to relieve thus the pressure exerted by the Turks upon the Brigade's position.
7. The necessity of delaying one day before pushing forward to the final objective.
8. The difficulty of moving other than in single file through much of the country.
9. The failure on the part of Colonel Monash to verify personally the line under construction on August 7, before committing his Brigade to the advance upon the morning of the 8th.

It has been said that "an objective is gained, only after preparing for every eventuality, including those which do not, but easily might, occur." Over-riding all the disadvantages the Brigade had to contend with, the valour of the men might easily have won the day if the error of locality had been rectified immediately. That this was not done on the morning of the 7th August rests with the Brigade and Divisional commanders.

Out of a battalion strength of 720 men, approximately 400 were reinforcements and 120 transport. These 520 men had reported for duty at various intervals while the unit was resting in Rest Gully. Added to this number are, of course, the details—wounded men who had returned from Egypt, Malta and England with various drafts, and the Battalion Headquarters staff which included signallers, A.M.C. and others. It will be seen therefore that the Battalion was practically a new one and, what was especially important, one which had not performed a single large-scale operation either in practice or in fact. Another serious factor was that many of these new men did not even know their platoon officers by name, and in some cases were quite unable to recognise their officers when seen under fire.

It was a pity that the intricate manoeuvre the Brigade was asked to perform could not have been the subject for a tactical exercise. That the operation appeared to be simplicity itself upon paper is where its real danger lay. The objective of the High Command was the heights of 971, or the extreme summit of Abdel Rahman Bair. This height formed the apex of a triangle of which the base was the sea, and two ridges the sides. The right-hand ridge—that nearest to the old Anzac line and running down into the sea—was known as Chunuk Bair, and the left ridge cutting the skyline and running down to the connecting ridge into Suvla Bay, went by the name of Abdel Rahman Bair. The 4th Brigade's objective was the Abdel Rahman Bair, but to reach this point it was necessary to proceed along the Beach to the extreme left of the advance, turn into the Arghyl Dere, then due east along its course until the junction of two depressions was reached. Here the 13th and 14th Battalions were to swing to the north, forming a series of outposts, and the 15th and 16th Battalions were to continue straight ahead and attack the Abdel Rahman Bair, which formed the northern slope of Hill 971. The Indian Brigade under General H. V. Cox, who afterwards commanded the newly-formed 4th Division in Egypt and France, was to attack the summit of 971. In the meantime, the New Zealanders were to attack and occupy the heights of Chunuk Bair—an operation that was to be performed in its entirety before the 4th Brigade made its final movement. A number of feints were resorted to on other parts of the Anzac front for the purpose of keeping the Turks busy and preventing their hastening reinforcements to the northern zone. The principal of these attacks was the now memorable engagement of the 1st Infantry Brigade at Lone Pine. This Homeric episode, one of the most gallant of the War, more than fulfilled expectations. In addition to this feint and the others planned, the 10th and 11th British Divisions, under General Stopford, were to make a landing at Suvla Bay and push forward to objectives on the high ground—Chocolate and W. Hills. The spot known as No. 3 Outpost, then in the possession of the Turks, was to be mopped up by an English regiment to open the gateway to the beach along which the 4th Brigade had to travel to reach its starting point. As it happened, the Suvla Bay landing was delayed and delay in warfare has ever proved disastrous.

On the morning of August 6, General Monash addressed the officers and non-commissioned officers of the Brigade at the head of Rest Gully. He outlined the whole plan of attack, making special mention of the Lone Pine feint and

placing particular stress upon the landing to be made by British troops at Suvla Bay. He expected that these troops would be seen by his men swarming over the Chocolate Hills when daylight broke on the 7th. As it happened, the troops were seen, but unfortunately not where the Brigadier had forecast. The reason why the advance was to be made with bayonet and bomb only was also explained to the men, and an order was issued that in no circumstances was indiscriminate shooting at small parties of Turks to take place. White distinguishing patches on the back and the arm were to be worn by all men—a necessary precaution owing to the number of regiments (English, New Zealand, Australian, Sikh, and Ghurka) which would be taking part in the battle. The password for the engagement was "Godley" and the countersign "Success."

After leaving the meeting, the officers of the 15th Battalion explained everything to their men. Captain Frank Moran, "B" Company, who was commanding the scouts and the vanguard, infused his men with his own bubbling enthusiasm. Captain Herman Cannan, who was in command of the advance guard, "A" Company, called his non-commissioned officers to his quarters and went into minute details regarding the Company's activities during the battle. He allotted to Number 2 Platoon (commanded by the 6th Reinforcement officer, Lieutenant Foster) the task of keeping in touch with the main body by means of throwing out quantities of paper every hundred yards, enabling those following to pick up direction without waste of time. If, as did happen, the platoon was compelled to take part in the fighting, it could leave a trail behind it which would enable its despatch carriers to find their way to and from the firing line to headquarters with ease.

The question of water was a very serious one. The mere bottleful that was issued per man, was not to be heedlessly used, but was to be conserved to the last moment of endurance. Orders were issued that on no account were the men to take water from the Turkish wells until a doctor had examined the water and declared it fit for drinking. This was due to the alleged practice of the enemy of poisoning all such water when retiring over his own country.

On the night of August 6, the 13th Battalion led the Brigade out of Rest Gully, closely followed by the 14th, and they passed the starting point—Number 5 Supply Depot—at 9.35 p.m., and in accordance with prearranged orders arrived at Number 3 Outpost. At this point the 13th Battalion came under fire from stray bullets that whistled down from the ridges of Chunuk Bair, where the New Zealanders were

already in action. Here, the column was held up for half-an-hour until the arrival of Major Overton and his guides. It was not until 10.30 p.m. that the head of the column at last moved forward. No opposition was met with until it turned into Taylor's Gap, where the enemy was encountered in force. This time three companies of the 13th Battalion were compelled to deploy and deal with him. This done, the column once more moved across the Arghyl Dere and formed up on a wheat field. It was at this point that the 13th and 14th Battalions detached themselves from the column and took up the Outpost Line according to the plan previously outlined. This line faced north from Knoll 9200 to Abdel Rahman Bair[1]. So far the whole operation was said to have proceeded according to plan, but not quite in accordance with the time-table set by General Monash.

To follow clearly the 15th Battalion's movements, it is necessary to revert back to Rest Gully. From this starting point the unit fell in behind the 14th Battalion and followed the same line of march as the 13th and 14th. The 16th fell into the column directly behind the 15th, with General Cox's Ghurka Brigade bringing up in the rear. The alternate opening and closing of the column increased to maddening proportions the further the units travelled. In the first mile the pace was reasonable, but after that barely 150 yards would be negotiated before a halt was called, and the whole line would remain stationary for some ten to fifteen minutes. Strict silence had to be observed during these compulsory stoppages. The bombardment of the Fleet was at its height and the destroyer on the flank swept the hills with its searchlight.

There had been a long stop at No. 3 Outpost, where the dead of the English regiment that had captured the Post lay thickly about the line of march. During this halt, Private Bert Thompson, of "A" Company, was wounded. It was after passing this Post that the first Turk prisoners were seen. Some more were met with about half-a-mile beyond it.

Through the steep country to the Battalion's right the New Zealand Mounted Rifles were assaulting in deadly silence line after line of the enemy's outposts. Stray shots from the fighting up above whistled over the heads of the men.

The 15th column of march was as follows: "B" Company (Capt. Frank Moran) supplying scouts and advance party; "A" Company (Capt. Herman Cannan); "D" Company (Major Eccles Snowden); and "C" Company in reserve under

---
(1) 13th Battalion War Diary.

the command of Captain H. C. Horne[1]. It was in this order that the unit entered the gully—by some called Olive Gully —the point from which the 13th and 14th Battalions had branched off. Here a long halt was made. This gully, lined on both sides with olive trees, afterwards became advance Brigade Headquarters. At the moment Major Overton and his guides were busily leading other units into their positions for assaulting the high ground to the right flank of the 15th Battalion's advance. All this country was presumed to have been cleared of the enemy before the 15th and 16th commenced to assault the heights of Abdel Rahman Bair. But this was not done, and when Colonel Cannan, whose headquarters were established directly behind the leading company, managed to secure Major Overton's[2] services, the Battalion had moved but a hundred yards out of the shelter of the olive trees when their scouts were fired upon. These enemy parties secreted in a gully running parallel to the Battalion's front, were dislodged by "B" Company in a short, swift, silent charge, and the column moved on. But stiffer opposition was encountered when the Battalion was crossing some open country. Colonel Cannan found it necessary to deploy the whole of "B" Company so that the advance would not be delayed. But the fighting developed to such an extent that "A" Company as well as "B" became engaged.

The leading platoon of "A" Company, Lieutenant Foster's No. 2, was ordered to line a ridge on the north bank and prepare to assault the enemy's position. As No. 2 deployed for this manoeuvre the platoon came under heavy rifle fire. Captain Cannan, who was leading his men, immediately stayed the assault, thinking that the fire denoted a heavier number of Turks than was generally supposed, and he called up another platoon to aid No. 2 in the charge. It is now thought that what Cannan took for heavy fire directed upon his men was, in reality, the backwash from the fighting proceeding further along on his right flank. Some amusement was caused by the actions of Private Mark Lambert, a

---

[1] The Officers taking part in this battle were: Commanding Officer Lieut.-Colonel J. M. Cannan, Second-in-Command Major H. R. Carter, Adjutant Capt. T. P. McSharry, Sig. Officer Lieut. N. O'Brien (Headquarters Staff). The Company commanders and Subalterns were: "A" Company—Major Herman Cannan, Lieuts. W. T. Mundell, J. G. Vidgen and R. W. Foster. "B" Coy.—Capt. Frank Moran, Capt. Jack Hill, Lieuts. J. C. Browne, D. M. Gillies. "C" Coy.— Capt. H. C. Horne, Lieuts. W. W. P. Fish, S. L. Stormont, Fred. Youden.

[2] The amount of work allotted to this officer was out of all proportion to what any human being should be asked to accomplish. Major P. J. Overton was killed on the morning of August 7, when leading Indian troops into position.

6th Reinforcement lad, who was rather deaf. This soldier stood on top of the ridge while bullets whistled all round him continually asking why they did not get on with the charge. His Corporal (Hayes) endeavoured to explain to him what was wrong, but Lambert, with hand cupped to his ear, could not understand a word Hayes was saying. Private Joe Taylor, better known as "Scotty," under the impression that the assault had started, crossed the ridge alone, and stumbling down the steep slope with all speed, came to grips with four Turks. Taylor was an old Imperial soldier who had served with the Black Watch. He despatched two of his opponents with the bayonet. Of the remaining two, one took to his heels and the other closed with Taylor, his bayonet catching Taylor in the chest. Taylor, in his endeavour to jump free, tripped and fell on the broad of his back. The Turk held on to some bushes to prevent himself slipping and, in doing so, hooked his bayonet guard in the bush in such a manner that he was unable to free it. Taylor, who was above his opponent, took advantage of his enemy's difficulty with his rifle, and leaned over the Turk and took a grip of his ear. Then commenced a tussle. Obtaining a second grip, the now unarmed men fought to a finish. Taylor, using all his great strength, kept forcing his opponent's head back, and when the platoon tumbled over the ridge, Sergeant Hanley, Corporal Hayes and others swarmed around the two men. Taylor gasped out, "Put a spike in him!" but the Turk was already dead from a broken neck. Urging the boys on into the charge, Taylor[1] fell out of the fight and went down to the dressing station to have his wound attended to.

"A" Company pushed on then and gained some three to four hundred yards, fighting for every inch of the way. In this hand-to-hand fighting, Chippendale and several others were wounded. The enemy appeared to be in parties of twenty to thirty, and as the country was very broken and very steep, their well-hidden riflemen had clear warning and ample time to train their weapons upon the advancing scouts. The sound of a woman screaming was heard clearly during this advance, and later, when the men entered the gully, women's shoes and other garments were found.

The 16th Battalion, under the command of Colonel Pope, was in close touch with the 15th, but it had tailed out during the advance. Colonel Cannan, realising this, didn't relish being attacked by strong forces while the supporting unit was unable to protect his flank. In the course of an hour

---

(1) Taylor was only absent a short time from the fighting and finally lost his life on August 27.

from 3 a.m. to daylight, Cannan sent three messages to General Monash, all of which stressed the need for the 16th Battalion to keep in close touch, and mentioned that the 15th was continuously meeting with strong opposition. These messages were conveyed by Signaller Wellard and delivered to the Brigadier verbally. Wellard, writing about events at this time, said that on the first two trips he made to Headquarters he was halted by staff officers some distance from General Monash's quarters and subjected to a cross-examination before being allowed to see Monash personally. On the occasion of his third visit, one of the officers remarked: "It's the same man. Let him through."

What deeds of heroism were performed before the light of day will never now be known. The weakness of the night advance plan compared with a daylight operation was apparent at this stage. The enemy was well hidden here, there and everywhere. Officers and N.C.O.'s were compelled to take the greatest risks in controlling their platoons and companies. They could see only a few men on either side of them. Sounds of heavy grunts, stabs and blows were heard as a section of the advancing men stumbled upon successive nests of Turks[1]. All the time lives were being lost and men were falling wounded. The experiences of two members of "D" Company will give an idea of the class of fighting. At this stage, three companies were involved—"B," "A" and "D." "C" Company were as yet in reserve. Part of "D" Company became engaged in a hand-to-hand struggle with an ambushing party of Turks. Among these men were Privates Len. Johnston and V. J. Wickins, who were cousins. About 4 a.m. Johnston emerged from a bayonet scramble minus his hat and rifle, having been disarmed by a Turk. Noticing in the darkness a dead man beside him, he seized the man's rifle and, picking up the hat, placed it on his head and continued to advance. During a lull after daylight he was asked by a friend where he had got his new hat. Removing it, he looked inside of it and saw his cousin's name printed on the sweat band. Johnston was an original "D" Company man and was wounded two days later and evacuated. Wickins was a 6th Reinforcement and had only landed upon the Peninsula on August 2.

---

(1) Colonel Jack Craven, D.C.M., writing about this period of the advance, said: "We had rushed a body of Turks holding a dry creek bank, and a great bayonet fight took place. We reorganised in the dark on the other side of the creek bed, and the only soldier I could see in the darkness was Signaller Billy Metcalfe, who said: 'Come on Jack, I suppose we will have to take the bloody hill on our own now?'"

It was during this fighting that Colonel Cannan again made contact with Major Overton and his scouts for the purpose of verifying the unit's position. The 16th Battalion had in the meantime closed up on the 15th, and an hour before dawn a bloody hand-to-hand tussle took place on the left. There, the mixed members of the various companies, headquarters, signallers and some of the 16th Battalion, fought a deadly battle to a bitter finish. At ranges of less than five yards, men were standing erect, firing point-blank at each other. One 16th man is credited with bowling over three Turks without removing his eyes from his sights, but he himself fell to a Turk bullet after his third shot. The wounds inflicted by shots fired at such short range led to the circulation of many reports that the Turks were using dum-dum bullets.

As this section of the advance was at a standstill, efforts were made to dig in. Pitifully shallow holes were tortuously torn in the hard and unyielding ground while men lay on their sides, firing a round every few moments. The living and the dead lay together. Dying Turks and Australians could have touched each other as they passed on. When the full light of day swept across the scene, the enemy could be seen retreating through a deep gully to the right toward 971. The position was held. It was now necessary to consolidate it. It was a rough line some hundred yards in length, but it presented a solid face to the enemy, and was connected up throughout excepting for a short stretch on the right flank. Into this position the reserve company, " C," was ordered to move.

The men of "C" Company were sitting in fours listening to the fighting taking place on their immediate front and left flank when the order reached them to seize and hold the spur some 220 yards away in front. It was believed then that the Battalion was facing a spur of the Abdel Rahman Bair. That this was not so was discovered too late to prevent the disaster that followed. Abdel Rahman Bair was not visible to the unit from the position it was occupying, for it was in the wrong gully—one closer to the sea than intended by Major Overton[1]. The ridges opposite "C" Company were occupied by Turks, though few showed themselves to the advancing troops. A regular nest of machine guns on a smaller knoll on the right flank, brought a devastating enfilade fire to bear as some 50 men of "C" Company moved forward. The fire almost swept the attackers off their feet, but those still standing forced their way toward their objective. More than fifty yards were covered by these men,

---

(1) C. E. W. Bean's Official History of the War—"The Story of Anzac."

who were now quite leaderless, when orders reached them to retire. In this skirmish Corporal Charles Quinn and another original member of "C" Company, Private L. W. Johnstone, lost their lives.

It was at this spot a remarkable duel took place. Nearby was a hedge, the boundary of an old cultivated patch of ground, and in this hedge were concealed two Turks. When some of Lieutenant Fish's platoon moved towards it the Turks leapt to their feet, evidently with the intention of retiring before superior numbers. As the two Turks stood staring at the Australians, one of the advancing party ran rapidly ahead dropped upon his knee and opened fire upon the leading Turk. The man fired at imitated him. Both men fired again and both missed their targets. The other members of "C" Company stood still and watched the battle with interest. Barely five yards separated the antagonists, but either from nervousness or from over-anxiety, the duelists failed to hit each other. Three shots were fired by each man without result. Then the "C" Company man sprang to his feet and charged with the bayonet. The Turk ran swiftly away until he had gained some twenty yards upon his opponent, when he wheeled suddenly, took careful aim, and fired. His shot struck the Australian just above the knee. The wound proved fatal to the Australian, for mortification set in before he could be evacuated. Describing this incident, Percy Toft said the company was so absorbed in watching the contest that the other Turk took advantage of the fact and faded away.

When daylight finally lit up the scene the Battalion found itself upon a ridge overlooking what was said to be the Kaiajik Dere but which afterwards was found to be the Asma Dere[1]. Colonel Cannan was in the company of Captain Moran. They stood on the place where the line was to be dug. Both these officers were extremely dubious as to whether they were on the right ridge[2]. As it was now too late to push on any further, and no guides were handy even

---

(1) The Story of Anzac.

(2) Col. Jack Craven writes: "Going along the top of the ridge at dawn I came across about eight 15th men and eight or nine Turks all wounded. Most of the Turks were bayoneted in the neck. One 15th man asked me: 'Did we get there?' Some of the Turks shut their eyes when they saw me coming but I nudged them and signed a cross on my arm and pretended to lift a stretcher. They understood this action and smiled sickly. When the stretcher party arrived nearly all these men were dead. There was a white tent in the valley under the big hill opposite, but no shots were fired at me. Later this hill was occupied in force by the enemy."

if required, they decided to dig in where they were. So the men were set to work.

Regarding that digging many sad stories are told, for one and all agree it was the toughest portion of the Peninsula on which they had ever been asked to construct trenches. Shortly after the digging commenced, Colonel Cannan noticed a large body of men slightly north-west also digging in. Under the impression that it was the enemy, he turned to Moran and exclaimed: "For God's sake make a supreme effort to take that ridge or we will be annihilated." Moran immediately collected his men for the assault and then one of the number noticed the white arm bands worn by the party digging. It was then learnt that they were a Wiltshire regiment.

No sooner was this problem solved when a party of Turks slightly north-east of the 15th, but only about eighty yards distant near the head of the gully, opened fire upon the Battalion[1]. As the men were bunched together at the time a number of them were hit. Private "Bluey" Blake, who had been amusing the men around with jokes while he was digging, was among those hit. Blake's favourite sally which he made just prior to his death was: "When I am drinking beer at the Marble Bar in Sydney I won't know you blokes." Captain Moran's revolver was cut from his belt during this rally by a Turk bullet. The Colonel of the 16th Battalion, Pope, was moving along with some of his men slightly to the right of the 15th position, and they also came under this fire. Drawing his revolver, Pope called to his men to follow him and raced toward the enemy. The 15th men nearby dropped their picks and joined in the rush. The enemy broke to the north and ran directly into the 13th Battalion lines, which battalion afterwards reported capturing 100 or so prisoners. A few Turks were captured by the digging party—three falling into the 15th's hands.

It was after midday and the by-now thirsty troops decided to risk the poisoning of the wells and get water from them. Sergeant Fred Hanley of "A" Company loaded himself up with waterbottles and set out with this purpose. Hanley said later that upon leaving the trench he made his way to where he thought the nearest hole would be. On his way down he met some men who had secured water and they gave him the necessary direction, warning him

---

[1] "Two signallers, S. W. Lockwood, a very small man, and W. S. Metcalfe, a huge fellow, were sent to find out if the men on the opposite ridge were Turks or British. They ran into a body of Turks and returned with three prisoners. Metcalfe had his rifle slung and a prisoner held by the scruff of the neck in each hand."

that all holes were covered by snipers, many of whom the men believed were hidden behind the Australian line. The hole lay in a small flat about one hundred yards from the bed of the Arghyl Dere. There were a few men lying dead around the well and Hanley decided upon making a dash for it, which he did, jumping into the well. To his astonishment he found himself in over three feet of mud, and the water he had risked so much to obtain was a thick soup-like mixture, so thick that he could hardly swallow it.

A considerable number of casualties occurred during the digging in, the principal ones being Captain J. Hill, second-in-command of "B" Company, and Captain Horne commanding "C" Company. Now the line was stationary, Colonel Cannan had established his headquarters in a fixed position and the signallers in this section of the line decided that it was time they reported to him. So they drew lots as to who should go, and the first chosen was Private Dick Marshall. This signaller had just left the position to go to Headquarters when the first shrapnel shells burst above the trench. Marshall was hit by this burst, receiving several wounds. With Marshall wounded, Wellard was the next chosen, and he negotiated the short distance safely and reported for duty.

Up to this stage in the Gallipoli campaign the signalling section had not had an opportunity to operate effectively. But in this advance their resources were utilised to the fullest extent. There is not a member of the original unit who cannot recall to mind Old Tom Hensler, an ex-Imperial soldier, while the names of Sparks, Wellard, Stigvart, Butler, Marshall, Hopwood, Paddy Kelly and many others, will be easily remembered. The signallers were under the command of Lieutenant N. O'Brien, who was wounded during this engagement and did not return to the unit.

Some idea of the intense heat during this August fighting might be obtained from the following: A young chap, shot in the upper part of the body, was stripped of his clothes by the stretcher-bearers so that they could bandage the wound. He was left lying there for a short time before being removed to the beach, and in that time his skin turned to a lobster red. The hard digging throughout the day and the intense heat combined to wear the troops down to shadows of their former selves. At midnight a half-bottle of water was issued to each man. It was all the fresh water that was available. The battalion then was relieved by an English unit and told to steal what rest they could preparatory to carrying on the advance before daylight.

The men were by now no means satisfied with the progress being made. In the morning, they had viewed General

Stopford's Suvla Bay landing force moving steadily forward into the hills and among themselves had decided that midday would see the Tommies linking up on the left flank. One eyewitness of this advance said: "As the sun rose I looked at Chunuk Bair. I could see some of our troops entrenched well up and others making their way there. Their bayonets flashed like mirrors in the morning sun. Suvla Bay, with the sun shining on it, was a wonderful sight with its fleet of transports, warships, destroyers, trawlers, pinnaces and barges. They had by this time quite a number of troops landed, and as they moved out to the south and north around the salt lake, it looked a walk-over for them, as the country could not be strongly held, otherwise we would not be able to "dig-in" in the open as we were then doing. The enemy, if he had any reserves to spare, would have brought them north during the night. The lines of skirmishes looked lovely as they moved across the flat country and we made sure that connection with us in the forenoon was certain. A few shrapnel bursts with very little other resistance from the enemy, and they dug in. I, like many others, looked upon them with disgust."

There was no action upon Gallipoli Peninsula, excepting, perhaps, the landing itself, which paralleled the attack by the Fourth Brigade upon the heights of Abdel Rahman Bair on the morning of August 8. The whole of August 7, as previously stated, had been spent in digging, and when the battalion was relieved for the few hours preceding the time when the assault would commence, many of the men were at the stage when they were too tired to sleep. So they kept awake talking in whispers until at 2 a.m. they were called out. Premonitions of coming disaster were common, and many men confided to their friends their last wishes. Among these was Private James Young, who confided in Fred Hanley that his real name was James Russell, and that he had served at one period of his life in the British Navy.

When a disaster of such appalling magnitude occurs as that which befell the 4th Brigade on the morning of the 8th, it is impossible to obtain a true picture of the scene. From Sergeant Fred Hanley a clear-cut narrative of his experiences has been obtained, and as this N.C.O. probably travelled further inland than any other member of the 15th Battalion, and lived to tell his story, I will relate it in full as he has given it to me. He writes:

"We moved down behind our lines for some distance towards the coast. There were a lot of British troops moving up on our right. We were travelling west on the south side

of the Asma Dere. We turned north through a broken part of the Dere. Crossing the Dere in single file we kept close touch with each other, as some parts of it were very broken and there was a chance of the line being disconnected. We halted for a few minutes on the north bank of the Dere. Captain Cannan walked back to Lieutenant Mundell and spoke to him for a few minutes. Corporal Hayes, who was close to them, told me that the captain shook hands with Mundell and remarked that he would not see it through. Just then our scouts came in and reported. Captain Cannan walked away from Mundell to take his position at the head of the company. That was the last time I saw him alive.

"We crossed out of the north side of the Dere still heading north. When the company was about clear of the Dere, a terrific rifle fire broke out upon us from the lower slope of the Kaiajik Dere. As the men were in close touch with each other, Lieutenant Mundell called out to deploy and assault the position. We now faced east in skirmishing order. Our right flank was moving along the north bank with our left flank bare to the north. The day was just breaking, and the enemy was about three hundred and fifty yards distant Hayes told me after the battle that two Turk scouts were seen by him just as he topped the north side of the Dere. These men ran to the north.

"Although we could not see the enemy when they opened fire on us, we kept moving in the direction of the fire. We were crossing a wheat field that had recently been reaped and stacked. When we got to within some two hundred yards of the enemy we could see them. About this point in the advance Lieutenant Mundell passed along the order to skirmish from the right, which we did. Visibility was bad, but we could now clearly see the enemy. They were not entrenched, but in lines across the spur. The lines ran from south to north, their left flank resting on the Kaiajik Dere. Their first line of men were sitting, the second kneeling, and as the spur got steeper, the lines of men stood up and fired over one another. It enabled them to bring about eight or nine lines of rifle fire to bear upon us. Up to this time, it was the worst rifle fire I had ever experienced in the open. We had a lot of 6th Reinforcements with us, but I must say that I never saw men show finer courage. Our line moved forward as one man without a bend in it. Besides the heavy fire we were moving under, I could see as we drew closer to the Turks, that they greatly outnumbered us. Sergeant Auchtcholonie, our platoon sergeant, looked quite a boy, and he was wonderful that morn-

ing. He was a born soldier. Although we were moving under a heavy volume of fire we did not have many casualties. Our quick movement and the bad visibility accounted for this. When we got to within one hundred yards of the enemy I could see the Turkish officer directing the fire of his men on our right flank. He was swinging his arms about and pointing in that direction. We were having a good few casualties on the right flank so I called upon the men around me to try and hit the Turk officer. Hard as we tried we couldn't, and he continued directing the fire. A few minutes later the right flank found trouble in keeping up with the main body[1]. The ground was rather broken with lots of little gullies that drained into the Dere, but the rest of our company was moving over level country. I sent word to the right to keep up, for every man would be needed to strike together when we charged, especially with the enemy outnumbering us and led by officers like the one we were looking at. A bayonet clash was certain. The right flank had just advanced level with us when Lieutenant Mundell brought forward his men into line, and we were waiting for the left flank to draw up also, when 'Nugget' Gray, on my right, drew attention to a party of troops moving up from the Dere. The light was still insufficient for us to make out who they were. I reported to Mundell, who said to watch them closely. As I rejoined 'Nugget' I could see these troops were now near the top of the Dere and appeared to me to be square on the left flank of the Turks. We soon discovered they were Sikhs. The enemy was completely unaware of their presence, for all their attention seemed to be concentrated upon us. About 75 yards now separated us from the enemy, and I was expecting the word to charge any moment, when the Indians appeared on the top of the Dere within bayonet reach of the enemy. The Indians let out one scream and went straight at the Turks. The officer in charge of the Turks, who was standing about twenty yards from the edge of the Dere, looked round and summed up the position in a second. He rushed towards the Indians with his arms extended. His men rushed in front of him and tried to form a solid line. I could see the Indians swarming up over the top of the Dere as we ran forward. It was a wonderful sight. The best move I ever saw at the war. Just as the Indians struck, our men gave a cheer and leapt

---

(1) It was apparently at this stage of the advance Lieutenant Foster lost his life. As his platoon awaited the order to advance and conform with the general movement, Foster failed to move. His Sergeant (Eric Simon) threw some earth at Foster hitting him. Concluding that he was dead the platoon conformed to the advance.

forward. We joined in with the Indians' left flank, our line extending from the south to the north, the Indian line running west to east. On the west end, the enemy stood their ground for a few moments, then they broke to the north. Those we could not reach with the bayonet we shot at from the hip as we ran. I heard a chap laughing like anything and glanced round to see the reason why. He was laughing at the numbers of Turks running parallel to us.

"I could see into the north-east as far as Anafarta. I had only about half-a-dozen men with me at this time and thought it was foolish to run about in the hills with so few men. So I decided to wait until some of our men turned up. This gully drained into the Asma Dere. It ran directly north, but where we were, on the right-hand side of the gully looking north, the bank had broken away and caused a bay About five yards down from this point there was no cover whatever in the gully until reaching the Dere. As the hill was very steep from here to the Dere I had a good view of the road running from Anafarta into the Asma Dere. I saw a Turk leading a mule with two boxes of small arms ammunition. He was going down the Dere along the road to Anafarta. We shot the mule down at four hundred and fifty yards. I cannot say how long we were there when a 14th Battalion officer[1] with 14 men appeared about eight yards to the north of me on the west side of the gully. He looked across to the north-east at a very high spur that ran straight west off 971. This spur rises straight up on the north side of the Asma Dere and forms the north bank of the Dere, the Anafarta road leading into the Asma Dere coming round the extreme west point of the ridge.

"The officer stood on the bank for a few moments then said: 'There is the ridge, men. Come on!' With that he rushed across the gully. The officer and the first six men got across safely but the last eight men fell dead from a burst of machine gun fire, directed down the centre of the gully. The fire came from the north, and so perfect was the range that not one of the eight men moved after falling I then said to my men: 'Come on, let's join him.' I leapt

---

(1) The 14th Battalion officer in question was Lieutenant Leslie Luscombe of "C" Company in that unit. This company along with "D" Company of the same battalion had come into action on the 15th Battalion's right flank, between our unit and the Indian Brigade. Lieutenant Luscombe's No. 9 Platoon and Lieutenant Curlewis' No. 11 Platoon each penetrated to the three small ridges held by the Turks in front of the main position on the Abdel Rahman Bair, but were too small numbers to effectively perform any manoeuvre. Curlewis was mortally wounded early after crossing the gully.—Vide "History of the 14th Battalion" by Newton Wanliss.

into the gully and ran toward the spur. I never saw my six men again. I do not know what happened to them.

"As I was running, I met a Turk running down the hill just to the right of me. I fired at him and missed, but with my second shot I got him. As I fired I heard a voice say: 'For Christ's sake don't.' I glanced down and saw lying at my feet, a 15th Battalion man who was then unconscious. He was badly wounded and I did not know him. I crossed the Dere and walked up on to the ridge on the north side, where I saw another 15th man badly wounded and just breathing his last. I did not know him either. Where I saw this man was evidently as far as our people advanced in the north-east. As I turned to come back down the ridge I saw a Turk coming down the Dere. He was unarmed and threw up his hands. I then heard some of our people talking. They were a few yards down the Dere, so I pushed the Turk in front of me and went down to them. It was the 14th Battalion officer and his men[1]. They had two prisoners with them. Just where I met this officer there was a large small arms ammunition dump—40 or 50 boxes carrying two thousand rounds to the box. As I joined the officer he asked for a volunteer to carry a despatch back for 150 or 200 men, so that he could hold the ridge on the north bank of the Asma Dere. I volunteered to go. He commenced writing, then asked me what time it was. I was looking at one of the prisoner's watches at the time and without thinking said, 'It is near nine o'clock.' 'No!' he replied, 'It is not that time.' He then looked at his own watch and I am not sure whether he said 10 minutes to six or 10 minutes past six, but it was one or the other. Completing the despatch the officer shook hands with me, and I stepped out on the south side of the Asma Dere and started to walk slightly south-west. I had not gone thirty yards when I came under heavy rifle fire from the ridge on the north bank of the Asma Dere. The bushes about me cracked like whips from the bullets, and I

---

(1) This gallant body of men included among their number Pte. J. Mathers of our Bn. Besides the Officer Commanding, Lieut. Luscombe, the following 14th men were with him: Sgt. N. Neyland, Cpl. G. E. Kerr, Pte. J. Masterton, Pte. H. N. Brown, Pte. W. Williams, Pte. W. H. Stringer, Pte. J. Passmore, Pte. H. Foxcroft, Ptes. T. H. Dowell, W. E. Warnes, Hennessy, P. O'Connor, B. Calcutt. They formed a barricade of the ammunition boxes found, and only when completely cut off and practically the entire party wounded or dying, did they surrender.

GROUP OF OFFICERS, FRANCE, 1918.
Capt. P. J. G. TOFT, Lt. E. VOSS, Lt. E. F. CHATAWAY, Lt. F. R. MUDGE,
Lt. E. S. ROBINSON, Lt. T. S. SLOAN, Lt. K. McKAY.
IN FRONT: Lt. W. RYAN.

Captains T. B. HEFFER, J. C. BROWNE, H. KOCH, S. V. O'REGAN.

"BABBLING BROOKS."

H.Q. 15 BN. SIG. SECTION.

thought it was only a matter of seconds before I would be riddled"[1].

"I went like a scalded cat for the gully where I had first met the 14th Battalion officer. I made for the point where I had come out of it, for I felt certain I would be a dead man if I struck it where the officer and his men crossed. A burst of machine-gun fire struck the opposite side of the gully as my feet landed in its blood-soaked bed. My feet flew from under me, as I slipped, and the gunner evidently thinking that he had me ceased firing. I then heard a voice up the gully calling to me and found it was Jim Morgan. I crawled on my hands and knees up to where Morgan was. Jim was wounded in the foot. He had a few men with him. Jim Young (Russel) was lying dead at Morgan's feet. He was hit first in the hand and Morgan had about another eighteen inches of bandage to complete the dressing of his wound when a bullet struck Young in the upper part of his body, killing him instantly. Morgan told me that once I left the spot I would be killed. As the despatch had to go through, I took off all my equipment so it would not handicap me. I advised Morgan to try and get back to the Kaiajik Dere, then saying good-bye to him, I followed practically the same line as we had taken during our advance.

"On my way back, I saw fifty of our men three hundred yards to the west of me. They were running north-east and were cut down with machine-gun fire from the north. I arrived in the Kaiajik Dere just below where the Indians attacked, and seeing a 16th Battalion officer, gave him the despatch. He read it and said: 'It is too late. A retirement has been called along the whole line.' I said: 'What about the officer and his men out there?' He said: 'Don't worry. They are probably on their way in now.'

"Corporal Pat Hayes, with several other members of the 15th walked over to me at this moment. We could hear the enemy coming in from the north calling 'Allah!' as they came. I was looking down the Kaiajik Dere, for we were well up towards the head of it, when an officer with about

---

[1] Lt. Luscombe in a letter to me stated: "It seemed impossible that he could live."
It was not until twenty years later that the story of this man's escape from death became known. The historian of the 14th Bn. History, Mr. Newton Wanliss, referring to this incident says: "Reinforcements were badly wanted, and a 15th Bn. man (one of the party) volunteered to carry back a message requesting them, but was killed by shrapnel while crossing the ridge en route." A footnote relating to this passage says: "Unfortunately the name of this gallant man is lost." In the course of correspondence with Lt. Luscombe the identity of this 15th man was firmly established as Hanley.

D

twenty men, some hundred yards away, hearing the Turks give their war cry, rushed to the north bank of the Dere with his men. They seemed to get just their head and shoulders over the bank, when there was a burst of machine-gun fire from the east and they all rolled backwards into the Dere. The whole of the left bank of the Dere came under enfiladed fire from the slopes of Abdel Rahman Bair, and it was under cover of these machine guns that the enemy was working in from the north. The position was desperate. There were some forty Indians nearby under a British officer—some of the men who had attacked that morning.

"There was a strip of land running down the centre of the Dere forming another gully. Behind this strip was very much like Dead Man's Ridge. Hayes and I got about ten men together and lined the ridge. We had a field of fire of some three hundred yards, and we thought we might put up some sort of stand. Our wounded were drifting in as the Turks advanced and I saw Morgan come in. An order was then sent to us for all men to go down the gully to where our machine guns had a possie on the north bank of the Dere. They had a good field of fire to the north. These guns were under the command of Captain Rose. These were the guns under the fire of which the enemy's attack from the north broke down, and the ones that fought our rearguard action. A message came through from Headquarters asking the commander of the guns if he wished to be left connected with Headquarters. He said: 'No. Leave me twenty-five men with the guns and I will carry the retirement through successfully.' Lieutenant J. C. Browne was entrusted with the command of the platoon which acted as advance guard. The feat was brilliantly accomplished."

A totally different story is to be told regarding the left flank of the Battalion in this attack. Captain Moran's scouts and the advance guard led by Captain Locke, 4th Brigade staff officer, were the first to come under fire. Their left flank, owing to the inertia of the British commanders at Suvla, was fully exposed to a rolling up movement from the north. This fact worried our Colonel considerably and Cannan urgently desired Brigade to send the 14th Battalion and portion of the 16th Battalion into a position to support his unit, and safeguard, if possible, the encroachment of the enemy from that direction. Unfortunately, the 14th Battalion, which was the supporting battalion to the 15th in this fight, swung into position on the 15th's right flank and only one company was able to be diverted in the direction Colonel Cannan desired. The 16th which was closely follow-

ing the 14th had also opened out into skirmishing order and closed up in active support of the 14th. The 13th Battalion was reserve for Brigade and was not to be used except in extreme emergency.

The left flank of the 15th Battalion, after driving in the Turk outpost line and whatever scouts the enemy had near to hand, entered the wheatfield, north of the "A" Company men, of which Hanley was a member. Hanley's section of "A" Company was practically the centre of the 15th advance, for on his left were "B" Company and on the right "C" and "D". When "B" Company entered the wheatfield it was met with a terrific fusillade of machine-gun fire. So intense was this fire that scarcely a man remained unwounded. In an effort to preserve this flank, Colonel Cannan immediately ordered two platoons of "A" Company to aid "B" and "D" in that sector. These platoons were under the command of Captain Herman Cannan, the C.O's. brother. In performing this movement it is presumed that Captain Cannan was killed. "B" Company, as far as is known, was practically leaderless. Captain Moran had fallen out of the fight with a bad wound in the shoulder, Lieutenant Gillies, who had been wounded twice, is believed to have lost his life when leaving the line to get his shoulder, which was bleeding profusely, treated by the doctor. There was no shelter whatever from the devastating accuracy of the Turkish fire and Cannan, realising that no good could possibly eventuate by leaving his men so exposed to annihilation, reluctantly ordered their withdrawal, he himself retiring with them.

In Hanley's narrative he mentions their joining up with the Sikhs in the charge finally made by the centre of the 15th line. But, immediately the Indian troops saw the left flank of the attack falling back, they conformed to the movement. One of their officers, questioned in regard to this action upon the part of his troops, said: "They are the best troops in the world just so long as the whites do not retire. If they see the white men beaten, they are useless!" While Moran's and Cannan's companies, together with our "D" Company, had been moving east, "C" Company commenced to veer south-east. Several spurs led from the high ground they were on down into the low country, and the company pushing along one of these, mainly in single file, was, owing to the darkness, unable to decide whether it was on the right spur or not. An enemy machine-gun on the right flank of the company was doing a lot of damage and hampering movement. Lieutenant Stormonth altered his direction to fall in with his senior officer's orders, and led his men in a

wild dash across the crest of the ridge to the reverse slope. There, to his astonishment, he found the ground sloping away at a steep angle beneath his feet, and he and his followers disappeared over the edge and down into the gully, the same one which "A" Company had already penetrated further up. In Stormonth's case, however, no path down the mountainside was chosen, and he and a number of his men fell twenty or thirty feet to crash almost insensible at the bottom. There they lay, expecting every moment that the other waves of "C" Company would follow the same course and link up with them. But, the other waves of "C" Company did not do so. Lieutenant Fred Youden's platoon came under heavy machine-gun fire and though it is known that Youden and a few men did actually go over the cliff and into the gully, no trace of them was ever found.

> The story of Youden's fate as told by Private H. Ludbey, who was a "D" Company runner attached to Headquarters is that he was sent on a message to Youden who had a mixture of "C" and "D" Company men with him, two of these men being Sergeant Rose and Private Charles Armstrong, both of "D." Youden was wounded and Ludbey was bandaging his hand when suddenly a party of Turks appeared in the gully. A shot was fired by the Turk officer at Youden and he fell to the ground. Then a volley was fired into the remaining men of whom Ludbey, alone, survived, though he was seriously wounded in several places. Armstrong and Rose, with a few men who were behind Youden, smelt a rat at the first shot and streaked for cover, and effected their escape. The Turks ratted the dead men for tobacco, boots and puttees (including Ludbey, who was alive but shamming dead). They then passed on further up the gully looking for new prey. Ludbey, when all was quiet, crawled to the various men to see if they were dead and when he found they were, he collected what paybooks and identification discs he could and then crawled painfully up the hillside and managing to attract the attention of some 16th Battalion machine-gunners was carried in by one of their number. Then he was passed down to the 14th Battalion dressing station where Captain Loughran attended to him. On the way down Ludbey saw Major Carter and told that officer of his experience.
> It was after the retirement that Major Carter, in addressing some of the men behind the position taken up by Captain Rose and his machine-gunners, told the story of Youden's death, but in his recital stated that the Turk officer called upon Youden and his men to surrender which they did. Immediately upon their laying down their arms, the Turk gave the order to fire and a volley came. Rose and Armstrong were mentioned as being two of the party and their escape was managed in the manner described by Ludbey.

Lieutenant Fish's platoon directed by the Adjutant, Captain McSharry,[1] only reached the edge of the gully, being almost wiped out before it got there. One of its members, Percy Toft, sought to find a way down into the bed of the dry watercourse. He went a considerable distance down one of the paths, but as no one came with him he was cautious. When he discovered a party of Turks calmly walking towards him, he streaked for home. Upon rejoining the remnants of the platoon on the top of the gully Toft found

that one of them, an original man, "Darky" Townshend, was badly wounded by a bullet through the chest. The precarious position these men were in was such that the movement of head or limb brought immediate fire upon them, and the longer they stayed where they were the less likelihood there was of their ever getting back to the main body.

This retirement of the 4th Brigade probably ranks as the most tragic in its history, excepting that of Bullecourt in France in 1917. Stunned by the fearful carnage, the men of "A" and "B" Companies were yet loath to leave their mates lying wounded and unattended on the slope beneath them. Many heroic and desperate, but futile attempts, were made to rescue a lost pal or answer a pleading voice for help. The wounded knew the fate awaiting them if they fell into the hands of the enemy, and it is on record that more than one wounded man pleaded with his friends to leave him and make good their own escape.[2]

Of the great number of missing—more than 200 of those who moved forward that morning—only 17 men and one officer (Lieutenant C. L. Stormonth) were taken prisoners. Stormonth, who was unwounded, related how he fell into the hands of the Turks. After his fall into the gully he lay doggo for some twenty minutes fully expecting, as mentioned before, that another wave of "C" Company would pick him up. As the time passed and no further men attempted the descent, he decided to move along the gully to the place where "A" Company had already passed. Making use of what shelter there was, he made slow progress, but, when he thought he had covered the distance necessary he raised himself slightly to see if he could locate some of "A" Com-

---

(1) Colonel Jack Craven, D.C.M., then Sergeant J. Craven, relates: "I was with McSharry when crossing the wheatfield. A murderous hail of machine-gun fire opened from the enemy on the ridges—a trifle high at first, but deadly when they got the range. We could see the strike of the bullets at our feet. Several men picked up stacks of wheat as camouflage but the number of casualties was ghastly. Signaller Paddy Kelly was one of the many killed here and when McSharry and I helped to pull him into the bushes he said: 'Never mind me, I'm done for. Look after yourselves.' I then took a message from McSharry to the 14th Battalion and on returning met Major Snowden, who was slightly wounded, the bullet passing through his water bottle into his buttock. I placed him under cover and then learnt that the order for retirement had been given.

(2) Sergeant Eric Simon, who was wounded in the shoulder, stopped to succour another wounded man, but found it impossible to aid one who could not walk. The man passed to Simon his last message to his people in Australia, all of which the sergeant took down in writing. Months afterwards when he was in France, Simon received word from Australia that the insurance due upon this soldier's death was paid to the relatives upon production of the letter.

pany. To his astonishment he found himself looking down the barrel of a Turk rifle. Rising to his feet, he discovered that he was in the presence of several of the enemy. These men, by means of signs, conducted him to a Turkish officer who happened to speak English. From this man, Stormonth learned of the complete failure of the 4th Brigade attack for the first time. The officer informed him also that the Battalion was exceptionally lucky, as a large body of Turks just missed cutting them off altogether. This news Stormonth received with joy, for he was then certain that the rest of the Battalion had not suffered the same fate as himself.

The seventeen men taken prisoner were—Corporal H. Hodsdon, Privates A. H. Jenkins, L. S. Hodges, J. Kelly and Skelton (all of whom died of wounds in Constantinople), Corporal Green and Privates Kerrigan, J. Mathers[1], A. Nelson, and W. P. Jones (all of whom died of illness in various parts of Turkey), and Private I. S. New, who was killed in an accident. The six remaining men, who with Lieutenant Stormonth returned to Australia after the war, were Sergeant W. Bailey, Privates J. Thomas, J. Beatie, E. C. Foster, A. Carpenter, and W. Mackay. The last-named, who had two serious gunshot wounds in the back, was captured nearly 48 hours after the others. Mackay was an original "A" Company man and he relates that he lay in trepidation throughout the whole of the night of the 8th while large numbers of the enemy searched out and killed all the wounded they could find. When he was at last discovered, he naturally expected the same fate as that which had befallen his comrades, but the Turks decided to make him prisoner instead. Mackay was sent to hospital and then to a convalescent camp. It was while he was convalescing that he struck a Turkish officer who had hit him between the shoulders with his swagger cane. Mackay remonstrated with the officer in the first instance, only to receive a second stroke. With one vicious punch to the jaw he stretched the Turk officer unconscious upon the ground. A Turkish sergeant in charge of the guard rushed to his officer's assistance, only in his turn to see stars. The rest of the prisoners present including Lieutenant Stormonth, seized Mackay to prevent him doing any more damage. For this act, Mackay received the severe punishment of the bastinado. He was then confined to a fortress for a short time before being allowed once more to associate with his

---

(1) Private Mathers was taken prisoner with the 14th Battalion party under Lieutenant Luscombe.

fellow-prisoners. From the details that can be gathered from various prisoners-of-war from Turkey, the men mentioned above were exceptionally lucky to escape from the country alive.

The casualties among officers in this engagement were exceptionally heavy. Excluding Lieutenant Stormonth, there were seven other officers reported wounded and missing. They were: Major D. H. Cannan, Lieutenants R. W. Foster[1], P. Gibson, J. G. Vidgen, D. M. Gillies, F. C. Youden and P. J. Platt. Foster and Gibson were 6th Reinforcement officers, the former in command of the Queensland section and the latter the Tasmanian. They had joined the unit with their men on August 2 and were extremely unlucky to be thrown into a big scale operation in such difficult country as Gallipoli, without first of all becoming familiar with the men in their platoons. Lieutenant Dave Gillies was promoted to commissioned rank on June 12 and though little is known of the fate of the other officers, it is known that he was wounded twice and is stated to have left the line to have his shoulder attended to, and is thought to have been killed on his way back to the dressing station. That was the last seen of this splendid young athlete and popular officer. Lieutenant P. J. Platt had not been in action with the unit before although a 1st Reinforcement officer. He was one of the officers who took part in the dummy landing made in the Gulf of Saros on April 25. Lieutenant F. C. Youden was a musician from Bundaberg and during the days at Lemnos Island prior to the Landing had enlivened the nights with many a tattoo on the piano, and was also the acknowledged accompanist to all the vocal efforts of the men—good, bad, or indifferent. He was one of the first N.C.O's. to be promoted to commissioned rank, had been wounded at Quinn's Post on May 9, and is known to have been wounded in this engagement before finally disappearing. J. G. Vidgen was a well-known athlete and like Youden and Gillies an original member of the unit. He was promoted to commissioned rank on July 31. Members of the Battalion will recall Vidgen's little brother, who, dressed in uniform, virtually became the unit's mascot before embarkation in Australia. Lieutenant Vidgen at this time was the youngest officer in the 15th, being then only 18 years of age. All the men above mentioned were finally reported killed after the most exhaustive inquiries were made as to their whereabouts in Turkey.

---

(1) The apparent death of this officer is previously mentioned.

Of the officers wounded, Captain Frank Moran was the only one to die from his injuries. It is stated regarding Moran that he died of a broken heart after learning of the losses sustained by the Battalion. There was probably no more universally popular officer in the 15th Battalion. He was a bundle of energy and enthusiasm, and a disciplinarian of the type Percy Toft aptly describes as "in a nice way." His men swore by him, and the worst laggard in the company followed his leadership without cavil. Time will not efface the memory of this gallant little man. Besides Moran, Captain Jack Hill, M.C., and Captain H. C. Horne were wounded on the 7th. Hill did not return to the Battalion, being finally evacuated to Australia. He was the first officer in the 15th to receive the Military Cross, and excluding Colonel Cannan, who at the termination of the Gallipoli campaign was awarded a C.B., was the only officer in the unit to receive a decoration on Gallipoli. Captain Horne returned to the unit for a short period and was then transferred. Lieutenant N. O'Brien, Signalling Officer before referred to, also failed to return to the unit, transferring to the Desert Corps. Lieutenant Luxmore, a 1st Reinforcement N.C.O., was promoted to commissioned rank on July 31. He also did not return to the unit, transferring at a later date to the 46th Battalion and then to the Chinese Labour Corps in France. Lieutenant C. Davy, wounded on the 7th, did not recover from his wound to rejoin the unit.

It is impossible to give the names of all the N.C.O's. and men who fell in this battle, but every member of the 15th will recall "Old" Tom Williams, sergeant-major of "A" Company. Williams had served in numerous campaigns as an old Imperial soldier. He was an original sergeant in "A" Company and was respected by all who had contact with him. Known as "Old Tom" he was never known to boast of any of his achievements, and with all his knowledge of warfare did not explain how a thing should be done, but set an example in action which the newcomer could follow if he wished. At the time he was wounded, Williams carried in a haversack upon his back the company roll. The bullet that finally caused the old warrior's death, entered his chest and passed out his back, drilling a hole through the haversack and the roll book within. "Old Tom" knew it was his death wound.

The retirement was in full swing and during it, Jack Hynes[1], who was a noted stretcher-bearer in the first

---

(1) The late Captain Jack Hynes, D.S.O., M.M. (F). Died from gas in Randwick Military Hospital.

months on the Peninsula, saw "Old Tom." Stooping down, he picked the old man up, and throwing him across his shoulder began the four hundred yards journey to safety. "Old Tom" urged Hynes over and over again to let him lie and make good his own escape. But Hynes was not leaving the most beloved man in the company behind, and finally struggled with his precious burden to safety. Tom Williams lived just long enough to see England again before passing away in the presence of his wife and children. Among the wounded were a number of men who at a later date were to receive commissions in France. These included Lance Corporal H. R. H. Lack, Sergeant Eric Simon, Private W. S. Missingham, and Signaller A. M. (Dick) Marshall.

The three Battalions which took part in the charge remained in reserve until 6 p.m. on August 9, the reserve Battalion, the 13th, holding the brigade frontage during this period. Upon the 14th and 16th Battalions moving forward into the front line position the 15th remained in bivouac. On this day Lieutenants C. M. Johnston and J. J. Corrigan reported back for duty from hospital.

At 8 a.m. on August 10 a fatigue party of 150 men from the battalion under the command of Major Bert Carter was sent to dig an inner line of defence for the 29th Indian Brigade. The men marched slightly over a mile to the position and then commenced digging on the exposed forward slope of a hill. Although subjected to the enemy's fire, the trench was five feet deep by 3 p.m. at the cost of one casualty—Private Jack Hynes, who was hit by a sniper's bullet. As the men were leaving the trench they were called upon to support the Indians who were at that moment being heavily attacked. Carter was wounded while directing this movement across an exposed piece of ground. Major Carter[1], from the formation of the unit, had acted as its second-in-command. He was universally popular, being familiarly known as "Bert." This officer did not rejoin the unit, being evacuated from hospital to Australia, and there discharged.

Within half an hour of the return of the fatigue party to the bivouac at 5 p.m., heavy rifle fire and bombing from the direction of the position held by the 13th Battalion was heard. A messenger from this battalion arrived in the camp asking for help. Colonel Cannan lent them some bombers. A little later, a messenger arrived to say the enemy had entered the trench and the colonel immediately

---

[1] The late Major H. R. Carter, Insurance Manager, Brisbane, Queensland.

sent "D" Company to the 13th's aid. Besides "D" Company another 50 men were shortly on their way to give added support. All these men came under the command of Captain Norton Russell of the 13th Battalion. The 15th's casualties in this affray were: Killed 2 and wounded 18. One of the killed was Private J. E. "Bluey" Williams, an original of "C" Company. The two deaths were caused by a shell that landed in the support trench where the men were awaiting orders. Among the wounded was an original "A" Company man, Private Jack Hetherington.

The day following, the fatigues became the most unpleasant of all—the day the dead were buried. This task, distasteful as it was, solved the mystery of the whereabouts of many of the missing. Among the bodies discovered outside the 3rd Outpost was that of Private Jack Booker. At this point, a fierce fight evidently took place, for in the one group lay the bodies of 10 Turks and 9 men of the 15th. For three days following, the fatigues consisted of making roads for mule traffic, while the nights were taken up in the peaceful pastime of occupying posts in the front line. Besides these duties, others—the carrying of rations and water, digging of communication saps and supporting trenches—were added for extra weight. The heat, which during the whole campaign had been intolerable, was evidently favourable to the breeding of flies, for they now settled about the troops in swarms. Added to this discomfort was the ever present stench from the dead.

On August 16 the battalion moved up once more into the front line and occupied three hundred yards of trench on the right flank of the 13th Battalion. It stayed here until August 21. On August 18, owing to the marked shortage of officers in the unit, a number of men were promoted from the non-commissioned ranks. These were: Sergeant W. H. Nicholls, W. Cummins,[1] R. B. McIntosh, E. Terry, G. Thorpe, and A. Mitchell. On August 21, men from the 13th and 14th Battalions under the command of Major Herring, co-operated with a force under General Russell in an offensive movement against the Kaiajik Dere. The 15th Battalion's task was the construction of a communication trench to the right of the Kaiajik Dere to enable water and ammunition to be passed through to the attacking party during the night. At 5 a.m. the Battalion moved out under cover of darkness and setting to work with a will, soon had their trench completed. The 13th and 14th Battalions on

---

[1] Cummins upon appointment was the youngest officer in the battalion just 19 years.

the left flank swung into their new positions, but the 9th Army Corps (British troops) who had the best part of a mile to cover—their objective being the Chocolate and W. Hills—failed in their aim.

If the advance made by the English troops on August 6 and 7 had caused much heartburning, their splendid discipline and steadiness under fire during this advance—even though it did not succeed—proved a source of wonderment and admiration to the watching Australians. The battalion's task had been of the easiest and only two casualties occurred. The position the unit now occupied was held for another six days. It was during this period that the death of our popular medical officer, Captain Guy Fitzmaurice Luther, took place. Luther had been attending to several casualties caused by snipers firing upon a certain point in the communication line. He was wearing around his neck a large red bandana handkerchief. An officer and some men came to Luther's dressing station on their way up to the front line. To show them the dangerous sector in the communication line, Luther accompanied them, and at the spot where so many casualties had occurred, a sniper's bullet struck him in the head. The cry for stretcher-bearers was answered with alacrity and when it was known that the Doc. was the casualty, in the shortest time possible, four other doctors arrived upon the scene. Dr. MacDonald of the 16th Battalion, who throughout the campaign had been a close friend of Luther, examined the wounded man, and the expression upon his face when he rose to his feet dispelled all hopes for the Doc's. recovery. Luther's own stretcher-bearers bore him gently to the beach where he passed away about an hour later without regaining consciousness.

It is difficult to recall all Luther's gallant band of workers at this date, but among them were Paddy Lee, W. P. Darby, Jack White, Middleton, Jack Cooper, Keith Murray (badly wounded in the August advance), Tom Coogan (killed in the August advance), Atkins, and Corporal Lamb.

On August 27 an attempt was made to dislodge the Turks from their trenches opposite No. 5 Post. Fifty men from "A" Company under the command of Lieutenant W. W. Coombs were placed under the command of Lieutenant-Colonel Adams, 14th Battalion, for this engagement. The whole force was working in conjunction with General Russell's men. The position to be captured was known as the high ground of Kaiajik Aghyl[1]. An intense bombardment

---

(1) Better known as Hill 60.

of about two hours by field and naval guns began at 2 p.m. At this period of the war the troops thought this something out of the ordinary. The moment the barrage ceased the men of the first wave from "A" Company's trenches leapt out into the open and sped toward the Turk line. They were met with a enfilading machine gun fire which brought them to earth. Hugging the ground for whatever cover they could find they awaited the second wave. This wave failed to gain the flying start the first one had got and the moment the men topped the parapet they were swept off their feet. But some of them managed to reach the forward position of the first wave and both parties joining forces they leapt out in the face of the hail of Turkish lead. Of the 50 men who took part in this charge, only ten escaped injury. Caught in the middle of No Man's Land where a slight depression gave the survivors a precarious shelter, the living debated what was the best thing to do. To go forward was impossible—to retire was equally so. After some delay, Sergeant Fred Hanley was sent back with a message stating that to continue the charge was hopeless. Hanley, crawling most of the way, managed to reach safety and sought out Lieutenant J. J. Corrigan, who was with a party of 50 "D" Company men under the command of Captain Salier acting as reserves for General Russell. Corrigan immediately saw Captain Margolin of the 16th Battalion, who advised that they get back the best way they could.

Upon receipt of this order the men in the open endeavored to retire. Owing to their exposed position when climbing over our parapet, suggestions were put forward that the parapet be pulled down to enable the wounded to come in. Unfortunately while this was being done, six wounded men lost their lives. Among those killed in this fight were three of "A" Company's original landing force upon Gallipoli—Privates J. R. "Scotty" Taylor, whose lone battle with the four Turks on the night of August 6 has already been recorded; D. Robertson and C. McAlister. Private J. J. N. McKain, another of this band was seriously wounded. The following day second Lieutenant A. Mitchell was wounded. This officer after his return to the unit in Egypt, transferred to the 47th Battalion and is best remembered for his long association with the 4th Brigade Machine gun Company in France.

The Battalion remained in the position they occupied (No. 4 Post) until August 31, when No. 5 Post, previously held by the 16th Battalion, was also taken over. The position of the men during this time in the line had reached

almost the limit of endurance. The total effective strength of the unit, excluding all Headquarters and details, was but 82 men. Percy Toft, who during the latter end of August, was promoted to sergeant, states that the night he took over the platoon there were only four men in it: Privates E. Bryans, Joe Coogan, Jack Ingram and himself. The conditions were vile, and the lack of water prevented the men even obtaining a wash. Some endeavoured to shave or wipe their faces with the little tea they were willing to spare, but the majority of them neither shaved nor washed. One Headquarter's signaller admitted that the stain of blood from a wounded comrade remained on the back of his hand from August 6 until he was evacuated with sickness at the end of the month. The lice and flies brought sickness in their wake, and man after man fell a victim to dysentery or enteric fever. Throughout the whole war there was probably no position held by British troops so nauseating and soul-destroying as this section of the Anzac line during August and September.

On August 31 a big Turkish attack was expected and all looked forward to getting some of their own back. The attack, however, did not materialise. On September 1 the Essex Battalion entered the front line but the unfortunate remnant of the 15th still remained there to teach the men of this Battalion their work. On September 6 the Essex unit was relieved by a Norfolk Battalion but the 15th still stayed on to instruct the new comers. This they continued to do until September 11, when they filed out of the front line down into Hay Valley preparatory to sailing from the Peninsula on the 13th for the long promised rest on Lemnos Island.

On September 13 the Battalion embarked upon the transports Abbassia and Osmanieh. The strength of the unit at this time was—Officers 11, other ranks 136. Besides Captain Coombs and Second Lieutenant Mitchell wounded, Captain T. P. McSharry had been evacuated sick, also Second Lieutenants R. B. McIntosh and G. Thorpe. Arriving at Lemnos Island on September 14, the men marched out to Sarpi Camp, West Mudros.

CHAPTER V.

LEMNOS ISLAND, THE EVACUATION AND BACK TO EGYPT.

The men were not given very strenuous work during the first days in Sarpi Camp. For a fortnight, they fed themselves up until all the elastic spring came back to their aching bodies, while the nights of undisturbed rest gradually tuned up badly frayed nerves.

Percy Toft has given some idea of the pleasant things to be obtained upon the island. "Grapes," he says, "were in season and plentiful. Almost a basketful could be purchased for one shilling. The fruit was small in size compared to the Australian eating grape. Evidently it was grown for wine. There was a monastery nearby and fresh eggs and butter could be bought. The prices were reasonable and the monks were very kindly. A Greek sold bread from a bakery cheaply. His bread was delicious. One Saturday I joined a large queue of waiting soldiers to obtain some bread for the week-end. I found myself at last in a crowded room ten feet square. The bread had only just come out of the oven. It was roasting hot. The only possible way to make an exit was to wrap one end of the bread in your tunic and put the other end under the noses of all who were in your way."

Even route-marching is a pleasant memory to those Gallipoli veterans who rested at Sarpi Camp. Toft declares that "one route march lives in my memory. We went through two Greek villages—Therma, a Greek watering place, and Castre, a fortified city and the capital. In the grounds of a large monastery we were permitted to roam and make purchases of coffee and biscuits. A feature of this place as in other places on Lemnos, was the fine brick wells with their crystal-clear water. These wells were centuries old. Women followed the ancient custom and still drew water from them. Never before had I seen so many hornets, nor any so large. They were from one to three inches in length, and black in colour with the brightest gold markings. They flew among us but molested no one."

On the slope of Mt. Therma were two marble baths which were fed by the hot springs higher up the mountain. These baths were privately owned and troops were allowed within, upon payment of a nominal fee. This privilege was taken

advantage of by many of the men, for the baths, though small, some six feet in length, were always at a temperature of 100 degrees Fahrenheit and enabled one to have a good scrub down.

On Saturday nights, concerts were held in a natural amphitheatre upon the island and patronised by all but the gamblers. The artists included New Zealanders as well as members of the 4th Brigade. But the star turns of all were the short speeches, generally a quarter of an hour, delivered by the Brigadier, Colonel John Monash. The magic of his elocutionary powers seemed to cast a spell over the men. It was probably this ability upon the part of Colonel Monash that stood him in such good stead when he attained to the higher commands. This officer did not at any time become part and parcel of the men's lives. He was unknown except by name to most of them, and even in the early days in Egypt little was seen of him. Upon Gallipoli Peninsula he was to us an unknown figure. All that mattered apparently was that he gave the orders and we obeyed them. Upon Lemnos Island Monash came nearer to the hearts of his men in the 15th Battalion, which was part of his command, than he was ever to be.

On September 21 Major General Sir A. J. Godley inspected the Australian and New Zealand Division. An inspection was always a bad sign, though in this instance it did not prove so.

The Battalion at this time was under the command of T/Captain G. F. Dickinson—Lieutenant Colonel Cannan being in hospital and Major Eccles Snowden upon leave.

On October 20 the 7th and 8th Reinforcements of the Battalion arrived at Lemnos and were taken on strength. These reinforcements were under the commands of 2/Lieutenant W. J. Cooper, 2/Lieutenant J. H. Wilson, who had brought the 8th Tasmanian Reinforcements from Australia, and 2/Lieutenant G. M. Williamson. 2/Lieutenant F. Lane, who had commanded the 7th Tasmanian Reinforcements, was left behind in Egypt sitting on an unfinished courtmartial. On October 25 mumps broke out among the new troops and all the reinforcements were immediately quarantined. They were kept in isolation until October 31 when the Battalion once again embarked upon the Osmanieh and sailed for Gallipoli. The strength of the Battalion had now increased to 13 Officers and 453 other ranks. 2/Lieutenant W. H. Nicholls was evacuated sick to hospital the day before

On the night of November 1 the sea was exceptionally rough and though the Osmanieh stood in close to land it

was impossible to disembark the men owing to the difficulty of transporting them into the open boats in such a sea. So the vessel sought shelter in the small harbour at Imbros. This was an apparently enchanted island to the troops when upon Gallipoli, but proved on close acquaintance not such a desirable spot.

The following night, November 2, the sea having moderated, the vessel again approached the coast and stood to for the purpose of landing its men. When the sleeping men were awakened to go ashore one of the number asleep on the deck failed to answer the call, and it was discovered that he had been killed by a stray shot from the Peninsula that had lodged directly in his forehead.

At this period the 14th Battalion was short of officers, and on November 12 2/Lieutenant G. M. Williamson from the 15th., 2/Lieutenant Fox from the 13th and 2/Lieutenant Cumming from the 16th were sent on loan to that unit. 2/Lieutenant Williamson finally transferred to the 14th and his services to the 15th were lost for all time.

While the battalion was in Hay Valley Major Snowden returned and took over the command. Sickness was still rampant and T/Captain Bill Mundell was compelled to leave the unit with dysentery, thus losing his promotion and reverting back to a 2/Lieutenant. T/Captains W. W. Coombs and J. J. Corrigan were both ill with yellow jaundice, but were doctored within the lines to save losing their promotion. 2/Lieutenant E. Terry was also ill and in hospital.

The addition of wounded men returning from hospital increased the Battalion's strength to 537 other ranks, while the number of Officers had again been reduced to 11. On November 21, Lieutenant F. R. North joined the Battalion.

It was on November 28 that the blizzard came, and in the morning astonished troops awoke to find themselves mantled in snow. As luck would have it, this day was the day upon which the whole Battalion was to bathe. It was the first time a bathing parade had been ordered in the 15th Battalion, and the little gods who control the fortunes of the mere rank and file had no intention that their plans should be interfered with by a mere snow storm. Out in the cold blast the men stripped naked and there received at the hands of the cooks sufficient thawed ice to fill a dixie. And this was their bath—hot water bath? No wonder so many writers say: "Strange fellows, these Australians." There was a quart of water per man, a small strip of flannel—the same quantity as used for rifle clean-

ing—as a sponge, and three or four men pooled their water and washed each other down.

On December 10, "C" Company under the command of T/Captain C. M. Johnston and 2/Lieutenant Eather, together with half of "D" Company under the charge of 2/Lieutenant Wilson were detailed off to take over the duties of Beach Garrison at Anzac.

Lieutenant Wilson, writing about this time says: "It was obvious to us that Anzac was being evacuated. Stacks of stores had their 'interiors' removed, leaving only outside shells of cases, etc. We had suspected evacuation some time before in Hay Valley, when we found biscuits, bully beef, etc., being removed from our local dump and taken to serve out to positions further back."

And so it transpired. The Battalion left Hay Valley on the night of December 13 and embarked on s.s. Carron.

The departure of the 15th Battalion from the Peninsula was as unobtrusive as its arrival on that now far off day, April 25, 1915. To them, it was no valiant gesture which in the course of time would become legend for the countless generations of Australians as yet unborn. There were no brief farewells—no vain regrets. To other units of the A.I.F. was given the task of holding the long thin line until the entire force had evacuated; the prospect of fighting a valiant rearguard action against an overwhelming enemy; the honour of holding the breach to the last man. And it was given them for no other reason than that they had been chosen to lead the actual landing upon the historic April 25. But, the Brigade that had held the key to the Anzac position, the Brigade that had faced the enemy in the open more than any other Brigade in the Australian forces; whose dead lay north, south, east, and west upon that tortuous terrain, greater in numbers than that of any other Australian unit, had to fade away in the night, days before the final flourish.

The few surviving members of the original Battalion were in a sad minority. Excluding officers, not fifty men remained, and of those fifty there were very few indeed who had not spent a term in hospital recovering from wounds to rejoin a month or so later as details from convalescent camps in Egypt and England. It is doubtful if one member of the 7th or 8th Reinforcements fired a shot in the direction of the enemy. They had learnt the art of fatigue work; had seen and heard the whine and explosions of shells; the crack of the passing bullet. They had become in the short space of time Anzacs, and as such were to be looked upon during the years of fighting in France. They

were veterans of the unit. From their ranks were to come many gallant men, some of whom attained commissions upon the battlefields in France. They were to form the nucleus of the new Battalion, which in the days at Tel-el-Kebir, came into existence. They had imbibed the glory of Anzac and they never lost it.

The 15th Battalion holds the doubtful honour of having the most casualties[1] of any unit in the A.I.F. that landed upon Gallipoli Peninsula. In the cemeteries at Steele's Post, Courtney's Ridge, Quinn's Post, Pope's Hill, Shrapnel Gully, the Beach and on Hills 60 and 971 lie their dead—the founders of the unit's history. The reckless gallantry of the defenders of Quinn's has become legend. Few, very few, can recall the deeds of heroism, the days of unremitting activity, the nights of anxiety, the rows of dead sentries awaiting burial at the break of dawn. Few can recall to mind the smashing attacks launched by a ferocious foe upon the little fort; the blood-red eyes of its defenders, aching for the want of sleep, peering along rifle sights, automatically aiming their shots into the dense mass of fanatical followers of the Prophet. Only those who helped in the defence of Bloody Angle and its environments preserve such memories.

The old hands were given no opportunity to bid farewell to their friends lying buried at the foot of that death-trap. Others were given that honour—the honour that rightly, by all the canons of fairness, should have been the 15's. There is no sentiment in warfare. Sentiment is a sign of weakness and must be stilled.

In the official list compiled of the number of officers and men in the 15th Battalion who became casualties during the Gallipoli campaign the following figures are given:—

	Killed in Action	Died of Wounds	Wounded in Action	P.O.W.
Officers	20	4	10	1
Other Ranks	419	107	510	17

Besides the above, 7 men died from disease, making the total casualties 1095. As these figures have been quoted in several official histories, and as it is impossible to check the figures given as regards the other ranks, I am for the purpose of record giving a complete list of all officers killed or wounded upon Gallipoli Peninsula.

(Killed in Action) 20: Captain W. O. Willis, 2/5/15; Majors J. F. Walsh, 28/4/15; H. Quinn, 29/5/15; D. H. Can-

---

[1] The Official figures are placed at 1,095 all ranks.

nan, 8/8/15; Captain S. W. Harry, 10/5/15; Lieuts. L. J Waters, 26/4/15; L. N. Collin, 9/5/15; T. Robertson, 27/4/15; F. L. Armstrong, 10/5/15; D. S. Freeman, 30/4/15; A. G. Hinman, 10/5/15; H. P. Armstrong, 10/5/15; J. F. Plane, 8/8/15; K. H. Anderson, 9/5/15; E. G. Wareham, 9/5/15; F. C. Youden, 8/8/15; D. M. Gillies, 7/8/15; J. G. Vidgen, 7/8/15; P. Gibson, 8/8/15; R. W. Foster, 8/8/15.

(Died of Wounds) 5: Captains H. F. G. Luther, 26/8/15; F. Moran, 20/8/15; Lieutenants Kessells, 4/5/15; N. Dickson, 26/4/15; H. G. W. Smith, 10/5/15.

(Wounded) 27: Majors J. F. Richardson, 26/4/15; R. E. Snowden, 2/5/15; Captains C. F. Corser, 1/5/15; F. Moran, 2/5/15, (D) 8/8/15; H. C. Davies, 2/5/15; B. Sampson, 10/5/15, 17/7/15; J. Hill, 7/8/15; Lieutenants N. T. Svensen, 10/5/15; A. Douglas, 2/5/15; G. F. Dickinson, 1/5/15; C. E. Snartt, 2/5/15; L. G. Casey, 10/5/15; N. O'Brien, 8/8/15, Captain H. C. Horne, 7/8/15; Lieutenants C. Davy, 8/8/15, W. W. Coombs, 27/8/15; W. F. Eather, 5/8/15; E. M. Little, 29/5/15; J. C. Browne, 8/8/15; F. C. Youden, 9/5/15; A. E. G. Leitch, 29/5/15; H. Koch, 29/5/15; Corbett, 3/5/15; G. King, 29/5/15; J. E. Sparkes, 19/5/15; C. H. Luxmore, 7/8/15; A. Mitchell, 28/8/15. (Prisoner of War): Lieutenant S. L. Stormonth, 8/8/15.

The voyage from Gallipoli to Lemnos Island was uneventful and the battalion disembarked at Lemnos Island on the day following. They had left behind in Hay Valley one man ("Old" Dave Waterfield), who was discovered after its departure, and collected and packed off to the unit the following day. The Anzac Beach garrison under T/Captain C. M. Johnston left four days later.

On December 23, Captain Johnston with 100 men sailed on the H.M.S. Ionian as an advance party to Egypt. Their Christmas dinner consisted of corned beef and carrots and a pudding with little fruit within it. It is said that no crumbs fell beneath the table. This party arrived in Alexandria on Boxing Day and proceeded immediately to Tel-el-Kebir, arriving there on the 28th. The next day they were in Ismailia to erect tents for the other members of the unit.

The rest of the Battalion had its Christmas dinner on Lemnos Island and on Boxing Day embarked upon H.M.T. Ascanius, leaving Mudros Harbour the next day and arriving at Moascar, Egypt, on December 30. From here they marched to their camp site at Ismailia.

The unit had left behind three officers at Lemnos Island. Captain J. J. Corrigan, and 2/Lieutenants Cooper and Wilson. This was due to accommodation, a matter which was

rectified later and the three officers joined the unit again at Ismailia on January 5, 1916.

EGYPT ONCE MORE.

To the battle-scarred veterans of Gallipoli Egypt proved a blessing. There the urgency of time seemed non-existent for they trod the sand of all time—the thousand thousand years or more of this world's existence. It was a period of healing. Days passed uncounted in their passing. Somewhere, the unit's ultimate destiny was being planned, but of this it was blissfully unaware. Its very being seemed of small moment and the few parades held were of a trifling nature. Idleness had laid its mantle over the camp and as yet it had not grown irksome.

Details from England, Malta and Egyptian hospitals poured into the camp during the first few days at Ismailia. Old hands sought out old hands, and talking quietly together, fought once more their battles and conjured to their minds first one and then another of the many friends who had gone West.

The first reinforcements to link up with the unit after its return to the desert were the 9th and 10th under the commands of Lieutenants F. W. Lane[1] and H. M. Brettingham Moore. These men arrived on January 8. On the 20th of the month two promotions to commissioned rank took place—Sergeants A. L. Langborne and W. A. Brooks. The latter, unfortunately, became seriously ill with enteric fever eleven days after his promotion and died in hospital on March 2. The death of this popular N.C.O. gave to the 15th Battalion the only fatal casualty among the officers during its two terms in Egypt. Among the men, the deaths did not total double figures. Lieutenant Langborne did not long remain with the Battalion, for a few weeks later at Tel-el-Kebir, the machine-gun section was absorbed by the newly-formed 4th Brigade Machine-gun Company, and the entire section, including Lieutenants Langborne and A. Mitchell, was transferred to brigade and became a separate entity.

Among the men transferred was Private J. J. Dwyer, who at a later stage in France gained the coveted V.C.

On January 21, the Battalion left Ismailia for Moascar, where route marches into the desert became the order of the day, and a stricter form of discipline was enforced. Leave to Cairo, however, was frequent, and almost any man

---

(1) Lieutenant F. W. Lane, who transferred shortly after joining the Battalion to the 47th Battalion, was killed while serving with that unit on 28/3/18.

with a credit in his paybook or with friends to aid him, was given permission to go.

On February 27, Colonel J. H. Cannan returned from hospital and resumed command of the Battalion from Major Snowden. Captain T. P. McSharry attained his majority about this time, and Captain J. J. Corrigan took over the duties of Adjutant. The orderly room was then in the hands of Sergeant Maurice Cook, an 8th Reinforcement N.C.O. who had as his assistant Private E. S. Robinson—better known as "Bags"—from the same reinforcements.

The day Colonel Cannan arrived back with the unit the Battalion entrained for Tel-el-Kebir, and there encamped near the site of Sir Garnet Wolseley's victorious battle against the Egyptians in 1882. Souvenir hunters searched enthusiastically in the hope of unearthing a Damascus blade with jewel-studded hilt and gold-embedded scabbard, for the rumour was that such a weapon had once been found. Until the day of our departure the thought of treasure trove continually attracted the gullible, though what was unearthed was not worth the sweat and labour expended upon it.

During the stay at Tel-el-Kebir, the 11th, 12th and 13th Reinforcements for the Battalion arrived. But the formation of the 4th Australian Division had commenced, and practically all these men were transferred in a body to the sister unit of the 15th, the 47th Battalion in the 12th Brigade. Besides the reinforcements transferred, a number of the old hands of the 15th were added to them for the purpose of strengthening the new unit. The first to be transferred was Major Eccles Snowden, who assumed command of the 47th and became Lieutenant Colonel. He took with him Lieutenant Eric Terry as Adjutant, Lieutenants F. R. North, J. N. Wilson and F. W. Lane were also transferred, most of these officers obtaining their captaincies and command of companies. Company Sergeant-Major Bell of "C" Company went over also, accepting the Regimental Sergeant-Majorship of the 47th. Among the other N.C.O.'s to transfer were Sergeant Franz Koch of "A" Company and Corporal Taylor of "C."

The transfer of men to the 47th had been a big drain upon the Battalion, but the drain had only commenced. Men had to be found for the new artillery brigade then in formation, and for the 4th Divisional Signalling Company formed shortly afterwards. To this was added the new Battalion formation known as the 4th Pioneers. Among the original members of the 15th Battalion Headquarters Sig-

nallers who transferred to the 41st Battery were Signallers J. E. Wellard, Sigvart, J. Guy, J. Hawks, and Les. Gillingham.

The command of the new 4th Division was entrusted to the little Imperial Officer, Major-General Sir H. V. Cox. This officer had done most of his soldiering in India and at the Suvla landing was in command of the Indian Brigade. He was a thorough student of warfare and a very capable commander. He was immediately nicknamed "Robin-Redbreast" and the name stuck until his transfer back to India after a period in France.

As we were now a separate entity, the severance of the 4th Brigade from the New Zealand Division under the command of General Godley became an accomplished fact. So far as the rank and file were concerned, the change over took place practically unnoticed except for a combined concert at which the singing of the Maoris was particularly appreciated. Among the officers, dinners were held, and an enjoyable time was spent bidding adieu to old comrades.

On March 7 three officers reported to the Battalion. They were Lieutenants Malcolm McGhie, A. R. Niven and J. M. Watson. On March 11 Lieutenant D. S. Jopling came into camp. On March 16 C.S.M.s J. H. W. Fraser of "B" Company and E. K. Carter of "A" Company were promoted to commissioned rank. E. K. (Nick) Carter's appointment made him the youngest officer serving in the unit, he being a few months younger than Lieutenant Dal Cummins. Both these officers attained their captaincies before reaching the age of 21 years. On March 18, 2/Lieutenant N. McGhie reported and 2/Lieutenants R. B. Glasgow and F. Martyr were taken upon strength. Both these men came from the 2nd Light Horse. Glasgow was a brother of the 13th Brigade commander, Brigadier General William Glasgow. Martyr was a man of splendid physique. He was unfortunately killed in his first engagement at Pozieres. Bob Glasgow was wounded going into Pozieres, but returned to the unit and became one of its best-known Company Commanders.

On the 26th of the month the three days trek to Serapeum began. This journey through the desert, though taken in easy stages, was a severe test to the men, many of whom were still weak from wounds received in Gallipoli, while the reinforcements had not yet accustomed themselves to the sand. Attached to the column were a number of camels utilised for carrying Quartermaster's gear and provisions. To some of the men the prospect of joining a camel corps and riding the beasts of the desert instead of trudging

on foot, appealed strongly. The few who did so, however, did not appear to appreciate the life and rejoined the unit at a later stage in France.

What might have proved a very serious accident happened to Private Wally Eastment, who was attached to the Quartermaster's store and travelled with the camel train Eastment was passing one of the camels when it suddenly attacked him, seizing him by the elbow with its teeth and shaking him viciously. The native drivers rushed to Eastment's assistance. So severe was the bite that it was a long time before the unfortunate man fully recovered.

This was the first march that equalled in any way the marches indulged in prior to leaving for Gallipoli. The men's comfort was carefully studied and the meals en route were equal to those received during ordinary camp life. On the last day of the march, however, the watercarts belonging to the Battalion were sent on ahead. An order was issued warning the men not to drink the water from the Sweetwater Canal. As no other water was obtainable, this order was continually broken, though it was realised that drastic after effects might ensue. When the end of the journey was in sight and the trees outlining Lake Tinsah were clearly visible the first men fell out. At the pontoon bridge which stretched across the Suez Canal, the men ignored discipline altogether, and discarding their clothing dived into the Canal's cool refreshing waters. Colonel Monash riding along the ranks remonstrated with them for not completing their journey, a mere matter of a mile to where the camp lay. The undressed and partially unrobed men were in a roguish mood and immediately began their time-honoured count. One-two-three .... At the first sound General Monash put spurs to his horse and galloped away[1].

The new camp, situated about a mile from the banks of the Canal, had little to recommend it, for it was subjected to the worst sand storms the unit was to experience while in Egypt. Duty men had to be found here also for all classes of work, from guarding the Canal to digging and renovating trenches or dragging the sand over a large area so that footsteps or marks of intruding Turks could be easily located, and a thousand and one other duties which to new and old hands alike seemed to be discovered by those on Brigade and Division solely to make what might have been a pleasant holiday as unpleasant as it was possible to conceive.

---

(1) Major Toft in "Playing a Man's Game" gives the total number of men who completed the march as 147 out of a total of over 600.

It was from this camp that the first anniversary of Anzac Day was kept by the troops. It took the form of water sports held on the Canal and to its banks came thousands of men who had one idea—to enjoy themselves thoroughly. Probably never in the history of the unit was there such a day. General Monash had ordered in his Brigade the wearing of two ribbons, red and blue, by all troops who had served on Gallipoli Peninsula, while those whose service had been in Egypt or on the waters coming from Australia wore the blue ribbon alone. The surprise of the afternoon was the arrival of the then Prince of Wales, and his appearance to the troops resulted in a wild burst of cheering. Shortly afterwards, while thousands of naked forms were sporting in the water or sunning themselves upon the Canal's banks, a wild shout broke the peaceful scene and men disappeared under the water in all directions, for a woman suddenly appeared upon the canal controller's ship. Naturally she soon left the carnival.

Shortly after Anzac Day the unit moved camp to the bank of the Canal itself. The change was a welcome one in more ways than one. In lean-tos and sand dugouts, quarters were found overlooking the water and it was not infrequent to find the water's edge occupied, night after night, by sleeping forms who tumbled into the water at daylight to awaken themselves. Throughout the day, as the duties were of the lightest, the men swam, and every steamer passing up or down the waterway was greeted by dozens of forms swimming about it, yelling for the latest news or chasing arduously tins of tobacco thrown to them by those aboard the vessel.

At this stage, the Lewis Machine Gun Section was formed. The command of the men who were to use this new weapon was given to Lieutenant Dal Cummins. Several men had been sent to the school of instruction in the gun held at Zietoun from Tel-el-Kebir. Among these was Billy Murdock. Murdock was an original member of the 15th Battalion, having joined it at Enoggera after his return from the Rabaul Expedition for which he had volunteered at the beginning of hostilities. As a bugler in the early days he was well known. He was made the senior sergeant. At Pozieres he received the D.C.M. and was shortly afterwards commissioned, but at Gueudecourt he became a casualty and fell into the hands of the Germans. After three attempts to escape from various prisons in Germany, he finally succeeded and returned to the unit at the completion of the

war, serving with it in France and Belgium after the Armistice.

Private Cecil Crowther, who became a Lance-Corporal in the first list of promotions for the machine gunners, rose to a sergeant and was taken prisoner at the same time as Murdock. The second sergeant appointed was J. Heron, who had but recently transferred from the A.S.C. No other appointments were made at this time, but shortly after the unit's arrival in France Leslie was appointed corporal, and shortly afterwards, as a sergeant, became attached to the Pay Corps, and did not see service any longer with the unit. Jack Rae was appointed Lance Corporal, and received his commission in France. He also collected a Military Medal and Military Cross. Among the Gallipoli men who joined the Machine Gun Section were Private A. B. "Taffy" Roberts from "A" Company, afterwards killed at Pozieres; Privates E. "Yerram" Bryans, T. P. Chataway, "Fatty" Ellis, E. M. Middleton, who lost an eye while in France, and W. Adams from "C" Company; Privates E. Robinson, J. Stewart and Dave Wilson from "B" Company (from which company also came Rae and Heron). From "D" Company came Privates Reason, Etchell and E. Chalk, besides several other men, thirty-six in all, whose service with the gunners was of shorter duration. As the value of these guns both in attack and defence became more fully recognised, the original small complement of thirty-two men, excluding the N.C.O.s, was considerably augmented, until with the extra weapons granted to the battalion before Pozieres it was found necessary to allot so many guns to each company in the unit, and draw upon such companies for reserve men and for rations.

On April 27, Lieutenant A. A. Plane reported for duty and in the following month Lieutenant T. B. Heffer reported and Lieutenants Dave Dunworth and W. J. Jamieson marched in on the 20th. Lieutenant Jamieson became Signalling Officer for the battalion but unfortunately was accidently wounded at Bois Grenier, France, on June 25 and did not see any further service with the unit.

During the month of May rumours were rife as to the probable destination of the Brigade in the near future. When the Quartermaster, Captain Fred Craig, began to check over all kit in the men's possession and at the latter end of the month withdrew one blanket from each man, various parts of Asia were suggested as the next scene of action. This furphy was quickly dispelled when lectures regarding our behaviour in France became the order of the day. On

May 31, 1916, packed to suffocating point in open trucks, we were trundled violently down to Alexandria and embarked on s.s. Transylvania, the ill-fated vessel that was torpedoed on its return trip to Egypt after our debarkation at Marseilles.

It was with some regret we bade goodbye to Egypt, for its great open spaces enabled us to breathe freely and its warmth had the friendly and familiar touch of distant Australia.

* ◊ ◊ *

CHAPTER VI.

AND THIS IS FRANCE.

It was with an interest almost amounting to enthusiasm that the men lined the decks on June 7, 1916, as the Transylvania steamed slowly into Marseilles Harbour. The three Battalions—13th, 14th and 15th—together with 4th Brigade Headquarters, disembarked during the afternoon, and marching through the city to the railway station, entrained for the long journey to the North of France.

The trip through the Mediterranean had been disturbed by the startling news of the Battle of Jutland, and the tragic tidings of the sinking of the H.M.S. Hampshire with Earl Kitchener aboard was received just before entering Marseilles. But, with the first sight of France these two great events were banished for the time being from the mind. This was the land of chivalry, of a thousand romances, of extremes of joy and sorrow. The visible signs of mourning were noted in every woman seen and in the dour and frequently fierce glitters of hate in the eyes of the men when speaking about the common enemy.

Far in the north the drums of war beat an incessant tattoo day and night, and far away down south another mourning robe was donned, and yet another and another. It was the first time we had noted the effect of the great tragedy upon those who stay at home. Brave hearts smiled and cheered, but not in the way of the English. The cheering contained a note of vicious exultation and admiration for the stalwart men of whom much was expected owing to the valour they had already shown upon Gallipoli Peninsula.

The train journey to the North of France was a tour de luxe to troops used to open trucks and the broiling sun of Egypt as the trains dragged their weary way across the desert. But in France, there were orchards and farms, vineyards and pasture fields, quaint villages and tree-lined rivers, and at every stop, instead of the dirty howling Arabs, there were meals in abundance and white people chattering about you while you ate. Day and night the train travelled north. To the majority of Queenslanders the contrast with the rolling plains and the coastal jungles of their native State was particularly apparent. The green of the fields and the trees was a darker hue than most of that

seen in our sunny land. Paris was passed during the night—the only blot upon an otherwise pleasant journey—and craning heads from carriage windows declaimed in emphatic tones that they at least could see the Eiffel Tower. At midnight on June 10, under cover of a light drizzling rain, we detrained at Bailleul, and walked a mile to our billets at La Maison Blanche. There, for the first time since leaving Australia, straw lay beneath our blankets in the open airy sheds where we were billeted.

The day following being a Sunday, the morning was devoted to idleness and drying of clothes, and the afternoon to an exploration of the near neighbourhood. The smallness of the farms proved a novelty to those who came from farming districts in Queensland and Tasmania, and many of these men, desirous of improving their knowledge of intensive farming, conversed with the farmers on the methods of agriculture used in the two countries. The middens at the back of all the farm houses astounded the Australian born, who, unfamiliar with this method of conserving animal manure for field purposes, admitted its economy, but disliked intensely its close proximity to the residential quarters. Many of these men declared themselves stronger adherents than ever to the artificial manures in general use in Australia.

From June 10 to June 15 practically no serious training was undertaken by the battalion, for it soon became obvious after one short route march that the feet of the men had to become accustomed to the cobbled roadways of France before anything else could be accomplished. That we were not in the country for a holiday became apparent when steel helmets and gas respirators were issued.

The change over from the slouch hat to the helmet was not at first acceptable. It did not come into general use when out of the line, and where the old hat always popped up was from the most unexpected quarters. The gas respirators were another matter. If the helmet protected the head from flying splinters or ricochetting bullets, the bag respirator with its unpleasant smell of chemical and its stuffy, choking sensation when breathing, was the only safeguard against the devastating effects of gas. So gas drill became the vogue. On June 15, the 4th Brigade having been temporarily attached to the 2nd Australian Division, was ordered to relieve the 7th Australian Infantry Brigade in the line of trenches at Bois Grenier.

Two days later the relief took place, and the 15th Battalion, as reserve battalion to the Brigade, occupied billets at

Jesus Farm. From this point, officers and N.C.O.s were sent to the front line to familiarise themselves with trench warfare as it was conducted in France. Men were also detailed for the new arm of the service—the Stokes Gun—a trench mortar which was to prove of great value. The bombers under Lieutenant Brettingham Moore started intensive training and the Lewis Gun crews under Lieutenant Dal. Cummins did likewise. The rations of the men at this period, though equal if not better than those received at any time since we had left Australia, were apparently quite insufficient for hungry men, for every house where eggs were obtainable was raided by the troops. Champagne could be purchased at five francs a bottle, and though somewhat on the green side, it found numerous buyers. White and red wines cost considerably less. Cider was obtainable for those who did not indulge in the harder tack and beer by those whose money began to run short. The beer was much below the average of the worst types of English or Australian beer. In fact, unless previously informed that it was beer, it was in most cases unrecognisable as such. It never became popular with the men.

On June 24, Lieutenant W. J. Jamieson, Signalling Officer, became the first officer casualty in France, being accidentally wounded while cleaning a revolver. He did not see further service with the unit. On June 27, the 13th and 14th Battalions relieved the 16th and 19th in the front line, and on the 30th the 15th Battalion moved out of Jesus Farm and took over the reserve trench held by the 20th Battalion. This position was known as the Bois Grenier Reserve Line. The 1st Australian Infantry Brigade occupied the trenches on the right flank and the 6th Australian Infantry Brigade those on the left. On the same day Sergeant A. M. Marshall of the Signalling Section was promoted to commissioned rank in place of Lieutenant W. J. Jamieson.

To the men used to the type of warfare on Gallipoli Peninsula the new manner of fighting appeared peculiar. Star shells fired at night from the German line cast their reflections throughout the area where the unit now was. Interspersed with rumours as to what was happening or likely to happen, were the sudden alarms from the gas sentries. During the course of these alarms many curious things occurred, for in the men's haste to place the respirators over their heads it often happened that the eye spots were at the back of the head instead of in their proper position. The cooler thinking men immediately reversed their helmets without any undue fuss, but those who were

slightly nervous, imagining that a black cloud of gas was destroying their vision, choked and spluttered into their respirators. One officer in the unit worked himself into such a frenzy that he fell down under the impression that he was dying.

During the night fatigue parties were continually at work making the trench system more bearable. The new earthworks in several places and the movement of men along the system in daytime attracted Fritz's artillery at last, and the first fatal casualty of the 15th Battalion in France occurred on July. 4. During the occupation of the Bois Grenier Reserve Line those Gallipoli veterans who had seen the longest service on the Peninsula were granted English leave. The claims of quite a number of men were put forward, and from these two N.C.O.s, Q.M.S. Jack Hynes of "A" Company and C.S.M. Blacklow of "D" Company were chosen. Among the officers the claim of Captain J. J. Corrigan was successful.

On July 8, 2/Lieutenants P. K. Landy and N. R. Fogarty reported for duty. On the night of July 11-12 the Battalion was relieved by the 31st Battalion, 8th Australian Infantry Brigade, and moved out to its old billets at Le Blanche Maison. The next day at 4 a.m. it entrained at Bailleul Railway Station for Candas, where it detrained and marched to St. Ouen. The first stage of the trek to the Somme battle had commenced.

On this day a vital change took place at Brigade Headquarters. The Brigadier—General Monash—transferred his command to Brigadier-General C. H. Brand, D.S.O. Of this the rank and file were not wholly aware until the Brigade parade on July 21. From the aloofness of General Monash to the companionship of Brigadier-General Brand was a radical but very welcome change. "The Brig" or "Old Steve" as General "Charlie" Brand became universally known throughout the brigade, was a very human man. His gallantry was of the highest order, and there were fewer errors in his judgment than many officers of senior rank could claim. His thin, soldierly figure was a welcome sight among all ranks. His constant thought was for his men's welfare and his earnest efforts to divert the minds of his men from a tragedy they had just faced was appreciated and silently applauded far more than he ever knew. Those men present at his farewell to the Brigade, prior to his departure for Australia in October, 1918, upon his Anzac long service leave, will recall the almost broken figure of their leader and friend who

spoke from the heart. Brand had become so much part of his brigade that to visualise it without him was impossible. As the years roll by and the greater figures on the stage of the world war drama fade from our memories, that of Charlie Brand becomes more firmly entrenched in the hearts and minds of those who served under him, more so even than in the heyday of his military career.

At 1 p.m. on July 16 the Battalion left St. Ouen and marched to Naours. Here on July 21 the new Brigadier was introduced to the brigade. This introduction did not auger well for the future, for the sentences passed on several delinquents were read out on the parade and the speech of the new Brigadier was most condemnatory. On this day also 2/Lieutenant A. V. Jackson reported for duty. On July 22, the longest march the unit had yet done in France took place. It began at 9 a.m. and after an inspection by General H. V. Cox at Flessells, the battalion returned to billets at 3.30 p.m.

Naours did not keep us very long, for on the 25th we left at 9 a.m. for Herrisart. On the 27th, Herrisart was left behind and the unit tramped into Warloy about 2 p.m. These marches revealed that the feet of some of the men still needed much attention. The bootmaker, Sergeant Cawsey, was probably the busiest man in the unit next to the medical officer, Captain Powell, round about this time. Feet were being continually washed with permanganate of potash solution and socks changed as frequently as they were available.

On July 28, the 2nd Australian Infantry Brigade marched through Warloy on their way back from the Pozieres engagement. The men of the brigade obtained all the information they could as to what was before them. Far from disconcerting them in any way, the fearful stories told by the returning men—all of which were probably more than true—only added spice to the adventure At night a concert was held and those who felt inclined drifted from the tales of carnage to the distant scenes of romance recalled by the "Ivy over the Cottage Door" or "My Ain Folks," and spent a thoroughly enjoyable evening. On July 30, Sergeant Jack Craven, an original "C" Company man and afterwards on Headquarters Signalling Section, transferred to the 14th Battalion with the rank of Lieutenant and took over the command of that unit's signallers.

It was at Warloy that a series of brigade exercises were carried out under day and night conditions. The first night operation the 15th engaged in was, to say the least, some-

what of a failure. This was the result of a rather curious incident. The men under Captain Walter Coombs of "A" Company were manoeuvring about in the dark when they stumbled upon some sheep in a pen, evidently part of a butcher's flock ready for the killing on the morrow. A wag in the company passed the word along that the sheep were to be released and driven in the direction of the enemy. Not suspecting that a trick was being played upon him, Captain Coombs opened the gate, and four frightened sheep scampered away, bleating pitifully into the darkness. The recovery of the sheep was ordered almost immediately and there started a wild sheep chase in the dark which completely disorganised the whole movement.

General Brand, by no means pleased at such an intrusion into his well-laid plans, ordered the manoeuvres to be carried out again on the next night. Happily the whole program passed off without a hitch.

The unit left Warloy on August 4 and passing through Senlis marched into the Brickfields at Albert, to bivouac at 11.45 p.m. The heavy cannonade in the Pozieres sector was clearly heard and star shells were visible shooting high into the sky. The whole of the next day was spent sharpening bayonets, collecting ammunition, and repairing equipment, while those who could steal a moment to themselves scribbled hasty letters home. In the late afternoon, General Sir William Birdwood held an informal chat with the men, and was heartily cheered by them as he departed. A few minutes after he left, the first of the enemy's shells to disturb our peace arrived, bursting with a resounding crash in the narrow street between the Brickfields and the Cathedral. This was swiftly followed by another, and after scattering a few more in the neighbourhood of the cathedral the battery threw a few into the fields itself for luck. So far as is known no casualties resulted from this desultory effort.

When night fell, the roll was called. The time for action had arrived. Those officers who were to remain behind were detailed off, and leaving them, as we thought in perfect security, the battalion marched out of its camping ground into the heaviest shell fire it was ever to experience during its long term in France.[1]

---

(1) The officers left in reserve were: Lieutenants W. T. Mundell, Walter Cooper, W. H. Nicholls, P. Landy, Eric Francis, R. B. McIntosh.

GROUP OF 15 BN. OFFICERS, NEUVE EGLISE, FRANCE, 1918.

GROUP OF 15 BN. OFFICERS, PHILLIPEVILLE, BELGIUM.

BACK ROW: Ohlsen, Hunter, Smith, Mudge, Loveday, Thorpe, Jamieson and Drane.

MIDDLE ROW: Lees, Drybrough, Hocker, Hamilton, Toft, McKay, Voss and Ward.

FRONT ROW: Francis, Bradley, Richardson, Sampson, Johnston, Robinson, Corser and O'Bryan.

No. 10 PLATOON, C. COY., 15 BN.

CHAPTER VII.

POZIERES AND MOUQUET FARM.

The series of battles on the Somme which opened on July 1 were designed to end the deadlock on the Western Front where the opposing armies had entrenched behind great belts of barbed wire and concentrated vast numbers of field-pieces of all calibres, machine guns, and every kind of weapon then known in war. Actually they constituted an assault upon one of the mightiest of the bastions the Germans had constructed in the long line of their defences extending from the North Sea to the Swiss frontier. The soil in the Somme area was peculiarly favourable for the excavation of elaborate dugouts, and some of them were thirty, or even forty feet deep and were capable of maintaining a whole company in perfect security during the heaviest bombardment.

For months, every nerve, both at Home and in the trenches, had been strained in a united effort to ensure that nothing would be left undone in the attempt that was to follow to bring the war to an end. Vast stocks of ammunition of all kinds had been accumulated and stored within convenient distance of the British front. Scores of miles of deep communication trenches had been dug, and the British and Australian infantry had been equipped down to the last proverbial boot-lace. The Somme was to be the real baptism in France of the Australian divisions that a few months previously, had emerged from the bloody heights above Anzac Cove with a name for dash and daring that no other troops before, or since, have surpassed. Unhappily it was to take toll of many thousands of their ranks, but the deeds of these men around Pozieres, and Mouquet Farm and Flers, were in a way to glorify the sacrifices they made.

On July 8, the 4th Australian Division was suddenly ordered to follow the rest of the 1st Anzac Corps to the Somme. By the 14th there had been concentrated in the area west of the Amiens-Doullens Road the three divisions of the Corps. The Australian part in the operations began with the attack of the 1st division on Pozieres, which was later followed with a second attack on Pozieres Heights by the 2nd division. The ensuing weeks were to provide some of the fiercest fighting of the whole war. During the first week of August the 4th Division, of which the 4th Brigade

formed part, had been on or near the edge of the battlefield. The brigades of the 2nd Division had been so badly mauled by this time that the 4th Division was sent in to its relief. The 12th Brigade was ordered to undertake the immediate relief of the 5th and part of the 7th Brigade, and the 4th Brigade, being a veteran formation, was to relieve the 6th and make an attack on the night following the relief. The relief was to take place on the night of August 5/6.

The 15th Battalion[1] left the Brickfields to enter the front line at Pozieres at 6 p.m. on August 5. The route lay through Albert via Tara Hill and Sausage Valley. Turning to the right, the column of men moved down from the higher ground into the cobbled streets of Albert. As the column passed under the huge bronze statue of the Virgin Mary, suspended at right angles to the basilica of the cathedral, clasping within Her arms the Child of Sacrifice, face after face in the marching line glanced upward. Through the ruined city they strode, the metallic strokes of their boots resounding from wall to wall, to echo eerily in neighbouring streets and lanes. The distorted shadows of the shattered buildings lengthened with the last rays of the departing sun. Near at hand the guns spoke; in the middle distance the crash of bursting shells continued unabated. Towards these sounds the column marched.

As the column rounded Tara Hill and marched towards Sausage Valley, the bombardment reached its height. The crashing of the British guns drowned the howl and screech of the retaliating shells. At Chalk Pit the first halt in the advance took place. Here a heavy enemy barrage was tearing the country to pieces and lashing the saps with an appalling ferocity. So severe was this fire that the unit retraced its steps to Wire Trench and from here sought to gain entrance into the saps leading to the front line. But again

---

(1) The officers entering the line with the battalion, in this the first serious operation undertaken by the unit in France were as follows: —Commanding Officer Lt. Col. J. H. Cannan, C.B., Adjutant Captain J. Koch, I.O. Lieutenant T. B. Heffer, Sig. Officer Lt. A. M. Marshall, Liaison Officer with 7th Suffolks Regiment Lt. E. K. Carter, "A" Company Captain C. Corser, Lieutenants F. Martyr and Fogarty. Sergeant A. B. Shrubb was granted commission rank the day following, thus giving a third subaltern to this company: "B" Company—Captain Snartt, Lieutenants R. I. Arnold, J. H. T. Fraser and J. M. Watson; "C" Company—Captain C. M. Johnston, Lieutenants D. Dunsworth, R. B. Glasgow and N. McGhie; "D" Company—Captain J. J. Corrigan, Lieutenants H. Brettingham Moore, A. A. Plane and A. R. Nevin. The officers left in reserve at the Brickfields, most of whom were called upon within the course of two days to replace casualties, were: Captain W. W. Coombs, Lieutenants W. T. Mundell, W. H. Nichol's, E. Francis, P. Landy, W. Cooper, R. B. McIntosh, D. S. Jopling, J. C. Browne.

another barrage blocked the way. Into this barrage the commanding officer, Colonel J. H. Cannan, with his Adjutant, Captain Harold Koch, the R.S.M., C. S. Goss, and C.S.M. Lack of "B" Company led the way, followed by the Lewis Gunners under Lieutenant Cummins and "B" Company under Captain Snartt. Disorganisation of the line of march took place immediately, and the only men to arrive in the front line that night except the headquarters staff, were two platoons of "B" Company and the Lewis Gun Section.

The epic feat of the Lewis Gunners in reaching the front line that night deserves to be recorded. From the moment they entered Wire Trench, barrage after barrage swept upon them. In the blackness of the night the faint lights discernible from the enemy's flares, which apparently rose from three sides of them, showed nothing but mud and desolation. The guides to this party were either killed, wounded or lost. Hampered by the extra panniers of ammunition the gunners were compelled to carry; tripped by the broken wires lying everywhere along the sap; crawling over dead and wounded; afraid to leave the sap in case they should fail to find their way back to it again; crouching in the mud and rain for long intervals while Fritz slashed them unmercifully with every form of high explosive; hearing the incessant calls for stretcher-bearers that throughout the long journey never ceased; the grumblings at the slowness of the guides; the explosive oaths; the howls of pain; the violent concussion when shells made direct hits—all these things created a bedlam which defies description. Although helpless as a rudderless ship in a cyclone, the battalion still fought on. At midnight, exhausted and weary, the men struggled painfully into the shelter of Gibraltar. There they met the Adjutant Captain Koch, who immediately ordered them to continue upon their way. Out into the blast once more they went, until almost dropping in their tracks, they arrived in the support line. There they were left to fall asleep where and how they could, too exhausted to worry about the shrieking inferno around them. The credit for this remarkable feat rests with Lieutenant Dal Cummins and his N.C.O.s, Sergeant W. Murdock and Corporal Jack Rae. Both these N.C.O.s worked hard and courageously throughout the night, while Rae personally made trip after trip down the line to encourage the men to keep touch with each other. Many lives were lost and numbers were wounded. Among the latter were Private Bill Adams, whose wound did not allow him to see any further service with the unit, and Private Jimmy Sigvart.

The experience of "B" Company—that is the two platoons Nos. 5 and 6 commanded by Lieutenant J. M. Watson and Sergeants Lulham and A. Robinson respectively with the officer commanding the Company, Captain Snartt—has been described by Lieutenant (then Sergeant) Andy Robinson who writes: "After leaving 'K' Trench we moved out into the open towards the left. Our leaders were immediately enveloped in a terrific shellfire, and losing their guide became completely lost. One particularly large shell fell between 5 and 6 Platoons killing Privates J. Lamberten and Hedge and wounding Corporal R. Luxton. No. 6 Platoon became separated from No. 5, while the rest of the battalion retired down 'K' Trench. The position was so confused that Private J. Montgomery and I made the men of our platoon stay with the wounded until after a long search we found the 24th Battalion in the front line. Sergeant Lulham was killed, but I do not know at what time. Just on daylight we discovered most of the 24th near us sitting in funk holes in natural positions, dead from concussion. Unable to take over from the 24th we were sent to a support trench to await the 15th coming in. From this position we were driven out by shellfire, Privates Barrow and Prescott being killed and the Lewis Gunner, Sergeant Jim Heron wounded. In order to escape from this I climbed over the back of the trench and was shortly afterwards wounded by rifle fire. The number of dead Germans about was surprising, and the trenches were so full of dead that it was impossible to move. The Australian dead were mainly of the 24th Battalion. One 24th man lay on top of a number of Germans who had apparently been bayonetted by him. He still clasped his rifle firmly in his hands."

The remaining platoons of "B" Company together with "A," "C" and "D" Companies had been turned back at "K" Trench. A brief description written by an "A" Company N.C.O. of that section's endeavour to enter the front line that night, was probably the same experience as that of the two other companies. It was estimated at one time that about half of the casualties of the 15th Battalion at Pozieres occurred that night. In "A" Company alone over 70 men are stated to have been wounded or killed. Sergeant-Major (then Lance-Corporal) J. Fleet writes: "We left Albert in the evening and expected to be in the support line in a few hours. Instead we were tramping up and down all over the place till the early hours of the morning. We suffered quite a number of casualties, for no one seemed to know where we were or where we were going. Travelling through

narrow trenches in full marching order, falling or walking or slipping upon dead men, wire overhead, wire underfoot, feet tangled in wire, wire around your neck, wire tangled in your rifle or your gear—it was a hell of a night. Everyone was in a terrible frame of mind. At dawn we found ourselves about half-way from where we had started, and had to get into our position in broad daylight. About a mile behind Gibraltar Sergeant Eric Simon was skittled in the sap. Half of our platoon was wiped out with one shell. Poor Oscar Sutton, an original and a fine soldier, was badly hit in the stomach. He was in great agony lying in the bottom of the trench. We could not help treading on him. I heard one man say as Oscar groaned, 'Sorry Oscar,' and Oscar said 'Never mind me. I understand boys.' Ernie George, another original, was wounded also but not so badly as Oscar. We yanked him out and he eventually reached Australia. Passing along Orchard Road—near Gibraltar—we were in full view of the enemy and he pasted us with coal boxes and shrapnel, making a fearful mess of my platoon. I kept yelling 'Keep going for the trench in front.' Fritz landed one shell near the 60ft. dugout Dr. Powell was in later. The stop was fatal. The next shell dropped among them. The Adjutant, Captain Harold Koch, was in the trench. I think he was there all night. Billy Woodridge got off with what we thought a slight hit in the thigh. Was surprised to learn he died in England.[1] Gorston and Goulton were wounded, the latter going round and round in circles quite silly from shock. Jim Page, a fine chap, a 1st Reinforcement, was also wounded. I watched him limping down the road. No trace was ever found or word heard of Page again. He just limped into the air. The next shell killed Corporal Frank Bruce,[2] a foot or so in front of me, also a few new lads. We breathed a sigh of relief for the bit of cover."

---

(1) Pte. W. I. Woodbridge was one of three brothers who joined the 15th Battalion in Rest Gully on Gallipoli Peninsula. In the attack by the unit at the time of the Suvla Bay landing, Mick (J.M.P.) Woodbridge was killed. The last member of this family, Paddy, was wounded in the charge at Pozieres, part of the casing of a shell severing the heel from his foot. Gangrene set in and at a later date the leg was amputated.

(2) Corporal F. A. Bruce was 32 years old at the time of his death. He was an original member of the unit. In relation to this soldier a curious case of coincidence is recorded. Bruce, during the charge from Pope's Hill on Gallipoli, was wounded with a bullet that passed through both his thighs without damaging the bones. He crawled into a small dugout until help came and within the dugout found a young 16th soldier whose wound was similar to his own. The 16th lad was Bruce's nephew.

The appalling muddle of this relief was no doubt intensified by the heavy bombardment by the enemy of all approaches to the front line. But the outstanding fact to the men seeking to penetrate the barrages was the indecision displayed by their guides on that night. Certainly these unfortunate men may have known the saps in daylight, but they failed to recognise them at night when destroyed by shellfire, and the point remains that the guides were quite unable to give the officers and N.C.O.s any idea whatever of their bearings. In the few instances where groups of men, thoroughly fed up with movement restricted to about five yards an hour and the enfilading shell fire that smashed their temporary shelters to smithereens and inflicted casualties, sought to find their own way across country, they were either driven back into the saps by the ferocity of the barrage or destroyed by it.

It was the unit's first real experience of concentrated shellfire, and the first taste of warfare for many of its ranks. It was impossible to penetrate this devastating curtain of fire in platoon or any other form of close formation without suffering heavy casualties, so throughout the early morning the Battalion filtered through in small parties, led either by an N.C.O. or an officer. The only officer wounded during this relief, Lieutenant Bob Glasgow, was in "C" Company. When the relief was completed the members of the 24th Battalion disappeared, doubtful in their minds as to whether it was safer to remain in the front line or to make the dash back to the rear through those shell-rocking saps.

During the brigade's occupation of the front line in Pozieres, an interesting experiment was carried out by General Brand, the commanding officer, in the form of a forward canteen in Cheese Road, near Brigade Headquarters at Gibraltar. As so many men can remember being able to buy many luxuries in this way the following details supplied by General Brand himself are interesting. The General writes:—

> "It was not a canteen in the ordinary sense of the term, but a forward depot at Brigade Headquarters near Cheese Road, not far from Gibraltar. From this advance depot supplies as ordered were delivered right into the front line by special carriers. The cash was collected on delivery............ The turn-over during the brigade's first period in the line was about 900 francs. Only these men forward of Battalion Headquarters were entitled to purchase. I have only a record of the first lot of supplies: 3 cases tinned fruit, 3 cases tinned sausages, 4 cases of cake, tobacco, biscuits and cafe au lait. All sold out. Depot replenished next time the Brigade went in. Does not sound very wonderful, but when the conditions at that period were considered it was a good effort."

The trenches held by the 15th Battalion were in front of Pozieres Village, or at least the site where the village had

been, and lay principally along the edge of Brand's Road, a partially sunken road passing west of Pozieres towards the village of Courcellette lying north-east behind the German lines. At the junction of "A" and "C" Companies the trench took such an acute angle turn, that from one portion of "D" Company's line the backs of their "C" Company friends could be clearly seen. This was the furthermost point and nearest part in the salient to the German line. This shorter section of trench held by "C" Company joined up with a section of No. 6 Platoon, 14th Battalion under the charge of Sergeant Douglas Mortimer of that unit, situated some 100 yards in front of the rest of the platoon commanded by 2/Lieutenant H. S. Dobbie.

The two companies of the 15th occupying the other and longer arm of the angle—that along Brand's Road, facing toward Mouquet Farm—were "A" and "D" Companies under the commands of Captains Cyril Corser and J. J. Corrigan. In front of this part of the line, strong points were pushed out from the trench and manned during daylight by Lewis gunners and grenade throwers. The distance from the enemy positions and "C" Company's sector was roughly from 420 yards to 450 yards, while on "A" and "D" Company's front they were 800 to 1000 yards away. As with all salients, enfilade fire from both sides was a constant menace. Directly behind the positions of "A" and "D" Companies, some hundred yards away, lay Tom's Cut, the support line. This trench, running parallel to the front line and to the other main artery into the front line, the Centreway, joined a section of trench, an original front line, some 100 yards behind "C" Company. One section of this discarded front line was at this time occupied by the 14th Battalion. Over the salient every variety of shell the Germans commanded was fired. The larger calibre shells, however, were less used than the smaller "whiz-bang" or hated "coal box."

The greater part of the front line system occupied by the Battalion was shallow and in parts it was nothing but a shambles. The dead lay everywhere, partially buried within the parapet or parados, or lying exposed within the trench and the open country to the immediate front. Narrow, shallow dugouts with galvanised iron roofs or no roof whatever, were the only shelters for the men, if they could be termed such, from the hail of lead that never ceased throughout the occupation of the line. At times, however, its ferocity abated sufficiently to allow for the clearance of debris. The unfortunate supporting troops in Tom's Cut suffered at all times from the barrages. Over all, during

the hours of daylight, swarms of brilliantly coloured flies—of the blowfly variety—left the bodies of the dead to settle upon the living. The rain on the night of the 6th added to the general discomfort and misery. Men slept while lying in pools of water at the bottoms of the trenches with nothing but their oil sheets as cover, or propped up in the evil-smelling holes called dugouts to snatch a few seconds rest. Shell shock cases were few, though four members of another battalion were discovered tearing at the earth with hands and teeth. They had to be strapped down to stretchers before they could be removed from the line.

After an apparently quiet afternoon for Pozieres, Fritz commenced a bombardment of the 14th's position and included in his fury the sector held by the connecting 15th Battalion's No. 11 Platoon under the command of Dave Dunworth. This bombardment did not lift until the break of day. In the 15th Battalion practically the entire section of trench held by No. 11 Platoon was blown to pieces. The men surviving this onslaught were drafted into the trenches of No. 10 platoon, commanded temporarily by Sergeant Percy Toft. Most of No. 11 platoon became casualties. Among those to survive the bombardment were Corporal Frank Barnes and Private Jimmy Henderson, the youngster who was the first casualty in "C" Company on Gallipoli Peninsula. At dawn, the enemy attacked on the 14th Battalion front. He was met with a fusillade of rifle and machine gun fire which evidently demoralised him. On the right flank the 14th Battalion men under Lieutenant Jacka, V.C. hopped out and engaged the charging Huns with the bayonet. On "C" Company's frontage Lieutenant Dunworth, collecting the remnants of No. 11 Platoon, did likewise and the astounded Germans promptly surrendered. The prisoners captured in this rally were—15th Battalion, 20 other ranks—14th Battalion, one officer and 100 other ranks.

The rest of the day was reasonably quiet and enabled the men to improve their trenches slightly and make themselves a little more comfortable. The cleaning up of the trenches was a most necessary and unpleasant duty. In this depressing graveyard the faces of the partially buried dead had assumed the green coating not unlike that of newly-cast bronze. Their sightless eyes and their grotesque postures created a sense of unreality that illustrations of Dante's "Inferno" assume. Horror poured upon horror had numbed the men's senses until almost anything was bearable. The crashing shells had lost all power to disturb the working parties. With picks and shovels and even

with their hands alone the work of clearing up the wastage of war went on. Bodies were reburied, and those recently killed were placed ready for stretcher-bearers and burial parties to tender the last rites. Discipline had triumphed. Never again was shellfire in France to prevent the men of the 15th Battalion from moving forward. Private Dan MacMillan of "C" Company summed it up when questioned about the shellfire at Pozieres: "You call that rough?" he exclaimed. "Wait until you get into something really rough."

Throughout the night of the 7th, heavy shellfire continued to fall on the Brigade's position. When darkness fell, picks and shovels were collected from the various dumps, and sapping parties dug toward the German line. These saps were ultimately to be completed by the parties detailed off for the following night when the 15th Battalion was to charge. As a protection for these sapping parties, patrols entered No Man's Land, and formed screens against sudden attacks, and strong fighting patrols, one under Lieutenant Malcolm McGhie, constantly moved about on the lookout for German patrols or anything of a suspicious nature. The patrol under McGhie brought in a prisoner during the night. A "B" Company patrol under its combative leader, Corporal Roy Proctor, unfortunately lost two of its number—Privates Walsh and Butler. A search was made for these two men by Proctor and Private Durough, but the bodies were not recovered. That same day Corporal Proctor became a casualty from shellfire.

Daylight on the 8th was devoted to preparations for the attack to be launched by the Battalion against the system of trenches immediately to their front known locally as Circular Trench, but officially by an intricate system of numbers. This attack was to be made in conjunction with the 7th Suffolk Regiment on the left flank. Stokes guns, trench mortars and Vickers machine guns were all moved up into position preparatory to the charge. The 16th Battalion, the supporting unit in the assault, moved forward to Wire Trench, and later in the day pushed forward a company to "K" Trench in readiness to give active support to the 15th Battalion if needed. From this Battalion came the sapping parties.

The attack was to be made in three waves. Two platoons of each company, together with a proportion of Lewis gunners, formed the first wave. The succeeding waves were made up of the other two platoons of each of the four companies, together with the remainder of the Lewis gun teams Captain Cyril Corser commanded the first wave—a change

which took place owing to Major Johnston's Company being on the extreme right flank—Major C. M. Johnston was in charge of the second wave, and Captain Jack Corrigan the third. The officers taking part in the charge were Lieutenants "Taffy" Nicholls[1], David Dunworth and Norman McGhie with "C" Company; Lieutenants R. I. Arnold, Jim Fraser and J. M. Watson with "B" Company; Lieutenants F. Martyr, A. B. Shrubb and N. R. Fogarty with "A" Company; and Lieutenants Brettingham Moore, A. R. Nevin and A. A. Plane with "D" Company. The whole advance was preceded by scouts and bomb-throwers.

The attack was launched at 9.20 p.m. The first wave was on the tape laid some thirty yards in advance of the front line, and when the barrage fell this wave moved quickly forward, escaping much of the back-lash which the awakened enemy threw over. During the advance of the first wave a shell landed in "C" Company's ranks killing that fine young soldier, Sergeant Stan Cousens[2]. Another shell accounted for the happy-go-lucky Paddy Lieper, who fell badly wounded and by some mischance was missed by the stretcher-bearers for two days before he was rescued. Both these men were original members of the company. Before half the distance had been covered shells began to fall thick and fast in the right half of the advancing troops, while a heavy and accurate machine gun fire swept No Man's Land. "C" Company had no difficulty in capturing their objective, where they set to work immediately to make themselves secure.

At the very outset "B" Company unfortunately lost their three officers. "A" Company's commander, Captain Corser,

---

[1] Lieut. Nicholls had been called up from reserve to replace Lieut. R. B. McIntosh, who was wounded shortly after entering the line when on a message to the Suffolk Regiment for Colonel Cannan. Nicholls arrived in the trench but a few minutes before the charge took place.

[2] Sergeant Stan Cousens had a premonition of his coming death and made reference to the fact some twenty-four hours previous to the charge. The First Reinforcement, Pte. A. B. "Taffy" Roberts, who was killed while leaving the front line to proceed to England on leave also had a premonition. While occupying the Bois Grenier Line with the Lewis Gunners, Roberts conducted a small trench newspaper for the purpose of amusing his friends. In the third issue of this paper he foretold his own death within one month. As he was on the roster for leave to Great Britain at the time the prophecy was laughed at. He also foretold the promotions of Sergeant W. Murdock, Corporals J. Rae, and J. Heron, and Pte. E. Robinson to commissioned rank, all of which at the time was considered highly amusing. Roberts and Page (who was killed as described by Sergeant Major Fleet going into Pozieres) were two of the first reinforcements who landed in Gallipoli with the original Battalion on April 25.

had covered about half the distance when he fell with a machine gun bullet in the stomach. On the way back to the line Corser saw and spoke to Lieutenant Arnold who was lying wounded and lying in a shell hole awaiting aid from the stretcher-bearers. Shortly after Corser left Arnold, a shell landed in the same hole, killing Arnold outright. Apparently the only point where the enemy's trenches were penetrated at this juncture was where Lieutenant Fred Martyr with one or two men crossed the objective. He fell mortally wounded and his body was recovered two days later.

On the left flank Lieutenant Brettingham Moore led his men into a machine gun cross-fire. This was caused through the failure of the 7th Suffolks to advance on his left flank. The strong points held by the enemy in this sector of the line, laid down such a heavy curtain of fire that the men struggled with heads down as if moving into a fierce hailstorm. Moore's men fell all round him, among them was Sergeant Romilly whose leg was shattered by a bullet. Moore's batman fell dead beside him. Private R. McKendrick also became a casualty and Moore himself was wounded in both hips. Struggling forward to the wire he found an opening and leapt into the German trench. To the left of Moore, Lieutenant A. A. Plane with a few men from the second wave had also found an opening and entered the German line. Plane fell badly wounded into the bottom of the trench.

Before most of the second and third lines could get out of their trench, the German barrage fell and much confusion occurred. This barrage covered not only the trench itself but the ground for some twenty to thirty yards in advance of it. Through this, the two lines attempted to force their way, with disastrous results. Lieutenants W. H. Nicholls and Norman McGhie, along with Lieutenant N. R. Fogarty were wounded and Captain Corrigan had only gone a few yards from the trench when he was hit by a piece of high explosive. Sergeant Farr, the senior N.C.O. in "D" Comany, then took command of Corrigan's men and carried on. In the short space of a few minutes, "C" Company was left with two officers, "A" Company with none at all and "D" Company with two; Bretttingham Moore, wounded but still in action, and Lieutenant A. R. Nevin. Lieutenant Dave Dunworth on "C" Company's left flank was endeavouring to connect with "A" Company, which at this period had not entered the front line. "C" Company with most of its N.C.O.s intact was rapidly consolidating its position. On their extreme right a Lewis gun team under the command of Pri-

vate Dave Wilson, containing those splendid soldiers Privates Douglas Clarke, Archie Brown and George Goodfellow. had overrun their objective, and, taking up a position forward of the new front line, held on to it until Wilson became a casualty with a bullet in the lung. They then fell back into their correct position taking Wilson with them. Long before morning, "C" Company's position was such that it would have been a difficult task upon the part of the enemy to dislodge it. Much of the credit due for this, rests with the various N.C.O.s—C.S.M. Eibel, Sgt. Percy Toft who had command of a platoon, Corporals Turner, "Afghan" Parker, Frank Barnes, Joe Lay and several others. The work of the gun teams under Privates Newton (who at a later stage joined the Flying Corps), Doug. Clarke and Joe Coogan also deserve mention.

Probably the first two men to enter the German line on the "A" Company front after the disastrous attempt by Lieutenant Martyr were Lance Corporal Jack Fleet and Private Archie Forrest. Fleet had been hit twice on the German wire, once in the head and once in the feet. He was lying in a shell hole watching a machine gun in a German outpost firing over his head. He had not seen a soul for some time when, glancing round, he saw some of "A" Company close to him. Crawling to another shell hole he found the company bomber, "Lofty" Wheeler, who was badly wounded. Wheeler and Fleet bandaged each other's wounds, and then both men began to crawl about to see what was doing. Meeting Forrest, Fleet parted with Wheeler and he and Forrest began collecting bombs from the wounded and dead, with the intention of attacking the post from which the machine gun was doing such damage. Having collected sufficient bombs they moved forward to the German line as a British shell landed and destroyed the gun crew. Crawling under the wire the two men entered the German line. Here they met two Huns, and Forrest hurled a bomb, killing one and wounding the other. Around them in the trench they found piles of ammunition and bombs of different types, all neatly arranged in crevices and bays. A few seconds after their encounter they were joined by Privates Charlie Wood and Billy Missingham who were followed almost immediately by a Lewis gun crew.

When Lieutenant Moore entered the German line on the right of "D" Company's sector he had a hectic time with some of the garrison. Quite alone, this officer accounted for five Huns before a bomb blew him into a dugout in the side of the trench. From this shelter he disposed of three new

assailants with his revolver and then ran for it. Around the first traverse he met a corporal and three men from "D" Company with a wounded comrade and half a dozen Germans about them. At the point where he met them he stumbled over the body of Lieutenant Plane, who cried out to him: "Save me Brett." Pulling Plane around the corner, Moore and his men routed the pursuing Huns. With the arrival of two other men he left them to hold that portion of the trench while he found out what was happening on his left flank. Meeting a party of twelve men who shouted the password "Queensland" he commandeered two of the party. Privates Jaynes and Andrews, and bombing and shouting their way along the trench, they finally arrived at the left flank and there consolidated in a huge crater. Jaynes was the sole occupant of the post, and Andrews the only guard upon the communication trench leading from Mouquet Farm into the trench they were holding.

Writing home to his mother about this period of the battle Lieutenant Brett Moore said: "I was the only officer in the trench, and had two N.C.O.s (Sergeants W. Domeney and Fleming) and about twenty men holding 150 yards of trench[1].......... We fixed up poor old Plane as well as we could, but we couldn't do much. He was in great pain, having both a leg and an arm broken, and very badly smashed up in addition. I sent messages by volunteers back to the Colonel over "No Man's Land" on which the Germans had put down a heavy barrage every hour during the night, but got no reply, and only lost my men[2]. I found later only two out of six got through ...." About 4 a.m. the two German machine gun crews to his right front who had caused so much trouble throughout the night, began crying "Kamarad" and waving a white flag. Their surrender was accepted and thirty Germans and two machine guns—both of which the Huns had put out of commission —were brought in. Moore and his men then explored 300 to 400 yards of new trench, but could not locate the enemy.

There is no doubt that the heavy loss among officers caused a serious dislocation of the plans laid down by the

---

(1) Beside Sergeants Domeney and Fleming the men in the trench system with Lieutenant Moore were Sergeants Watkins, Corporals Steele and Lambert, who acted as a runner, "Farmer" Parker, Mick O'Brien, Wilf Beaumont, Steve Andrews, Gus Harman, Grenadin and Jack Trull and A. B. Smith.

(2) Corporal Lambert successfully negotiated the dangerous road back to Battalion Headquarters with a message and returning through the barrage area once again sought to carry a message through for Moore, but was killed between the two positions.

commanding officer, Colonel Cannan. Leaderless, the men were in a quandary as to exactly what should be done. For hundreds of yards on either side of the small groups of "D" and "A" Companies who were in possession of the German line, there was an unoccupied trench. Feeding this trench was a series of saps. When daylight came, and the positions of the various garrisons could be located, the enemy came up the saps and bombed the few men out. During the disorganisation of the charge far too many men had found their way back to the original jumping-off line, while dotted all over No Man's Land in shell holes were groups of two and three men waiting for daylight to obtain their bearings. As day began to dawn, Lance Corporal Rae, Lance Corporal Missingham and other N.C.O.s sought to recover these men and lead them to the captured position, but the hour was too late. Colonel Cannan was compelled to make his decision before dawn and owing to the reports received that decision meant retirement. The decision was influenced also by the hopeless failure of the Sussex Regiment on "D" Company's left flank to secure even a footing in the German line, thus leaving the whole of that flank in the air.

Just on daylight Lieutenant Moore received his orders to retire, though reinforced but a few moments before by some men collected from No Man's Land. With his men, the captured guns and the prisoners, two of whom were detailed off to carry Lieutenant Plane back home, "D" Company made its way back to the original line[1]. The "A" and "C" Company men still continued to hold their positions. Fleet and his small group were determined not to budge an inch, but to hang on to what they had captured as long as possible. Before daylight Lance Corporal Missingham had made contact with the 16th Battalion digging party and vainly sought to entice them to come to Fleet's assistance. The party, however, were under other orders and at the moment were already leaving their work to retire to their Battalion's position in reserve. About mid-day, this group of men fell in with the general order for retirement and made their way back to the jumping-off position. Before the retirement of this small group, "Do you know what" McLean had barely got his usual preamble out before voicing an opinion, when a large shell landed wounding him badly. Carrying McLean, the party had scarcely gone fifty yards when shells began to fall thickly among them and three more were either in-

---

(1) Sergeant Domeney and Corporal Steele were the last men to leave the trench. Steele, unfortunately, was killed by a bullet in the head just as he stepped on to the parapet of the jumping-off line.

jured or killed. By superhuman efforts the few remaining men managed to bring home those still living to the original front line.

"C" Company now remained the only company in the captured trench and C.S.M. Eibel, foreseeing that a retirement must take place when the British guns reopened on the German line, immediately commenced clearing the trenches of all wounded. This remarkable soldier had set an example in coolness and courage unexcelled in the unit. He was aptly and well-named "Iceberg" and had for a close companion in this respect the imperturbable Jack Rae. Both these N.C.O.s were to receive commissions in the field

By 1 p.m. on the 9th, most of the attacking parties from "D," "B" and "A" were back in their original front line, but "C" Company still hung on though their flanks were in the air. When Lance Corporal Jack Rae retrieved his gunners from the position where he had left them between "A" and "D" Companies' positions, he joined "C" Company and took over command of three Lewis guns upon their right flank. These guns were under the command of Privates W. M. Middleton and McLeish and a third man, whose name has been forgotten. With a plentiful supply of ammunition and a good field of fire no fear for the safety of the company was felt by them.

It was rather unfortunate that in "C" Company, by some error of judgment, the whole of the flares necessary for the instruction of the supporting artillery should have been in the hands of one man, and when he fell the only flares recovered were the barrage ones which were not needed. Throughout the greater part of the morning and early afternoon an aeroplane was despatched to pick up the exact position the 15th Battalion men were holding. Sweeping low while subjected to heavy machine gun fire from the enemy the pilot failed to locate our trenches although all manner of queer devices were used by the infantrymen to enable him to do so. While the various men who had occupied the German line were making their way back in small batches, Colonel Cannan sent to the Brickfields for the remaining officers of the unit to fill in the gaps caused by the casualties. Fifteen officers had fallen— 3 were killed and twelve wounded. N.C.O.s had taken over command of most of the platoons, while the "C" Company sector was reinforced by Lieutenant Malcolm McGhie and his section of bombers. Lieutenants Cooper, Landy and Browne were brought from reserve and sent to "D" Company and Captain Walter Coombs was brought up to command "A"

Company along with Lieutenant W. Mundell. Every officer with "B" Company had been wounded excepting their commander, Captain Snartt, while its personnel had been reduced close to the low level of "A" Company. "C" was by far the strongest company of them all, and when the plans for the attack of the 9th were issued, "C" Company was to assault the same trenches as they had the night before. Captain Harwood's Company of the 16th Battalion was to attack on their left, then "A" and "D" Companies of the 15th Battalion with Major Percy Black's Company of the 16th Battalion on their left flank. The assistance of the Sussex Regiment was dispensed with altogether. The time set for the charge was 8 p.m.

At this hour a short barrage—an exceptionally good one—was thrown on the German line and the men moving shortly before its conclusion were well clear of their jumping-off line before the Germans retaliated, and upon the cessation of the British gun fire rushed their objective which they occupied without any great difficulty. On the "D" Company sector, however, some of the men had penetrated too far on the left flank—that connecting with Major Black's Company of the 16th Battalion—and were recalled to the correct line. It was while he was making the connection with the 16th that Lieutenant Cooper[1] fell accidentally wounded, his leg being amputated at a later stage. When this happened, Lieutenant J. C. Browne took over command of the company. As no counter attack took place the position was rapidly consolidated and the following day the Battalion, relieved by the 16th, made its way back to the Chalk Pits and became the reserve battalion to the brigade.

The total casualties for the unit in this engagement were 90 killed and 370 wounded. Three officers were killed —Lieutenant A. B. Shrubb of "A" Company, who was promoted to commissioned rank on August 6 and killed in the trench before the commencement of the charge of August 8, Lieutenants R. I. Arnold, "B" Company, and F. Martyr, "A" Company, who had come from the 5th Light Horse prior to leaving Egypt. The only original officer left in the Battalion at this period, excluding Colonel Cannan and Captain

---

(1) Lieutenant Walter Cooper had proved himself this night a determined combative leader and his loss at this juncture was deeply deplored by his men. The young lad who fired the shot was overcome with remorse and as his leader was being carried past him, the boy burst into deep sobbing. Cooper, though in considerable pain, spoke to the lad. "Don't worry," he said, "it was only an accident, boy." After the amputation of his leg this officer joined the Flying Corps and was Adjutant to his unit when the Armistice was signed. It was while serving with the Flying Corps he was awarded an M.B.E.

Craig on Headquarters Staff, was Captain Snartt. Captain C. Corser was among the wounded and was not to see any further action with the 15th though he rejoined his unit just before the Armistice. Of the original men who had been promoted officers at various periods the following were wounded: Lieutenants R. B. McIntosh, W. H. Nicholls, J. H. W. Fraser and Captain J. J. Corrigan. The other officers wounded were: Lieutenants J. M. Watson, A. A. Plane, who had been transferred from the 7th Light Horse, Norman McGhie, R. B. Glasgow, Brettingham Moore and Captain W. J. Cooper.

The percentage of Gallipoli men who fell in this engagement was noticeably large, while many of those who did not lose their lives were so badly injured that they did not return to the unit. Besides Sergeant Stan Cousins of "C" Company, two well-known original men—Private Frank Dunn and stretcher-bearer McKenzie lost their lives. McKenzie, who was acknowledged by all as the doyen of stretcher-bearers, lost his life through the premature burst of one of our own shells just as part of "A" Company entered Sausage Valley after leaving the front line. The fearful injuries he received caused his death some twelve hours later. Among the original men of "D" Company to be killed were Lance-Corporal G. M. Steele, Privates T. V. Baker, H. F. Edwards and E. O. Heawood.

Probably the largest number of decorations ever awarded for a single engagement in which the 15th Battalion participated were awarded for this battle. To the men of Gallipoli it came as a great surprise, for there, the scarcity of honours was so noticeable that a continuance of such a policy was to be expected in France. Three officers were awarded the D.S.O.—Major C. M. Johnstone, Lieutenant Brettingham Moore and the Medical Officer, Captain Powell. Two were the recipients of the Military Cross—Lieutenants David Dunworth and Malcolm McGhie[1]. Among the D.C.M.s awarded was that of Private George Williams. This fight was Williams' first engagement and throughout it he had shown a fearlessness as a runner that was to be associated with his name until August 1918 when he lost his life outside Lihens. The Lewis gunner, Sergeant W. Murdock also received a D.C.M. To the men who had kept

---

(1) Lieutenant McGhie transferred to the Brigade Transport a few days after the unit left the line. When asked in the transport lines one day why he left the 15th he replied: "When I enlisted I enlisted as a horseman, not a b........ yabbie." The allusion being of course to the mud of Pozieres and Mouquet Farm.

the communications open fell a considerable number of Military Medals—runners and signallers taking the larger portion. Among the Headquarters runners who secured the decoration was the midget aborigine, Private Madge, of whom it was said a "coal box" turned him white. To see this little chap speeding down the saps while barrages were falling was a sight for the gods. Associated with Madge was the famous runner "Skinny" Hansen, to whom speed in delivering a message was his first and last thought. He also received an M.M. Probably the hardest earned decoration at Pozieres was that gained by the "A" Company runner, Private Stuart Cameron. This youngster, the life and soul of his friends without the line, would, when within it, accomplish anything asked of him, but only after he had overcome a paralysing form of inner fear. He was completely helpless for a second or so as he thought of those shell-lashed saps, then to his lips would come the only song he was ever known to sing: "Who's afraid of the Big Black Bear," and throwing himself forward, away he would speed through the heaviest of the shell fire and deliver his message. To Sergeant Percy Toft, who commanded a "C" Company platoon throughout the whole term in Pozieres, came a Military Medal, and to Corporal Jack Rae of the Lewis Gunners a like decoration. Corporals Frank Barnes and G. Parker were also awarded Military Medals.

With the relief of the 15th Battalion by the 13th at midday on August 10, the unit congregated in Wire Trench, and sorting itself out compiled its casualty list. On the night of the 11th a call for Lewis guns was received from the 16th Battalion and six guns were handed over to them. At 4 p.m. the following day the 13th Infantry Brigade relieved the 4th Brigade and the unit marched back to the Brickfields. Leaving this area on the 14th it made its way by easy stages through Contay and La Vicogne to Warloy. One day was spent at Warloy only to return to La Vicogne and to move from there to Halley, to Talmas, and Vandencourt Wood, where the battalions arrived on August 24. Remaining there for two days, the unit set out once more for the Somme, and reached its destination, the Brickfields outside Albert, and taking the old route through 1st Avenue, "K" Trench and Tom's Cut, it relieved the 24th Battalion in the front line at 3.45 a.m. on the 27th. Heavy rain was falling.

On the way into the line a large shell fell into the sap through which the men were walking and Lieutenant Eric Francis and 13 men of "B" Company were either killed or wounded. While the Battalion had been out of the line a

considerable change had taken place in its personnel. This had become necessary because of the heavy casualties among the officers. From the ranks the following N.C.O.s were commissioned on the 19th August—R.S.M. C. S. Goss, Sergeant J. P. G. Toft, C.S.M. H. A. Eibel, Sergeants W. Murdock, A. V. Watkinson, W. L. E. Domeney, E. Binnington and M. H. Gray. The appointment of these men filled some of the gaps in the platoon commands and all served during this trip into the line excepting Lieutenant Gray who was accidentally wounded by a Lewis gunner during practice on August 25[1]

Mouquet Farm was without doubt the filthiest spot the Battalion ever entered during its service in France. The large number of unburied dead lying about in the mud, their bodies swollen to outrageous proportions, emitted a stench equalled only on Gallipoli. In front of "B" Company Headquarters, where Captain Snartt resided, the air was so foul that all visitors to Headquarters quickly lit cigarettes or pipes and blew clouds of smoke through their nostrils in an endeavour to kill the odour. In front of "C" and portion of "A" Company's trenches dead men stood erect, waist deep in the mud which had set about their bodies, just as if they were advancing towards the enemy lines. Trenches and saps and the sunken road near the farm were almost entirely built of the German dead, and the continuous shelling of the position stirred up the buried bodies, hurling them into the air and spraying their limbs over the living within the trench system. So nauseating was the whole position that strong men were freely sick and non-smokers chain-smoked with a rapidity that burnt their mouths and noses.

Mouquet Farm itself was held by the enemy and was a veritable fortress. Built of concrete interlaced with steel, the dugouts were capable of housing a Battalion or more of men. From these dugouts a series of saps led to strong points, also built of concrete, in which machine guns could fire at all angles upon troops advancing toward them. When on the night of the 27/28th the 14th Battalion made an attack upon the two principal strong points of the farm

---

[1] Lieutenant Gray's career with the 15th Battalion seemed fated to be a chapter of accidents. An original member of the 15th Battalion in December, 1914, the choice of a vacant commission in the unit lay between Gray and Frank Armstrong. Armstrong was Colonel Cannan's choice owing to his greater experience. Gray contracted typhoid fever and was left behind when the Battalion sailed for Egypt. Rejoining as a reinforcement when the unit got to France he served at Pozieres until the accident referred to ended his service with the A.I.F.

designated on the trench maps as 54 and 27, the advanced posts of "B" Company, 15th Battalion which were on the right facing strong point 77, were manned solely by Lewis gunners under Corporal Jack Rae. The 14th Battalion, numerically far too weak for such an assault, was led by Captain Hansen of that Battalion and Lieutenants P. J. Hayes, F. Anderson, A. R. Dean and Quinn. The attack was timed for midnight and, at 11.55 a trench mortar barrage was put down and the men started on their way. The 15th men watching the assault were astounded to see German machine gunners appearing from out of the ground barely thirty yards away from their position. It was not dreamt for a minute that the enemy was so close. One Lewis gun crew under McLeish moved forward and, taking up a position in a disused trench, opened fire upon the two enemy guns. Both guns were put out of action, but only after a smart duel in which Corporal Rae and several other gunners had a narrow escape, because a third gun, unseen by them, came into action while they were engaging the other two.

At midnight August 29/30 the Battalion, less "D" Company, was relieved by the 13th Battalion and sent into reserve in Crater Trench. Here the most unpleasant duty was undertaken of supplying nightly fatigue parties to the front line. To the men who participated in this work, the mud of Pozieres is a lasting memory. Through the saps leading to the turn-off to Mouquet Farm, parties of 150 men trudged up and down, invariably under heavy shell fire, continuously losing men in the congested saps and often as not—especially the first two days—unable to reach the front line. When the second night proved a fiasco, the saps were ordered to be kept clear until the working party was in position. The total casualties sustained by the unit during these fatigues amounted to 13 killed, 67 wounded and 7 missing. Among the men killed were Private Jack Kilgeur of the Lewis Guns Section and Private Athol Harvey, "D" Company, one of the originals, who was three times wounded on Gallipoli Peninsula and met his death while on fatigue, under the command of Lieutenant Billy Mundell.

On August 30 another vital change took place in the 15th Battalion. Colonel J. H. Cannan who had commanded the unit from the beginning was promoted to the command of a Brigade in the newly-formed 3rd Division to which General Monash had gone but a short time before. Lieutenant Colonel J. H. Cannan, at the time of his promotion was probably the only A.I.F. Battalion commander who had landed in Gallipoli on April 25, 1915, and who was still com-

manding his original unit. With Captain W. O. Willis, his first adjutant, he had watched and guided the Battalion through the first difficult days in Australia; on through its adolescent stage, the strenuous training days on the sands of Egypt, the anxious days at Lemnos Island, and the piecemeal landings of his companies in Gallipoli. This was no easy task where men are ruled more by tact than by fixed and unswerving army rules.

He was a reserved and silent man and extremely hard working. In the great game of soldiering—especially to those who are the pawns and who hold, as they do, commands that move to fixed objectives chosen by the person overlooking the whole board, luck plays a very great part. Cannan had more than his share of the bad luck that culminated in the disaster to his battalion during the Suvla Bay operations in Gallipoli. The tragic blundering of the old and out-of-date commander of the British Landing Force, General Stopford, in failing to move forward to his objective when nothing barred his way, laid bare the whole flank of Cannan's attacking force, enabling the Turks to close in from the north in a rolling-up movement. Cannan's decision to retire was made, according to a Turkish officer in conversation with one of his prisoners[1], just in nick of time, preventing as it did the complete annihilation of his Battalion. At Pozieres this officer was compelled to make a similar decision when the English Regiment on his left flank failed to attain its objectives. His judgment was vindicated the following night when the position was reoccupied without the aid of the English troops and with but trifling casualties. He was only 34 when promoted to Brigadier-General and must have been one of the youngest Brigade Commanders in the British Forces. It was during the time in which Colonel Cannan and Lieutenant T. P. McSharry of the 2nd Light Horse were associated at Quinn's Post in Gallipoli—the Colonel as Permanent Commander of the Post and McSharry as permanent adjutant—that Cannan, attracted by the personality and gallantry of McSharry, determined to secure that officer's services for the 15th. This he did a month later, and immediately appointed McSharry Adjutant of the Battalion. These two officers, with commendable skill, handled the delicate task of transferring troops and officers to the newly forming units of the 4th Division at Tel-el-Kebir. In the ensuing months McSharry rose to second-in-command of the unit and when the Colonel left to take over his Brigade command McSharry

---

(1) Lieutenant S. R. Stormonth, 15th Battalion.

took control of the 15th. He was to lead the Battalion for all but a few weeks short of two years. This was exceptional luck for the unit, for nothing so disorganises a Battalion as continual changes in its command. Both men naturally made friends and enemies, as every commander of individuality must. They were opposites in almost every particular, the one tall and well knit, the other small and of jockey weight, which earned for him the nickname of "Jockey Jack." Cannan had a splendid speaking voice while McSharry possessed a small voice with more than its share of biting sarcasm if matters did not go his way. Each was unafraid to exercise his own judgment, where matters adversely affected the Battalion, and both secured the utmost from their men when the occasion demanded it. The more difficult task had fallen to the lot of Colonel Cannan, and his successor inherited a complete working unit whose record of bravery had already become a byword in the A.I.F.

There is no ceremonial leave-taking of commanders in these days of modern warfare and the Battalion awoke one morning to learn that Colonel Cannan had already left for England to take over his new command.

The Battalion left Crater Trench on September 2 and marched to Warloy for baths and fresh clothes. Due to the mud and slush in which the unit had been working, the men's feet were tender and sore and it was a weary crowd of troops that moved out the following day for Rubempre. A party of 13 men under Lieutenant Toft who had been to Rubempre to receive their Military Medals from General Birdwood, rejoined the unit before it left Warloy. At Rubempre gas drill was practised and the furphy immediately gained ground that the unit would be going to Belgium for a rest. On September 6 it marched to Greaincourt, arriving there at half-past twelve. The following day a few reinforcements arrived—a mere 75 for the whole Brigade. On this day while the Lewis gunners were practising, one of their men was accidentally wounded. On September 8, the Battalion marched from Greaincourt to Doullens and entrained at 12.30 p.m. for Hepeutre where it detrained at 6 p.m. From this siding they marched to Quebec Camp near Reninghelst arriving at 8.45 p.m.

CHAPTER VIII.

ST. ELOI AND BOORLARTBEEK.

In September, 1916, the Ypres salient with its bloody past had assumed the appellation of a "rest area." As such it remained until the British offensive at Messines in the second half of 1917. The 4th Brigade was to recuperate, and what better way was there of recuperating than living within sound of the guns, and within reach of reasonably large towns, where there was some contact with civilisation. The Battalion had increased in strength by the addition of details and a few reinforcements to Officers 33 and Other Ranks 595. This number of officers was increased on September 9 by the appointments of Sergeants R. L. Moore, M.M., T. C. McCormick and Corporal F. E. Barnes to commissioned rank. A week later C.S.M. W. Goninon of "D" Company was also given his commission. Of these four officers Lieutenant Goninon alone saw the end of the war. Rex Moore was unfortunately blinded in a bombing accident and Frank Barnes lost his life at Bullecourt. Lieutenant McCormick did not see much more service with the unit but returned to Australia shortly afterwards.

On the 16th the Battalion moved into the trenches at St. Eloi, relieving the 102nd. Canadian Infantry Battalion. The specialist sections took up their posts on the night of the 16th, and throughout the 17th small bodies of men penetrated the line relieving the Canadians. At 9.25 p.m. on the 17th the relief was completed without the loss of a man. The front line strength of the Battalion was Officers 21 and Other Ranks 368. It was distributed throughout the system as follows:—"C" and "D" Companies under the commands of Captain David Dunworth and Lieutenant A. R. Nevin took over the forward line with 11 Officers and 254 Other Ranks; "B" Company under Captain F. A. Leslie (who had transferred from the 4th Pioneer Battalion to the 15th on August 29), with 4 Officers and 68 Other Ranks held the reserve line, the Old French Trench, and "A" Company under Captain W. W. Coombs was situated in reserve at Voormezeele Switch. "A" Company was numerically the weakest company, a mere 46 men, for it had not recovered from its heavy losses at Pozieres.

The trenches throughout the system were composed of sandbags placed tier upon tier on top of the sodden ground.

Built to a standard pattern, the traverses laid down as regular as cogs in a wheel, appeared to the men used to the solid, deep constructions of Gallipoli, as quite inadequate shelter for heavy gun fire. In parts of the line no parados existed, while in other sections—such as that between the 15th and 16th Battalions on the left flank—an open space of some fifty yards was unoccupied. These unoccupied spaces were known mined areas, and were patrolled by the Lewis gunners throughout the night. It was the duty of these men to rush the crater should the Hun explode the mines while they were in the line. Guarding the one between the 16th and 15th were those splendid gunners Privates Ernie Chalk and Joe Reason, both afterwards taken prisoner at Bullecourt along with Etchell, an M.M. winner, and several others of this Tasmanian crew.

Behind the line lay the partially demolished buildings of the town of Ypres, foremost among which were the battered walls of the famous Cloth Hall, whose beauty in the full moonlight night was enjoyed by all within the line.

Throughout the area occupied by the unit, were millions of rats. The trenches teemed with them to such an extent that officers got in much needed revolver practice. The men camped in the dugouts in support spent many sleepless nights as these brutes were so persistent that they gnawed their scalps and their toenails. During the whole term in the line enemy shelling was desultory except for the second last day when Fritz put down a heavy barrage on the forward trenches. The only other shelling objected to was that of a Belgian battery which got its ammunition once a week and just as regularly once a week—preferably on Sunday—blew part of the 15th Battalion's parapet down. On the Battalion's right flank—the 13th Battalion's frontage—an enemy searchlight swept the intervening No Man's Land at night. This action brought reminiscences from the Gallipoli men of the "destroyer on the flank" during the Suvla Bay operations. The day following the occupation of the front line "A" Company's commander, Captain Walter Coombs became a casualty. This was his second wound in the head and being more serious than the one he received in Gallipoli, he did not see any further service with the 15th. Captain W. T. Mundell took over command of the Company.

Practically the whole of the time spent in this sector was devoted to fatigue work. There appeared to be no section of the trench system which did not require something done upon it. When the rain fell the place was a quagmire

and many of the saps and support trenches were quite uninhabitable. Drainage for these sections and duckboarding of other sections went on every night, while the number of bags filled to replace gaps in the front trenches was enormous. With the rain, came the fear of trench feet which had been declared a crime, so permanganate of potash washes were the order and French chalk was supplied in liberal quantities. Rubber knee boots were also issued, but these were discarded whenever possible because they softened the soles of the feet.

Besides the fatigues, without which no soldier could possibly be happy, a system of patrols was organised. There are more patrol stories told of this sector than any other front the Battalion occupied in France. It may have been the quiet of the front that encouraged Colonel McSharry to stir his officers to extra activity. A proposed Brigade stunt in which three of the Battalions intended to raid the German line simultaneously fell through after quite an amount of preliminary patrolling had taken place. The night before the raids Lieutenant Rex Moore, in conjunction with the Battalion Intelligence Officer, Lieutenant Percy Toft, took a party of bombers out to look over the position to be attacked. This party, consisting of the bombing sergeant, Farr, and Privates Charlie Godfrey, Paddy Sammon, Ted Clancy, Ted Tutty and one or two others eventually congregated in a shell hole only a few yards away from the German line and, during a whispered debate as to whether it would be wise to attack on such a quiet night without a preliminary barrage, Farr suddenly sneezed. The effect was electric, and the shower of bombs that greeted the interruption of the stillness sent everybody back to their own lines, fortunately without a casualty.

Members of another patrol party lying within easy reach of the German trench who were listening to a German working party changing over, burst into laughter when they heard a Hun say clearly: "I've had enough of bloody shovels —I want a pick to-night."

On the night of the 20th a patrol picked up a German officer and his batman who had become lost, and brought them into Headquarters. These two men gave the Brigade experts quite a lot of work extracting information from them. Three nights later Lieutenant A. R. Nevin, of "D" Company, set out with a patrol and, venturing too far, met his death. Nevin, in his anxiety to secure something of importance to report, had left his patrol some distance away and ventured closer to the line on his own. Although search was made for

his body it was not recovered until after the war, when he was buried in the Menin Gate Cemetery along with some 50 other 15th Battalion men who had lost their lives at different times in the Ypres sector.

The Battalion I.O., Lieutenant Percy Toft, was transferred to Brigade as Intelligence Officer on September 15, Lieutenant Frank Barnes taking his place on Battalion.

If the Germans were busy constructing trenches and improving their position, the 15th Battalion was doing likewise. In all the work done, the casualties had been very light, only two men were killed and four wounded. Then, like a bolt from the blue, came the bugbear of salvage. Every man coming out of the line was greeted with the notice: "HAVE YOU TAKEN UP YOUR SALVAGE TO-DAY?" It was no good saying you hadn't any, for you were sent back to the front line again to find some. Lieutenant Domeney and other officers were appointed to see that this work was carried out, and the dumping grounds for salvage began to look like the scrap yard of a city incinerator. All the debris of warfare was collected and dumped into the salvage heaps. Everything made salvage and everything from a 15-inch shell to a jam tin and scraps of wire netting was acceptable. Each unit was credited in its accounts with what was collected. What the 15th Battalion earned is not disclosed, but it should be a goodly sum. One thing the salvage business did was to cause much more argument among the men than any other order issued by the Higher Command as to whether or not England was at the end of her resources.

On October 2, General H. V. Cox, commanding the 4th Australian Division, accompanied General Sir Reginald Kidston on an inspection of the Battalion's lines. From October 5th to the 7th, fine weather set in—a very welcome change from the wet weather. On the latter date the 13th and 16th Battalions were relieved, and at 5.30 p.m. on the 8th the 51st Battalion relieved the 15th and the unit marched back to billets at Ontario Camp.

Upon the return to this camp, it was learnt that three days previously three more promotions had been made to commissioned rank. These were Sergeant John Ingram, of "C" Company, who was replacing Lieutenant Nevin (killed in action), Sergeant J. M. Rae from the Lewis gun section, replacing Lieutenant Landy, who was returning to Australia on October 4; and Sergeant W. Missingham, of "A" Company, replacing Lieutenant Jopling, who was returning to Australia on the 7th of the month. Both Missingham and Ingram had a short run as officers with the Battalion for at Bullecourt both were taken prisoners of war. Jack Rae became

Intelligence Officer of the Battalion and served until the battle of Hamel, when he was seriously wounded and did not recover until after the Armistice was signed. Rae undoubtedly was one of the best I.Os. the Battalion ever saw, and his work in that field, and his contempt for danger, placed him in the front rank of combatant soldiers in the Brigade.

On October 10, an inspection took place of the new area at Zillibeke, which the Battalion was to take over. Officers, N.C.O.'s, runners, and specialists, all made journeys up to the front line, looked over the position, and returned to lead their comrades in later. On October 12, General Plumer inspected the Brigade. General Plumer, who in 1917 was to become better known to the 4th Brigade than any other Corps Commander outside of Generals Birdwood and Monash, and whose name was already familiar to many members of the Brigade for his service in the South African War, was the least like a military leader of any man they had so far seen. With his cherubic countenance and his ever-present monocle, he reminded the men of the Australian High Commissioner in London, Sir George Reid, and they always expected from him some witty remark or bright sally in the best Reid tradition.

At 8 p.m. on the same day the specialists of the Battalion left Ontario Camp and entered the front line at Zillibeke, taking over from the 4th Australian Battalion.

The new front line was much more active than that of St. Eloi, for the enemy engaged in a constant trench mortar duel with the British batteries in rear. On the first day 2/Lieutenant J. Ingram was wounded. At night, patrols searched for the body of Lieutenant de Winton of the 4th Battalion, who had been lost the night before during a raid. As de Winton's body was supposed to lie in front of "B" Company who were occupying the line of trenches at the Bluff near Hill 60, Corporal Roy Proctor was instructed by Captain Leslie to find the body if possible. Proctor's patrol was, unfortunately hit by a shrapnel burst and Private Reuter was killed and Private Davey wounded. Bringing Davey in, Proctor waited for the shelling to cease and then recovered Reuter's body. A search was then made for the body of de Winton but without avail. When daylight came "B" Company kept a keen lookout for the missing man and during the morning Sergeant A. Robinson located the body, and recovered it at nightfall with the aid of Private W. Jackson.

Rain fell continuously throughout the 18th and 19th, and on the latter date the Battalion was relieved by the 6th London Regiment—better known as the Post Office

Rifles—and all but the Lewis gunners and a few other details returned to Ontario Camp. The gunners later rejoined the unit after they had remained for a time with the London Regiment to see that everything went well with them after the explosion of a mine in the area. On October 21 the unit marched to Godeweersvelde, where a presentation of ribbons was made by General Birdwood. On the 25th the Brigade left for Caestre and there entrained for Pont Remy, which it reached at 6.30 a.m. on the 27th. The winter had now begun to set in, and for the next seven weeks the men wallowed in mud, morning, noon and night.

THE SOMME WINTER.

The 1916-17 winter in France tested the Australian troops more than any other experience they were to undergo. The intensity of the cold, especially the driving bitter winds that swept the country at intervals, and the sharp frosts that followed on an already snow-frozen ground, seemed to penetrate every joint of the body. The winter clothing already issued consisted of cardigans, sheepskin jackets, mittens and balaclavas, all of which came into constant use. Fuel for the fires within the huts—when one lived in huts and not tents—was plentiful, and roaring stoves were kept going day and night.

The men grumbled, as was to be expected, at the large number of fatigues that came their way. The majority of them did not at first realise that they were the reserve battalion for the Brigade, and through all their grumbling also failed to realise that they were really the favoured battalion of the 4th Brigade. They at least had freedom of movement and enough exercise to keep the blood circulating, whereas their unfortunate sister battalions were living in mud one moment and ice the next, diligently preserving the British line from being washed away at Flers.

For ten days, during which it rained most of the time, the men helped to construct roads and railways near Buire-Sur-L'Ancre and Meault. They also juggled with train loads of shells destined for the artillery. A fatigue party of 4 Officers and 220 men was stationed at the Anzac Railhead on the light railway system running up towards Flers. These men were left behind on November 16 when the unit marched to Pommiers Redoubt where they camped in tents in a field of mud. Fine but cold weather was experienced while occupying these quarters, but on November 19 and 20 snow began to fall. On the 20th the 220 men at Vivier Hill were recalled and fatigues were then utilised for hut building as

well as unloading munitions at Montauban rail siding. On November 22, part of the Battalion left for the new camping area at Bazentin. The rest of the unit followed the next day. Here duties were allotted that kept the coldest man warm. Ammunition was unloaded at the Quarry under Major Waters. Ammunition was again handled at Deauville for the Light Railways under Colonel Fewtrell. A pump guard was supplied for Pommiers Redoubt. Another guard was furnished for Bazentin House and another still for Carlton Camp. Parties were also supplied for railway and road construction, hut building and timber carrying.

The 12th Brigade was relieved by the 4th Brigade on November 25. On the 26th, the 14th Battalion took over the front line held by the 48th Battalion at Bull Road, near Flers. Instead of following the normal course of events and moving forward with the rest of the Brigade, the 15th Battalion remained on fatigue as reserve battalion for the Brigade.

A considerable amount of sickness, especially in the form of severe colds, attacked the men while at Bazentin Camp. The Medical Officer, Captain Powell, had a long string of men to attend to day after day. Where possible, most of these men were allotted light duties, consisting of cleaning up and replacing the duckboards in the neighbourhood of the camp. The appalling mud in the area was carried into every hutment, so the cleaning of the duckboards served a good purpose.

Throughout the month officers and N.C.O.s trudged to and fro in small parties to the front line so as to familiarize themselves with the ways into and out of the various sectors. The awful carnage that took place at Delville Wood and in the adjacent Longueval Wood became a familiar sight, for the bodies of the slain still lay above ground, and in some cases fatigue parties were utilised to bury them. When the ground froze, burials were impossible until the coming of the spring.

Over this camp a long-distance high velocity enemy gun used to fire nightly at the railway close by but during the course of the unit's stay in the camp not one of its shells fell within its boundary. The transport lines, however, came in for a very heavy shelling one morning but luckily escaped with few casualties confined to the horses and mules.

An officer who was to become well-known to the 15th Battalion joined the unit on December 9. This was Lieutenant Simon Porter, who afterwards commanded "B" Company at the battles of Polygon Wood and Hamel, where he received

the wound that cost him his life. With Porter came Lieutenant A. M. Pedersen, whose short stay with the Battalion terminated at Bullecourt when he was wounded.

December 12 saw the arrival in the camp of the 20th Reinforcements for the Battalion under the commands of Lieutenant E. M. Bradley and James L. Drybrough. The former took over command of the Battalion's transport, a command that he held for some considerable time. At a later date he became commander of "D" Company. This solidly built officer quickly built up a reputation for himself as one of the finest soldiers in the Battalion. He was the soul of dependability and was beloved by all with whom he came in contact. His nerve was astounding, and the story is told of him that at Hamalet while walking across the open to the front line, a shell landed at his feet and hurled him into the air with the force of its explosion. Bradley landed back on his feet in no way dismayed, but he had hardly gone another few feet when a second shell repeated what the first had done. This time Bradley was wounded but continued on his way into the front line to command his men. Drybrough was unlucky enough to be wounded in his first engagement at Bullecourt but he returned to the Battalion the following year and served with it until the termination of the war.

Christmas Day was a holiday for all but an unfortunate Officer and 25 men who were detailed to unload an ammunition train. The day was spent quietly and the men were given a splendid dinner under the circumstances. In the Officers mess a special function was held. An autographed copy of the menu card forwarded to me by the late Captain E. K. Carter giving a list of the officers present on this occasion should prove interesting. The autographs on the card include Captains F. A. Leslie, W. Cummins, W. H. Nicholls, F. W. Craig, (Q.M.), David Dunworth, W. T. Mundell, A. H. Powell (M.O.), Lieutenants E. K. Carter, A. M. Pedersen, E. Binnington, J. M. Rae, Percy Toft, G. Urquhart, W. A. Kenyon, S. F. Porter, J. N. Drybrough, F. E. Barnes, E. M. Bradley, R. L. Moore, B. S. Atkinson, J. M. Watson, R. J. Luxton, W. S. Missingham, J. H. W. Fraser, W. Murdoch and H. A. Eibel. Major J. J. Corrigan was also present at this dinner, being in command during Colonel T. P. McSharry's absence. Mundell was in reality a Major at this time but was unaware of the fact and signed the card "Capt." The Quartermaster Hon. Captain Fred Craig had also received his promotion to Hon. Major but like Mundell did not know of his promotion. The Adjutant of the Bat-

talion, Captain Harold Koch, was also missing from the dinner. Of the Officers who signed the card on this the 15th's first Christmas in France, Captains Leslie, Nicholls, Lieutenants F. E. Barnes, J. M. Watson, and Eibel were to give their lives before four months had elapsed. Captains Mundell, S. F. Porter and Lieutenant J. H. W. Fraser were also to fall before the war ended.

The first two foreign decorations to be awarded to the 15th Battalion appeared in orders on January 1, 1917. They were the Serbian Star (2nd Class) and the Serbian Silver Medal. These awards went to C.Q.M.S. Jack Hynes of "A" Company and Private R. V. Wilson of "D" Company respectively. Hynes had but a short time before been awarded the British Military Medal. Another decoration awarded at the same time was a Military Medal to Lance Corporal W. Gillespie.

On January 9, the Battalion broke camp and marched to Melbourne Camp at Mametz. Here again fatigue work was the order of the day, interspersed with specialist training and gas helmet drill. On the 21st the weather showed us what it really could do, and a heavy fall of snow followed by continuous frosts became the rule. But the days were bright and sunny and the atmosphere keen and bracing. In the huts at night the men crowded around the stove fires or along the pipes leading away from them so as to keep warm, but most of the men coiled up in their blankets early in the night.

On January 22, signallers and guides visited the front line at Gueudecourt for orders had been received that the next day the battalion would relieve the 46th Battalion of the 12th Australian Infantry Brigade.

CHAPTER IX.

GUEUDECOURT AND LAGNICOURT.

The 15th's relief of the 46th Battalion took place on January 24 and 25. The countryside was frozen, and the Somme was a solid block of ice—an occurrence so rare that nobody had witnessed such a phenomenon for eighty years. On its way the Battalion moved through what was left of Delville Wood, crossing the broken and twisted earth where one of the bitterest struggles of the whole war had taken place during the previous summer.

Here, the grotesque shapes of what once were human beings lay carpeted with snow. Some of them had become part of the frozen earth itself where they awaited the warmth of spring and the burial parties.

As company after company passed through the wood the flat country around Flers came into view. Across this expanse of snow the Battalion picked its way. "A" and "B" Companies took up their positions in Bull Trench in support. "C" and "D" moved forward into the front line where they took over from the companies of the 46th.

The Gueudecourt positions lay forward of the village between two ridges, the higher of which was occupied by the Germans. The British line, as always seemed to be the case, lay in the hollow. In the wet weather the position was almost untenable, and in the dry season a constant source of danger to its occupants due to the superior observation of the enemy. The saps which ran from the ridge where the village of Gueudecourt once stood were so shallow that movement in daylight rarely escaped observation by the German snipers and gunners. The line had really never been completed and Shine Trench occupied by "D" Company consisted of only a few holes. At the junction of the centre sap and Shine Trench was a trench known as Grease Trench, which branched sharply to the north-west. It was well named, for it was uninhabitable even in fine weather. Beyond, and adjoining it, was another trench in which "C" Company took up its position. The junction of Shine and Grease Trenches was manned by a platoon of "D" Company under Lieutenant C. S. Goss.

Generally, the conditions in the line at Gueudecourt were only made bearable by the continuous state of fine weather. Owing to the shallowness of the saps it was im-

Capt. S. V. O'Regan, M.C.
Mentioned in Despatches.

C.S.M. J. FLEET,
D.C.M., Medaille Militaire (France).

Major C. F. CORSER.

Capt. G. LUTHER.
Killed in Action.

Capt. S. A. RICHARDS.

Capt. C. S. GOSS, M.C.

Sgt. P. McCoy,
D.C.M., M.M., 1914-18
Major 62 Bn. (A.I.F.) 1939-45

Capt. D. Dunworth, M.C.,
1914-18.
Lt.-Col. Director of Recruiting for
Queensland.
(Second World War)

possible to bring food up to the front line except under the cover of darkness, and when it did arrive it was usually frozen. However, the introduction of tommy cookers did much to relieve the situation, and the frozen bread and bacon of the morning meal became more palatable after being thawed out. The hot night meal also arrived cold, and like the morning meal had to be warmed up in the line[1].

The question of tea was solved by the issue of dry tea for the men to do their own brewing. During the night, men with picks and entrenching tools would hack out large chunks of ice from the nearby shell holes, cache some for the next day's supply of water, and melt the rest for their evening or morning brew. Some idea of the intense cold may be gauged by the fact that when "A" Company left Melbourne Camp at Mametz for Bull Trench at Gueudecourt, the two "A" Company Sergeants Eric Simon and Jack Fleet, filled a thermos flask with scalding hot coffee, intending to drink some when they got to their destination. This flask—for all its guarantee—had its contents frozen long before Bull Trench was reached. The temperature at this period was stated by Sir John Monash in "Letters to My Wife" to have been 2 degrees below freezing point during daylight and 12 degrees below at night.

During daylight the men cleaned the trench store ammunition. The Battalion had in the past taken over much front line ammunition that was in a bad state due to too infrequent inspections, but never in its history did it find such a mess to clean up as this one. The cases of S.A.A. were frozen together in solid lumps and the clips within them were rusty and unworkable. The mills bombs were in a similar condition. From many of them the pins could not be extracted, and many failed to explode when put to use. The men were set to work to clean up the conglomeration of trench stores with strips of rifle-cleaning cloth and oil while a keen wind blew through their trenches freezing them to the marrow. The shallowness of the trench system precluding any movement by day, except that absolutely essential, resulted in boots becoming frozen to the feet, and they had to be chopped away when the time came to remove them. Men with frozen feet were numerous and even the fatigues and night patrols did little to ease the torture.

---

[1] Amongst the various experiments made by the Quartermaster at this time was the use of petrol tins embedded in straw for the conveyance of food. Unfortunately these tins were washed out instead of being burnt out with the result that all food which arrived in the forward areas was strongly impregnated with petrol.

The principal fatigues were the attempts at deepening Possen and Eve trenches. Here, with every blow of the pick splinters of ice penetrated hands and faces, causing cuts and scratches that were most difficult to heal.

About 10 p.m. on January 27, Captain W. H. Nicholls was talking to some of his N.C.O.s and men when a large shell from one of our own howitzers fell in among them. Nicholls, Sergeant Havers, Privates H. D. Anderson and "Bandy" Mann were killed and Privates Sillett and Jim Nicholls, along with some others, were wounded.[1] Captain "Taffy' Nicholls had returned from England a short time before, and during his stay in Blighty he had married. He was to have left the unit for the Training Battalion in England the following morning. This game and popular little officer, whose name will always be associated with "C" Company of the 15th at Quinn's Post in Gallipoli, was deeply mourned by all who served under him.

The following day "A" Company relieved "D" Company, with the exception of the post occupied by Lieutenant Goss, and "B" Company relieved "C". This relief took place about 3.30 a.m. and at daylight Fritz commenced a systematic shelling of "A" Company's position, mainly with five nines. In this shelling Privates W. Murrell and R. Parkinson were wounded, Murrell so seriously that he died some time afterwards.

"The hail of shell lasted for three hours," Sergeant Eric Simon wrote when in hospital a few days later.

"It tore huge holes in the earth, threw great clods of earth and fragments of shell hundreds of yards, smashed the telephone wires and killed four and wounded half-a-dozen men. The 'grumps' fell like hail, and the small number of casualties with such a great expenditure of ammunition was little short of marvellous."

The following afternoon "A" Company got a similar dose of shelling from a different direction. The next day "A" Company was relieved and sent back into support to prepare for the coming attack.

The Battalion staff work at Gueudecourt was not up

---

(1) Lieutenant Colonel D. Dunworth writes: Captain W. H. Nicholls was killed about 10 p.m. I had just returned from a patrol with Sergeant Havers and the latter had returned to his post in front of my shelter where Nicholls was resting. I had gone to the left flank of the Company to talk with Sergeant Redmond, when I saw a display of lights, and realised that one of our own shells had fallen on a box of Verey lights on top of my shelter and exploded them. This howitzer of ours had dropped a shell in a vacant part of the trench earlier in the afternoon, and later on dropped another shell on our front line, killing two of the men.

to its usual standard. It was known that Stormy Trench, which was the objective in the coming attack, was one of the key positions in that sector of the German line, and even though it was already suspected that the Germans were retiring on to their famous Hindenburg Line, there could have been no excuse for assuming that the assault on Stormy Trench would meet with only little opposition. Apparently Battalion Headquarters considered that the latter would actually be the case, as companies were sent into the fight with a totally inadequate supply of bombs, and with no provision made for their support once the position was occupied. Added to this, the failure of the artillery to cut the wire in front of "C" Company—a fact which was reported before the attack commenced—resulted in the Company making a futile demonstration against a wall of entanglements and being compelled to retire with the loss of many of its best men.

According to the Official Historian, Mr. C. E. W. Bean, General Holmes, who had assumed command of the 4th Australian Division, did not specify the time at which the attack was to take place. It was merely to be one of several other demonstrations intended to test the activity of the Huns after the winter. However, the day of the assault was fixed for February 1. Now the merest novice in the study of warfare knows that light plays a great part in all operations, whether in attack or defence. In choosing February 1 for the attack no allowance was made by the staff for the fact that on that day the moon set at approximately 4 a.m. Until day broke, then, the defenders of the newly won position would be fighting blind against an enemy who knew the whole lay of the ground and would consequently be fighting at a distinct advantage during the hours of darkness between the setting of the moon and daybreak.

Stormy Trench was deeply constructed with all the usual dugouts and with deep communication saps leading back to another position known as Sunray Trench which in its turn twisted downwards to a junction in Stormy Trench almost opposite the junction of Eve Alley and Shine Trench in our own network. Grease Trench on our left which connected with the main communication sap, Fugitive Alley, was unoccupied by the Battalion except for a Lewis gun team under the command of Lance Corporal E. K. Chalk, who had with him Privates J. Reason, E. J. H. Etchell, L. G Webb and A. E. Cleaver. These men remained in Grease Trench throughout the whole operation, being in touch with Lieutenant Goss' Headquarters at the junction of Fugitive

Alley and Grease Trench. They were to safeguard any outflanking movement from the north-west. Grease Trench was to be the jumping off point for "A" Company, and "C" Company was to go over from Shine Trench and capture Sunray Trench in the German line. As it was impossible to enter either of these jumping off places in daylight, the two companies had to enter the line the night before, and move off into their starting positions early the following evening.

"A" and "C" Companies were under the command of Major W. T. Mundell and Captain David Dunworth respectively. Dunworth's company was in the peculiar predicament of having only one officer—Dunworth himself. The Company had entered the line with two captains only, one of whom, Nicholls, being killed on the 27th. Having no subalterns Lieutenants W. Domeney from "D" Company and Tom Heffer from "B" were loaned to "C" Company. Heffer had recently been intelligence officer for the unit, the "C" Company officer Lieutenant Percy Toft replacing him. Toft having recently been transferred to Brigade Headquarters. Lieutenant Frank Barnes from "C" replaced him on Battalion Headquarters as I.O. Of the other "C" Company officers, Lieutenant E. Eibel was at a school of instruction, and Lieutenant Jack Ingram was still in hospital with wounds. Besides the two officers lent to him, Dunworth was finally given a third, Lieutenant R. B. McIntosh, from "A" Company, who was put in charge of the carrying parties The "D" Company men holding the trench opposite Sunray Trench were commanded by Captain Harold Koch, who had recently been adjutant of the unit, which position was now held by Captain Basil Atkinson. The "A" Company officers attacking with Major Mundell were the ex-Lewis gun sergeant, Lieutenant W. Murdoch, and the popular youngster, Captain E. K. (Nick) Carter. The two companies "A" and "C" combined, totalled about 150 men, and they were to capture the 600 to 700 yards of trench which constituted one of the strongpoints in the German position.

Lieutenant Tom Heffer, in writing about this engagement, says: "At 2.30 we turned out into a calm moonlight night. It was cold as charity but beautiful. We were soon under way in single file to our jumping-off trench, and well settled down in it by dawn. We had a rather lazy day of it chatting and smoking. Our 60lb. trench mortar bombs and our heavy artillery had a go at the enemy wire on the front we were tackling. As Fritz's trench was only about 75 yards to 100 yards from ours, we should really have been

withdrawn to escape the back-lash of our heavies, but movement out of the trench in daylight was impossible, as in many places the communication saps barely hid a man lying down. We were peppered with showers of frozen earth and fragments of shell which came hissing into the snow about us, but had great luck in getting no one hit, though shells were falling close to the trench both in front and behind. The wire was not cut, so the attack was off so far as "C" Company was concerned, though "A" Company had a go at its objective. To assist them 50 of "C" Company under Captain Dunworth, Lieutenant Domeney and I had a go at the strongpoint which formed the right of "A" Company's objective."[1]

At seven p.m. the barrage fell. The line of men stood up and moved out, walking close up to it, ready to leap forward when it lifted. For the first and only time in the whole night's operations luck was with the attacking force. The Germans did not think that the effort upon the part of the artillery was a barrage. When the two minutes elapsed, and the barrage lifted, the men dashed forward into the barbed wire. Previous to this they had kept a perfect line, moving, as Lieutenant Heffer says: "Over the snow in great style just like a practice manoeuvre." Pulled up short by the wire the "A" Company men sought for an opening, and on Captain Carter finding one, he rapidly drew the men towards it and shepherded them through. So swiftly was the manoeuvre accomplished that the men were

---

[1] Lieutenant Colonel D. Dunworth, writing, says: "I realised late in the afternoon that the failure to cut the wire in front of "C" Company necessitated a change of plans. I got in touch with Colonel McSharry and told him that I would send one party of my men under Domeney to attach themselves to "A" Company and assist them, and that I would take action to prevent the enemy in front of our position from interfering with "A" Company. With this in view I took a party to attack a strong post on the right of "A" Company's objective, and ordered Lieutenant Heffer with another party to attack on the right of "C" Company's objective in an endeavour to force an entry at that point. Domeney's party linked up with "A". Heffer was unable to find an opening and was wounded. My party engaged the German strong post in a bombing attack, and kept them from enfilading "A" Company. Realising that "A" Company had reached its objective I withdrew my men and got in touch with McSharry to let him know the position. He ordered me to place the balance of my men at "A" Company's disposal and to return to Battalion Headquarters to hold myself in readiness to organise a counter attack if necessary. Later on McSharry realised the seriousness of Mundell's predicament and authorised me to take over men from "B" and "D" Companies to go to Mundell's support. As I took this matter in hand I was informed that the Germans had recaptured the trench, and while endeavouring to complete arrangements for a counter attack McSharry cancelled the arrangements on the grounds that we were too short of bombs."

in the German trench before the German officers had come up from their dugouts. Heffer, who was on the extreme right flank of the charge, leapt forward to the wire slightly in advance of his men when a bomb burst beside him driving a piece of metal through the middle of his thigh. As he fell to the ground a big explosive burst and he rolled into an ice floored shell hole and lost consciousness. Corporal Roy Proctor was killed at the outset, being hit on the head by an egg bomb. "C" Company's fighting tornado, Sergeant Peter Mulvey, became tangled up in the wire, and from this position hurled bombs and explosives at the Germans until, wounded again and again, he finally fell dead across the wire. The failure of the fifty men belonging to "C" Company to enter the trench through the barbed wire necessitated their withdrawal. Their losses were not heavy, but they were unfortunate ones. Besides the loss of Sergeant Mulvey was that of Sergeant Peter Drummond, whose injuries were so severe his leg had to be amputated.

On the right section of "A" Company's attack the "A" and "C" men under the command of Lieutenant W. Domeney forced an entry into the trench and immediately closed up that flank by the erection of a barricade. On the left flank of the company a similar barricade was erected under the supervision of Lieutenant W. Murdoch. Left in command of this barricade was Sergeant Bert Johnson of "A" whose fine work throughout the whole night called for special mention.

The three Lewis guns that went into the attack were in charge of Sergeant Cecil Crowther. Corporal Steve Moran had one gun on the left flank, Lance-Corporal R. G. Clark with another gun was in the centre and Lance Corporal George Goodfellow was on the right flank. The centre gun under Clark had a splendid field of fire to the right flank, and during the attack upon Domeney's position in the early part of the night it secured excellent targets until a trench mortar bomb from the enemy registered a direct hit, and Private George Peopples was so severely wounded that he died an hour afterwards in the trench. The gun itself was knocked out of action. The left flank gun was firing down a wide communication sap known to the men as the "Mule Track." All these guns were some fifteen to twenty yards forward of the captured position.

The task of mopping up the dugouts in which the Huns were secreted fell to the lot of Sergeant Farr of the Battalion bombing section, who in company with Sergeant Eric Simon systematically went about this duty. In all 52 prisoners of all ranks were captured and everyone who saw them

admitted that they were very poor samples of Fritz's fighting machine. While the dugouts were being bombed a violent attack developed on the right flank. This position was difficult to defend because a communication sap feeding it from slightly lower ground entered the trench at the point where the barricade had been erected. From the centre of the captured position the ground fell away in a gradual slope to the right barricade, and it was from this lower ground that the enemy consistently sought to regain entrance to the trench. When the first attack was launched Lieutenant Domeney sent for assistance from Major Mundell's men occupying the centre, and Sergeant George Ludlow, Private George Black and several others were sent to reinforce him. With the assistance of Clark's gun in the centre and Goodfellow's on the right, Domeney's small garrison which included Sergeant Jack Fleet, Private Archie Forrest[1] and a few others beat the attackers off. Ludlow and his few stalwarts were sent back to the centre position again but they had barely arrived there when an attack was launched on the left flank. In a hectic bomb fight in which Sergeants Johnson, Crowther, Corporal Rowe, and a few other men were prominent, word was sent to Mundell for assistance. Mundell, afraid to weaken his centre in case it should be attacked, advised them to handle the situation themselves. This they did.

During these two attacks the severe shelling of the captured position ceased and the enemy's artillery now concentrated all its force upon the open country lying between the new position and the old trench line, so as to prevent supports or ammunition getting through to the garrison. The two attacks upon "A" Company's flanks had practically exhausted the supply of bombs brought over by the men, but luckily, a supply of the enemy's egg and stick bombs was discovered and Sergeant Farr, assuming the role of instructor, passed along the trench showing the men how to use them. The problem of bombs being solved for the moment, the more serious matter of the condition of the

---

(1) Private Archie Forrest lost his life in this engagement. After a counter-attack had been driven off, Forrest against all advice clambered over the parapet and went searching for the enemy further afield with nothing but his pockets full of bombs. He was never heard of again. At Pozieres this young soldier of small physique was known as the "Pocket Dynamite." With his favourite weapon the Mills he would venture anywhere. Absolutely fearless he was a natural fighter. There is a marked similarity between Forrest's death and that of the "C" Company youngster Byrne who lost his life in a charge from Quinn's Post, Gallipoli, on May 9, 1915, except that Byrne's favourite weapon was the bayonet.

Lewis Guns arose. Clark's gun was out of action with a direct hit; Moran's gun was practically useless owing to continual stoppages.[1] Goodfellow's was still operating with a limited field of fire and did do so until the last moment, so a Vickers Gun manned by the men from the 4th Brigade Machine-gun Company was hastened up to the front line and passing through the barrage took up a position in the centre from which point a field of fire was secured to both flanks.

With the aid of the unexpected supply of German bombs a fresh attack was easily beaten off. But the question of ammunition, especially bombs to deal with the trouble from the saps, which even at this early stage had almost proved tragic, was to worry the men throughout the night.

The "C" Company men, who had been under the command of Lieutenant Tom Heffer, now found themselves under the command of Corporal Goodger, and were set to work sapping through to the captured position. The work was started when some of the party were instructed by Lieutenant Jim Fraser of "B" Company and Headquarters to form a carrying party. Lieutenant Goss was then instructed to keep going with the sap and for this purpose a number of "D" Company men were used.

The party of men under Lieutenant Fraser hastened down to Brigade Headquarters and collected boxes of bombs. In crossing No Man's Land where the enemy's barrage was falling, a number became casualties but the remainder of the party secured an entry into the trench, delivered their precious loads, and offered to assist "A" Company with the defence. Private Paddy Lennan, who with Charlie Godfrey had been a tower of strength, told the "C" Company men to get home as quickly as they could as it wasn't their fight. After they had gone the boxes were opened and the bombs distributed among the defenders, only to be discovered they were not detonated. Just then the enemy launched an attack upon the centre and right flanks. This attack used up a considerable number of the egg and stick bombs being held in reserve, and Major Mundell, in doubt as to the advisability of holding on when his force was being depleted

---

(1) In the attack made by the 13th Battalion three days later upon Stormy Trench strict orders were issued by Captain Harry Murray that the Lewis guns should be free from all oil whatsoever, and taken into the attack with every working part dry. This officer was convinced that the oil was responsible for the stoppages owing to the fact that it froze. Whatever the real cause the 13th guns had no trouble whatever.

every moment with the mounting casualties, and the supply of bombs running short, sent Private Paddy Sammon with a message to Headquarters.

The German barrage had increased in its intensity about this time. Sammon, venturing out between the two positions, became enveloped in the hail of shell and soon became lost. Wandering about between the two lines a large "coal box" fell near him and a huge chunk of ice landed on his head. Dazed and ignorant of his bearings he was found by Sergeant Jack Fleet and Private Hawkins —the latter wounded—who had been sent by Mundell to Headquarters to get a supply of bombs. The three eventually made their way through to Colonel McSharry. Obtaining the bombs and a party to carry them, Fleet led them through the barrage to the post, but many of the men became casualties, only four reaching the line.

Fleet's return to the trench coincided with another enemy attack. The trench was now full of casualties. The German Red Cross men who had been captured earlier in the evening turned to and gave a very much needed hand. It was impossible to evacuate these men due to the intensity of the barrage. Major Mundell put up the S.O.S. but there was no response from our artillery. Then he sent two men for information as to why the artillery would not respond to his messages. These men lost their lives crossing to the old line. An idea of the intensity of the barrage may be gathered from a description by Lieutenant "Dick" Goss. "Hell," he says, "was let loose. I never saw so much metal thrown into so small a space, before or after." Among many of the men who survived the inferno there was much argument as to whether the British barrage had been placed between the two trenches by accident instead of on the new objective in front of Stormy Trench. In "D" Company alone, 28 out of its 60 members became casualties, yet where the Huns were congregating time and again on the right flank for the purpose of attack, not a shell fell.

It was known at this period that nothing but reinforcements, bombs and a good light could possibly save the situation. Mundell in desperation turned to Sergeant Fleet once again to get a message through to the Colonel. Fleet, one of the first men wounded in the charge, made his way back for the second time to Battalion Headquarters and upon delivery of his message was informed by Colonel McSharry that the men were to retire. With this order he made his way back, arriving just as the light was fading and the right flank and centre was being heavily attacked

with bombs. Private Paddy Lennan, an original who had fought like a tiger throughout the night, Sergeant Eric Simon and a number of others became casualties. At Lennan's request Simon left the trench. Writing from hospital some days later Simon said: "It became very dark about 4 a.m.—the moon had gone down. The enemy artillery began to pound us and then when it stopped a very strong bomb attack was made on our right. Exhausting their few bombs, and losing heavily, the right fell back to where I was, about seventy yards from the original right. The enemy's bombs were exploding around us everywhere—in the trench, on the parapet, and behind the trench. We could not see an enemy anywhere, but the bombs continued. A bomb exploded beside me, as a man of my platoon, Paddy Lennan, was speaking. The explosion knocked me silly for a moment, and I reeled round the corner. Recovering, I called, 'Paddy Lennnan, are you there?' 'Yes, Eric, got a bad one,' he answered. I could just discern him, badly wounded, working his way along the bottom of the trench with his elbow. By this time what was left of the right was driven right in on us. Bombs fell thick, casualties were occurring. We tried to make a stand, but had no bombs. The rifles were useless. We could not see the enemy who must have been in the trench and the saps."

A few moments later, as Simon was attempting to get some bombs from Lennan's[1] back where he had a bag slung, another bomb landed wounding him. In the rally on the right flank Lieutenant Domeney had been wounded and evacuated. In the general chaos that followed, it was impossible to evacuate the desperately wounded and the non-walking cases. Lennan died from his wounds while in the German's care. Lieutenant Billy Murdoch, who had been wounded in the knee, became a prisoner of war. Murdoch had been wounded early in the fight but had carried on through most of the night until he finally collapsed. The Lewis Gun sergeant, Cecil Crowther[2] also

---

(1) Sergeant E. Simon in his letter referred to Paddy Lennan urging the men to stand and fight, though himself seriously wounded and incapable of rising from the ground.

(2) Some of the men on the left flank were unaware that a retirement had been ordered. Sergeant Cecil Crowther writing says: "At the time things were getting hot. Their counter-attack had started in earnest. For some reason or other I walked round the parapet straight into a German officer with an army right along the trench. This was just before daylight and it was pitch dark. They grabbed my revolver and seated me against the trench with about a dozen of our boys."

became a prisoner of war along with Sergeant Bert Johnson ⁽¹⁾; Private Sid. Clark, whose leg was amputated while a prisoner, Private George Black and a number of others.

The retirement took place just as the ration parties with the rum issue were struggling across the open to the captured position. These optimists, some of whom actually got into the trench, dropped their precious loads and fled. During the retirement two good soldiers, Privates Harry Penny and Billy Hawkins were killed. Sergeant George Ludlow, who with Major Mundell and Sergeant Fleet were the last to leave the line, became tangled up in the barbed wire and while getting free was wounded by a bomb.

It is apparently the rule in the British Army that no decorations are awarded to a unit which suffers a defeat. The fact that greater gallantry is displayed more often in defeat than in victory does not seem to carry any weight. One man, however, was rewarded for his work on this night, Sergeant Jack Fleet, who received the notification that he had won the coveted French Medaille Militaire, while in hospital recovering from his wounds. This young soldier received a shower of congratulations, among the senders of which were Colonel McSharry and nearly every officer then serving in the Battalion.

The Battalion's casualties for this engagement were 52 killed and missing and 87 wounded. The prisoners captured by the unit were 2 officers and 50 other ranks.

At 8 o'clock that night the Battalion was relieved by the 13th Battalion, which took over the front line system preparatory to their charge on Stormy Trench on the night of the 4th. On this night the 13th supported by one company of the 14th Battalion under Captain S. M. Hansen, (who died from wounds received in this engagement), attacked the position under the leadership of Captain H. W. Murray, and after fighting throughout the night kept command of the post and ultimately made it secure. Their captures were 2 officers and 75 other ranks. Their casualties were 2 officers and 41 other ranks killed, 5 officers and 167 other ranks wounded, and 18 missing—out of a total fighting strength of 671 men. The casualties

---

(1) Sergeant Bert Johnson writes: "Towards daylight there were only about eight men left in our particular position. I asked Corporal Rowe to hold on until I got instructions from Major Mundell. As things were getting pretty hot I ran down the trench. About twenty yards down I met Cecil Crowther and asked him where the boys were. He did not know. I then ran to Mundell's position and imagine my surprise when I found it."

in the 14th Battalion Company were 72, of whom 27 were either killed or died of wounds.

While the Battalion was in Gueudecourt "B" Company suffered several casualties among whom were Sergeant Roy Proctor, who was killed and Sergeant "Goddy" Crow who was wounded. Proctor's commission in the 25th Battalion was on the point of going through. Like many other men he had a premonition of his end and before the hop-over he had confided his fears to Private Bill Crummy. His loss was keenly felt in the company. The 12th Australian Brigade relieved the 4th Brigade on February 9 and the same day the 15th Battalion left Perth Camp, where it had been in reserve, for Becourt.

On the 11th of the month Lieutenant A. C. Loveday joined the Battalion but the following day he was seconded for duty with the 4th A.L.T.M. Battery with which unit he served practically throughout his whole term in France.

An unfortunate accident occurred on February 21 while the bombing officer, Lieutenant R. L. Moore and his men were practising. A bomb exploded and killed Sergeant Farr, who had been associated with the bombing section from the time when it was first formed, and badly injured Lieutenant Moore, who lost his eyesight. The loss of Moore was deeply regretted by all ranks. He had been a very popular N.C.O. while serving with "D" Company and was equally popular as an officer. He was an original of the Tasmanian company. Moore was the second officer in the Battalion to be blinded, the previous one being Lieutenant Maurice Little at Gallipoli. Both were due to bomb accidents.

The Battalion remained at Becourt until March 23 when it marched to Crucifix Wood. In the interim it had held its sports meeting on the 10th though the weather was still cold following a very heavy fall of snow on the 5th. A number of field exercises in which the whole brigade took part had also been held, skirmishing and open warfare exercises being in anticipation of a different form of fighting with the German retirement to the Hindenburg Line. On the 15th the unit marched to Bazentin-la-Petite and an advance party was sent on to Grevillers, where they camped on the 26th. The next day they were in Favreuil, where they were employed making shelters in a reserve line of defence. These shelters in this defence line were to be used as billets, in accordance with orders that troops were to be removed from the shelled areas. The ground was carpeted with snow, in many places six to eight inches deep, and the whole surface frozen over.

On April 3 the Battalion took over the outpost line on the northern outskirts of Lagnicourt from the 52nd Battalion, 4th Australian Division. This position came in for much indiscriminate shelling by the enemy. During the occupation, the outpost line was advanced three hundred yards towards Queant without meeting any opposition. The 49th Battalion on the left flank also advanced its line to a distance of some three hundred yards. A further six hundred yards was gained on the night of the 4th and the 49th Battalion again kept pace. Some enemy patrols were met with but they fell back without offering any serious resistance. The 9th Battalion of the 3rd Australian Infantry Brigade—fellow Queenslanders—relieved the 15th Battalion on the night of the 6th and the unit marched back to Favreuil.

Battalion Headquarters during the occupation of the Lagnicourt sector was situated in a small dugout built under a house on the left of the village. The building was a prominent landmark and members of the Headquarters staff had referred from time to time to the fact that it was not shelled by the enemy. This was thought to be very peculiar, and created some uneasiness in the minds of the occupants. Upon the day of the relief, while clearing up the quarters for the new tenants, Colonel McSharry spoke to Lieutenant Rae about booby traps. A small box connected by wires was discovered in one corner hidden under some rubbish. Sensing a trap—they were plentiful enough during the German retirement—all speed was made to vacate the place and the incoming unit was advised not to occupy the position. The next day the mine exploded.

The number of casualties during the short time the line was held by the 15th had not been heavy, but on the day the Germans launched an attack on the unit's right flank some heavy shelling took place in "B" Company's sector. This flank was just south of Queant, which the enemy captured only to be driven out again some days later by the Third Australian Division. Lieutenant Simon Porter in charge of "B" Company withdrew his men to a flank. One of the many shells flying around landed in the Lewis Gun position some thirty yards in advance of the line held by Lance Corporal G. Goodfellow and his team. This shell severed an artery in Goodfellow's leg. Unaware that the platoon had vacated the trench, Goodfellow raced to it for aid, but collapsed on the parapet and died after being hauled into the trench by men who had hastened back to help him. This young soldier had proved himself

one of the best gunners the unit possessed. The only officer casualty was Lieutenant Simon Porter who was wounded on the day of the relief.

Upon return to Favreuil preparations were begun for the attack on the Hindenburg Line, which came to be known as the First Battle of Bullecourt.

During the intervening time after Gueudecourt a number of new officers had been appointed and others arrived from O.C.B. courses in England. On March 18, Q.M.S. Wesley Goninon was promoted to commissioned rank with Lance Corporal E S. Robinson of the Lewis Gun Section, who had recently returned from hospital. Other officers who reported for duty were Lieutenant J. T. G. Proctor, who had transferred from the 4th Australian Divisional Headquarters on February 21; C. C. Drane, Orderly Room Corporal from "C" Company who had returned from an O.C.B. course in England on March 20; Captain S. V. O'Regan from the A.M.C. replacing Captain Powell, who had been medical officer for the unit since Captain Luther's death on Gallipoli on March 7; Chaplain Captain C. Lonergan who was replacing Father Tighe from the 6th Infantry Brigade on March 26; and Lieutenant M. J. D'Arcy on April 2.

In Doctor O'Regan the Battalion gained a medical officer who will be remembered as long as members of the unit foregather. His slim boyish figure made him appear exceptionally young for a fully-fledged medico. It was within the line that the "Little Doc" shone. When the "Little Doc" was awarded the Military Cross for his work at Bullecourt, it is safe to say that no more popular decoration was ever awarded an officer or man in the Battalion. So overcome with shyness was this remarkable man when he stepped out upon the parade to receive the honour from the hands of General Birdwood, that the vociferous applause that greeted his appearance, completely unnerved him, and the continuation of the handclapping and calls of "Good Old Doc," "Good Old Stan" only made it more difficult for him to locate his place in the ranks.

CHAPTER X.

BULLECOURT.

The year 1917 was one of unending battle. It was a year of monstrous and desperate conflict. All the roads of war were crowded with men and guns and the battered remains of men and guns. It began with the great German retreat from the Somme.

The Australian divisions had won the heights of Pozieres just as the winter snow and ice had begun to settle over the awful wreckage of war before Christmas, 1916.

The ferocity of the Somme fighting had been too much for the German forces. After the thaw, they started on their great withdrawal to the Hindenburg Line. The decision to make this move had been come to late in the previous year at a time when German Headquarters viewed the situation with the gravest concern. The effect of the continued onslaughts on Verdun, the ferocity of the Somme fighting, the unmistakeable signs of unrest on the home front as a result of the food shortage and the introduction of rationing, and the terrible casualties of the previous summer fighting, all combined to produce in the minds of the German High Command, then composed of Hindenburg and Ludendorff, a feeling of the profoundest gloom. Ludendorff placed on record an opinion that if the war should continue without the collapse of one of the Allies, the defeat of Germany was inevitable.

The German positions on the Somme were far from satisfactory from the defence point of view, and the coming of winter had emphasised the necessity of finding more suitable ground to accept battle. Furthermore, the British thrusts along the Somme had left a German-held bulge extending northwards to Arras which provided an awkward salient which invited envelopment as soon as the Allies were prepared to renew the offensive in the Spring.

Actually the strategic conception for the Allied operations after the thaw was based on the envelopment of this bulge, although the Germans did not know this at the time. The idea of eliminating this bulge and automatically shortening the line and thus relieving a number of battle-weary German divisions, had been exercising Ludendorff's mind for some time, and ever since September he had been building the enormous system of fortifications some

twenty-five miles in rear which came to be known as the Hindenburg Line.

British Intelligence had heard much of its immense strength from German prisoners, and our airmen had sighted portions of it from time to time. So that when a report came in on February 24 that some of the German trenches in the northern sector of the Somme had been found abandoned, while it was greeted with the greatest surprise by the troops, it was not altogether unexpected by British Intelligence. On March 15, the last German posts were withdrawn and the Allies cautiously felt their way forward. As the Germans moved back, the country was laid waste behind them and their dead and broken batteries were strewn in obscene heaps over the landscape. The French villages they had occupied were gutted by the explosions of countless mines. Everything was destroyed, and the completeness of the destruction the history of war had not before known.

The great fortified Bapaume ridge with its hedges of wire was abandoned, and the Australians who occupied it on St. Patrick's Day looked upon the plain beyond that stretched out to the Hindenburg Line. There followed a series of isolated fights for the villages the Germans sought to hold as the main body of their forces withdrew behind the great masses of wire in front of their newly prepared positions. These outposts were mostly fortified and were garrisoned by the pick of the German infantry. The bloody fights around Le Barque, Boursies, Noreuil and Hermies and Lagnicourt, culminating in the attack on the Hindenburg Line at Bullecourt, provide a chapter of heroism in A.I.F. history excelled neither before nor since.

The events that led up to the first Battle of Bullecourt need to be explained. In November 1916 the Allied Commanders-in-Chief met to discuss their plans for the Spring of 1917. The outcome of these discussions was a decision to resume operations on the same grand scale as the Somme in the previous year, the complete success of which was thought to be only prevented by the onset of winter. It was decided that early in February, the British Fourth and Fifth Armies should resume their offensive on the southern side of the German bulge between the Somme and Arras while the British Third Army was to strike on the northern side of the bulge from the general direction of Arras itself. The whole scheme, however, had to be revised with the withdrawal of the German forces to the Hindenburg Line. That portion of the plan applying to

the Third Army was retained with minor adjustments to meet the new situation. The Third Army moved forward early on the morning of April 9 and with the aid of the new British gas shell which proved most effective in paralysing the defending artillery, the infantry made encouraging progress until they met with a stiffening resistance as they approached the Hindenburg Line. In an attempt to relieve the pressure on the Third Army, the Fifth Army under Lieutenant-General Gough, launched a converging attack from the south. The Fourth Australian Division, now part of Gough's Army, was at this time facing that section of the Hindenburg Line behind the wire of which stood the villages of Bullecourt and Riencourt.

The heavy bombardment which preceded the attack of the Third Army was the subject of much interest to the men in the 15th Battalion, who were awaiting orders to move forward from their camping ground at Favreuil. The Arras offensive was of a pattern similar to those along the Somme in the previous year, which consisted of a heavy shelling of the area to be attacked prior to the advance of the infantry.

General Gough, commanding the 5th Army planned to break the German line between Bullecourt and Queant and penetrate as far as Riencourt, creating a gap wide enough for the cavalry to sweep through and make a lightning dash to the rear of the German forces occupying the line from Bullecourt to Arras. The plan was feasible enough as plans went at this stage of the war. But originality was sadly lacking, as frontal attacks upon entrenched infantry had from the earliest days proved extremely costly.

When the first orders for the Australian attack were issued, the rank and file who were to take part in the engagement thought highly of the proposal. The barometer of collective thought was at "Fine." The plan provided for a creeping barrage, a form of barrage that was universally used during the Messines attacks in the second half of the year with remarkable success. This barrage was to fall upon the first objective then travel slowly by a fixed time-table to the second objective, then settle on the third objective—Riencourt. Twelve tanks—the new arm which had not yet proved itself—were to follow the barrage, clean up the machine-gun posts in each objective, and after a pre-arranged signal from the guiding tank the infantry were to follow and mop up the Germans who were left in the trenches. Flank barrages were also to be laid

down upon Bullecourt and Queant. The attacking Battalions were to be the 14th and 16th Battalions which were to take the first and second objectives, and the 13th and 15th Battalions were to pass through the 14th and 16th and take Riencourt. On the left flank the 46th Battalion of the 12th Australian Infantry Brigade was to assault Bullecourt, and further still on the left, nearer to Arras, the 62nd British Division was to "stand to" until the Australian objectives were secured. It was then to assault the German Line directly to its front. On the supposition that all would prove successful, the 13th Australian Light Horse was to show the way to the 17th Lancers (Imperial Regiment) through the gap to Riencourt, thus enabling the mounted troops to perform their encircling movement.

The plan appeared to be feasible, and it had just that touch of audacity, combining as it did, mounted troops and the "something is going to happen at last" feeling, so that the men were fully keyed up to all the possibilities. In this spirit the men left their shallow trenches in the snow at Favreuil and marched the seven miles to Noreuil on the night of April 9.

The British line in front of Bullecourt ran almost parallel with a railway which ran approximately east and west and after skirting south of Bullecourt took a slight turn and passed through the northern outskirts of Queant. The railway was about 2,000 yards north of Noreuil where 4th Brigade Headquarters was established. A sunken road running through Bullecourt ended at the railway embankment from 300 to 500 yards north of the British line. The Hindenburg Line in front of Riencourt had two deep well-constructed lines of trenches about 100 yards apart, connected by a number of saps and concrete tunnels 10 feet underground which enabled the enemy to return to the line should he be driven out. Before the first line of trenches was a belt of barbed wire in places 50 to 60 feet deep with a number of lanes which enabled the German patrols to enter No-Man's-Land. Between the wire and the first line of trenches in the sector over which the 15th was to advance were two 15 feet tank traps. Between the first and second row of trenches was another deep belt of wire. Slightly to the right of the position to be attacked, the German line forked, and two rows of trenches and wire passed in front of Queant and two other rows passed in rear. Bullecourt on the left flank was similarly protected. Running from the line of trenches directly back to Riencourt were several deep saps through which the German

front line could be speedily reinforced. The distance from the proposed starting point—the sunken road—to the German line was approximately 800 yards, apparently without the slightest indentation in its snow covered surface sufficiently deep to conceal a man. Throughout this elaborate system of defence were a number of specially constructed concrete machine-gun posts.

The battle of Bullecourt was the second occasion on which the 4th Australian Infantry Brigade was called upon to attack as a Brigade [1]. All the various arms belonging to the Brigade—the 4th Machine-gun Company, 4th Trench Mortar Battery, and its other sections—were operating.

The fighting strength of the 15th Battalion was 440 men. Nearly 100 men of the Battalion were either transport, cooks, or other details, forming the largest nucleus probably ever left out of the line for a single engagement [2]. This nucleus was placed under the command of Second Lieutenant C. C. Drane. Of the officers chosen to lead the unit in the charge none were above the rank of Captain. They consisted of the four Company Commanders—Captain J. M. Watson, "A" Company; Captain F. A. Leslie, "B" Company; Captain David Dunworth, "C" Company; Captain R. D. McIntosh, "D" Company. Neither Watson who received his promotion on February 7, nor McIntosh promoted on November 30, 1916, had commanded a company in the line. McIntosh, who was the original armourer sergeant of the Battalion, was well known to "A" and "C" Companies but quite unknown to "D" Company which he now commanded. Watson who went into Pozieres with "B" Company and was there wounded, was quite unknown to "A." The "B" Company commander, Captain Leslie, like Captain Dunworth in "C," had held command of his company from St. Eloi, a matter of twelve months. He was immensely popular as a leader and always affectionately referred to as "the man with the red hair." Dunworth was popularly known as "Legs Eleven." Several young officers who had not previously been in action with the Battalion and who, in fact, had never seen front line work, were given commands of the various platoons. These were Lieutenants J. T. G. Proctor, M. J. D'Arcy, W. D. Kenyon, A. M. Pedersen and J. L. Drybrough. Second Lieutenant R. J. Luxton had command of a platoon in "D" Company. This officer had

---

(I) The previous occasion the Brigade attacked as a complete unit was in Gallipoli on August 8, 1915.

(2) 33% of the active strength of the unit was left as a nucleus in case of disaster.

seen service in South Africa but this was his first experience of warfare in France. Besides these officers, Lieutenant A. M. Marshall of "D" Company, who had been associated with the signalling section from its inception, and Second Lieutenant G. H. Wilkins of "D" Company, who was promoted a short time before, also took in platoons.

On the night of the 7th, the cavalry to take part in the attack filtered into the valley at Favreuil where the 15th Battalion was billeted in trenches, and erected their horse lines immediately in front of the unit. In the morning the snow-covered valley was a black mass of men and horses. In the early afternoon of the 8th a German airman attacked the observation balloons directly behind the 15th Battalion's trenches and destroyed two of them. The occupants leapt to safety by a parachute descent. Evading the heavy fire from anti-aircraft, machine guns and riflemen on the ground, the airman flew low over the area until at last he returned to the German lines. It was impossible that this visitor could have failed to see the congregation of troops at Favreuil. The incident caused much uneasiness among the men.

April 9 dawned with the discovery that 38,000 bombs sent forward to Brigade Headquarters were not detonated. To the 15th was allotted the task of rectifying this under the supervision of the Brigade Intelligence Officer, Lieutenant Percy Toft. About 9.30 p.m. the same day the Battalion left Favreuil with the intention of being on the jumping-off line in time to advance at 4.30 a.m. the following morning. This same night an officers' patrol which consisted of Captain A. Jacka, 14th Battalion, and Lieutenant F. Madge and H. F. Bradley of the 16th Battalion, was sent out for the purpose of discovering how strongly the German line was held. They were also to ascertain the amount of damage done to the German barbed wire by the British artillery. The night was freezingly cold. During the time the 15th were marching to Noreuil a change in the plan of attack took place. The officers' patrol which had gone out early, returned and reported the enemy's wire "badly smashed in some places, but in others it was still intact." From the same source came the report:

"Considerable enemy movement in front of our own line in the shape of strong patrols" and a suggestion that the position should not be attacked until the barbed wire entanglements were destroyed.

Immediately following on this came the order to attack

the Hindenburg Line in the morning, and to the consternation of everybody the creeping barrage was to be dispensed with. The concluding sentence of this remarkable document baldly stated:

"The tanks will crumble down the wire."

The 15th Battalion commander, Lt. Col. T. P. McSharry was quite unaware of the alteration in plans until the unit arrived at Noreuil, and accompanied by Captain Dunworth he visited General Brand's Headquarters. It was then about midnight, according to Captain Dunworth. Entering Brigade Headquarters, says Captain Dunworth, "We found General Brand apparently despondent." The news that the barrage was to be dispensed with came as a thunderbolt. The two officers suggested to General Brand that he ask for the barrage as well, but the reply was "the tanks could not operate with artillery".[1]

"In vile humour we rejoined our unit and got into position, and deployed along the railway line about 1600 yards east of Noreuil," Captain Dunworth goes on. "That was our only shelter—a permanent way three feet (about) high. We had to use ground sheets to blanket our torchlights whilst we endeavoured to explain the new instructions to our officers and N.C.O.s. We waited, ready, but no tanks came . . . as it got near to daylight our exposed position became dangerous, and at the last moment (between 4 and 5 am.) we got orders to retire. As we pushed through Noreuil the enemy began to bombard the village. One expected to see a shambles made of it. Our men were ordered to 'break across country' and make their way home individually. Heavy snow began to fall. It obscured the German gunners' view and probably saved many lives, but it made the return to Favreuil an extremely tedious march."

There were several casualties this first night. Three men, Sergeant Goodger, Private G. H. Needs and another member of "C" Company were wounded when a shell fell among them while sheltering on the railway line awaiting the arrival of the tanks. Several other members of the unit were wounded during the return to Favreuil, where they arrived shortly after 7 a.m. There it was known almost immediately that the unit would go forward the same night with the intention of carrying out an assault at the same

---

(1) Lt. Col. Dunworth writing says: "To the best of my memory McSharry at my suggestion asked General Brand for a barrage as well, but a reply that the tanks could not co-operate with artillery was given by the Tanks Officer present, who appeared to have little confidence in his own tanks." How ridiculous was this assertion was proved at Hamel and on August 8, 1918.

hour the following morning if the tanks should get there in time.

At 10.30 p.m. on April 10 the Battalion moved forward to Noreuil. This time the members of the unit were not in a pleasant frame of mind. The muddle of the morning was ever present in their minds, and there was a total lack of confidence in the Army Commander amongst all ranks. The opinion that the enemy was aware of the impending attack, and the thought of advancing in the face of heavy machine-gun fire over 800 yards of level country did not exactly inspire trust in the Command. With the men in nucleus were left more farewell messages to relatives than in any other engagement in which the Battalion took part.

There was a further hitch just prior to the beginning of the advance. The twelve tanks which were to replace the artillery, and lead the way to the infantry, were apparently in difficulties again. One tank, in fact, was out of action before zero hour, and the Colonel commanding reported that his tanks would not be in position at the appointed hour. As eleven tanks only could now be depended upon and these were to arrive late, Colonel Drake Brockman, commanding the 16th Battalion, made the request for zero hour to be put forward fifteen minutes. This request met with the peremptory command to "Stick to programme."

The 15th Battalion Headquarters staff, consisting of Lieutenant-Colonel T. P. McSharry—commanding officer, Captain E. K. Carter, Adjutant, and Lieutenants F. E. Barnes, Intelligence Officer, and J. M. Rae, Special Duties, was now at a standstill until the attack commenced, Rae, who was in a state bordering on complete exhaustion, for he had been travelling about all night making contact with the battalions upon both flanks, obtained permission to go forward to the starting point. While in the sunken road where part of the unit was awaiting zero hour, he reported that the enemy's machine-guns were particularly active, so much so that several casualties occurred among the men. One man, wounded in the stomach by a machine-gun bullet, lay at Rae's feet. When Rae called for stretcher-bearers, the man coolly said to the officer: "If we are defeated, Mr. Rae, do you think the enemy will come as far as this?" "No," replied Rae. "I don't think so." "Then I will give myself a chance to live," replied the man. "I'll stay here to-day. Will you take my haversack and waterbottle away from me, for I am told that if you eat or drink with a wound like mine you're gone." Rae did as the man requested and made him comfortable for his long wait.

That there was plenty of activity in the German line was apparent to everyone. Sergeant Guy Luttrell, of "D" Company, one of the few N.C.O.'s to return from the attack, says: "While lying out in front of the sunken road awaiting zero hour, I noticed green lights fired in the air from the enemy line. Obviously a signal, for we were met with a hail of machine-gun and rifle fire just as soon as we moved off in artillery formation and further on heavy stuff joined in. I only saw one tank on the move, and that on our right."

At 4.47 a.m. the 15th Battalion deployed into artillery formation and, under heavy fire, followed in the wake of the 14th Battalion, through which it had ultimately to pass. Of the six tanks allotted to the 4th Brigade for the attack only three were in position when zero hour arrived. These moved forward at 4.30 a.m. Across the expanse of snow moved the four lines of the leading battalions—the 14th on the left and the 16th on the right, keeping perfect distance and stepping out as if upon a parade. Behind these four lines of skirmishing troops came in artillery formation the other two units—the 15th behind the 14th and the 13th behind the 16th. The three tanks taking part in the operation were upon the right flank. Light snow was falling. When about half the distance had been covered, for some inexplicable reason two of the tanks suddenly stopped their forward movement and opened fire upon the enemy's trenches. The heavy shell and machine-gun fire which had greeted the troops almost from the commencement of the attack had mostly kept high, but immediately after the peculiar action of these two tanks, the snowing ceased, and the machine-gunners, their targets now visible, poured a deadly cross-fire into the advancing men. Leaving the tanks behind and pressing forward with all speed, the 14th and 16th Battalions came to the wire entanglements. There were but few openings and, with unsurpassed bravery, they either cut their way through the wire, or rushed through the openings and jumped into the German line. One tank made its way forward to this position after the infantry had captured it, but in attempting to get through to the second objective, it was knocked out by a gun in Queant.

The two rear battalions, in artillery formation at the time this was happening, came under a terrific hail of fire from the German artillery and machine-guns. One shell falling into a 15th section wiped out every man. When this happened, the battalion opened out into skirmishing order and raced madly forward to the barbed wire to aid its sister units. As the men rushed through openings in the wire and the track made by the one tank, they were raked unmerci-

fully with a fire of machine-guns that swept them again and again off their feet. At least 100 of the 15th Battalion fell when moving along the wire seeking the entrances or when passing through them when they were found. The by now sadly depleted 15th joined up with the 14th, and the two battalions leapt with fury at the second belt of wire, and hacking and slashing their way through, secured a footing in the second objective. The cost of this heroic charge proved heavy. Upon the wire hung many brave men. On the right flank that fine soldier, the pride of the 4th Brigade, Major Percy Black of the 16th Battalion, lay dead—killed while calmly cutting his way through the wire to make an opening for his men. In the 15th sector many men had fallen, and one officer, "C" Company's commander, Captain Dunworth, was wounded. Still some hundreds of yards ahead lay the battalion's final objective.

Up to this time the 15th had lost four officers: Captain R. B. McIntosh and Lieutenant G. H. Wilkins, of "D" Company, Lieutenant J. Drybrough, of "B" Company, and Lieutenant, A. M. Pedersen, of "A" Company. All these officers were hit before the first line of trenches was captured.

On reaching the second objective, things were in a chaotic state. The four units were thoroughly mixed, and Major Harry Murray, of the 13th Battalion at once set about consolidating the whole line and became leader of the attacking parties. The right flank of the brigade rested where the Queant-Riencourt road cut through the Hindenburg Line, and the left flank of the 13th and 16th Battalions where the Noreuil-Riencourt road crossed the trench. Adjacent to this latter point was a communication trench running back in the direction of Riencourt. Up this trench men from the 13th Battalion under the leadership of Lieutenant B. Rose bombed their way until they met with heavy opposition. Following a fierce counter-attack, they were compelled to consolidate. Captains Dunworth and Leslie, of the 15th Battalion, working independently, gathered together numbers of the 14th and 15th and attempted to storm Riencourt across the open. Leslie's attempt failed at the outset. After obtaining the assistance of Lieutenant Luxton of "D" Company, and a "D" Company Lewis gun team, two of whose members were Private W. Elliott and Sid. Collins, they leapt out of the trench in the direction of Riencourt. A blast of machine-gun fire met them and Leslie fell dead. Within a couple of seconds, Luxton was also killed, and the few men with them were driven back into the trench. Writing about this, Sergeant-Major P. J. Fleming, of "D" Company said: "The position that we had

when we reached the Hindenburg Line was right in front of Riencourt, with Bullecourt on our left. We had as our objective Riencourt, but found it impossible to get past the last of the German trenches owing to the machine-guns[1] being placed in the top stories of the buildings."

Captain Dunworth, writing about the final effort he made to get to Riencourt, says: "Our casualties had been heavy, but we had to make an effort to get to our final objective though it appeared suicidal. I gathered about a score of men (including, I found out afterwards, some 14th men whose colours were much like ours in the poor light) and pushed forward. We had got some distance, as far as the six roads[2] when a concealed machine-gun opened on the men after a rifle bullet in the left shoulder had put me temporarily out of action. From what I can gather, the machine-guns played on the men until they were wiped out. After a while, finding the Germans' attention elsewhere, I crawled on my stomach to a trench running from the captured trenches back to the supporting lines, and made my way back to the second line we had taken."

Upon the return of Dunworth to the trench, he despatched a message at 7.10 a.m. to Colonel McSharry per pigeon asking for S.A. ammunition and rifle grenades. This message finally reached McSharry at 9.50 a.m.[3], but even at this late hour, it was impossible to cross the intervening space with the necessary supplies. As early as 5.15 a.m. Lieutenant Jack Rae, and an officer of the 17th Lancers, British Cavalry Division, endeavoured to get forward to the front line via the left flank. After going only a short distance, both officers were wounded by a sniper who had been overlooked by the mopping-up parties during the advance. Rae and his friend streaked for cover, while the sniper poured rapid fire into them. While Rae was negotiating some barbed wire a 5.9 shell landed at his feet and he was wounded in the knee. He made his way to Battalion Headquarters before receiving treatment, and there informed Colonel McSharry that he thought it was impossible to establish

---

(1) Lieutenant Rose's party, 13th Battalion, reported: "Saw crowds of gunners, firing from roofs and upper windows of the village, untroubled by our shells."—"The Fighting Thirteenth," by Captain T. A. White.

(2) It is evident that Captain Dunworth is alluding to the point where the Hendicourt-Bullecourt-Riencourt and Noreuil roads meet.

(3) Lieutenant-Colonel Dunworth states: "The pigeon sent by me would go to Corps Headquarters. Years afterwards General Birdwood said to me that on receipt of the message he immediately went to Gough and asked to be allowed to withdraw us, but it was too late."

communications. None of the runners despatched by the 15th from the captured position had managed to cross safely to McSharry. An attempt was then made by Lieutenant F. Barnes, the I.O., at the request of Colonel McSharry, to obtain communication with the 15th through the centre or right flank. Barnes, though wounded, did actually penetrate into the trench system, but after collecting what data he could, lost his life while returning to Battalion Headquarters. Two ammunition parties then attempted to get through, but both were wiped out to a man.

In the desperate fighting that took place all along the line under individual officers or N.C.O.'s—any cohesive action whatsoever being impracticable—a number of officers and N.C.O.'s showed exceptionable courage and fought with the individual tenacity of tigers. Among them was an original "C" Company man, Lieutenant Ernie Eibel, who was promoted to commissioned rank after Pozieres. Eibel, whose coolness under all circumstances was a byword in the unit, died without it forsaking him. Known as "Iceberg" Eibel from the early days in Gallipoli, he was fatally wounded during an attack upon his part of the trench. Taking a number of papers from his pocket, Eibel gave them to one of his men saying: "Take these documents to Captain Dunworth and tell him I'm finished." "But," said the astonished man, who was quite unaware that Eibel was wounded, "You are not dead?" "No, but I will be by the time you get to Captain Dunworth," was the calm reply. "He saw the inevitable end," writes Captain Dunworth, "and died bravely." Everybody who knew "Iceberg" Eibel can well picture his last moments.

Besides Eibel, the well-known N.C.O.'s, Sergeant-Major "Yank" Power, of "B" Company, and Sergeant-Major Charlie Emerson, of "C" Company, proved themselves towers of strength. Two finer fighting men the 15th Battalion seldom saw. Power, with his outbursts of rage that were levelled against foe, officer or man, was notorious. Emerson, with his strength and coolness and cold-blooded determination not to budge an inch, was every bit as ferocious as Power, though quieter, and he must have proved a thorn in the enemy's side right up to the moment that he was forced to surrender.

Sergeant-Major Fleming, of "D," also became a prisoner of war and, with these three senior N.C.O.'s, a number of officers and men among them, Private David Waterfield, who was badly wounded, fell into the hands of the enemy. Without bombs or any form of ammunition to repel the repeated counter-attacks, they were finally completely surrounded and cut off. During the last few critical moments before

the whole defence crumbled and a retirement was ordered by Major Murray, Dunworth, who had been wounded for the third time, gave orders to those around him, who were unwounded or slightly wounded, to try and make their way back, while the more severely wounded held the line. Unfortunately this gallant action only enabled a very few men to get back, for most of the retiring troops were cut to peices by machine-gun fire. At 11.15 a.m., the 46th Battalion of the 12th Brigade, operating on the left flank, was seen to be retiring. This caused the plight of the 4th Brigade to become more precarious, and five minutes later members of the 15th Battalion began the dash back to safety.

Out of the total attacking force, only 52 men returned, and of this number there were very few N.C.O.'s, and not one officer. Of the N.C.O.'s, Sergeant Guy Luttrell, of "D" Company, managed to escape. Two Lewis guns were, by some strange chance, rescued, but few of their crews got back. In all, 16 guns were lost. Throughout the morning and the afternoon the stretcher-bearers worked hard to recover the wounded. In the morning the German gunners fired over and over again upon these brave men, but in the afternoon they permitted them to recover the wounded in peace. Captain Stan. O'Regan, the Battalion Medical Officer, performed marvels, ably assisted by his Sergeant, Cyril Bull. With an absolute contempt for danger, he won the admiration of everyone who came in contact with him.

Of the officers who took part in this engagement, not one returned unwounded, while of Battalion Headquarters Staff, the Battalion I.O., Frank Barnes, lost his life, and Lieutenant Jack Rae was wounded. Of those who actually took part in the charge, five were killed. They were Captain F. A. Leslie, J. M. Watson[1] and Lieutenants Luxton, J. G. T. Proctor, and Eibel. Luxton, who was a 13th Reinforcement, had seen service in the South African war, in which he was taken prisoner by the Boers. Captain Leslie was deeply mourned by his company. The officers wounded were: Lieutenants A. M. Pedersen, J. L. Drybrough, W. D. Kenyon, G. H. Wilkins, and the two Company Commanders, Captain R. B. McIntosh and Captain D. Dunworth. The latter was also reported missing, and then prisoner of war. Dunworth was the only officer wounded who failed to get back to the battalion. Those taken prisoner of war were: Lieutenants W. Missingham, J. Ingram, A. M. Marshall, M. J. D'Arcy, A. V. Watkinson, and E. Binnington. Lieutenant Jack Craven,

---

(1) Captain Watson and Lieutenant Proctor were reported missing and P.O.W. Their bodies were recovered after the war.

Signalling Officer, of the 14th Battalion, who had served with the 15th Battalion throughout Gallipoli, was also wounded in this engagement.

The 15th Battalion's casualties[2] were placed at 19 officers and 264 other ranks, in the report forwarded by Colonel McSharry to Headquarters after the engagement. In reality, 20 officers were regarded as casualties. This was the second occasion, as mentioned before, that the 4th Australian Infantry Brigade had operated in an engagement as a complete unit. The first was the attack upon Abdul Rahman Bair on Gallipoli Peninsula, an operation somewhat similar to this engagement in that in both instances the men were subjected to concentrated cross-fire from machine-guns. In the Gallipoli battle, 10 officers and 380 other ranks had fallen, and of these only one officer and 17 other ranks became prisoners. In the Bullecourt affair no less than nine officers were made prisoners of war, all of whom returned to Australia at the termination of hostilities. A large number of the men were also made prisoners at Bullecourt, and the greater proportion of these arrived home safely. Among those who died of wounds in Germany was young Private Albert Jolly of the Lewis Gun Section, and Private Dan Tudor of the same section, who died while working as a prisoner of war in the salt mines of Germany. Besides Dave Waterfield from "D" Company, the Lewis gunners, Lance-Corporal E. Chalk, and Private Joe Reason, were both seriously wounded and fell into the Germans' hands. From the same gun crew, Private A. E. Cleaver was also made prisoner. Corporal R. J. Clark was also among the wounded taken prisoners.

On April 12 the battalion left Favreuil and, entraining at Bapaume, detrained at Albert and marched to some huts at Mametz. The depleted ranks were a pitiful sight as the unit trailed through the snow to Battalion Headquarters and, led by their Colonel, marched to the entraining point. At Mametz on the 14th General Birdwood addressed a ceremonial brigade parade and conveyed messages of congratulation from the Commander-in-Chief. Messages were also received from Generals Birdwood and Holmes, but no amount

---

(2) The official casualties of the 4th Brigade were:—

	Officers.	Other Ranks.
13th Battalion	21	546
14th Battalion	19	582
15th Battalion	20	380
16th Battalion	13	623
4th A.L.T.M. Battery	1	30
TOTAL	79	2,260
4th M.G. Company	5	99

of words could offset the bitterness that prevailed throughout all ranks. The talk of "bad luck" in the failure to hold the line was extremely pathetic when the least assistance from the artillery in the initial stages might have turned the tide.

One of the few inoculations much enjoyed by the men took place at this camp. They have had the effect of taking the minds of the men off the recent disaster. They also enjoyed much needed baths. Ribemont became the Battalion's new home on the 18th. Sports were held, and a series of N.C.O. classes were begun. On April 20 nine new officers were appointed from the ranks. These were: C.Q.M.S. J. T. Hynes, from "A" Company; Sergeants M. J. Logan, L. A. Hocker, "B" Company; W. P. Jones and H. G. Maegraith, "C" Company; A. B. Smith, B. J. Shaw, and G. W. Luttrell, "D" Company; and P. R. A. G. Ohlson, Lewis Gun Section. Next day the following officers reported from O.C.B. units in England—2/Lieutenants M. A. Cook, Orderly Room Clerk, 15th Battalion; George Hurry, from the 27th A.S.C.; C. E. Northover, from the 4th Field Ambulance; A. Coutts, from 12th Field Ambulance; and W. J. Hines, from 4th Divisional Headquarters. On the 26th, Signalling Sergeant B. C. Newlands, and original member of "D" Company, was commissioned and on the 30th Captain Burford Sampson returned to the unit, and on the same date 2/Lieutenant Josiah Francis joined up. By May 1, with the arrival of reinforcements and the return of hospital details, the unit had increased to the respectable strength of 500 men. With this new blood in the Battalion, Bullecourt became but a memory.

A medal parade was held in fine weather at the brigade church parade, and 12 members of the Battalion received Military Medals or ribbons from the hands of General Birdwood. The next two days were spent in sports. The Divisional Rifle Battalion and Team Match was won by the 15th Battalion with its sister Battalion, the 47th, second. The platoon match was won by the 47th, with the 15th third. The tile shooting competition was held on the 9th, and it was also won by the 15th. The next three days a Divisional Boxing Tournament took place which did not reflect much glory upon the battalion, as the men were rather out of form. On the last day of the tournament, the 12th, General Birdwood, who had been appointed to an English command, bid farewell at a parade of the Division and made another distribution of medals and ribbons.

On May 5, 2/Lieutenant G. H. Joubert marched in from an O.C.B. course in England. On the 6th, R.S.M. H. R. H. Lack, of "B" Company, was promoted to commissioned rank.

On the 17th of the month 2/Lieutenant R. Carew, ex-31st Battalion, reported from an O.C.B. course.

During this term out of the line the unit had enjoyed splendid weather, but when on the 16th they entrained at Edghill Railway Siding and detrained at Baillieue to march 13 kilos to Doulien village, rain fell. The unit was billeted in farms about the village—the companies being very scattered. The countryside was looking its best and the crops were ready for harvesting. The strength of the battalion while here grew to 719. Fine weather continued and, on the 26th, the Army Commander, General Plumer, together with General Holmes, commander of the 4th Australian Division, reviewed the brigade. On the 29th there was another boxing tournament, at which were present no less than seven generals: Birdwood, Russell (the New Zealander, well-known to Gallipoli men), Monash (previous commander of the 4th Brigade), Holmes, Glasgow (also well-known to the 15th, and brother of Captain Bob Glasgow), Robertson, and Charlie Brand. The following day all surplus gear was dumped at Doulien, and the next day the brigade marched to Neuve Eglise and there bivouacked in tents. On June 1, officers and N.C.O.'s commenced their visits to the front line and, on the 3rd, the "A" Company Sergeant, Eric Simon, was promoted to commissioned rank. Two days later Lieutenant G. A. Thorpe reported for duty. The attack upon the Messines Ridge by the 2nd Army Corps was about to begin.

◆ ◆ ◆ ◆

CHAPTER XI.

MESSINES AND POLYGON WOOD.

The sound of the guns had scarce died down in front of Bullecourt during the summer of 1917, when the Australians were sent to take part in the great series of battles that began with Messines and ended with the Third Battle of Ypres.

Dominating the British trenches in the "Salient" in front of the city of Ypres was the great hog-backed Messines-Wytschaete Ridge, from behind which the German artillery for over $2\frac{1}{2}$ years pummelled the British lines with every kind of explosive then known to man.

In the middle of 1916 General Plumer and his staff conceived the idea of tunnelling under Messines and, for a whole year, they prepared their plans for the great attack that came to be known as the Battle of Messines.

While the rest of the British forces were fighting on the Somme, the Second Army, under Plumer, hung on to the "Salient" and waited for the day that was to be theirs. Allied tunnellers worked feverishly day and night and packed the galleries under Messines with over one million pounds weight of ammonal. By June, 1917, everything was ready—guns, railways, tanks, and every conceivable engine of destruction invented for the mass killing of men.

During the week previous to the attack, British guns of every calibre with ever-growing violence, spread destruction in the German forward and back trenches. Great belts of fire were mapped out, and for days before Messines went skyward, many of the German garrisons were pinned to their tunnels without food, and without any possible chance of relief. On the night of June 6 there was a thick summer fog over all Flanders and the sky was livid with the flashes of bursting shells. In the dark fields before Messines the waiting infantry watched the awful splendour of it all, and listened to the savage whine of the German shrapnel in reply.

Just before dawn on the following day, June 7, there was a low rumble that grew in terrifying intensity until it swept all other sounds before it. From out of the bowels of the earth there gushed up into the sky a mighty volume of scarlet flame, until the whole countryside was illuminated by a fierce red glow. The earth trembled and surged violently to and fro. The heights of Messines had been rent by an explosion that had altered the very geography of the country-

side. Stumbling in among the shell-holes, British and Australian infantry scrambled over the wreckage towards the German lines. The Battle of Messines had begun.

The 4th Brigade's part in it was of minor importance. It remained in reserve to be called upon if required. The 15th and 16th Battalions were at the river La Douve and La Plus Douve Farm, when the bombardment began. After standing by for twenty-four hours and learning that all objectives had been taken, the brigade returned to its tents at Neuve Eglise. We saw a number of prisoners being drafted to the rear and they were so shaken and nerve wracked by the barrage that all the fight appeared to have gone out of them.

On the 8th the brigade moved forward again and relieved the 1st and 2nd New Zealand Infantry Brigades, who were in support to part of the 12th Infantry Brigade, then holding the front line in what was known as Owl Trench. "A" and "D" Companies relieved the 2nd Otago Regiment and "B" and "C" Companies the 1st Canterbury Regiment in the neighbourhood of Gooseberry Farm. The following day the backwash from a big shell mortally wounded young Sergeant Eric Hobson, who was walking about at the back of the parados. Hobson had come to the battalion as a reinforcement sergeant while the unit was at Tel-el-Kebir. One of two rosy-cheeked boys—compulsory trainee lads—he and the other, Leonard Hocker, who had since obtained his commission, were inseparable and were known to members of the unit as "the twins."

The 46th Battalion, 12th Australian Brigade, was relieved by the 15th Battalion in the front line on the night of June 10. The positions occupied by the various companies were: "A" and "B" under the commands of Captains E. K. Carter and Burford Sampson in Owl Trench; "D," under Captain W. Domeney along the Black Dotted Line, and "C," under Captain R. Glasgow in Oxygen Trench. Owl Trench was situated to the north of Hun's Walk, and feeding it from Blauwen Molen was a communication trench locally known as Fanny's Cut. Almost east of Owl Trench, some five to six hundred yards away, lay Gapaard Farm, supposedly in the hands of the enemy. On the southern side of Hun's Walk, close to the continuation of Owl Trench, was Steignast Farm, while north of Gapaard Farm again lay Les Quatre Rois Cabt. The task set the battalion was to discover whether Gapaard Farm and Les Quatre Rois Cabt were occupied, and if they were, to force the enemy out of them, and establish strong points on which further consolidation would be made by the units following the 4th Brigade. The general idea evidently in the whole plan of operations was to keep the enemy

15 BN. RUGBY TEAM, FRANCE, 1918.

BACK ROW: Patterson, W. Stone, Ralph, ——, J. Thompson, ——.
MIDDLE ROW: Cox, Cunningham, J. Clancy, P. Pringle, Ferguson, McKeiver, G. Swepson, Bowers Jnr.
FRONT ROW: Willcox, Robinson, Mackay, Sampson, Cook and Pilkington.

15 BN. SOCCER TEAM, FRANCE, 1918.

L./Cpl. C. REDDIE.

Cpl. J. E. WELLARD, M.M.

Pte. J. T. HUTCHINSON,
C. de G. (Belgian).

Cpl. L. HANSEN, M.M. and Bar.

continually moving and so prevent his showing a solid front, and settling down into a permanent entrenched position before renewal of the advance could be made by British Arms. Under cover of all this activity the reorganisation of the British units and subsidiary units was taking place.

"A" Company established its headquarters in a pill box, and this came in for some heavy shelling. One large shell landed in the doorway, burying Captain "Nick" Carter, the C.S.M., Jack Fleet, and the company runner, Archie Bowman. The two former, though badly shaken and cut about by splinters, were not evacuated, but Bowman sustained a badly sprained back and was sent to hospital. A signaller who was on the point of entering when the shell landed was also injured. On the same day, Private Vince Murphy was killed by shell fire and, Privates "Nigger" Lennan and McDonald were wounded, the latter seriously. McDonald had been left with the "nucleus" but, refusing to stay there, had made his way up to the front line and rejoined his comrades only a short time before.

Once the unit had settled down in the front line system patrols were sent out. Gapaard Farm was left for "A" Company to tackle and the job fell to Lieutenant Percy Toft, the ex-"C" Company officer who had served a term on Brigade Headquarters. Toft's advance was to be a daylight one, but when passing up the sap, his platoon was fired on and in the distance he could clearly discern the observation balloons of the Huns operating as if everything was stable. The numerous furphies that cavalry were patrolling and had passed through the British line in an endeavour to pick up traces of the enemy did not sound sense to Toft. Once in the front line he and Lance-Corporal Paddy Sammon decided to investigate on their own account first, and after venturing some five hundreds yards were finally halted by rifle fire from some trees within the farm. Satisfied that the place was occupied by some Germans at least, they retraced their steps to the 15th's lines. That night with his platoon of some thirty men he took possession of the farm, in doing which he captured two field guns. Les Quatre Rois Cabt was occupied without any trouble whatsoever, so the front line was immediately pushed forward nearly a half mile, and strong points were constructed in the new position before relief by the 11th Cheshire (English) Regiment, at 3 a.m. on the 13th.

Prior to this, however, a strange occurrence took place in an "A" Company patrol. In connecting up and making the new line permanent, a considerable amount of digging had to be done. To protect the digging parties, each outpost system had to supply patrols which passed backwards and for-

wards between posts to cover the working parties. In one of the patrols were Privates F. Alfred, who was a boxing associate of Charlie Godfrey, and George Pratt, an ex-bank manager and one of the oldest men in the battalion. Pratt had shown himself an excellent soldier at Pozieres and Mouquet Farm and was a proved and trusted man. These two took their duty seriously. In charge of one of the working parties was Lance-Corporal Sheppherd, who was also a boxing man and, like Alfred, a very fine soldier. Between Alfred and Sheppherd there had sprung up an enmity which increased in intensity as the days went by. This particular night, when Pratt and Alfred approached Sheppherd's working party, words were exchanged between the two men. Sergeant "Ham" Irwin, as was his custom, visited his patrols frequently throughout the night and, setting out as usual to find Alfred and Pratt, could not locate them until he had ventured quite close to the German position, where he suddenly saw movement in front of him. The movement was caused by George Pratt, whose bandy legs and bowed shoulders were easily distinguishable, circling round and round two figures, apparently engaged in a death struggle. Hastening, as Irwin thought, to his men's assistance and fully expecting them to be at handgrips with a German patrol, and poor old George Pratt engaged in a life and death struggle, he discovered Sheppherd and Alfred fighting out their long enmity with bare knuckles. Both men were in a bad mess, for they had pasted each other with considerable skill, but the lashing they got from their sergeant's tongue soon stopped the fight. Pratt, Irwin learnt, was merely acting as referee to the contest. The two combatants obeyed him with the same promptitude as they would have done if confined to a roped square in the Brisbane Stadium, and not a shell-pocked No Man's Land within easy reach of a German patrol. Alfred was to lose his life in the battle of Polygon Wood.

As the men were making their way out of the line after being relieved, a distance of five yards was kept between them owing to the heavy shelling of the communication trench by the enemy. Movement was slow enough as it was, but a young chap in Lieutenant Carew's platoon kept getting his rifle tangled up in the telephone wires, causing halt after halt. The abuse from the men only flustered the lad more than ever until finally his voice rose in a wail: "Mr. Carew, I'm stuck!" Big Sandy Munro, sergeant to the platoon, lost his temper and, leaping out of the sap, strode wrathfully along the top to the delinquent. "Stuck, are ye?" he roared. "I'll stick ye! I'll murthder ye!" Peculiarly enough, the threat solved the lad's difficulties, for

his rifle did not become entangled again. During this relief the "B"Company platoon under the command of Lieutenant George Hurry, who had Sergeant J. Steele and Corporal C. McKinna and machine-gun section from Number 7 Platoon with him, was, through some mishap, overlooked. The following morning Lieutenant Toft went up to the line to investigate. The unit occupying the front line knew nothing about Hurry and his men. Hurry's position was an isolated one, but he was in no way worried about the fact. Toft went straight out to the post, which consisted of shell holes, and brought the platoon in. The battalion fell back to Red Lodge in Ploegsteert Wood, "A" and "B" Companies occupying the underground galleries there, and "C" and "D" Companies tents. From this point numerous fatigues came the unit's way until on the 17th they moved back to the old camping ground at Neuve Eglise.

H.R.H., the Duke of Connaught, visited the 2nd Corps on June 27, and members from each battalion in the 4th Brigade were chosen to represent their units on a parade at which H.R.H. inspected them. The 15th Battalion party consisted of 2/Lieutenant J. T. Hynes, of "A" Company, with C.S.M. (Afghan) G. Parker, of "C" Company, Lance-Corporals P. J. Sammon and P. C. Rawlings, and Private Riglan.

The next day the battalion returned to the galleries and tents in Ploegsteert Wood preparatory to again relieving the 1st and 3rd New Zealand Infantry Brigades in the front near La Truile Farm. This relief was effected on the 30th. "C" and "B" Companies relieved the Wellington Regiment, the former in the front line; and "A" and "D" Companies, the Auckland Battalion "D" Company in the front line. On this day 2/Lieutenant N. C. Whitehouse, one of "C" Company's Lewis gunners, returned from an O.C.B. course in England and was posted to "C" Company. A complete change of landscape had taken place during the short term out of the line, for rain had fallen in the interval and the whole countryside had been turned into a vast bog. The battalion was holding about 1,500 yards of front from La Trouve Farm on the right flank to the River Douve on the left. On the opposite bank of the river was the 3rd Australian Division.

The appalling mud, combined with the shelling day and night of all communication saps, added to the difficulty of moving to and fro. The saps were, in many instances, knee deep in water, and in other parts even waist deep, and through this thick muddy soup the men waded. On the right, the village of Warneton was seen to be in flames. The last day in the month saw heavy rain falling which added to the general discomfort. "C" Company, under the com-

mand of Captain R. Glasgow, came in for a considerable amount of strafing from the enemy during this term in the line. Glasgow's headquarters were situated in Uncle Trench, close to Ultimo Avenue, and about two hundred yards in the rear of Au Chaslau Cabaret. The front line position was held by a series of outposts—six in all—covering the two company front, each post consisting of some twenty to thirty men. On the night of July 1/2, Lieutenant C. C. Drane's Post had a surprise raid by the enemy. After a fierce tussle, the Germans were driven off, our losses being one man missing and six wounded. The following night the same post was again raided, but the garrison was not to be caught napping again and, after a brief set-to, the Germans decamped. At 10 p.m. three H.E. shells scored a direct hit upon Lieutenant S. A. Richards' listening post. The four occupants of the post were lifted violently into the air and flung some distance. The corporal in charge was seriously wounded and the other three so badly shaken that they were evacuated. On the night of July 3, an inter-company relief took place and "C" Company fell back into support in St. Andrew's Drive. From here they supplied working parties to dig a trench at the corner of the support line and Antonio Avenue, but the position was continually shelled. On the night of July 10 Lieutenant Nelson took the "C" Company men along to the work, but they were heavily strafed and lost four killed and three wounded. On the night of the 11th the party was under the command of Lieutenant Richards and again got a severe strafing, one shell accounting for the four sappers supplied by the engineers. All four were killed. In face of this the engineers abandoned the proposed work considering that it was far too dangerous.

On the same night as Lieutenant Drane's post was first raided, the enemy heavily shelled the front line system and this, combined with falling rain, made matters very unpleasant. Fatigue parties were at work all along the front line. One of these parties came into contact with a German patrol, which had ventured too close, and in the ensuing melee five of their number became casualties. On the 2nd the weather brightened up, but to minimise the effect of the better weather on the spirits of the men, Fritz decided to paste the countryside with heavy shells. It was during the shelling of support and reserve positions on this day that Major-General W. Holmes, commanding the 4th Australian Division, was killed. At the time of his death, he was accompanied by the Hon. W. A. Holman, Premier of New South Wales, who was reviewing matters for himself at close hand. General Holmes had only been appointed to the Division on

January 1, 1917. A very fine youngster in the 15th Battalion, Private James Booth, met his death also on this day when a high velocity shell landed directly into the front line.

Large numbers of enemy planes had been operating daily from the beginning of this term in the line. Some displayed considerable daring and flew very low over the front. On the night of July 3rd, "A" and "C" Companies took over the line and wiring parties were sent out to erect entanglements over the major part of the front. Heavy shelling continued day and night, most of which was concentrated upon the Ultimo communication sap which was in continuous use. The work of the runners and guides in this sector was most difficult. Special mention must be made of the work of Private George Williams, whose uncanny habit of leading working and fatigue parties to their correct locations was remarked upon by everyone.

On July 6, No. 3 Post was heavily shelled, and Private Stevens was wounded. This same night there was some gas shelling. By some unfortunate mischance the carrying parties to the front line were unaware that the position was being gassed, and the result was the following day many men became ill, vomiting throughout the day and suffering from the most intense pains in the head and sore eyes. As they were not completely disabled by the gas, they refused to leave the unit. This was the first occasion that what came to be known as mustard gas was used against the battalion.

The front line companies were relieved on the night of July 7/8 by the 14th Battalion. The 16th Battalion on its right flank was relieved by the 13th. Falling back into reserves "A" Company went to Bunhill Row, consisting of dugouts and breastworks, "B" Company to Prowse Point, "C" Company to Ontario Avenue and part of "D" Company to Ontario, and the others to the near neighbourhood of that trench. Battalion Headquarters established itself at St. Yves Post Office.

The night before this relief the enemy heavily shelled Brigade Headquarters, one shell hitting the mess about 7.30 p.m. and wounding the Brigadier, General Brand, the Brigade Major and another officer, and killing the Intelligence Officer, Lieutenant G. Mills. Mills, who was from the 13th Battalion, had taken over the position of I.O. from Lieutenant Percy Toft of the 15th Battalion on April 12.

About this time there were more casualties amongst the nightly fatigue parties than there were in the front line. On the night of July 12, while on a front-line fatigue, seven men were hit, the last to be brought down by the bearers being Private Davies, who died on the way down. On the

13th there were five casualties and, after this fatigue was finished, the 52nd Battalion, 13th Australian Brigade, relieved the 15th, and the Battalion marched to De Schule Camp on the Bailleul-Armentieres Road. The casualties officially reported for this trip into the line were nine killed and 22 wounded.

During the six weeks around Messines several officers left for a term of duty with the 4th Training Battalion in England. Among these were Lieutenant Leonard Hocker and Captain G. A. F. Smith. One officer had left for the Anzac Corps School, and Lieutenant W. J. Hines left on the 24th June. Two went into hospital sick—Captain J. C. Browne on June 26 and Lieutenant P. R. A. G. Ohlson on July 1.

Enemy aeroplanes attacked the back areas on the night of July 16, dropping bombs along the routes in and out of the line. The battalion vacated its camp and took to the open fields. A considerable amount of damage was done to hutments, camps and houses nearby. On the 18th 2/Lieutenant Andy Robinson returned from an O.C.B. course in England and was posted to "B" Company. A brigade inspection was held the next day, and there was a route march of ten kilometres. The men rather enjoyed this, for it was through undulating country that had practically escaped the ravages of war. Crops were looking their best and the general greenness was a pleasant contrast to the mud the men had recently left behind.

On Sunday night, July 20, enemy planes again came over and dropped bombs into adjacent horse lines, ten horses being killed and five wounded. On the 21st, Sergeant C. F. Barwood, of "B" Company, was appointed to commissioned rank, and on the same day Lieutenant J. M. Rae returned to the unit after recovering from wounds received at Bullecourt. On the 22nd a bath parade was held, though the unit had to march nine miles to the canal to have it. The rest of the week was spent in training, and on the Saturday General Birdwood arrived and inspected the various companies at their daily routine work. It was intended on the Sunday to hold a church service at which medals and ribbons won were to be presented. But with Saturday night came heavy rain and as Sunday continued wet, the service was abandoned. Another promotion in "B" Company took place on August 1 when Sergeant C. G. R. French was given commissioned rank.

In pouring rain on August 3 the battalion moved forward to Hillside Camp near Neuve Eglise. In torrents of rain the men had to erect their own shelters for the night. Soaked to the skin, they obtained what comfort they could and the

next day moved to the western slope of Messines Ridge, taking over the support lines with Battalion headquarters at Ploegsteert. Here headquarters came in for a strafing so severe that entrance to and exit from the place was impossible, so the location was changed, and headquarters occupied jointly with the 13th Battalion that unit's headquarters. 2/Lieutenant A. F. Nicholson joined the unit from the 13th Light Horse and was posted to "A" Company on the 4th.

The new headquarters was heavily shelled on August 7 and five or six members of the staff were wounded. On the 7th and 8th large fatigue parties were drawn from the battalion for the tramway construction job which had suffered so severely from enemy shell fire. The Engineers always hoped that it would be completed when Fritz grew tired of destroying it. On the night of the 8th four officers and 200 men were employed on this job, and during one strafing there were seven casualties which included Lieutenant "Jerry" Carew. This terminated Carew's service with the battalion. As an N.C.O. in his previous unit he had won the D.C.M. On the same night Corporal J. Hall was killed. The previous day the "A" Company runner, Private R. R. Row was wounded, and on August 10, during a heavy shelling of "B" Company's quarters, their company commander, Captain Burford Sampson, was slightly wounded.

Fatigues continued until August 14. The men worked very hard, considering the deplorable conditions under which they laboured. When the brigade originally took over this position, they took it over as a one-battalion front. The 16th Battalion was the first unit to hold the front-line sector. It was followed by the 14th, the 15th relieving the latter unit on the night of August 13/14. "A," "C," and "D" Companies went into the front line with "B" Company in support, "C" Company on the left flank being at Gapaard Farm.

The battalion held the front-line trenches until the night of August 20/21, when it was relieved by the 13th Battalion. There was so much mud that very little work had been done. The enemy shelled the front line system consistently, but the casualties were few. On the night of the 15th, Corporal Driscoll was fatally wounded, dying some hours later at Doctor O'Regan's dressing station. Our own artillery was also active during this term, particularly on the night of August 15/16, when it laid down a heavy barrage along the German sector. A trench mortar battery situated in Kiwi Farm caused a lot of trouble and a keen watch was kept upon it.

The night of August 17 spelt tragedy for "C" Company for young Lieutenant H. C. Whitehouse and three other men

were killed on outpost duty, a shell landing directly among them.

A reinforcement officer, Lieutenant J. C. Willis, was posted to "C" Company on the 20th. In private life Willis was an actor and had toured Australia extensively, being well-known in Queensland as a member of the "Dandies" Company. Two days later another reinforcement officer, 2/Lieutenant G. R. Baillie, joined the unit and was posted to "A" Company, and on the following day 2/Lieutenant C. H. Lyon reported back from an O.C.B. course in England and was posted to "B" Company. The night before the relief took place, Major William Mundell, who commanded the battalion during this term in the line because Lieutenant-Colonel T. P. McSharry was undergoing treatment in Steenvoerde for malaria and trench fever combined, was killed on the wire near Gapaard Farm. This was the only occasion that an officer actually commanding the battalion in the front line was killed. In his quiet way, Major Billy Mundell had firmly established himself in the affections of his men in "A" Company, the company with which he had been connected since the formation of the unit. His promotion from the ranks had been rapid. He and Major J. J. Corrigan were the only men from the ranks to reach field rank throughout the 15th Battalion's history. Mundell landed in Gallipoli with the first of the 15th Battalion parties. He was in the second list of N.C.O.'s to be promoted in the field and had practically taken part in every engagement until the one in which he met his end. That he had a premonition of his fate was a well-known fact, for he had openly spoken about it in the mess before entering the line.

An unfortunate incident took place on the night of Mundell's death when a young officer recently arrived with the unit, and in the line for the first time, sent a working party out to repair some barbed wire that had been badly cut by the enemy's shell fire. Forgetting that he had sent the party out, he threw a live bomb in among them under the impression that the enemy was attacking. As a result of this disastrous happening one man was killed and another so badly injured that his brain was impaired. This was the second occasion such a thing had happened in the battalion, the previous one being on Gallipoli when a young reinforcement officer shot a man dead. This same night a whizzbang landed among the "B" Company cookers and Private Peno was killed. The following night Sergeant George Ludlow fell unconscious to the bottom of the trench. When the stretcher-bearers, Private Shearer and another bearer, carried him from the front line they were under the impression

that he was dying. But Ludlow had succumbed to trench fever, which at this period was beginning to make itself felt in various forms. On this same night Colonel McSharry returned and took over command of the battalion.

The relief of the battalion by the 13th was completed before midnight on August 21, and the unit marched to Neuve Eglise. The following day the new Commander of the Division, Major-General Sinclair-MacLagan, paid his first visit to the unit. The battalion remained six days at this camp and then moved forward again, relieving the 16th Battalion in the support line east of Messines Ridge. Heavy rain fell throughout the night of August 26/27. To the surprise of everyone, at 4 p.m. on the 28th, the 16th Manchesters relieved the unit, and it marched back to the camping ground at Neuve Eglise between Dranoutre and Crucifix Corner. Next day the battalion held its sports and visited Palmer baths. On the 30th August, the unit marched to Lamotte Wood, where some of the men were in billets and some in tents. During August two officers, Lieutenants C. F. Barwood and A. F. Nicholson, were evacuated to hospital. Lieutenants J. T. Hynes and C. C. Drine to the 4 Training Battalion and, on September 1st, Lieutenant J. P. S. Toft also left for a term of duty with the 4 Training Battalion.

On September 1, the brigade embussed in about 170 motor buses and travelled via Merville and Aire to Lisbourg, where the 15th Battalion debussed and marched about two miles to Predefin. Here, between Lisbourg and Crepy, brigade practise stunts were engaged in, ready for the new hop-over. The Second Army Commander, General Plumer, attended the exercises as a spectator and critic. The unit remained here for eighteen days before embussing again on September 19, and travelled via Fruges, Aire and St. Omer to Wallon Capel, where they expected to remain for a week. On the 21st however, they were on the road to Steenvoorde, ten miles away.

POLYGON WOOD.

With the elimination of the great German bulge south of Ypres by the capture of the Messines-Wytschaete Ridge, the Allied offensive was resumed further north, to end in the mud of Passchendaele, which German writers have called "the supreme martyrdom of the war."

The whole operation got the name of the Third Battle of Ypres. After an intensive bombardment extending over the best part of fourteen days, the great stroke, with which it was hoped to destroy German resistance in the north, was delivered on July 31. The Germans adopted a

system of defence which was to prove most troublesome from the very commencement. It had for its main object, not so much to preserve every inch of ground, as to prevent a breakthrough, while inflicting the maximum amount of loss to the attackers.

The forward areas of their defence system were organised as a kind of fortified outpost line. Here there were no connected trenches, but a series of strong points housed in concrete structures which were afterwards nicknamed "pill boxes" from their general appearance, and which, in some instances, were capable of accommodating anything from a platoon to a company. In addition to their natural strength, they proved to be particularly suitable for the defence of the flooded country through which the British advance was to take place. Their capture by unaided infantry was somewhat of a problem, and they certainly achieved the purpose of breaking up the attacking columns before they encountered the main trench system in rear of them.

Throughout August there was hard and prolonged fighting on both sides of the Menin Road as the Australians pushed on towards Passchendaele. The Fourth Brigade came into the picture towards the end of September to take part in the battle of Polygon Wood. The position to be assaulted was just short of Broodseinde Ridge. The distance to be covered was the best part of 1,000 yards. This advanced position was known to the men as the Blue Line and ran through part of Jetty Wood on the 5th Divisional front, then west of Melenaarstheek to south-west of Zonnebeke village. It was exceptionally strong and the country to be traversed was pockmarked with shell holes and was a sea of mud.

The brigade assault was divided into two stages. The 16th Battalion was to secure the Red Line, and the 14th and 15th Battalions the Blue Line. The 13th Battalion was to be in reserve. The artillery was to lay down a creeping barrage. Three minutes after zero it was to advance at the rate of 100 yards in four minutes up to a distance of 200 yards, after which it was to be slowed down to 100 yards in six minutes. The rate of its intensity was to increase after moving from the Blue Line, but at this line it would remain stationary for 100 minutes after zero hour. This, as will be seen at a later stage, caused some confusion.

In fine weather, on September 22, the brigade embussed for the Canal area near Ypres to relieve the 6th Australian Infantry Brigade. Numerically the 15th Battalion was, at this period—Steenvoorde—the strongest unit in the brigade,

its strength being 22 officers[1] and 750 other ranks. Debussing at the Canal, the battalion bivouacked near Belgian Chateau, leaving their 33 per cent nucleus at Carstre. On the 23rd the men drew their bombs and extra ammunition, then marched to the Ypres Ramparts and encamped. They left this position on September 25, halting for two hours at Gordon House to allow the moon to set so that movement across the low-lying marshes would not be observed by the enemy.

The city of Ypres, or at least what remained of it, bristled with all calibres of guns which belched and vomited their shells into the German positions. The distant German front line was lit up by a continuous succession of flares, proving that the foe was both alarmed and active. The plans for the attack were circulated to battalion commanders a few days before the hop-over. They provided for an advance in four waves, a platoon to each wave. The second wave would contain the moppers-up and the third and fourth waves the carrying parties. To indicate the position of the Red and Blue Lines, the artillery was to fire smoke shells from each battery as the barrage reached the objectives. The Australian portion of the attack stopped at the railway line at Zonnebeke, the final objective being on the eastern outskirts of Zonnebeke, facing Broodseinde. The southernmost part of the advance, which was of varying depths throughout, was nearer Reutel and included all that portion of Polygon Wood which was not already in British hands. South of the 5th Australian Division were English and Scottish troops, and north of Ypres adjoining the 4th Australian Division, were the English 59th and 3rd Divisions, which included the Royal Scots, Gordons, King's Own and other regiments. The whole advance from near Groanenbury in the south to near Winzig in the north was on a front of approximately six miles, and the deepest point to which the line advanced was about three-quarters of a mile. Co-operating with the troops was the 4th Squadron of the Royal Flying Corps, whose machines kept touch with the men on the ground by sounding a succession of "A" notes on their Klaxon horns. The infantry replied by firing red flares, this giving the location of their advance positions. Distinguishing badges were to be worn

---

(1) Officers entering the line for the Battle of Polygon Wood were:—
"A" Coy.: Capt. E. K. Carter, Lieuts. Guy, Baillie, Eric Simon, J. Willis. "B" Coy.: Capts. S. R. Richards S. Porter, Lieuts. A. Robinson, G. Wilkins, C. Lyon. "C" Coy.: Capt. R. Glasgow, Lieuts. J. W. Nelson, H. G. Maegraith, S. H. Joubert, B. A. Richards. "D" Coy.: Capt. W. Dominey, Lieut. R. V. Jackson.

by scouts, runners, signallers, carrying parties and moppers-up.

The 13th Battalion, 4th Australian Brigade, was holding the then front line near Helles, known as the Anzac Ridge Lines, and through this unit the brigade was to advance to the attack. To this battalion fell the duty of sapping through from the old position to the captured position and also the task of conveying messages expeditiously back to brigade. Major Marks, commanding the 13th Battalion, put his men to work sapping the night before the charge, with the result that the unit had completed almost half of the necessary work when the advance started. During the advance the battalion finished the saps and they provided much needed shelter for wounded being carried to the rear and ammunition parties working their way forward.

The position to be attacked was the higher country lying almost due east of the Anzac Line. Once on the move the troops travelled practically parallel to the Polygon Wood Racecourse. Before midnight on September 25, the brigade and battalion Intelligence officers laid the tapes. The three 4th Brigade battalions were in position by 4.50 a.m., an hour before zero, the 15th Battalion directly behind the 16th with the 55th Battalion on their right flank and the 14th Battalion on their left. So to eliminate any possibility of doubt as to the exact positions of the units, notice boards were erected on the flanks. The password for the charge was "Cobber." The night was exceptionally quiet for the Ypres area until 4.15 a.m., when the enemy, whether suspicious or not is unknown, began shelling the back areas with his heavies. As the 15th Battalion entered the saps leading through the marshy country to the starting point, two men were killed and five were wounded by one of these missiles. Crossing the ridge, the men sheltered themselves in the numberless shell holes to await the commencement of the charge. Their arrival at the set point was later than the time calculated. At ten minutes to six, the British barrage opened with a tremendous crash, and the 16th Battalion moved forward to the attack, the 14th and 15th Battalions following close on their heels. The first objective was taken at very small cost to the 16th Battalion, which took about 200 prisoners. The enemy's losses beside those taken prisoner, were stated to have been large. As the barrage was to remain safeguarding the 16th Battalion's new position until 7.30 a.m. before moving forward to the Blue Line, a number of the officers and men, whose watches evidently did not synchronise, kept moving forward into the British barrage, causing some confusion and a number of casualties. In

"A" Company's sector Sergeant-Major Jack Fleet, helped by Privates George Williams and "Skinny" Hansen, retrieved a number of the wounded, while those uninjured were ordered back to the main body to conform with the general movement. In Lieutenant Guy Baillie's platoon, a number of men penetrated the barrage and, while Baillie and Fleet were endeavouring to restore order, Colonel McSharry appeared upon the scene. Members of the 55th Battalion were also converging upon the 15th Battalion's sector and some of their members moved forward into the barrage as well. For the splendid work done by Fleet at this stage and at a later stage, he was strongly recommended by the 55th Battalion, through which unit he was awarded a D.C.M. Colonel McSharry, after leaving the junction of the 15th and 55th Battalions, moved along to the left, visiting each of the companies in turn. Lieutenant Andy Robinson, of "B" Company, relates how he was surprised to hear his Colonel's voice immediately after the line had moved forward, praising the men for the splendid way they carried out orders.

When the barrage lifted and began to move toward the second objective, casualties began to mount. "C" Company under the command of Captain Bob Glasgow was the most unfortunate of the four companies. When a gun from a battery, firing directly over their line of advance, fired short, two of "C" Company's officers, Lieutenants Maegraith and Joubert were seriously wounded. Joubert died the following day. Lieutenant Robinson, writing about this British gun, said: "It was really a thrilling sight to see the members of "C" Company fill up the break in the line each time a shell burst. Unfortunately the gun kept up with the advance and continually harassed them throughout."

In "A" Company's sector, Lieutenant Jock Willis was wounded, and in "B" Company Lieutenants G. Wilkins and C. Lyon became casualties, Lyon's wound proving fatal. As the battalion moved up the hill to its objective, Lieutenant Robinson in "B" Company fell—shot down by an enemy machine-gun at close range. About the same time Lieutenant Nelson, "C" Company, fell mortally wounded. "D" Company under the command of Captain W. Domeney had, up to this time, escaped officer casualties, though during the consolidation of its position Lieutenant R. V. Jackson became a casualty. As "A" Company, with some members of the 55th Battalion, approached the first "pill box," a number of Germans were seen emerging and Sergeant Fleet, closely followed by Privates Hansen and Williams, rushed in. Fleet fell in the mud at the feet of one of the Huns, and was on the point of being despatched when Williams took a hand.

Private Cyril Beadon, single handed, captured a German machine-gun crew with a long-handled German shovel as a weapon. He proudly exhibited the eight captured men for all to see. Two "A" Company stretcher-bearers—Privates Devries and Parker—performed wonders. Of the sixteen bearers on Headquarters Staff, nine became casualties. Among these were Privates Marshall and Moles, the latter an original member of the section. The depletion of the bearers' strength necessitated men being brought forward from the Field Ambulance units to supplement the remaining few left with Doctor O'Regan. O'Regan again proved himself a tower of strength and worked strenuously throughout three days without a moment's rest.

During the consolidation of the captured position, a considerable amount of sniping took place, and by the time the unit was relieved by the 45th Battalion at 10 p.m. on the Thursday night, September 28, the men had quietened most of these pests down. The two or three efforts at counter-attack were repulsed by a curtain of fire laid down by the artillery immediately upon request. Altogether, considering the magnitude of the attack, the casualties had been extremely light. The brigade casualties were:—

	Officers.	Other Ranks.	Total.
Killed	7	104	111
Wounded	17	448	465
Died of Wounds	3	6	9
Missing	0	9	9
	27	567	594

Among the 15th Battalion missing was the "A" Company Quartermaster, Sergeant Dick Fowler. Fowler took on the job of seeing that the rations were delivered in the front line in person, and his disappearance was a mystery until the termination of the war, when his body was recovered and placed in one of the new cemeteries then being constructed. Among the killed were Privates F. Alfred, who had represented the unit at several of the divisional boxing tournaments, R. M. Pleister, L. C. Bennett. T/Corporal, W. Denehey was wounded badly and left for dead by several of the stretcher-bearers owing to the fact that his face had turned black. Denehey's wife was communicated with by some of these men telling her of his death, but luckily she received a cable from her husband before the letters of condolence arrived. Of the officer casualties, three died of wounds— Lieutenants S. H. Joubert, J. W. Nelson, and C. H. S. Lyon; of those wounded Lieutenant J. W. Willis was the only one to

see further service with the Battalion, Lieutenants A. Robinson, H. G. Maegraith, G. H. Wilkins and R. V. Jackson returning to Australia for discharge. Two days before the attack on September 24, Lieutenant W. P. Jones was killed while attached to Brigade Headquarters as I.O.

A number of decorations were awarded for this show. Military Crosses were given to Captains R. Glasgow and S. Porter and Lieutenants S. H. Joubert, J. G. Maegraith, G. W. Wilkins. The two "B" Company N.C.Os, Sergeant "Goody" Crow, who was wounded in the head, and Corporal Kunkler also wounded, received Military Medals, and both were to receive commissions on their return to the battalion from hospital.

After the relief the battalion went back to the Ramparts at Ypres and there the roll call was held. On September 30 the unit marched to Halifax Camp. It remained at Steenvoorde until October 11, when it returned to Halifax Camp near Vlamertinghe, camping the next day in the tunnels at Esplanade Cut at the Ramparts on their way into the front line. At Steenvoorde a number of promotions were made to fill the gaps caused by the officer casualties at Polygon Wood. Those promoted on October 5 were: Q.M.S. A. B. Fenton, Q.M.S. J. E. Greenwood, Q.M.S. F. J. Merrell, Sergeants T. B. Sloan, W. P. Ryan, A. R. Kunkler, W. J. Spencer, J. Grant. On the 6th, 2/Lieutenant L. J. W. Taylor reported to the unit with reinforcements. On the 13th, the battalion left the Ramparts and moved forward on to Westhoek Ridge where it bivouacked in the open. The night was very quiet. The following day "A" and "D" Companies moved forward in close support of the 14th Battalion, which was occupying the front line. These support lines were heavily shelled with gas on the 15th, and 12 men became casualties. These shells were of the delayed action type and the casualties followed because the men were unfamiliar with their manner of working. The gas itself did not seriously affect them until 24 hours later.

The 14th Battalion was relieved on the night of the 16th. On the night of the 17th the unit connected up its flank with the 52nd Battalion on the right, and its patrols made connection with the 39th Battalion north of the railway line. The following night the 13th relieved the 15th Battalion which moved back to Railway Wood dugouts. In this trip to the line "B" Company lost a very popular officer in Lieutenant George Hurry. The men of his platoon set a guard over his body day and night until relieved, when they carried it through the mud and slush back to the Ramparts at Ypres, where the remains were buried by his Company Com-

mander, Captain Burford Sampson, and the members of the platoon, Sampson reading the burial service. Another casualty was 2/Lieutenant H. L. Kent, a newly-arrived reinforcement officer, who was wounded on the 18th, and did not see any further service with the Battalion.

On October 15, Lieutenant G. S. Heron, who had transferred to the 69th, returned to the battalion owing to the decision not to form the 6th Australian Division, and was posted to "A" Company. On October 22, Lieutenants E. H. Voss and G. S. Fewster reported for duty. Fewster came from the 4th Divisional Pioneers through an O.C.B. course in England, and Voss from the 4th Division Train, also through an O.C.B. course. Rumours that the 4th Australian Division was to be pulled out of the forward area and sent back for a three months' rest were going the rounds, but it was not until mid-November that this took place.

◆ ◆ ◆ ◆

CHAPTER XII.

TEMPLEUX-LA-FOSSE AND WINTER.

It came as a great surprise when on November 16 the long-promised three months' spell to the 4th Australian Division began. On that date the 4th Brigade was to march by seven easy stages from Crepy to Fricourt, situated near Abbeville. On the 15th of the month, the men had hot baths and those with scabies were treated with sulphur ointments as well as the hot-water cure. The march began on the morning of the 17th with an easy stage of seven miles to Torey. The following day 12 miles were covered to Compaigne, where games of football were played on the 19th. The 20th found the unit at Maintenay, three miles away, and on the 21st it was at Ligecourt, seven miles distant. Le Titra was reached before midday on the 22nd, and the next day the men marched into Friville, seven miles further on. In this village they settled down to enjoy the long-promised rest.

There were several rather pleasing features about this march, the principal one being the astonishingly good billets found throughout the journey. The easy stages of the march enabled the softened feet of the men to withstand the demands made upon them. Throughout the seven days only one man fell out and he was a case of notoriously bad feet. With the expectation that Fricourt was to be the 15th Battalion's winter quarters, the men set about making themselves comfortable. The winter was closing in quickly, but the intense cold felt in the neighbourhood of Flers during the 1916 winter was not expected to prove so severe closer to the seaboard.

The Brigadier, General Brand, set out a syllabus of training which included special lectures for officers and N.C.O.'s. It was during the course of a lecture, at which most of the Battalion officers and N.C.O.'s were present, that the General arrived in person. He was somewhat upset and informed all present that General Byng's forces in the near neighbourhood of Cambrai had suffered a reverse, and the 4th Brigade was under orders for an early move to the scene of operations. There was something more than disappointment at this sudden change from good times to bad, but, with a spirit that did the men credit, any ill-feeling was dissipated once the order to move arrived.

On December 5, in full marching order, the Brigade left by train for its destination. The 15th Battalion travelled as follows: "A" Company entrained at Woincourt at 3 p.m. and detrained at La Chapelette at 2 a.m. on the 6th and marched to Moislains, where it arrived at 6 a.m. The remainder of the Battalion entrained at Woincourt at 10 p.m. and detrained at La Chapelette at 8.30 a.m. the following day, arriving at Moislains at midday. The march in the dark hours of the morning along the ice-bound roads to Moislains by the men of "A" Company is unlikely to be forgotten. The lack of knowledge as to the distance the enemy was away, the intense cold, and the eeriness of the journey owing to the dearth of movement, led to many precautions being taken. The men were not allowed to smoke. Speech was conducted in whispers, and broken step was made at the crossing of bridges. The billets were half-buried in snow. They were the largest huts the unit had ever occupied, and the heavy blanket of snow lying on the long roofs resisted even the warmth created by the huge fires that blazed within. The change from the temperate climate of Friville to the Arctic wastes of Moislains was severely felt by all ranks.

In this camp, on December 11, a vote was taken on the Australian Referendum for compulsory service sponsored by the Prime Minister of Australia, the Rt. Hon. W. M. Hughes. The Battalion strength stood at 741 all told, and of this number 712 men voted. On the 12th, the Battalion played the 4th Field Ambulance football. On the 13th and succeeding days, brigade exercises were held. On the 17th, an order came to move to Templeux-la-Fosse. On this day, some three to four inches of snow fell to freeze as soon as it touched the ground. On the 19th, the unit started along the slippery road to its destination, where it was to take over a line of tents previously occupied by the 49th Battalion. From the line of tents the unit was to supply working parties for the new British Reserve Line then in course of construction a mile away.

The march to Templeux-la-Fosse had many unpleasant features and there was a considerable amount of grumbling among the men. Along the road the Divisional Commander, Major-General Sinclair-MacLagan, reviewed the unit. As the men had been picking their way with considerable care, owing to the slippery surface, this review proved rather a failure. The sudden call to the men to march at attention was disastrous. Lieutenant Grant, of "B" Company, was one of the first casualties, for his feet shot from under him and, falling heavily upon his buttock, he split that part of his

anatomy open and had to receive medical attention. Several other men sustained nasty falls, one man having his collarbone broken. In the transport, the water cart horse under the control of Driver Parfitt sprawled heavily upon the roadway when his driver attempted to salute, and a general mix-up ensued. A few bright exchanges then followed between the Divisional Commander and the Transport Officer, Lieutenant E. H. Voss, to be continued, after the transport had passed on, by the Commander and Colonel McSharry. By the time Templeux-la-Fosse was reached, the men in the unit were seething with rage. When it was learnt that a special parade was called for the afternoon, at which the Brigade Commander, General Brand, would inspect the men, they were almost on the verge of revolt.

By the use of considerable tact upon the part of Colonel McSharry and the Company Commanders, who were ably seconded by many of the N.C.O.'s, the good humour of the unit was restored, and the parade, the briefest ever held in the 15th Battalion, passed off without a hitch. The men then returned to their tents, and began a search for firewood with which to warm themselves at their oil drum braziers.

Christmas was spent at Templeux-la-Fosse, and the occasion was made as enjoyable as possible. The early morning visit of an enemy aeroplane flying very low, caused some anxiety, for the 16th Battalion had been bombed on the night of the 22nd and there had been frequent air raids during the previous ten days. Fritz, however, must have been in a convivial mood, for we were not raided during the whole period of our stay.

Early in the New Year a call for volunteers to serve in the Near East, encouraged some of the officers and men to volunteer. Among the very few chosen was Sergeant-Major "Afghan" G. Parker, D.C.M., M.M., who left for an unknown destination. A call for officers willing to serve in the Indian Army and the Rhodesian Police Force was also made and to the Indian Army went Captain W. "Dal" Cummins[1], who had only recently returned from the 6th Australian Division which had just been disbanded. Lieutenant J. H. T. Fraser, an original of "B" Company, also returned from the 6th Division and was posted to "A" Company, but a few days later took over the Transport from Lieutenant E. H. Voss, the latter returning to his company.

The weather was intensely cold on January 10 when the Battalion marched out at 3 p.m. for Peronne, where it entrained. Leaving Peronne at 6.30 p.m., the night was spent

---

(1) Captain W. Cummins transferred to 69th Battalion, 6th Australian Division, on March 22, 1917.

in the train and, at 9.30 a.m. the following morning, the men detrained at Bailleul where they were served with hot cocoa at the Y.M.C.A. At 11 a.m. they started their march to La Clytte, where they arrived at 3.15 p.m. and took possession of Murrumbidgee Camp. This camp was one of the filthiest the unit had ever occupied.

The Battalion remained here until January 20. During those days the whole camp underwent a transformation and fatigue parties were supplied daily for the dozen and one duties that fall to the lot of units in reserve. On the 20th the Battalion moved by the Light Railway up to Spoil Bank, and detraining there started up Olaf Avenue to the relief of the 45th and 46th Battalions of the 12th Australian Brigade, which were holding a line of outposts—part of the Belgian Wood and Chateau Wood groups in the neighbourhood of Wervieque. The area was better known to the rank and file as Hollebeke.

During the stay at Templeux-la-Fosse, three reinforcement officers reported to the Battalion. They were 2/Lieutenant G. Ward, on December 16th, 2/Lieutenant A. H. Moss on December 18th, and 2/Lieutenant E. P. Farrelly on January 8, 1918. On January 18th 2/Lieutenant L. J. Page, a "B" Company N.C.O., reported back from an O.C.B. course in England. On the same day Lieutenant J. W. Willis returned from hospital after recovering from wounds received at Polygon Wood.

It was also at Templeux-la-Fosse on January 2, 1918, that the Battalion lost its young and studious medical officer, Captain Stan. O'Regan, with his return to the 4th Field Ambulance. His place was filled by Major R. F. Craig. Craig was with the unit only for a short period. He did not become well-known to the men, for sick parades in those days were small in number. He left the unit to go to the 15th Field Ambulance.

HOLLEBEKE

Hollebeke lay south-east of Ypres, a matter of some two miles east of the old St. Eloi line held by the 15th Battalion during October, 1916. During 1914 the historic Chateau de Hollebeke was the main objective of a desperate attack by the 4th and 10th Hussars of the 3rd Cavalry Brigade. The Canal at Hollebeke turns sharply west before continuing its course to Ypres and hand to hand fighting during the desperate days of '14 took place almost daily. The pride of the German army threw itself valiantly against the thin British line, under, it was said, the eye of the Kaiser himself, who had arrived on the battlefield to watch his

victorious troops sweep through on the road to the channel ports. That they failed to get through is history. Nearly four years later, Australian troops were in the same area, covering almost the same ground. Rumour was rife that the great German offensive following the collapse of Russia and the signing of the peace treaty with Rumania, both of which calamities had released hundreds of thousands of German troops for the Western theatre of war, was to be launched in the neighbourhood of Hollebeke.

At midday on January 20, 1918, the relief began and was completed at 7.30 p.m. "B" Company under the command of Captain S. A. Richards, relieved the 45th Battalion. The two outposts belonging to the 45th which the 15th Battalion took over were relieved by Lieutenants Moss and Barwood under cover of night. The right flank outposts belonging to the 46th Battalion were relieved by two "A" Company platoons under the commands of Lieutenants E. Voss and W. Ryan. Two platoons from "B" Company, under the command of Captain J. C. Browne, went into support at Embankment Dugouts, and the two "C" Company platoons, under the command of Captain Gordon Smith, into the Ypres-Commines railway dugouts.

The outpost system was divided into four groups, and communication with it during daylight was extremely dangerous. The whole countryside was one huge bog and many of the craters on the edge of the tracks leading to and from the outposts were twelve to fifteen feet deep. As much barbed wire had to be erected, the unfortunate carriers for the necessary fatigue parties ran the risk of drowning, as the tracks were difficult enough to follow in daylight, let alone at night. With the intention of securing identification and perhaps a hint as to what the Hun intended in the matter of attacking, a strong raiding party was put into training from "C" Company under the leadership of two of the company's officers, Lieutenants C. C. Drane and J. Merrill. For some reason the scheme was dropped.

On the night of January 19, however, the enemy attempted a raid. Shelling the outpost system heavily for about half an hour, they attacked in the neighbourhood of Lieutenant Barwood's post and that held by Lieutenant Eric Voss and his men of "A" Company. The 16th Battalion post on Voss's right flank also came in for a heavy strafing and though there were no signs of the enemy other than two deserters who gave themselves up, the raid fizzled out so far as the 15th Battalion was concerned. On January 22, while "B" Company were undergoing an inter-platoon relief,

its lines were heavily shelled and a number of casualties occurred. Sergeant Ellis and four men were hit by a direct burst at the door of their pill box. Ellis, with both legs shattered, managed somehow or other to crawl to Captain Richards' dugout some distance to the rear and there secured aid. Both his legs had to be amputated. "C" Company relieved "B" Company on the night of January 24 and on the same night "D" Company, under Captain W. Domeney, relieved "A" Company, then commanded by Lieutenant H. R. H. Lack.

The fear of a German attack on the Kaiser's birthday was intensified by information supplied by one of the two prisoners taken. This led to the whole Brigade remaining on the qui vive all that night. Identification was secured when an enemy patrol was fired upon by our men and one of their number was killed, a search being made of his clothing. On the same night there was a bombardment with gas shells most of which landed in Olaf Avenue and Fusilier Walk. The 14th Battalion relieved the 15th on the night of January 29/30, and the unit moved back to Tournai Camp. The casualties during this term in the line were very few, numbering only 2 killed and 8 wounded. One of the killed was Private Fudge, whose father was one-time member for the Mackay electorate in the Queensland Parliament.

At Tournai Camp large fatigue parties were put to work on the new reserve line, which was being hastily constructed as a further line of defence should the German attack be launched in the northern one. The Battalion's strength at this period totalled 46 Officers and 675 Other Ranks.

With the addition of one platoon of the 16th the Battalion moved forward again on February 20 at 3 p.m. A halt was made at St. Eloi for tea, after which the same sector as that previously occupied in January was entered and the relief of the 46th Battalion, 4th Australian Division, took place. This time "B" Company took over the outposts system. "D" Company went into support, and "A" and "C" Companies into the reserve lines known as Railway Trench.

About 3 a.m. on February 25, the enemy shelled one of the Potsdam outpost groups held by the B Battalion with Trench Mortars and then attempted to raid it. The raid was a complete failure and two of the enemy were left in our hands. Our casualties were two men wounded. The following night an inter-company relief took place, "A" Company taking over from "D" in the front line. The whole area remained quiet during the stay in the line and on March 2 the unit was relieved by the 12th Battalion, 1st Australian

Division, the relief being completed by 2.45 p.m. The Battalion then marched to Kruistnaathoek and there embussed for Shankhill Camp, Neuve Eglise, which was reached at 4.30 p.m. Orders were issued here that the unit had to be in readiness to move at two hours notice.

The Battalion remained camped in Nissen huts until March 25. The peace was undisturbed, except for one night, when a long range high velocity gun placed a shell at the corner of one of the huts. The shell, a dud of big calibre, blew the man sleeping in the corner of the hut through the roof, his battered body coming to rest on the top of the building. His companion sleeping beside him was killed instantly, though his body did not move from its position on the floor.

March 25 saw the end of inactivity. On that date the Battalion embussed for a destination where it was to be caught up with the great events of the German push in the Spring of 1918.

* * * *

CHAPTER XIII.
THE BIG PUSH.

The year 1918 was one of the most momentous of the whole war. The release of German divisions from the Russian front following the Revolution and the approach of peace negotiations with the newly-born Soviet Government, resulted in a great troop concentration on the Western front.

Before the end of 1917, German Headquarters had come to the definite decision that if they were to win the war they must deliver a crushing attack in France before the American armies had fully mobilised. This was to be an early and supreme effort to shatter the Allies once and for all. With the American Army on French soil, the task of overwhelming the French and British forces was considered to be an impossibility. In the eyes of the German General Staff, then, "all that mattered was to get together enough troops for an attack on the Western front." With the failure of the last Russian offensive in 1917, the whole situation, in Ludendorff's view, was now more favourable to Germany than "one could ever have expected."

Early in the new year there began the greatest concentration of men and war material which the world, up to that time, had ever seen. German G.H.Q. even thought of transferring the 15th Turkish Corps to France. It was estimated that 30 divisions would be transferred from the Eastern theatre to the West. Between November 1, 1917, and the fourth week in March, 1918, the German divisions in France actually increased from 146 to 192. By the beginning of March the great offensive was believed to be imminent.

During the period of these great concentrations, the Australian divisions were in a quiet sector round about Messines and Armentieres. On January 1 they had merged into the Australian Corps under the command of General Birdwood. Some divisions were in the line. Others rested in the Calais area. Further south on the Somme was the Fifth British Army under General Gough. On its left was the Third Army in the Arras sector. The right of the Fifth Army joined the French left. The German plan aimed at driving a wedge between the French and the British and the rolling up of the British line to the Channel ports.

On March 21 the great attack was launched. When the first news filtered through, few of the rank and file of the rear divisions of Australians believed it, but when rumours

increased hourly, giving details of the rapidity with which the Germany forces were smashing through the southern sector of the British line, the men became anxious to see things for themselves. Their chance came soon enough for, on the afternoon of March 24, all officers and men were recalled to their lines. Packs and surplus gear were dumped, and the Battalion was ready to move off at an early hour the following morning. Reveille was set for 3.30 on the morning of March 25. After, the unit marched out to the embussing point on Waterloo Road, where, in conjunction with the rest of the Brigade, the embussing took place and the long journey to Bavincourt began. The route was through Steenwerck, Estaires, Merville, St. Venant, Lillers, and St. Pol, where an hour's halt was made for lunch. Thence via Maizieres, Avesnes, Barly, to Bavincourt, which was reached about 6 p.m. The I.O., Lieutenant Jack Rae, who, with his scouts had been touring France, visiting town after town as his orders were changed to fit in with the rapidly changing scene of operations, secured good billets for the men, but only after considerable difficulty. The inhabitants of Bavincourt were packed up ready to leave when Rae arrived in the village, and when he sought to arrange for the billets they were under the impression that he was an Austrian and part of the German advance formations. When they finally learnt that he was an Australian they put themselves out to please him. It was in this village, however, that the largest account ever served upon the 15th Battalion for damage alleged to have been done by their men while in billets was presented. The amount ran into thousands of francs, and considering the short stay of the unit and the length of time after their departure before the account was lodged—six months or more—the debt should never have been paid. As it happened, dances and boxing tournaments were conducted for the purpose of raising the money after the Armistice was signed, and the full amount of the alleged debt was met.

At 11.15 a.m. on March 26 word was received at Brigade Headquarters that the enemy had broken through with armoured cars at Hebuterne. This rumour was said to have been the work of German agents operating on our side of the line. Other accounts credited them with having been French farm tractors which the owners were anxious to avoid falling into the hands of the invaders. However, orders were received for the 4th Brigade to occupy a line from Souaster to Bienvillers. As the possession of Hebuterne was in doubt, everybody was uneasy, so General Brand went forward to reconnoitre the position for himself.

Prior to the General's visit to Hebuterne, Lieutenant Jack Rae, I.O., 15th Battalion, in company with another officer, had entered the village during the morning and found a number of German troops in an advanced stage of intoxication. They were in such a state that Rae and the other officer stood at the church corner in the centre of the village without being molested. When General Brand arrived a little later no Huns were to be seen, nor were there British troops, although Rae had made contact with a number earlier in the morning. After the order had been given to occupy Hebuterne, the officer in charge of one of the 15th Battalion's advance parties found directly forward of the position he occupied a captain and sixty members of a British unit. This man, unaware of his exact position, thought the Germans had completely surrounded him. Upon learning otherwise, he fell back with his men upon the Brigade's left flank.

Orders to occupy Hebuterne were received by the Battalion Commander, Lieutenant-Colonel T. P. McSharry[1] at 3 p.m. The Battalion was to move forward with the rest of the Brigade. A strong patrol sent out to contact the enemy, if possible, discovered that the south-western corner of the village was in German occupation and the north-western corner was occupied by a company of the 9th Welsh Regiment. The Brigade dispositions were as follows: 16th Battalion on the right flank, 13th Battalion in the centre, and 15th Battalion on the left flank. The 14th Battalion was held in reserve. Brigade established its Headquarters at Crucifix Corner.

There was no difficulty in occupying the village. The Company Commanders—"A" Captain Harold Koch, "B" Captain Simon Porter, "C" Captain Percy Toft, and "D" Captain E. M. Bradley—entered the village without opposition except in the case of "C" Company, which encountered a machine-gun crew and promptly took its members prisoner. "A" Company took one totally inebriated German in charge. The line occupied was an old French trench skirting the edge of the village. The night was very quiet and there was only intermittent machine-gun fire until near 4 a.m., when a few shells fell into the main street in the vicinity of the church. About daylight on the 27th the enemy commenced to shell the town, the front line and support trenches with mortars and artillery. The position of the men in supports was unenviable, for their trenches collapsed under the intensity of the barrage. So heavy was the bombardment on the

---

(1) Lt.-Col. T. P. McSharry went on leave this night to Paris and the Battalion was commanded by Major J. J. Corrigan for several days.

village that Battalion Headquarters moved into nearby trenches. The following day they left their new position and occupied another that was receiving less attention from the enemy shelling. About 11.30 a.m. on the 27th word came that the enemy were massing along the front. So soon as they were located a heavy rifle and machine-gun fire was poured into them. Originally advancing in twelve waves against the 13th and 15th Battalions, they veered to the right, taking advantage of lower ground, and attempted an attack upon the New Zealanders on the 16th Battalion's right flank. As an attack was still expected on the 4th Brigade's front, orders were issued for the 14th Battalion in reserve to move forward on to the 15th Battalion's right flank. At the same time the 13th Battalion was to advance its line slightly so as to include the cemetery south of Hebuterne.

Rather a peculiar thing was noticed during the bombardment of Hebuterne. This was a British aeroplane showing British colours flying in the German formation operating overhead. It was the first time during the war such an incident had been noticed by us.

The unit was now part and parcel of the 62nd British Division, and was to remain so for some little time. The 12th and 13th Battalions were further south in the neighbourhood of Villers Bretonneux. On the morning of the 28th another trench mortar barrage was laid down on the 15th Battalion's lines, the support lines again being the main sufferers, and in "C" Company supports Lieutenant Josiah Francis became a casualty. The enemy attacked the moment the barrage lifted, and was repulsed with ease. About 50 of them then attempted an attack upon one of "D" Company's posts, but lost heavily. Severe shelling continued until March 31, from which date it began to lessen. The Battalion's casualties had been light considering the value of the work done. They were: Killed 9, died of wounds 3, and wounded 59, including one officer. The Battalion strength at this time was: Officers 40, other ranks 677.

On April 1 two platoons of "A" Company commanded by Lieutenant Guy Baillie moved forward two hundred yards and occupied a system of trenches without loss. "C" Company, conforming with this movement, also advanced. On April 5 heavy shelling, interspersed with gas, again took place. The expected attack however did not develop, though the 16th Battalion heavily attacked on its front. Rain fell on the 6th, turning the countryside into a bog. The wet weather continued until the 9th, on the night of which the 15th Battalion was relieved by the 10th Royal Fusiliers, and the men marched back to Rossignol Farm. The total casual-

ties during this term in the line were: Two officers and 68 other ranks.

The second officer to fall a casualty was Lieutenant J. Fraser, Transport Officer, who was wounded. He was afterwards killed at the Battle of Hamel. The remarkable work done by Lieutenant J. M. Rae, M.M., calls for special mention at this point. During these operations he was instrumental in several changes which were made in the dispositions of the troops and he was of such service to the Brigade and Divisional Commanders that he achieved the unique distinction of receiving two Military Crosses at the one time—one Cross from the 4th Australian Division and one from the 62nd British Division. As an officer is not allowed to possess two Military Crosses—he obtains a bar if recommended a second time—Rae had to choose which one he preferred. He selected the recommendation of the 62nd Division.

Around about this time Percy "Darkie" McCoy won a D.C.M., having previously won the M.M. He finished up with the Unit to return safely to Australia and take part as a Major in operations against the Japanese in World War II in the fever stricken jungles back of Merauke on New Guinea.

At Rossignol Farm the men were to be held in readiness to move at a half-hour's notice. Baths were arranged and there was a general clean-up. On April 11, visits were paid by the 4th Divisional Commander, General MacLagan and Major-General Williams of the 37th British Division to which the 4th Brigade was at that time attached. MacLagan, in addressing the men, expressed the hope that the 4th Brigade would soon be attached once more to his division, a prospect which did not appear very likely at the moment, for the British commanders more than once stated that they could not do without us. On April 20 the Battalion moved forward from the support lines and occupied the front line held by the 16th Battalion. "D" and "A" Companies took over the front line. As in the former position, night patrols were continually on the move, but the enemy was rarely seen. The unit remained here until April 24, when it was relieved by the 2nd Wellington Battalion of the 1st New Zealand Brigade and moved by bus to Allonville. The casualties during this period in the line were: 1 killed and 4 wounded. The unfortunate death which occurred was that of a youngster with a mania for souvenirs. He had ventured out in front of Lieutenant Guy Baillie's position in broad daylight and was shot by a sniper.

During the Brigade's occupation of Hebuterne, the 13th Australian Brigade, under Major-General W. Glasgow, and the 15th Brigade, under Major-General "Pompey" Elliott, had

fought their great night battle at Villers Bretonneux. These two Brigades had seen exceptionally heavy fighting, and on April 26 a conference of all commanding officers was held at Brigade Headquarters, General Birdwood being present. It was then agreed that the 12th Brigade would relieve the 15th Brigade on the night of April 27/28, and the 4th Brigade, which was farthest from the scene of operations, would relieve the 13th Brigade on the night of April 28/29. On the 27th the 15th Battalion moved out of Allonville after leaving its nucleus in Allonville Wood and moved to Pont Noyelles, arriving there at 3.30 p.m. The following day the 13th and 14th Battalions took over the front line and the 15th and 16th went into supports. With the addition of details and reinforcements which were steadily arriving throughout this time, the Battalion had reached the strength of 57 officers and 955 other ranks. During the month two Reinforcement Officers, 2/Lieutenants F. Hohnen and G. H. Smith, joined the unit. Both were transferred the day following to the 47th Battalion. On the same day 2/Lieutenant E. G. Sellars returned from an O.C.B. course in England and was posted to "C" Company.

The Battalion remained in the support area near Villers Bretonneux until May 9. The casualties were exceptionally light, being 16 other ranks wounded. The duties had not been arduous, though much barbed wire was erected under the supervision of Captain W. Domeney who, at this time, was attached to Brigade Headquarters as Works Officer. One post which was manned by men from the 15th Battalion obtained identification during this term through a German liaison man who walked into their position by mistake.

At Blangy-Tronville, bathing in the Canal took place and this was much appreciated by all ranks. Daily batches of officers and N.C.O.'s visited the line south of Villers Bretonneux to familiarise themselves with the neighbourhood.

The Battalion moved forward again on the 14th into the support line near Villers Bretonneux, and there set to work under engineers to construct headquarters for the unit, dressing stations and generally to improve the line of trenches. The 16th Battalion took over on the right flank and a French regiment on the left. The artillery fire during this term in the line was consistently heavy and various movements of German troops were noted. On the night of the 16th the enemy aircraft were busy and bombs were dropped around Battalion Headquarters. The weather continued fine and warm. The lack of green vegetables began to have its effect here and many of the men suffered from an epidemic of boils. One young officer boasted of 72, which

necessitated his being evacuated. On May 18 the front line was taken over. On our left flank was the 13th Australian Battalion and on our right the 14th Australian Battalion, then the 2nd French Zouave Regiment. On the night of May 20 the Battalion was relieved by the 41st Battalion, and moved back to Blangy-Tronville, arriving there at 2 a.m. The casualties were: 1 killed and 8 other ranks wounded.

May 22 saw the Battalion on its way to Freschencourt, where it arrived at 4.30 p.m. Trench fever broke out in a mild form among the men at this time, and treatment for several days, sometimes within the billets, usually got them on their feet again. The first night at Freschencourt proved disastrous for "B" Company. Billetted in the village, the four subalterns of "B" Company, owing to the hot weather, were sleeping in a tent at the back. The enemy who had become very active with the bombing of the back areas by aircraft, visited Freschencourt this night and a bomb, landing at the entrance to the tent in which Lieutenants Keith Mackay, A. Kunkler, A. H. Moss and J. Grant were sleeping, exploded. Moss and Grant received injuries which proved fatal shortly afterwards. The astonishing thing about it all was that Mackay was at the entrance and escaped injury. Kunkler had a revolver in the head of his valise and part of the casing of the bomb penetrated the valise, cutting the barrel of the weapon in two, its owner escaping without a scratch. The two men furthest from the bomb received the greater force of it.

On the last day of the month the Battalion moved forward again and relieved the 55th Australian Battalion in the front line just forward of the village of Hamelet, lying in the low country outside Corbie. The Battalion was at this stage probably stronger than at any other time since Gallipoli. Its strength was 53 officers and 1009 other ranks. Four officers had been evacuated ill during the month and one officer, 2/Lieutenant Fred Stephenson, had reported back from an O.C.B. course and was drafted to "D" Company to which he had originally belonged. On the night of June 1, after the relief had been accomplished, wiring parties were sent out and trench-digging parties set to work. In charge of one of the wiring parties was Lieutenant J. Heron and, as he led his men across the open to begin operations, a machine-gun opened and Heron fell shot through the shoulder. Showery weather was encountered on the 1st of the month, but the days were warm and, as the supporting company for the time being was close to the Canal, the men spent their time swimming and thoroughly enjoying themselves. "A" and "D" Companies, under the commands of

Captains E. K. Carter and E. M. Bradley, took over the front line; "B" Company, under the command of Captain S. Porter, was in reserve, and "C" Company, under Captain R. Glasgow, in support. Directly in front of "A" and "D" Company's position was a large field of mustard, and through this "A" Company's patrols passed nightly to the road dividing the two companies that led from Hamelet to the left of Hamel village. It was through this mustard field on June 20 that Lieutenant Guy Luttrell, when on a visit to "A" Company's front, overheard a voice calling from No Man's Land and, upon making a search in company with another officer, he discovered a French soldier who had escaped from the German lines behind Hamel, where he had been held prisoner. The escape was made in broad daylight.

The same day an officer and seven other ranks from the 33rd American Division were attached to the Battalion for instruction. On the night of June 22 an "A" Company patrol, to which was attached an American officer and four N.C.O.'s, contacted an enemy listening post, a bomb from which wounded the officer. A curtain of machine-gun fire was immediately thrown round the patrol in an endeavour to entrap them. After lying quietly in shell holes for about an hour, the patrol withdrew, taking the wounded officer with them. The work done in extricating themselves from an untenable position was mainly due to the efforts of Sergeant Peter Bell and Corporal "Slogger" Richmond. On the same night 2/Lieutenant George Sellars[1], who had but recently been commissioned, lost his life. Sellars, who was in reserve, had been sent for by the Adjutant, Captain Tom Heffer, to replace Lieutenant C. C. Drane of "C" Company, who had left to have a tooth extracted. A "B" Company officer[2] had also left the line wounded on the same night. Sellars journeyed up to the line in company with Lieutenant J. M. Rae, who was replacing the "B" Company officer. Some twenty minutes after reporting to Captain Glasgow, Sellars was hit in the jugular vein by a fragment from a shell while in the company of Lieutenant Goninon. He was rushed immediately to Major Kennedy's dressing station, but he was found to be dead. Sellars' death cast a deep gloom over the unit, for he was one of the most popular N.C.O.'s in the unit.

On June 24 and 25 a fog settled over the countryside and at the approach of dawn on each day the front-line

---

(1) 2/Lieutenant G. Sellars returned from an O.C.B. course on 17th April, 1918, and on that date two Reinforcement Officers, 2/Lieutenants F. H. Hohnen and G. H. Smith, reported for duty. The two Reinforcement Officers were transferred to the 47th Battalion on the 18th April, 1918.

(2) Lieutenant Geoff. Ward.

troops vacated their trenches and moved out some fifty yards in front as a precaution against surprise attack under cover of the fog. There were more than the usual number of evacuations during this time in the line, as influenza and trench fever were rampant. A temporary hospital was dug in the embankment of the railway line adjacent to the Canal between Blangy-Tronville and Daours and camouflaged with green branches to avoid attracting the attention of aircraft. Doctor McDonald, a Queenslander, dealt with the majority of these cases, thus avoiding having to send them to the rear. Many of them recovered in the course of a few days and, after a short period in reserve, were drafted back to their companies.

The casualties during this period in the line were:— Killed—Officers 1, other ranks 11. Died of wounds—other ranks 1. Wounded—Officers 2, other ranks 34. The two officers wounded were Lieutenants J. Heron and G. Ward, the latter being hit through the muscle of the arm. On the night of the 26th the Battalion was relieved by the 52nd Australian Battalion and, passing out of the trenches, went into dugouts in the neighbourhood of the temporary hospital. Here on the 27th 2/Lieutenant C. M. Black, an original of "B" Company, returned to the Battalion from an O.C.B. course in England. On the 30th 87 reinforcements were drafted to the unit.

Preparations were now in hand for the Battle of Hamel.

◆ ◆ ◆ ◆

Capt. F. MORAN.
Died of Wounds

Capt. D. H. CANNAN.
Killed in Action.

Lieut. E. W. SIMON,
M.M. and Bar.

Major G. F. DICKINSON,
D.S.O., Russian Order of St. Stanislas,
3rd Class 'With Swords'.
Twice MID

Dvr. H. DALZIEL, V.C.

CHAPTER XIV.

THE BATTLE OF HAMEL.

The Battle of Hamel, fought on July 4, 1918, as a military operation was one of the most perfect actions of the whole war, as for the first time there was complete co-operation between infantry, artillery, tanks and aircraft—a form of co-operation the General Staff had been seeking ever since the disastrous experiment with tanks at Bullecourt during the summer of 1917.

With the exception of a few American troops employed with our battalions for instructional purposes, the attack on Hamel was an entirely Australian operation both in its design and the method of carrying it out. General Monash succeeded to the command of the Australian Corps towards the end of May, and almost immediately he and his staff set about finding a solution of the problem of Hamel. For some time it had been desired to straighten out the Hamel salient, and the capture of the ground east of the village and Vaire Wood would give better observation and would have the additional merit of depriving the Germans of this advantage. There was abundant evidence, too, that German morale was weakening under the strain of having to meet the persistent raids of the Australian infantry on their defences.

The task was allotted to the Fourth Australian Division, in the ranks of which were scattered some of the first American troops to reach France. The operation was a simple direct advance of tanks and infantry under an artillery and machine-gun barrage. Elaborate precautions were taken to ensure that it would be a complete surprise. No movement of lorries or troops was permitted during daylight hours. Nothing concerning the plan was committed to writing. The reinforcing artillery was moved into the sector under the cover of darkness into positions that had been previously prepared and camouflaged. Tanks were moved up by night, and the noise of their approach was drowned by low-flying aeroplanes. In order to further confuse the enemy, gas and smoke were used each morning for a week before the day fixed for the attack. On the actual morning of the attack the usual smoke was used, but without the gas, the result being that the German garrisons were caught with their gas-helmets on. To distract atten-

tion from Hamel itself, minor operations were undertaken north and south, and finally the Australian advance was not preceded by the usual preliminary bombardment and wire-cutting.

Everything was in readiness for 3.10 a.m. on July 4. Suddenly there opened with a crash, the fire of 326 field-guns, over 300 heavies and more than 100 Vickers machine-guns. The surprise was complete, and before the Germans knew what was happening, they saw the advancing infantry emerging from the protecting smoke-screen, almost on top of them. The 4th Brigade plan for the attack included the capture of Hamel Village and Hamel and Vaire Woods, all situated on higher ground with a spur just beyond them, and all of which overlooked the low country around Hamelet and the country on both sides of it.

The 16th Battalion objective was the capture of the two woods. The 15th Battalion was to attack on the north of the 16th and the 13th Battalion on the south of it. The 14th Battalion was the supporting Battalion to the Brigade. The 11th Brigade, with two Battalions, attacked on the left flank of the 4th Brigade and the 5th Brigade attacked on the right flank.

For the first time, the new Mark V tanks were to be used for this operation, and an air umbrella was to be formed of all aircraft available for dropping ammunition to the attacking forces and to assist in the location of enemy batteries and the direction of our own artillery fire upon the German gun positions. Phosphorus shells were also used to mark the position of the German line when the barrage fell.

Attached to the Brigade was a number of United States Army details. Two companies of the 132nd United States Infantry Regiment, part of the 33rd American Division, were divided between the companies and Headquarters sections of the Battalion, and the 131st American Regiment was split up between the 14th and 16th Battalions. There was some opposition at the time to American Regiments going into action with the Australian Brigades, but preparations were too far ahead for an alteration of plans so the Americans went into their first action in France under the direct command of Australian leaders.

On the 15th Battalion's left flank was the 43rd Australian Battalion. Here, Captain Percy Toft, with two sergeants and ten men from the 15th Battalion and two sergeants and ten men from the 43rd Battalion, acted as

liaison officer, and his duties were to keep constant touch between the two Battalions throughout the attack.

On the night of the 3rd July, the Battalion moved from its jumping off positions in two separate sections. The main force was under the command of Lieut.-Col. T. P. McSharry, and the second section, which included the Americans, was under the Battalion's Second-in-Command, Major Burford Sampson. While positions were being taken up at the starting point Captain R. B. McIntosh was wounded for the third time.

Just prior to the move forward the Battalion had been paid a visit by the then Prime Minister for Australia, the Rt. Hon. W. M. Hughes, who addressed the men shortly and wished them luck and a safe return to Australia after the final victory was won. On July 2 part of the Battalion relieved the 51st Battalion in a section of the front and support lines. The Medical Officer, Major Kennedy, who had recently arrived in the unit, and his second-in-command, Lieutenant Shramm of the 131st United States Infantry Regiment, moved forward with their personnel to Chalk Pit. The R.A.P. was in a tunnel cut into the rocks and shortly after their arrival the first four casualties were brought in—the result of gas shells which fell among two of the platoons. Indiscriminate shelling of the country through which the troops moved to the attack, continued throughout the greater part of the night. The officers commanding the four companies in the attack were:—Captain E. K. Carter, "A" Company; Captain Simon Porter, "B" Company; Captain R. B. Glasgow, "C" company; and Capt. E. M. Bradley, "D" Company.

The attack opened at 3.10 a.m. with a heavy barrage. Under cover of the noise the tanks moved out into the open. Unfortunately there were some early losses, caused by one of our guns firing short. Twelve were killed and about 30 were wounded. Lieut. Spencer, of "A" Company, collected a direct hit and died instantly. With the first lift of the barrage a heavy fire swept the first wave of advancing troops and caused a number of casualties. Pear Trench, from which the fire principally came, was one of the three main recognised obstacles, and the Battalion had been allotted three tanks to assist in its capture. There was a good deal of enfilade fire as well, which came from a nest of machine guns close to the Hamel Road. It was about this time that Dalziel won the first and only V.C. awarded to a member of the Battalion. Henry Dalziel was one of the volunteers of the Transport Company who went into the

fight to help make up the shortage of men in the unit which prevailed at this time. His company met with the most determined resistance from a body of Germans entrenched across the line of advance. It seemed that the defending troops had been little affected by the barrage, and the stubbornness of their defence threatened to hold up the whole advance. Dalziel took stock of the position, and saw that it was heavily wired. Crawling forward with a Lewis gun, he managed to get it into action from a place which afforded some measure of cover. An epic fight for mastery followed, but the accuracy of Dalziel's aim was too much for his antagonists. At one period, it was a case of three machine-guns to one, but Dalziel fought on, and little by little he overcame the resistance of his antagonists, silencing gun after gun in turn, and killing their crews. During this unequal duel he was wounded in the hand, but he continued to serve his gun, though he was losing much blood in the meantime. Having dealt with one group of German guns, he turned his attention to another gun, which suddenly opened fire from an unexpected direction. Dalziel's method of dealing with this new menace was typically Australian, and it provided a clear demonstration of the superiority of the Australian morale. He grabbed his automatic pistol and rushed the post, killing or capturing the entire crew with the few shots he had in his magazine. Needless to say he captured the gun as well. Despite his wound, Dalziel went on with the rest of the Battalion and took part in the final capture of the objective. At this stage of the fight, ammunition supplies became very low—a contingency that was partially met by dropping boxes from low-flying aeroplanes and Dalziel was not to be denied whatever remaining thrills there were to be got out of the battle. He went over open ground under a very heavy storm of rifle, machine-gun and artillery fire, and twice returned with a supply of ammunition for his Lewis gun until he was finally wounded in the head. His action contributed materially to the success of the operation and it did much to clear the way for the Battalion to achieve all that was expected of it. Finally the guns in Pear Trench were quietened by a stream of machine-gun bullets poured from Lewis-gunners firing from the hip as they advanced. This enabled the bombers to get in their work at close quarters and finally the trench surrendered.

At this stage considerable confusion prevailed. Some sections of the 16th Battalion were digging in between the first and second objectives considerably out of the position

they should have occupied. In the 15th, Captain Carter of "A" Company was a casualty, so too was Captain Porter of "B" Company. Lieutenant Jack Hynes took over command of "A" and Lieutenant Jack Rae "B" Company, but in consolidating the second objective Rae was wounded. "C" Company, under Captain Glasgow, had moved up into the central position, but the Company was not actually occupying the ground they should have held under the plan of battle. Lieutenant Toft came over from the flank to the "C" Company position just as Lieutenant Fewster moved out with a party of men to further exploit the new position. Fewster was killed as soon as he came in view of the enemy and any further exploitation in that particular direction was abandoned.

One of the stretcher-bearers, Private Shearer, who went into Pear Trench with Dr. Kennedy, says that "We rested until 10 p.m., when we moved up the winding saps to Battalion Headquarters. We waited with the infantry for two hours, and then we advanced through fields of wheat torn by shell fire and interlaced with barbed wire. Overhead, aeroplanes hummed and, before long, we heard on the morning air the reports of our bombs bursting on the village of Hamel. The crack of the enemy's flare-pistols seemed as though the users were within a stone's throw of where we lay concealed and silent. Dozens of these lights lit up the surroundings along our front and an occasional shell burst on our now deserted front line. With deafening noise, the guns poured shells upon a two-mile front, and shrapnel bursting short overhead wounded a number of our men as we moved through the wheatfield.

"At the pear-shaped trench (Pear Trench) heavy fighting held up the charge for a time. Here, in a battered dugout, were captured two large trench mortar guns and their crews. We established our Regimental Aid Post in the trench. The white chalk sides were stained with blood. The prisoners aided the stretcher-bearers bringing in the wounded. The tanks passed on and stormed the strong points near the last objective. Already aeroplanes were dropping machine-gun and rifle ammunition where the advance troops were consolidating on the ridge to the right of Hamel village. As often, tragedy and comedy met during the attack. While the sunken road was littered with dead and dying, the two doctors were having a hectic time and the stretcher-bearers were run almost off their feet. Kennedy glanced up during the rush to see where Shramm was, and found him squatted on the ground writing busily in a volume like a cheque book with his fountain pen.

" 'What the hell are you doing with that bloody pen?' he bellowed. 'Guess I'm making out my diagnosis chart!' replied the well-trained Shramm. 'Chuck the bloody book away,' snapped Kennedy to the unfortunate American medico, whose own peacetime D.M.S. had insisted that all casualties must be written up in his weird and wonderful case book. So Shramm scrapped it and set to work to give immediate attention to the wounded, minus red tape."

At this time there was a shortage in the 15th Battalion of S.B. armlets for the bearers and, in lieu of the regulation armlet a strip of ordinary white cloth lettered with indelible pencil was used, and practically every Yankee bearer wore one of these makeshifts. Sighting a Yank who wore one of them walking about doing nothing, Moles, a hard-bitten original stretcher-bearer, called to him for assistance. On his call being ignored, Moles burst into a stream of blasphemy which caused the astounded American blushing confusion. Then Moles discovered the American was not a stretcher-bearer but an officer with a wounded arm whose white band was a bandage staying haemorrhage.

The capture of Fear Trench was swiftly followed by that of Vaire Trench. The two left-hand companies, "A" and "B," were thus on their objectives. But, on the right flank, "C" and "D" Companies were held up by machine-gun fire from Hamel Wood and a strong point to their immediate front. These guns were finally dislodged by the tanks, and the two companies gained their objectives. Half an hour after, heavy formations of planes flew over the lines and continued till midday, when their control of the air was disputed by a flight of 35 German planes. During this fight some 25,000 rounds of ammunition were dropped by our planes.

The Battalion's captures in the engagement totalled 230 prisoners, two 8-inch mortars, one light mortar, 10 heavy and 45 light machine-guns, together with large numbers of rifles, ammunition, equipment and other material. Our losses were 3 officers and 32 other ranks killed, 9 other ranks died of wounds, and 6 officers with 190 other ranks were wounded. The American company with the 15th lost 13 other ranks killed, 2 officers and 44 other ranks wounded. In the 15th itself, Lieutenant J. H. T. Fraser, M.C., a Transport Officer, was killed while bringing rations forward during the night; Lieutenant W. J. Spencer was killed as already told. Lieutenant Fewster was killed after "C" Company obtained its objective and was embarking upon a minor operation. Captain E. K. Carter lost his leg. Lieutenants J. M. Rae and A. R. Kunkler were so severely wounded that they did not

return to the Battalion, and Captain Simon Porter so seriously that he died in London before the war ended. Two "D" Company Lieutenants—C. M. Black and F. Stephenson—were also casualties.

On the night of July 5, the Battalion was relieved at 2.15 a.m. by the 49th Battalion. After the relief, Major Kennedy who, in the short time he had been associated with the unit had made himself very popular, was transferred to Harefield Hospital, England. Captain Lance Hunter arrived in his place. There are many stories told regarding "Doc" Kennedy, but the manner in which he got his little wire-haired dog named Steve over to England is among the best. When Kennedy got to Boulogne he learnt that dogs were not allowed into England owing to an outbreak of rabies. As the leave boat was on the point of sailing, Kennedy gave Steve a whiff of chloroform, put him into a kit bag, and boldly walked aboard the ship. Steve woke up on English soil and during the Doctor's stay at Harefield made himself a great favourite with staff and patients alike.

* * * *

CHAPTER XV

THE BATTLE OF AUGUST 8, 1918.

The 15th Battalion moved from Querrien on August 1 and relieved the 2nd French Regiment of Zouaves in the front beyond Cachy village near Villers Bretonneux—a position better known to members of the Battalion as Hangaard Wood. The unit remained here for four days, being relieved on the night of August 4 by the 50th Battalion, A.I.F. Leaving this post, they moved to the Vaire-Sous-Corbie area and there commenced to make preparations for the great attack to be launched by the British forces on August 8.

At 4.15 on the morning of the 6th the enemy opened a fierce bombardment as a preliminary to their attack upon the 18th and 58th British Divisions north of the Somme. Their guns lashed the whole of the wooded areas along the Somme, causing considerable damage and confusion among the battalions of troops assembling or bivouacked ready for the attack. During the shelling of the 15th Battalion area a number of casualties occurred and by far the most serious of all was that of the Commanding Officer, Lieut.-Colonel T. P. McSharry. There are numerous stories as to how McSharry met his death, but the generally accepted one is that McSharry and his adjutant, Captain Tom Heffer, came out of their tents when the shelling began, to see to the well-being of the men. Finding a member of "A" Company badly wounded, the two officers obtained a stretcher and, placing the man upon it, were moving him to a place of safety when a shell landed close to the stretcher and McSharry and Heffer fell, the latter fatally wounded. Lieutenant Walter Hynes, who had replaced Lieutenant Eric Simon as Intelligence Officer only a short time before, suddenly remembered that he had left the papers relating to the plans of attack in his tent. Without realising that their recovery could easily wait till later, Hynes ran into his tent to collect them and, immediately upon reappearing at the opening of the tent, he was hit with the full face of a bursting shell. Thus, with one swoop, Colonel, Adjutant and I.O. of the Battalion were put out of action. In the whole history of the 15th Battalion no more disastrous upset to plans prior to a big attack ever took place. The loss of McSharry at this juncture was severely felt. Members of his battalion regarded him as the finest colonel in the A.I.F. Outspoken to a degree of bluntness that at times was most alarming, intermingled as it

often was with a caustic wit, he voiced his opinions in council without fear or favour, tearing to shreds any weaknesses that appeared to him apparent in any scheme of attack. His friends were innumerable, for his strong personality attracted friends and forced others into open enmity. There are hundreds of stories relating to his contempt for danger. In his carefree moments he could tell and appreciate a good joke, and it is known that in his diaries many a humorous incident is related, for he was a great collector of soldiers' tales.

In the presence of Major-General Sinclair-MacLagen, Commander of the 4th Australian Division, Brigadier-General Brand, J. M. Cannan, original Colonel of the 15th Battalion, Colonels Doust, Drake-Brockman, Marks and Crowther, the three last commanding the 16th, 13th and 14th Battalions, with staff and other officers and members of the Brigades of the 4th Division, Colonel McSharry was buried in the cemetery near Corbie at 6 o'clock on the day of his death. McSharry's funeral was a quiet one, for the men were not allowed out of the camping area to attend it. But, in the evening, small groups made their way to the cemetery to spend a few moments' contemplation at the grave which held all that remained of their much-loved Commanding Officer. These quiet pilgrimages continued until the troops left France, long after the Armistice was signed.

Colonel McSharry held the greatest number of decorations awarded to any member of the battalion, though, strictly speaking, the first award, that of the Military Cross, was earned while a member of the Light Horse. He afterwards, while Colonel of the unit, received a D.S.O. and Bar, and a C.M.G., and was awarded the Brevet rank of Major. Major Burford Sampson, Second-in-Command of the Battalion, at once assumed command of the unit. Captain Atkinson, then serving on Brigade, was brought back to act as Adjutant, and Lieutenant Eric Simon once again took over the duties of I.O. The preparations for the attack remained unaltered, and the men were given all particulars in relation to it that could be obtained.

On the night of the 6th the enemy again shelled the back areas, but the battalion suffered no losses. On the night of the 7th another bombardment of the camping areas took place and, while sweeping about with his guns, Fritz quite unintentionally set a tank alight in Orchard Wood. Concentrating upon this point, his artillery met with considerable success, and it was freely rumoured that eleven tanks had been destroyed. There is no doubt that a number of tanks were hit and others were badly burnt. It did not,

however, make any marked difference to the progress of the operation order issued for the Brigade.

At 1.30 a.m., on August 8th, the Battalion left its camping area and moved forward in the darkness to the first lining-up position just to the left of Hamel village—the left flank on the Somme Canal, and the right on the road passing from the left of Record Wood to the village of Cerisy on the river. Here the long line of men awaited the coming of dawn for the signal to advance. Although the Battalion at this time contained a large number of men whose battle experience was either very limited or none at all, its officers and N.C.Os were almost without exception veterans of the Gallipoli campaign, either having fought with the Battalion itself or with other units from which they had transferred. Major Sampson, in command, had landed on Gallipoli with the first boatload from the unit, and Sergeant Jack Fleet, of "A" Company, had stepped ashore from the same boat. Major Richardson, commanding "B" Company, was that company's original commander on Gallipoli, and Captain Glasgow, of "C" Company, had served with the Light Horse in Quinn's Post. Captain Domeney, the Tassie "A" Company commander, was another one; so, too, was Lieutenant Eric Simon. Captain Basil Atkinson, Adjutant, was an original, and Lieutenant Barwood was a Gallipoli reinforcement. Officers who took part in the 8th August advance were: Commanding Officer, Major Burford Sampson; Adjutant, Captain Basil Atkinson; Intelligence Officer, Lieutenant E. Simon; "A" Company, Captain W. Domeney, Lieutenants J. Greenwood, W. Ryan, T. P. Chataway; "B" Company, Major J. F. Richardson, Lieutenants E. Robinson, C. Barwood; "C" Company, Captain R. B. Glasgow, Lieutenants W. Goninon, L. Hocker; "D" Company, Captain E. M. Bradley, Lieutenant B. Shaw. All were in position before 3 a.m., and zero hour was timed at 4.20. Three objectives were marked out for the attack and were known as the Green, Red and Blue Lines. The Green Line ran from the Somme Canal about 1,000 yards west of Cerisy to 300 yards east of Abancourt, and the fringe of Marcel Cave. The Red Line, the 14th and 15th's objective, ran along the Somme River from Cerisy to Morcourt.

In the first stage of the attack the 11th Australian Infantry Brigade was to advance the 3,000 yards to the Red Line in front of Cerisy. At this point, the 4th Brigade was to pass through the 3rd Division in the following formation: 15th, 14th and 13th Battalions from left to right. At Morcourt the 16th Battalion was to pass through the 14th lines to Mericourt-sur-Somme, south-east of Chipilly Ridge; the 12th Brigade was to attack to the right of the 4th Brigade.

On the north side of the Somme Canal, English troops were to conform to the general advance. "D" Company, 4th Pioneer Battalion, was to operate with the 14th Battalion and also three tanks.

At 4.20 a.m. a heavy barrage fell and the 3rd Divisional men moved forward at once to attack the Green Line, capturing the position with ease. At 3.50 a.m. the 15th Battalion, conforming with the movement as laid down by Brigade, moved forward to its second forming-up position in front of Gailly Hospital. A very thick misty fog had swept up and enveloped the advancing troops, and visibility was limited to a few yards. Captain Domeney and Captain Glasgow conferred together by the aid of torch and compass to obtain their bearings. "B" Company sought their way along the Canal bank and the right flank of "A" Company had as their guide the main road leading into Cerisy. "D" Company although their left flank was touching the main road, found that their right flank was having difficulty keeping in touch with "B" Company of the 14th Battalion, under the command of Captain C. R. T. Cole. An engineering party under Lieutenant Lewis moved forward at this same juncture—a party of men who were to do excellent work when the bridge across the Somme at Cerisy was finally reached.

Four hours after zero, at 8.20 a.m., the barrage fell for the second stage of the attack, that upon the Red Line which, so far as the 15th Battalion was concerned, was the bank of the River to a point near Morcourt—the objective of the 14th Battalion. Directly opposite Cerisy was the village of Chipilly, and to its right Chipilly Spur, overlooking the low-lying country which formed the valley through which the River Somme flowed. Mericourt-Sur-Somme, also overlooking the valley, lay slightly to the right of Chipilly Spur. A sunken road passed through part of Cerisy village down to the bank of the river, and then up more steeply through the village of Chipilly. On the opposite bank of the Somme Canal the ground rose sharply from the junction of the Canal and the River, and, taking an acute turn, rose steeply to Chipilly Ridge, which ran from the left of Chipilly proper, flanking that village, which lay in the hollow, and terminating in the highest point overlooking Mericourt-sur-Somme.

From the Green Line to Cerisy Village was about 1,000 yards, and upon this line the men were lined up when, at four hours after zero, 8.20 a.m., the barrage fell for the second stage of the attack, that upon the Red Line. The whole earth seemed to be quivering with the shock of gunfire as the Battalion moved slowly forward in artillery formation toward their objective. Scouts from the 42nd Battalion

were ahead of the Battalion as they advanced, and as these scouts were encountered and passed, the position of the enemy was given to them.

Then the fog lifted and a remarkable sight confronted the advancing men. All along the right flank, and to the immediate rear, appeared nothing but advancing troops moving forward as if on parade, while dotted here and there were tanks chugging along at fixed intervals. A few shells from a worn gun in the British batteries were falling short, some of them dropping in among the "C" Company men of Lieutenant L. Hocker's platoon, but fortunately causing no damage. A German battery, presumed to be the one hidden in the side of Chipilly Ridge, landed some shells slightly in advance of the "A" Company platoon with its flank on the the River Somme, from the junction of the Somme Canal and road, but no damage was done. The men in Lieutenant J. Greenwood's platoon, close to which a tank was moving, opened out to give the tank a wide berth. Within fifty yards of the fringe of Cerisy village, the troops opened out into line formation, and a halt was made to allow the tanks to pass through. A machine-gun hidden in a house on the outskirts and to the right of the main road leading into Cersisy, opened fire upon "C" Company, and Captain Bob Glasgow was shot through the lung, Lieutenant W. Goninon taking over command. Lieutenant Hocker was wounded about this time also, and several other men were hit. Then the tank went through and, pumping shells into the house concealing the gun, brought the walls tumbling down. The gunners were seen streaking for cover down the village street. The crews of a 77 battery on the outskirts of the village had already deserted their guns, and as the order for advance was given and the men streamed into the village, large forces of the enemy could be seen on the opposite side of the river streaking for the line of trenches on the heights of Chipilly Spur.

As the men ran towards the village, keen on coming to grips with the enemy, a battery of Australian eighteen pounders galloped into action behind them and, swinging their guns into position, opened fire upon the streams of German troops covering Chipilly Spur. The 15th Battalion took its objectives with little or no opposition. In the whole history of the Battalion no easier victory had been won. Lieutenant Greenwood's platoon mopped up the dugouts on the right of the road near the bridge and occupied the river bank, while Lieutenant C. Barwood's platoon on the left flank were on the banks of the canal in the shortest time. A small island in the centre of the river was occupied by

Corporal Richmond, of 4th Platoon, and a Lewis gun crew, while other members of the same platoon led by Sergeant Peter Bell took some forty-odd prisoners from a Headquarters and Ambulance Dressing Station. The mopping up of the dugouts along the sunken road was carried out by Corporal George Williams.

On the right flank, "D" Company met with some opposition, but eventually, with the aid of a number of "A" Company men under Captain Domeney and Sergeant Fleet, the resistance was overcome and the enemy surrendered. The tank operating with this force climbed up on to the high ground to the right of Cerisy village and, swinging around a cottage, came into full view of the enemy battery hidden in Chipilly Ridge. A salvo of shells put the tank out of action just as Lieutenant Bernard Shaw led his men at the double around the front of the machine. A machine-gun burst from a gun on Chipilly Spur caught this gallant young officer and he was killed instantly. Shaw was very popular in the Battalion and his death cast a gloom over all the members of his platoon. This young Tasmanian's service with the unit was dated from the early days of Quinn's Post, where he was first hit. He had been in practically every engagement of importance in which the Battalion had taken part. Using a number of captured machine-guns, Lieutenant Greenwood's platoon, which was in the low country fringing the river in front of where Shaw was killed, brought a concentrated fire on the battery that was doing all the damage. Time and again the German gunners tried to get their guns into action, but the accuracy of the fire of Greenwood's men soon decimated their ranks and finally the surviving gunners took to flight.

Within a few minutes of the battery being silenced, a Sergeant and two men belonging to the English Regiment on the opposite bank of the river could be seen sneaking towards the battery's position. Men from our side of the river yelled encouragement to this small force, which finally arrived at the battery site and inspected the row of dead men leading from the dugouts to the guns. It was not until the arrival of the Intelligence Officer, Lieutenant Eric Simon, that the men in the 15th learnt of the heavy casualties the Englishmen had suffered and which prevented them conforming with the general plan of attack. Late that afternoon, American troops moved forward in their place and occupied the position on the opposite bank and completed the movement as originally planned.

The 15th Battalion casualties in this engagement were —one officer killed (Lieutenant B. Shaw), and seven other

ranks killed. Three officers were wounded (Captain Bob Glasgow and Lieutenant L. Hocker of "C" Company and Major Richardson of "B" Company whose place was taken by Lieutenant E. Robinson). Other ranks wounded totalled 27, and six other ranks were gassed.

The total number of prisoners captured was 350. Two 77 guns, two minnewerfers, 15 heavy machine-guns, and four light machine-guns were included in the booty. At midnight the unit was relieved and moved into support in the rear of the Red Line just outside Morcourt, to be again relieved on the night of the 10th and to move into trenches near Sailly-le-Sec.

* * * *

CHAPTER XVI

LIHU FARM AND JEANCOURT.

After their relief on the night of August 10, 1918, at a quarter past midnight, the Battalion marched to its new billets in trenches near Sailly le Sec. Throughout the march heavy shelling lashed all the roads and the neighbouring country, but fortunately without inflicting much damage. In the new billets, situated in an open field lined with hawthorn hedges, the Brigade canteen got in a supply of English beer, which was greatly welcomed, although it ran to only a quota of one small bottle per man. The number of teetotallers in the unit at this time was apparently above average, for some of the members obtained sufficient bottles to have a quiet and orderly party.

Three days later the Battalion was once more on its forward journey to the front line. Passing through Sailly le Sec, they crossed the Canal and passed through Hamel to La Motte and thence to Santerre. When skirting Bayonvillers, and when almost clear of the town, disaster overtook No. 3 Platoon of "A" Company, commanded by C.S.M. Fleet.

A big shell landed right in among the men, and nine of the platoon were killed and two wounded. Among the killed was Corporal George Williams, D.C.M., one of the youngest, if not the youngest corporal in the unit, but who at that period probably held more active front-line service in France than any other N.C.O. of his rank. Williams' fearlessness and outstanding courage on all occasions kept him in high respect throughout the unit, and his loss was keenly felt. At 10.30 p.m. the men were in billets in the sunken road lying between Bayonvillers and Lihu Farm, at no great distance from the railway. A conference was held of all senior officers and I.O.'s at which General C. H. Brand attended and gave a resume of what was expected when the line was actually occupied. A slight alteration in plans had taken place, and instead of the imminent hop-over, a series of silent preparations, which had at this time become the vogue, was contemplated.

The Battalion was still under the command of the Tasmanian, Major Burford Sampson, and three of the company commanders at this period were from the "tight little isle" also. They were Captain W. Domeney, of "A" Company, Lieutenant W. Goninon, of "C" Company, and Lieutenant C. W. Goss, of "D" Company. Two of these, Lieutenants Gon-

inon and Goss, were original members of the Tasmanian section of the 15th Battalion. Captain W. L. Domeney was a Gallipoli reinforcement from Tasmania. Lieutenant J. L. Dryborough, a Townsville man, was the sole Queenslander in command of a company. He had "B" Company. The Second-in-Command of the unit was Captain B. Atkinson, who was an Englishman, and the Adjutant was Lieutenant Eric Robinson, better known as "Bags." Lieutenant Maurice Cook was the Signalling Officer.

The relief of the 2nd Battalion at Lihu Farm was completed at five minutes past midnight on the 16th August, 1918, with only one casualty, and that man slightly wounded. Throughout the whole movement the enemy shelled Crepy Wood and its environs, but without doing any material damage to the advancing men. "B" Company took over the left sector of the Battalion front—about one hundred yards —and pushing out patrols connected with the 13th Battalion on the left flank. "A" Company, doing likewise, joined forces with the 46th Battalion on the right flank. The 46th Battalion at this time was commanded by Lieut.-Colonel J. J. Corrigan, whose rise from a private to a Colonel constituted the record achievement for any member of the Battalion. "C" Company passed into the support line, and "D" Company took over the Reserve Line.

On the night of the 17th August the front-line companies moved forward on a silent penetration manoeuvre and occupied a new set of trenches slightly in advance of the old French Line. The weather had remained fine throughout this period and enemy shelling, though at times heavy on supports and reserves, was light compared with many previous actions in which the Battalion had taken part. Battalion Headquarters situated on the fringe of the road, became the target for much of the shelling that took place, and Lieutenant M. Cook was slightly wounded. That same afternoon an astonishing mishap overtook part of an American force, whose cookers had arrived and planted themselves in the wooded hollow directly across the road from Battalion H.Q. adjacent to the first-aid post commanded by Captain Lance Hunter. Warned over and over again of the danger of the thick clouds of smoke arising from the cookers, several of the Americans thought they would climb nearby trees and a telephone pole, to see how far distant the front line lay. When the enemy opened on the cookers, a direct hit was scored on a full dixie of boiling stew. Several men were badly scalded and a number wounded, all being treated by Captain Hunter and his staff. Those up the trees and the telephone pole were amazed to see a direct hit on the base of

the pole and an American clinging frantically to half a dozen wires as the pole bounced about like a bucking horse. Cut and bleeding, the man was finally hurled to the ground and, semi-conscious, was borne off to receive first-aid.

One of the strongest drinks ever captured from the Hun was secured by the men from a German canteen secreted in the wood. This potent brew was commonly known as "Green Kummel." It was rumoured that German troops at the time of the big advance at the commencement of the year had been freely issued with this firewater so that they would face the prospect of heavy casualties with all the patriotic fanaticism that had been noticeable among them at the beginning of the war. If this were true, methylated spirits and boot polish is fruit cocktail by comparison.

Lieutenant "Sarky" Englert, reported with some reinforcements on the night of 21st August, and was posted to "C" Company, proceeding up to the front line immediately Englert was to become one of the Rugby football team members and made quite a name for himself as a player.

News that the Battalion would be relieved somewhere about the 27th August was brought in person by General Brand on a routine visit to the front line system. It took place slightly earlier on the night of 24/25th August.

Nothing approaching this relief had ever been experienced by the majority of the men in the unit. The few old hands of the Pozieres, Mouquet Farm, Messines and Polygon Wood sectors looked upon it as one of those queer misfortunes that—for no apparent reason whatsoever—just happen to a Battalion on active service. The 1st and 2nd Battalions of the 59th French Infantry Regiment were the relieving force. The 1st Battalion relieving the two 15th Battalion front-line companies, "D" and "C," and the 2nd French Battalion relieving the 15th Battalion's "A" and "B" Companies. It is doubtful whether the enemy had any knowledge that a relief was imminent, though for five hours Fritz laid down a heavy barrage of gas and H.E. shells, covering all saps into the front line, and support and reserve lines, besides lashing the roadway from Battalion H.Q. to the disused German hospital on the roal to Allonville.

At the meeting place of the 15th Battalion guides and the French relieving columns, the trouble started when a German H.E. shell landed directly in the roadway just as the parties met. A number of casualties occurred among both parties. From then onwards the French force was led through an ever-increasing hail of shell to their various positions in the trenches, our men marching out in good formation when relieved.

The gas used is stated to have been Yellow and Blue Cross, the former being better known as "Mustard Gas." It was stated by many who experienced it that much was dispensed from a shell which burst in the air and sprayed the gas in liquid form over everything and everybody within range. Many of the men began to feel itchy skin beneath their clothing, and about the neck and wrists. All exposed parts were quickly covered and everything possible was done to prevent any gas touching the skin. One of the first casualties was Lieutenant W. Ryan, who was hit by the nose cap of a gas shell near the hip. Of the other officers in the line, those gassed included Lieutenant Wes. Goninon. When leading "C" Company out, his men came under heavy shell fire and a piece of shell destroyed his runner's helmet. Goninon changed helmets and finished the journey without any protection. Captain W. Domeney was also gassed along with his two subalterns, Lieutenants Eric Simon and Jim Greenwood.

Buses were waiting in the neighbourhood of Battalion H.Q. to take the unit direct to billets in Allonville. This was much appreciated by the men, but it proved only a doubtful blessing. Within the crowded buses the gas put in the major part of its deadly work. The heat of the men's bodies seemed to generate the vapour until over fifty per cent. of those travelling were affected in some form or other. It is realised now that had the unit marched, as was so often the case in the early days, much heavy loss of men might have been averted, for the gas on boots and clothing would have been distributed into the air and blown away by the breeze.

The 46th Australian Battalion relieved the same night also suffered heavily from gas, while the relieving French units lost nearly 70 per cent. of their personnel. It was a very subdued unit for several days following its return to Allonville. The next day men twisted in agony or completely blind—for the time being—lay all over the village, many dropped in their tracks on the footpath or in the gutter, and others lay on the roadway. A willing crowd of helpers brought these men into the First Aid Post, and Dr. Hunter, after doing what he could in the emergency, despatched them as rapidly as he could to the hospitals.

Reinforcements and details arrived with the unit at this juncture and, by August 27 it had rebuilt its strength to 17 officers and 480 other ranks. From this number eight officers and 94 other ranks were detached for other duties of a routine nature. In the interim a Court of Inquiry was held into the reason for the large number of casualties in the 15th and 46th Battalions. The result of this inquiry completely exonerated anyone from blame.

Sports were held at Allonville and several very fine Rugby football matches were played. The fiercest and most exciting match was between the two Rugby States—New South Wales 13th Battalion and Queensland 15th Battalion. Foremost among the officer players were Lieutenants J. Hynes, Eric Voss, F. J. Merrill, B. R. Willcox, K. Mackay and "Sarky" Englert, and among the N.C.O.'s were C.S.M. Jack Fleet, Sergeant P. Bell, Sergeant "Slogger" Richmond, Patterson, "Wally" Stone, Cox, Cunningham, J. Clancy, R. Pringle, Ferguson, McKeiver, George Swepson, "Snowy" Bowers and "Togo" Lyons. The Australian Soccer team belonging to the Battalion and consisting of practically all Tasmanians, won the cup given for the teams competing in this code of rules.

The Battalion left Allonville on September 8, 1918, arriving at Biaches on the same day. A nucleus of 64 other ranks under the command of Captain Richards was posted to the Brigade Camp at Corbie. The Transport, under the command of Lieutenant Peter Ohlsen, arrived at Biaches two hours later than the main body, but in ample time to allow the men to sort things out and set to work and make themselves reasonably comfortable in the ruins of the town.

The following day a party of officers and N.C.O.'s went forward to look at a series of trenches in the near neighbourhood of Bouvincourt, into which the unit moved that night. The 16th Battalion occupied the left flank and the 13th Battalion the right flank; the 14th Battalion was in reserve.

The Rt. Hon. W. M. Hughes, accompanied by General Maclagen, paid the Battalion another visit on September 15. He delivered a short address to the men and passed on. During the month of August a number of men, all of whom were N.C.O.'s in the Battalion, were promoted to commissioned rank. During this month officers from other units and reinforcement officers arrived. The first of these to join the unit were 2/Lieutenants H. F. Stitz, on the 27th August; F. R. Mudge, C. M. Brook, D.C.M. (original members of the Battalion), J. H. Jamieson, F. N. Livingstone, G. F. Masterton, all of whom arrived on September 13. On this day the following N.C.O.'s with the Battalion were promoted: H. J. Bowers, W. H. Stone, R. Strangman-Taylor, T. J. Smith, G. Jamieson, and A. W. F. G. Crow, better known as "Goddy" Crow. This officer's promotion dated from August 20. Crow and Bowers were both original members of the Battalion. At this juncture, the Battalion was probably stronger in officers than at any previous time in its history.

JEANCOURT.

What is familiarly known as the battle of Jeancourt to members of the 15th Battalion is officially known as the fight for the outposts of the Hindenburg Line. It took place on September 18, 1918. This was the Battalion's last engagement. Three Divisions took part in the battle—the 1st and 4th Australian Divisions with the 1st British Division on the right flank. Part of a French Division and units of the 3rd British Army were also involved.

The forming up line for the 4th Division lay just forward of the two villages of Jeancourt and Vendelles, and for the 1st Australian Division from the left of Jeancourt to the left of Hesbecourt, the front for each Division being about 3,000 yards. As in the previous engagements, each objective was known by a colour, the first in this instance being the Brown Line, east of Le Verquier, which village was the objective of the 16th Battalion.

The 15th and 13th Battalions were given the task of flanking the village and consolidating on the Brown Line. The 16th Battalion at this point was to take over the Brown Line from the two sister battalions, which in their turn passed on to the second objective, the Red Line, approximately 2,000 yards further east to the edge of Ascension Wood. Upon these two first objectives being gained, the 14th Battalion was to pass through the Red Line and exploit the movement to its fullest advantage, about another 2,000 yards to the Blue Line.

Three tanks were re-allotted to the 4th Brigade, but they were restricted in their operations beyond the Brown Line. Mobile Field Artillery and Heavy Artillery co-operated. Four machine-guns from the 4th Machine-Gun Company were allotted to the 13th, 14th and 15th Battalions. Six mortars from the 4th A.L.T.M., two being posted to each of the attacking battalions, operated with the three units so far as the Red Line, after which the six guns were to proceed with the 14th Battalion to the final objective—the Blue Line. At this point they were to remain with the 14th Battalion, giving what support they could during that Battalion's consolidation of the position.

The 13th Australian Infantry Brigade, which was holding the line, was relieved by the 4th Australian Infantry Brigade on the night of the 16/17th September, the relief being completed at 11.50 p.m.

The strength of the Battalion at this juncture was 21 officers and 311 other ranks in the line, one officer and 78 other ranks left at the Transport Lines, and 9 officers and 51 other ranks left with the nucleus. With the small force of

men actually going into the fight, quite a number of original members of the Battalion, some of whom had returned from hospital, went into action. In "A" Company, with Captain Jack Hynes, an original, commanding, there were C.S.M. Jack Fleet, Corporal Gordon Smith and some others, while in "B" Company was Lieutenant "Goddy" Crow, in "C" Company Sergeant Bob Hunter and Lieutenant Wes. Goninon, and in "D" Company Lieutenant Goss.

"B" Company, under the command of Captain Josh Francis, who had returned to the unit after his wound at Hebuterne, took over the front line from the 49th Battalion. "C" Company, under the command of Lieutenant Wes. Goninon, relieved the supports company, and "A" and "D" Companies, commanded by Captains Jack Hynes and E. M. Bradley, took over the Reserve Line along the Railway Embankment. In command of the Battalion was Major Burford Sampson, with Lieutenant Eric Robinson as his Adjutant and Lieutenant Jeff. Ward as I.O.

The Battalion had settled down for the night in their new possies, when Lieut.-Colonel C. M. Johnston reported in from the 45th Battalion and assumed command from Major Sampson. Johnston, who was the third officer holding the rank of Lieut.-Colonel to command the Battalion, had been absent from the unit for over two years. He served for a considerable time on Brigade Headquarters as Brigade Major, and prior to his being in command of the 45th Battalion, he had held a temporary command of the Victorian 14th Battalion. It was very unfortunate for the Tasmanian officer that he should have lost the command of the Battalion for what proved to be the last action in which it was to participate during the war, but he had the consolation of knowing that he had commanded it in the most successful action—the engagement of the 8th August, 1918—in which the unit had taken part.

At 2 p.m. and 8 p.m., on September 17th, watches were synchronised at Brigade Headquarters, and zero hour for the following morning—5.20—given out. The 16th Battalion was on the 15th Battalion's right flank and the 12th Battalion of the 3rd Australian Infantry Brigade the left. A creeping barrage was to be used for the first two objectives after which mobile artillery would take up the role of covering fire. There was little shelling by the enemy this night.

Rain had fallen during the relief on the 16th and on the 17th also, and the morning of the 18th proved a dull, dreary and dismal one as the men assembled at the jumping off tape preparatory to the charge.

The barrage fell at zero-hour and, excepting for a few

shorts, proved an excellent one. The 16th Battalion attacked and mopped up le Verquier in a very short time, capturing no fewer than 450 prisoners. The 13th and 15th Battalions, following closely on the barrage, captured the Red Line by 9.35 a.m. A number of prisoners was captured, the majority of whom were passed through the 3rd Australian Infantry Brigade Area direct to the P.O.W. camps.

Owing to the greasy nature of the country, the tanks again proved ineffective, and failed to arrive at the starting point. Dummy tanks of all descriptions were used in the engagement, and these models were moved into various positions with the idea of misleading the enemy, which no doubt they did do quite successfully.

The number of prisoners falling into the 15th Battalion's hands during the engagement will never be known, but to "B" Company fell a German H.Q. Major and some 80 other ranks. These men were overlooking a position quite unaware that the Australians were so close to them, when Lieutenant "Goddy" Crow of "B" Company and his orderly, Private Musson, noticed them in the early hours of the morning and immediately rounded them up. The Sergeant-Major with the German officer was very upset over his capture, for having served throughout the war he was on the point of receiving his commission in the German Imperial Army—no mean feat for a ranker. His capture by the Australians lost him this honour. Lieutenant Crow said he had never before seen a man so crestfallen. Lieutenants Mackay and Crow consolidated this position and made everything secure for the incoming troops, who were to relieve them in the course of forty-eight hours.

No figures are given as to the actual number of prisoners captured by each Battalion in the Brigade, but the 4th Brigade's total was 49 officers and 1088 other ranks. Over 250 of enemy dead were counted upon the field.

There was at the time of this engagement a number of original members of the unit ready to leave upon long service leave to Australia. These men, unfortunately for some of them, had not been withdrawn from the line in a body. Some of them actually refused to be withdrawn to proceed on their leave, claiming that they preferred to continue serving with the unit. Among these was Corporal Gordon Smith, whose service with the Battalion as a runner and an N.C.O. had embraced practically every major engagement in which the unit had participated. Smith remained with the unit and was one of seven killed by a stray shell that landed among them just prior to their leaving the line.

Also among the number was C.S.M. Jack Fleet, who was

told that he had been specially selected for a trip home. But Fleet could not be persuaded to go, especially as he discovered that the period away would be mainly taken up with transport duty with only a week or ten days in his own State. The spirit of Jack Fleet on this occasion, as on a later occasion when he likewise declined to avail himself of 1914 leave, reflected that which animated most of all of the members of the Battalion, who figured that as they had seen the thing through so far with so much fighting and suffering in company, they would prefer to see it through to the end and to be in at the finish.

Another survivor of the original Battalion was C.S.M. "Andy" Skinner, who was also waiting about this time to go on 1914 leave but who preferred to remain with the unit to see it all out. He won the Military Medal at this, the last operation in France in which the Battalion took part. He had already won the D.C.M. at Mouquet Farm on the Somme in 1916. The determination of "Andy" Skinner at that time to see the business through to the bitter end was reflected in his determination to fight again in World War II. He achieved the unique distinction of being the only member of the original 15th to serve with the 2/15th Battalion (A.I.F.) to fight at Tobruk in the Libyan campaign, Syria, and later on with an administrative unit in New Guinea. He had then become a Captain.

A number of decorations were given for this engagement, including a D.S.O. to Captain Jack Hynes, and an M.C. to Lieutenant C. C. Drane of "C" Company.

On the night of September 22, the 4th Brigade was relieved, less the 15th Battalion which, from 10 p.m. that night, came under the administration of the 3rd Brigade.

The weather still remained unsettled, and the following day guides were sent out to meet the incoming Americans, who took over from 1 Platoon of "D" Company, two platoons from "A" Company and one platoon from "C" Company. It was during this take-over that "D" Company captured a German Staff Major and his orderly. As many papers of value were found intact upon these two men, they were transferred immediately to 3rd Brigade Headquarters for questioning. It was not until five minutes past one on September 24 that the relief was completed and the Battalion moved to Tincourt, going into billets in trenches at this point. The transport meanwhile had moved to Bouvincourt. On September 26 the 15th Battalion entrained at Tincourt at 8.30 a.m. and arrived at Longpre at 4.15 p.m. and marched to billets at Crouy two and a half hours later.

CHAPTER XVII

VICTORY AND HOME.

After the battles on the Hindenburg Out-Post Line the War hastened to its conclusion.

Most of the fight had now gone out of the German infantry, and the combined thrusts of the Allied Armies during September and October on the Western, Austrian, Bulgarian and Turkish Fronts soon brought the end in sight.

The clear evidence of the German decline on the Western Front, and Haig's determination that he would break the Hindenburg Line where the German reserves were thickest, persuaded Foch to seek victory during the autumn of 1918 instead of postponing the attempt until the spring of 1919.

On September 15, the Allied Armies attacked the Bulgarians on the Salonika Front, which crumbled in a few days.

Towards the end of September, the combined assaults of the Allied Armies fell on the Western Front and the line threatened to crack.

At about this time the German Supreme Command completely lost its nerve, and there came the first indications of the German anxiety for an Armistice.

By October 5, the British forces were through the strongest section of the Hindenburg Line and they faced the open country beyond.

Meanwhile, Allenby had struck at the Turks in Palestine, and his mounted divisions raced towards Damascus and Aleppo. Turkey capitulated on October 30.

In the first week of the same month the A.I.F. had fought its last battle in France at Montbrehain, which the Australian Official Historian, Dr. C. E. W. Bean, described as "one of the most brilliant actions of Australian infantry in the First World War."

By the end of October, the Austrian Army was split in two by a series of brilliant strokes on the Adriatic plain, where retreat became a rout, and Austria asked for an Armistice, which was signed on November 4.

With this wholesale desertion of Germany's Allies, the curtain began to fall on the Western Front.

At 11 o'clock on the morning of November 11, the World War came to an end.

The Armistice was signed in Foch's railway carriage in the Forest of Compiegne at 5 a.m.

The 15th Battalion was still at Crouy when the momentous news was flashed across the world.

The Battalion diarist naively records the event in these words: "The news was taken very quietly by the men, but the civilians were more demonstrative.

"In honour of the great event, bells were rung, flares were fired, and flags were displayed throughout the village, and the Battalion band played inspiring music in the village square.

"The ladies of the neighbourhood presented numerous bouquets and flower pots to the C.O. for the Battalion, and in the evening, an Officers' dinner was held, at which the matron and three sisters of the A.G.H. were present.

"On November 15, an exchange of flags between the Battalion and the inhabitants of Crouy took place to commemorate the signing of the Armistice and of our stay there. A very fine tricolour was given to the Battalion."

The men now looked earnestly forward to their return to Australia. Since their last fight at Jeancourt, the rest at Crouy and the exhilirating stimulus of inter-Company and inter-Battalion football matches, brought about a marked change in the outlook of all ranks.

During this period, the Battalion outshone itself on the football field, beating the 13th Battalion by 14 to nil, the 4th Field by 23 to 3 and the 13th Battalion again on October 25 by 8 to 6 which gave the 15th the Cup. On the following day the Battalion beat the 14th Battalion at soccer.

The Battalion left Crouy on November 14. A few days later, at Fresnoy-le-Grand, it was unofficially learned that the Brigade would form part of the Army of Occupation for a time, and that the Battalion was destined for Cologne.

The men were greatly thrilled at the prospect of going into Germany, but a few days later, at Sains, they were sadly disillusioned by the arrival of a number of British troops which were stated to have just come from England and who were reported to be going to Cologne instead.

There was considerable bitterness at the prospect of being done out of what the men so eagerly looked forward to—a trip into Germany to enable them to treat the Germans in a manner in keeping with their own treatment of the inhabitants of the French and Belgian villages during the years of the German occupation.

At about this time the ration situation was most un-

satisfactory and the men were getting worse and less food than at any period during the years of fighting.

Matters were not improved with irritating parades, during which most of the time was spent in learning to salute. With the approach of the cold weather in December conditions became almost intolerable and in the hope of relieving the situation an extra pay was arranged, but as there was no food to buy, things went from bad to worse, so bad indeed that on December 4, after the Battalion had gone on strike, Brigadier Drake-Brockman came down to the billets at Sains and ordered everybody out on parade.

The companies were quartered on the floors of a building which had been used by the Germans as an Auxiliary Hospital, but the men refused to leave their billets. When ordered to fall in, they hung out of the windows and told the Brigadier if he had anything to say he had better say it to them from where he stood in the lane. "What do you think you are going to do to fill in time while waiting to be repatriated to Australia," asked the Brigadier. "Play two-up," chorused the men. And that ended that. Brigadier Drake-Brockman then left, and sensing that there might be serious developments if the food question was not satisfactorily solved, he made immediate arrangements for a supply of rations to be sent down to the Battalion. When it arrived the men got at least one decent meal, but they were not persuaded to go on parade until they saw what the morrow would be like.

By way of a diversion, the Command arranged a competition in which the best dressed guard was granted an exemption from duty. This scheme caused no little amusement to the Battalion and inhabitants alike and as the men had more money than there was food to buy they were able to turn the competition into a money spinner by running a sweepstakes on the winner.

Towards Christmas, the Battalion moved over the Belgian border to Philippeville. Xmas Eve brought a surprise visit from Edward, Prince of Wales, which caused no little amusement in the hunt for those who mattered, as the Prince rode quite unexpectedly into the billets and none of the senior officers could be found until after a thorough search in every corner of the village.

With the approach of February, the men began to leave for England, and home, those with the longest service being sent away first, beginning with the originals who had embarked with the Battalion in 1914.

Original men from all over the place began to drift back to the unit for the purpose of joining drafts being sent back.

Lieutenant W. Murdoch, promoted a captain while a prisoner of war in Germany, found his way back to the unit for a few days.

Those members of the Battalion in London, or convalescing in Wandsworth and other hospitals, gave a dinner to a large number of prisoners of war who returned in a bunch to that city.

After touching farewells between the men who went on early draft home and those who anxiously waited their turn in Belgium and England, the Battalion strength began to dwindle, until towards the end of 1919 the last batch returned to Australia, to pass with their comrades into history, whose glory rises, "as it will always rise, above the mists of ages, a monument to great-hearted men; and, for their nation, a possession for ever."

CHAPTER XVIII.

POSTSCRIPT.

With such a magnificent tradition set up on the bloody fields of Gallipoli, France and Flanders, it was inevitable that the surviving members of the Battalion should set about perpetuating the great name the unit had earned during the fateful years of the First World War.

Eventually what came to be known as the Angels Remembrance Club, 15th Battalion, A.I.F., came into being. That was in 1935. Already, the world was heading for another cataclysm, although perhaps few people were ready to admit it at the time.

The men of the old 15th felt that it was a duty they owed to the men who had died so nobly to perpetuate not only their memory, but the tradition the Battalion had so gallantly established.

The primary objects of the Angels Remembrance Club are fittingly set out as follows:—

(a) To perpetuate the traditions of the 15th Battalion, A.I.F.

(b) To perpetuate the memory of deceased comrades, and

(c) To promote good fellowship amongst surviving members of the Battalion, and ex-members of other units for whom specified provision is made for membership of the club.

Before World War II. set the nations of the earth at each other's throats again, the Angels Remembrance Club maintained a close relation with the 15th Militia Battalion, Commonwealth Military Forces, and its members did much to help and encourage the new generation to understand the meaning of war and the necessity for preserving the spirit of the old A.I.F., which had evoked the admiration of peoples the world over. One of the first things the Club did to promote this spirit of comradeship with the sister militia unit was to present it with two cups, one for military efficiency and the other for sports to be competed for annually by the militia companies.

When Great Britain again declared war on Germany in September, 1939, the 2/15th Battalion A.I.F. came into being, and after the appointment of its Commanding Officer, Lieut.-Colonel "Spike" Marlan, first to enlist with the new unit was

an old member of the 1/15th, Captain "Andy" Skinner, who had fought through with the old battalion from Gallipoli to the signing of the Armistice on November 11, 1918. In the first World War Captain Skinner won the D.C.M. and the M.M., and in between the two wars curiously enough he served in the Permanent Forces as Area Officer to the 15th Militia Battalion. This association did much to help the Militia unit to realise what a fine formation the parent body had been.

Captain Skinner, by the way, carried the name of the old unit with him when he went to England in 1937 as a member of the Coronation Contingent to attend the crowning of King George VI. The name of the unit also went with him when he represented Queensland in the final of the King's shoot in Sydney and Melbourne.

One of Colonel Marlan's first acts after the formation of the 2/15th was to invite members of the Angels Remembrance Club to a ceremonial parade prior to the Battalion's departure for Port Darwin. On that afternoon there was formed the 2/15th Welfare Club, which, during the period of the last war, raised the best part of £6,000 for the benefit of the members of the Battalion and their relations. This fund was administered by a committee, consisting largely of women, under the able chairmanship of Mr. H. M. Witham, himself an old soldier, of the 1/41st Battalion, and a man who had become peculiarly linked with the old 15th Battalion through his marriage to Dr. Luther's widow. It will be recalled that Dr. Luther was the old Battalion's first M.O. He was killed on Gallipoli on August 25, 1915. His son served with the 2/15th during the second war.

Since the end of World War II., in which the 2/15th fought in the Middle East and in the South-West Pacific, and the 15th Battalion, C.M.F. in New Guinea and the Solomons, the three units have become so linked that each regards the whole as constituting a 15th Regiment. Every year services are held on Anzac Day and Armistice, or Remembrance Day, and members from all three formations attend at the crypt in Anzac Square, where there is a plaque, unveiled by Major General Cannan, the original Commanding Officer of the 1/15th in 1932, to the memory of fallen comrades. Incidentally two original members of the old Battalion came all the way from Tasmania to be present at the unveiling—Sergt.-Major Tom Turner and J. Dwyer.

The old Battalion, of course, marches in the annual Anzac parade. It is led by the President of the Angels Re-

membrance Club, irrespective of what rank he held during the first war or has held since. The Battalion's only V.C., Harry Dalziel, carries the flag, and members of the committee the banner.

Throughout the year the Club performs a regular round of duties to those of its members who are constantly passing on with the wearying of age to join their comrades of the battlefields. Funerals are arranged and attended with suitable honours and the sounding of the Last Post at the graveside.

Q.M. AND STAFF, 15th BATTALION, PHILLIPEVILLE, BELGIUM.

Pte. ADAM MILLER.

Cpl. H. D. ANDERSON.
Killed in Action.

15th BATTALION, A.I.F., 1914-18, ANZAC DAY MARCH, BRISBANE, 25th APRIL, 1945.

NOMINAL ROLL

of

Members of the 15th Battalion

Australian Imperial Forces

Showing only those who were actually
"Taken on Strength" of Unit.

WAR 1914-1918

LIST OF MEMBERS

No.	Name	No.	Name
5646	ABBOTT, John Charles	3322	ALLEN, Fursden Joseph
1155	ABEL, Arthur Edward	7743	ALLEN, James
6214	ABEL, John Llewelyn	3465	ALLEN, Norman Henry
6121	ABELL, Nugent Edward	3229	ALLEN, Thomas Fagan
2722	ABERY, Griffiths	3027	ALLEN, Wilfred George
401	ABRAHAM, Gilbert Harry	2721	ALLEN, William John
3113	ABRAHAM, Jabez	1303B	ALLEN, William Templeton
6456	ABURROW, Sydney Charles	7195	ALLENBY, John Thomas Harwood
402	ADAM, Charles Robert	1826	ALLEN-WATERS, Kenneth Charles Henry
2721	ADAM, William Watson		
714	ADAMS, Albert Ernest	3028	ALLISON, Robert Knox
325	ADAMS, Alexander Andrew	565	ALIKIN, Samuel
77	ADAMS, Clarence	1	ALLOM, John Norman
2496	ADAMS, Harcourt	1002	ALLOM, Owen Bertram
2551	ADAMS, Herbert	1152	ALLWRIGHT, Sydney Thomas
2101	ADAMS, John	3	ALNE, Carl
31	ADAMS, John Henry	5810	ALSBURY, David Alson
2665	ADAMS, Percy Robert Woodland	101	ALSOP, John
3686	ADAMS, Ralph Wilfred	6479	AMOS, Charles Henry
253	ADAMS, Sydney James	4359	ANDERSEN, Jacob Nielsen
1866	ADAMS, Thomas Charles	1451	ANDERSEN, John Martin
3443	ADAMS, Thomas Frederick	6458	ANDERSON, Albert William
642	ADAMS, William	6704	ANDERSON, Allan
2326	ADEN, Alexander	2102	ANDERSON, Bernard Joseph
2332	AGNEW, William	2380	ANDERSON, Claude
870	AGUTTER, Frederick	2328A	ANDERSON, Franklin
2382	AHERN, Francis Daniel	566	ANDERSON, Frederick Alexander
6703	AHERN, John Lindsay		
6457	AHERN, William Henry	1154	ANDERSON, George
1637	AHERNE, Reginald Percy	5975	ANDERSON, Harold Dean
2723	AIKEN, Norman	3029	ANDERSON, James
7193	AINSWORTH, Albert Irvine	7683A	ANDERSON, Joseph Lewis Gordon
4730	AIREY, Stanley Thomas		
1454	AITKEN, John	Lieut	ANDERSON, Kenneth Henry
4245	AITKEN, Robert	6868	ANDERSON, Peter Christian Sidney
3466	ALBION, Percy Miles		
3227	ALBURY, David William	1301A	ANDERSON, Thomas Gray
715	ALCOCK, Alfred John	2330	ANDERSON, Thomas James
3677	ALCOCK, Frederick Charles	2714	ANDERSON, Walter Edward
2552	ALCORN, Douglas John	254	ANDERSON, Walter Henry
1909	ALDERSON, Fairburn	7196	ANDERSON, Walter William
3174	ALEXANDER, Archibald Edgar	2103	ANDERSON, Wilfred John
3572	ALEXANDER, Frederick Bert	713	ANDERSON, William
1001	ALEXANDER, Harry	251	ANDREW, William
1851	ALEXANDER, John	6461	ANDREWS, Alfred Charles
564	ALEXANDER, Thomas	2554	ANDREWS, Arthur George
5259	ALFRED, Francis	3034	ANDREWS, David Lloyd
869	ALLAN, Jacob	403	ANDREWS, Edward
7822A	ALLARD, John Hayward	3030	ANDREWS, Edward Cecil
7681A	ALLASON, Sidney Ernest	1794	ANDEWRS, Frederic Colin
5255	ALLEN, Francis William	2051	ANDREWS, Roydon

HISTORY OF THE 15th BATTALION

No.	Name	No.	Name
2497	ANDREWS, Stephen	3475	AVENELL, Charles Norman Roy
6610	ANDREWS, Walter Ernest	2949	AVERY, David Robert
1301	ANSON, Edward	867	AVERY, Harold McLean
6931	ANSTIS, Claud Clement Godfrey	2860	AVERY, Norman Leo
		1153	AYERS, William Bruce
6385	ANTHONY, William	4731	AYLING, Edwin Thomas
3571	APPLEBEE, Leonard John	6708	AYLMER, Francis Alfred
3031	ARBERY, William John	3234	BACH, Phillip
7194	ARBUCKLE, Archibald	406	BACK, Herbert Stanley
1156	ARCHER, Alfred George	1781	BADKIN, John James
765	ARCHER, Francis Sydney	5031	BAGLEY, Arthur Alexander
567	ACHIBALD, William	2114	BAGLEY, Frank Wallis
4732	ARDIL, Leonard Pitt	7444	BAGSTER, William Henry
3230	ARGO, William	2889	BAILES, Harold Percy
7769	ARLETT, George	6947	BAILEY, Albert Lyall
2673	ARMITAGE, Henry Alfred	6468	BAILEY, Angus Joseph
10	ARMITAGE, Jack Wilfred	6467	BAILEY, Bertram Sydney Harold
1676	ARMITAGE, James		
5978	ARMSTRONG, Alton	3685	BAILEY, Eric Charles Rees
1003	ARMSTRONG, Charles	255	BAILEY, Michael James
Lieut	ARMSTRONG, Francis Leofric	1722	BAILEY, William
2/Lieut	ARMSTRONG, Hutton Perkins	1901	BAILEY, William
568	ARMSTRONG, James	Lieut	BAILLIE, Gavin Richmond
5817	ARNEY, Richard William	7776	BAILLIE, James
2/Lieut	ARNOLD, Ralph Irving	3237	BAIN, Robert Irwin
2084	ARNOLD, Reginald Joseph	7685A	BAIRD, Norman
1377	ARNOTT, James Allan		BAIRD, Roderick William (Served As)
3680	ARUNDELL, William Joseph		
103	ASHFORD, Leonard Joseph	3463	ZIELMAN, Roderick William
3002	ASHLEY, John	407	BAK, James Jensen
4428	ASHWIN, William	367	BAKER, Arthur Alexander
868	ASHWOOD, Harold	1304A	BAKER, Arthur John
3231	ASHWORTH, William Arthur	338	BAKER, Bert Henry
3679	ASPERY, Bertie Stanley	7744	BAKER, Carl John
6459	ASPERY, Percy Clarence	1305	BAKER, Claude Herbert
3681	ATHERTON, John	2822	BAKER, Daniel Henry
3683	ATHORN, Harold Ernest	4741	BAKER, Elver Cuthbert
3678	ATKINS, Arthur Frederick	2821	BAKER, Elwin Raymond
2948	ATKINS, Frederick John	5049	BAKER, Francis Shedrick
6221	ATKINSON, Alfred	3701	BAKER, Frank
Capt	ATKINSON, Basil Spence	408	BAKER, Frederick
6707	ATKINSON, Edward Hyles	3574	BAKER, George Albert
1378	ATKINSON, Leslie	4753	BAKER, Henry Kohlhoff
6481	ATKINSON, Thomas	7208	BAKER, John Joseph
1151	ATKINSON, Thomas Christopher	7206	BAKER, Terrence James
		Hon/Lieut	BAKER, Thomas George
252	ATKINSON, William Leslie	1164	BAKER, Thomas Vincent
1453	ATTEWELL, Arthur Harry	2723	BAKER, Victor Roy
6480	ATWELL, Edgar Albert	1716	BAKER, Walter Edward
1710	AUBIN, Albert Louis	3694	BAKEY, John Frederick
1302A	AUBREY, Joseph	6393	BALDWIN, Archibald Charles William
1702	AUCHTERLONIE, Bertrand		
591	AULD, Herbert Francis	7587	BALDWIN, Percy Harold
2765	AUSTIN, Edward William	1717	BALE, William
1469	AUSTIN, George	5333	BALL, Charles
2329	AUSTIN, George	2951	BALLANTYNE, Samuel Herbert
6460	AUSTIN, William Clarence	409	BALLARD, Abe

HISTORY OF THE 15th BATTALION

No.	Name	No.	Name
6942	BALLARD, James Vincent	Lieut	BARWOOD, Charles Frederick
2339	BALLS, John Irwin	2341	BASING, Walter Henry
3236	BALMER, William George	1603	BASS, Clement Stanley
726	BAMBERY, George Sweeten	2731	BASSETT, George Henry
725	BAMBERY, Timothy Richard	3250	BASSETT, Kenneth Cameron
6229	BAMFORD, John Joseph	4751	BATE, Richard Cornish
1672	BANDICK, Arthur	7850A	BATH, John
3698	BANKS, James Hatley John	5580	BATH, Thomas Joseph
5783	BANKS, William Henry	6226	BATTERSBY, William John
2432	BANKS, William James	3702	BATTIS, Francis James
7200	BARBER, Joshua George	590	BAUER, Charles Roy
6710	BARCLAY, Thomas	1634	BAUER, Frederick William
875	BARDEN, Henry Rupert Cecil	7086	BAUER, Walter Frederick
5332	BARDON, Peter Joseph	3896	BAULD, Stanley Gordon
3235	BARKER, Cecil Ernest	3688	BAUNACH, Francis William
4286	BARKER, John Thomas	1710	BAVINGTON, George Augustus
2219	BARKER, Thomas Lyneord		Leslie
2730	BARKER, William Henry	1677	BAXENDALE, Leslie William
1921	BARLOW, Jamieson Rupert	1468	BAXTER, Clarence Sydney
3626	BARNARD, William Henry	1720	BAXTER, John Robert
3573	BARNES, Clifford Aubrey	1308A	BAXTER, Neil
2/Lieut	BARNES, Fraser Eugene	5979	BAYLEY, John Thomas
1475	BARNES, Henry Bowen	1456	BAYLISS, John Godfrey
1715	BARNES, Herbert	5781	BEACHAM, Frederick Richard
1408	BARNES, Percy	874	BEACOM, Joseph Archdall
1638	BARNES, Russell Hedley	6946	BEACOM, John Crozier
1461	BARNES, Wilfred Paul	3576	BEADLE, George
256	BARNES, William	878	BEADON, Cyril Edward
1409	BARNES, William James	2108	BEAL, William
6211	BARNETT, Richard McNab	3689	BEALE, Bruce Duncan
104	BARON, John	3798	BEALE, Percy William
569	BARR, Andrew	3009	BEALE, Roy Dudley
3127	BARR, Henry Phillip	3696	BEAMISH, Henry
3909	BARRATT, Maurice	1004	BEARD, Edward Frank
3703	BARRATT, Samuel Verg	2883	BEARD, William
1410	BARRETT, Ralph	7687	BEATON, James White
1718	BARRETT, Thomas	1827	BEATTIE, John Irving
5033	BARRIE, John	3575	BEAUMONT, Wilfred
3053	BARRIE, Lewis Henry	257	BEAVERSEN, Joseph William
7803	BARRIE, Thomas James	6939	BEAVIS, William Henry
6944	BARROW, Eliphia Walter	6769	BECKE, Clive Druce Gervase
2557	BARROW, George Clarence	1856	BEDLINGTON, William
2274	BARRY, Bernard Thomas		Christopher
6711	BARRY, David William	6712	BEER, Reginald Stanley
4448	BARRY, James	722	BEESLEY, Arthur
4449	BARRY, William Francis	571	BEESTON, Henry
7811	BARRY, William Frank	4431	BEESTON, William Walter
716	BARTHOLOMEW, Edward		Stuart
	Charles	4738	BEHAN, Edward
2725	BARTHOLOMEW, John Bland	4254	BEHAN, John William
1247	BARTLE, Vivian Nicholas	5335	BEITH, Andrew
33	BARTLEM, Frank John	3007	BEITZEL, Frederick William
2/Lieut	BARTLETT, Arthur Harold	4359	BELBIN, Alfred George
3006	BARTON, Alfred	4733	BELCHER, William
6383	BARTON, Eric Paul	1163	BELL, Arthur
258	BARTON, William	2682	BELL, Edward Potter
1161	BARWICK, Joseph Thomas	6713	BELL, Henry

HISTORY OF THE 15th BATTALION

No.	Name	No.	Name
1458	BELL, Percival Thomas	5983	BIRD, Edward
2271	BELL, Richard Turner	7813	BIRKE, Henry Oscar
259	BELL, Terence	4259	BIRNEY, Thomas
3697	BELL, Thomas	5343	BIRRER, Otto
570	BELL, Thomas Henry	3239	BIRT, Herbert Hobday
1852	BELLENGER, William Ivan Victor	4143	BISH, Charles
		7801A	BISHOP, Charles Gustave Phillip
1160	BELSTEAD, Andrew		
6589	BEMI, Edward Lawrence	4260	BISHOP, Con
3691	BENDER, Harold Wilfred	1712	BISSET, David
613A	BENNETT, Douglas John	6936	BLACK, Alexander Stewart
6714	BENNETT, Edward Alfred	6716	BLACK, Arthur Herbert
871	BENNETT, Harry Amos	4754	BLACK, Charles Balfour
1417A	BENNETT, James	Lieut	BLACK, Charles Miles
106	BENNETT, Leonard Spencer	572	BLACK, George
6961	BENNETT, Leslie Edward	2558	BLACKETT, Robert
523	BENNEY, George Burleigh	2106	BLACKLOCK, Herbert John
4257	BENNION, Edwin Ellis	1006	BLACKLOW, Edward
1676	BENSLEY, Roland Gordon	1854	BLACKLOW, Fred
1405	BENSON, Francis McLellan	1915	BLACKMAN, Irwin Oxley
261	BENSON, Samuel Ernest William	1917	BLACKMORE, Frederick Spencer
		2726	BLACKMORE, Harry
3699	BENTLEY, George Weberley	Lieut	BLACKMUR, Albert Edward
411	BENTZON, Sydney Malcolm	1007	BLACKWELL, Henry Albert
7745	BENVENUTTI, Angelo	3577	BLACKWOOD, Henry William
3687	BERGIN, Philip	1306	BLAGDEN, Arthur Basil
1675	BERKINSHAW, William Ernest	109	BLAIN, James Gillespie
6859	BERNARD, George	5334	BLAINE, Edward Hugh
2666	BERNER, Henry	1309	BLAIR, William
1464	BERRY, Enos Thomas	3578	BLAKE, Arthur Charles
107	BERRY, John	1809	BLAKE, Charles Isaac
3178	BERRY, Michael John	724	BLAKE, Frederick
1012	BERRY, William Alexander James	1714	BLANDFORD, Leslie Charles
		5653	BLISS, Lionel Percy
410A	BERTRAM, Francis Dixon	7197	BLUNDELL, Harvey Ernest
5345	BESGROVE, Walter George	2336	BLUNDEN, Leslie Eldridge
4360	BESIER, Ernest Frederick	6960	BLUNT, Joseph John
609	BESSELL, Ernest Henry	2499	BOAG, Harold Leslie George
2688	BEST, Raymond Thomas	2729	BOARDMAN, William Vernon
4358	BETHEL, Wilfred Michael	5984	BODEN, Abel
5981	BETTRIDGE, Ernest Gordon	1005	BODEN, Herbert
7464	BETTRIDGE, Leonard Charles	2116	BOGE, Herbert
6941	BEUTEL, Fredrick Johann	34	BOGIE, Robert Dickson
6940	BEUTEL, Herman William	6950	BOGUE, William
4734	BEVERIDGE, Jack McIntosh	5985	BOLCK, Robert
405	BEVERLEY, Thomas	2344	BOLDERSON, Phillip Cyril
7842	BIANCHI, George	6870	BOLDERY, Ernest
1467	BIDDLE, Arthur Edwin	5986	BOLGER, Patrick Joseph
6463	BIDGOOD, Frank Alexander	3005	BOLLINGTON, Llewellyn
420	BIGGS, James Carter	6466	BOLT, Joseph Henry
5982	BIGGS, Robert James Marley	6224	BOLTON, Frank Percy
108	BILLETT, Alfred	1640	BOLTON, Leslie
614A	BILLINGHURST, David	260	BOLTON, Wilfred
3238	BINNIE, Charles George	4736	BOND, Donald Archibald
Capt	BINNINGTON, Edward	1913	BOND, John
1639	BIRCH, Leslie	5777	BOND, John Jacob
Lieut	BIRD, Benjamin Robert	2011	BOND, Richard

No.	Name	No.	Name
4026	BONDING, James Jacob	3242	BRAND, Stanley Jollie
6718	BONNEFIN, Francis Aleide Adrian	2667	BRANDON, James Thomas
			BRANGWYN, James Chesterfield
1905	BOOKER, Herbert Edward		(Served As)
4025	BOON, Horace		
7618	BOORMAN, Richard Newton	4771	CHESTERFIELD, James
6962	BOOTH, James Oliver Allan	1688	BRATCHFORD, Anthony James
4747	BOSEL, Charles Frederick	5543	BRAY, Francis
5339	BOSTON, Alfred John	6614	BRAY, John George
723	BOSTON, Percy Walter	5647	BRAY, William
1684	BOSWORTH, Henry Charles	721	BRAYLEY, Leslie Keith
2333	BOURKE, Argyle Michael	4737	BRAZIL, Martin Joseph
1310	BOURKE, David Christopher		BREADY, William John
110	BOURKE, Edward William		(Served As)
4750	BOURKE, John Joseph	2113	BRODEY, William John
6948	BOURKE, Joseph	Capt	BREMNER, Norman Frederick
2571	BOURKE, Thomas	873	BRENNAN, Francis Patrick
2334	BOURKE, William James	1158	BRENNAN, Patrick
1457	BOURNE, Henry	577	BRENNAN, William
4735	BOURNE, Oliver Gabriel	1682	BRETON, Harold
2498	BOWATER, William Edward	Capt	BRETTINGHAM-MOORE, Hubert Mansel
1463	BOWERMAN, George		
4068	BOWERS, Cyril John	876	BREWER, Arthur Livingstone
7205	BOWERS, Henry James	7787A	BREWER, George Warren
Lieut	BOWERS, Horace James	5990	BREWER, William James
971	BOWERS, Norman Harcourt	1920	BRICE, Jonathan Walter
2272	BOWIE, Joseph	2500	BRIDGES, Norman Clarence
1412	BOWKETT, John Henry	7203	BRIDGES, Willie
1411	BOWKETT, Thomas William	6723	BRIERTY, Aubrey Horace
1010	BOWLING, Horace	111	BRIGGS, George
6719	BOWMAN, Archibald David	2110	BRIGGS, John
5987	BOWMAN, John	4740	BRIGGS, Sidney
7454	BOWMAN, John	6938	BRIGHT, Archie Graham
2727	BOWRING, Albert	7692	BRIMBLECOMBE, Louis Hugh
1388	BOX, William Charles	573	BRINDELL, George
3692	BOYCE, William Percy Norman	7456	BRISCOE, Francis Charles
5988	BOYD, Henry Douglas	3255	BROAD, Peter
5341	BOYD, Hugh Gordon Walpole	264	BROADBENT, Herbert Oliver
1069	BOYD, John Henry	3245	BROADFOOT, Alexander
2337	BOYD, Joseph	1460	BROADHEAD, Douglas Henry Allen
1459	BOYD, Norman Howard		
12	BOYD, Robert	561	BROADHURST, Frank
5831	BOYLE, Eric Frank	2950	BROCKEN, James
5340	BOYLE, Patrick	1855	BROCKMAN, Edward Albert
2953	BOYLES, Charles William	3517	BRODIE, Daniel Colin
3243	BRACE, Frederick	7205	BRODIE, Robert Patison
262	BRACHER, Alexander William	2273	BRODIE, Thomas
6365	BRACKEN, Robert Cecil	3175	BROMFIELD, Cecil
Capt	BRADLEY, Ernest Martin	7199	BROMFIELD, Jack Mawdsley
6228	BRADLEY, Ralph Murray	1466	BROMLEY, Thomas Valentine
263	BRADNOCK, William Durant	2/Lieut	BROOK, Charles Munro
5989	BRADSHAW, William Edward	4443	BROOK, Edwin
1332	BRAITHWAITE, Arthur Joseph	5820	BROOKS, Arthur
3177	BRAMICH, Alden Bernard	6720	BROOKS, Edward James
4362	BRAMICH, Sydney Stewart	1853	BROOKS, Ernest Allen
2722	BRAMICH, Tyson Kenneth	3010	BROOKS, Ernest George
3246	BRAMPTON, Charles Edward	2728	BROOKS, George Henry

No.	Name	No.	Name
112	BROOKS, John Atkinson	2560	BRUCE, Henry
1009	BROOKS, Josiah Francis	114	BRUCE, Roderick Malcolm Livingstone
3579	BROOKS, Michael		
3580	BROOKS, Victor Allan	1602	BRUCE, Windle
2/Lieut	BROOKS, William Abercrombie	6724	BRUMPTON, Ernest Osborne
413	BROOME, Hider Stanley Filmer	7201	BRUNTON, Arthur Norman
265	BROOME, Geoffrey George	418	BRYANS, Edward
2692	BROSTROM, John	Lieut	BRYDON, Leonard Amyas
32	BROUGHTON, Travers Robert Rhys	5991	BRYER, Percival Samuel
		981	BUCHANAN, Alexander
1878	BROWN, Alfred	1911	BUCHANAN, Donald Spencer
872	BROWN, Allan Daniel	2338	BUCHANAN, John Corry
4430	BROWN, Andrew	1910	BUCHANAN, Leonard Alexander
4455	BROWN, Archibald Lorrimer		
1305A	BROWN, Arthur Benjamin	4748	BUCHANAN, Norman
1302	BROWN, Charles Richard	4743	BUCHANAN, William Colin
6937	BROWN, Charles Wilfred	1713	BUCKLE, William
1641	BROWN, Donald	4454	BUCKLEY, Arthur
4440	BROWN, Duncan	718	BUCKLEY, David
1918	BROWN, Duncan Sinclair	2396A	BUCKLEY, Edward William
625	BROWN, George	5336	BUCKBY, Patrick Denis
1306A	BROWN, George	3626	BUCKNEY, Arthur John
5652	BROWN, George Alexander	6464	BUGDEN, Clarence Robert
4859	BROWN, Gilbert Walter	3176	BULL, George Arnold
1159	BROWN, Harold Baylie	267	BULL, George Franklin
2275	BROWN, Henry	268	BULL, Robert Charles
717	BROWN, James	3	BULL, Thomas Henry
4266	BROWN, James Scott	7202	BULLOCK, Walter Henry
2010	BROWN, James William	4671	BUNNETT, Norman James
6590	BROWN, Joseph	5993	BUNTER, William Frederick
3686	BROWN, Lawrence	579	BURDEKIN, James Vivian
1259	BROWN, Oliver	2117	BURGIN, Harold George
3265	BROWN, Percy	1719	BURKE, Charles
1465	BROWN, Robert	416	BURKE, Harry
1681	BROWN, Robert Smart	3700	BURKE, Henry Arthur
7688A	BROWN, Reginald Victor	7747	BURKE, Martin John Joseph
1687	BROWN, Stanley James	2952	BURKETT, James
1156	BROWN, Sydney	6781	BURLING, Francis Ellis
1601	BROWN, Thomas	2052	BURN, Aubrey Francis
4453	BROWN, Thomas	4742	BURNE, Charles Radford
4745	BROWN, Thomas James	1455	BURNES, Thomas
419	BROWN, Thomas William	1462	BURNETT, Richard William
575	BROWN, Walter William	7812	BURNS, Harry
6465	BROWN, William James	1845A	BURNS, James Joseph
7098	BROWN, William James	6227	BURNS, John Ferguson Joseph
7809	BROWN, William Joseph	719	BURNS, William Henry
6722	BROWN, William Royal	6462	BURNS, William Murray
7463	BROWN, William Smith	2276	BURNSIDE, Albert
4276	BROWNE, Eric James	2115	BURRIDGE, Albert Dennis
574	BROWNE, Frederick Robert	1011	BURSLEM, Claude Henry
1379	BROWNE, George	6222	BURTON, Albert Edward
2109	BROWNE, Harry Michael	4749	BURTON, Arthur
576	BROWNE, Henry James	2724	BURTON, Herbert James
Capt	BROWNE, John Charles	3244	BURTON, Leonard
7782	BROWNING, Samuel	6597	BURVILL, Robert William
578	BRUCE, Francis Arthur	125	BUSBY, Alexander
1902	BRUCE, George Hamilton	580	BUSBY, George Howard

HISTORY OF THE 15th BATTALION 251

No.	Name	No.	Name
7687A	BUSIKO, John William	5669	CAMPBELL, Peter Patrick
6943	BUSTEED, Bernard	4756	CAMPBELL, Robert
7688	BUTCHART, James Scott	3259	CAMPBELL, William
1445	BUTLER, Edgar Henry	5786	CAMPBELL, William
5342	BUTLER, Edmund Campbell	6235	CAMPBELL, William Parke
2	BUTLER, Frederick	1473	CANE, Arthur William
6949	BUTLER, Fred	3179	CANN, Herbert Henry
2561	BUTLER, George Gray	Capt	CANNAN, Douglas Herman
76	BUTTERFIELD, Ernest	Brig-Gen	CANNAN, James Harold
3476	BUTTERWORTH, Frank Joseph	1768	CANNON, James
4361	BUTTON, Douglas Vivian	6898	CANTRELL, Henry Frederick
1071	BUXTON, John Cecil	3075	CAPP Henry James
5650	BYFORD, William John	7636	CARBERRY, Michael Joseph
2107	BYRNE, Eugene Gerald	2 Lieut	CAREW, Robert James
417	BYRNE, Henry Francis	3582	CAREY, Edward Roy
115	BYRNE, Herbert Horan	4478	CAREY, Ernest James
116	BYRNE, James	1857	CAREY, Jack Garbut
7477	BYRNE, Joseph Ambrose	6473	CAREY, James
3233	BYRNE, William James	866	CAREY, Thomas James
1912	BYRNES, John Thomas	421	CARLETON, Phillip Edward
4251	BYRNES, Leslie Joseph	2845	CARLILL, Daniel
1008	BYRON, John	1928	CARLIN, John Thomas
1169	CABALZAR, Reginald	5357	CARLISLE, Robert
	CADY, Alfred George Edward (Served As)	1858	CARLSEN, Arthur
		6390	CARLSON, Joseph Frederick
363	WILLIAMS, William	7216	CARLYLE, Charles Aubrey
882	CAFFIN, Edgar Atheling	7215	CARLYLE, Edward Harold
6729	CAIN, Edward John	7219	CARMAN, Thomas Andrew
1018	CAIRNS, Wilfred	1727	CARMODY, Walter
270	CAIRNS, William Burridge	269	CARNOCHAN, Alexander
5367	CAITHNESS, Alexander Thomas	1926	CARPENTER, Alfred Allen
2563	CALDERWOOD, James	581	CARPENTER, George Roland
7804A	CALDICOTT, William Henry	7693	CARR, Daniel
3911	CALDWELL, Erskin James	5347	CARR, George
6957	CALDWELL, Robert Ramsey	3258	CARR, Henry
3484	CALEY, William Joseph	5785	CARR, William
5353	CALL, John Robert	3718	CARR, William Henry
1957	CALLAGHAN, William Henry	2318	CARR-BOYD, John Gerald
4460	CALLOW, George	5994	CARRICK, William
1314A	CALLUM, William Findley	422	CARRINGTON, John
4272	CALNAN, Charles	1415A	CARROLL, Ivan Robert
1285	CAMERON, Andrew	1452	CARROLL, James
3706	CAMERON, Charles Stuart Kennedy	2564	CARROLL, James
		2349	CARROLL, John
3019	CAMERON, Ewen James	4766	CARROLL, John
5369	CAMERON, James Kenneth	732	CARROLL, John Thomas
6593	CAMERON, Ralph Owen	8	CARSELDINE, Duncan Stewart
6576	CAMERON, Selwyn Everett	6392	CARSON, John
1925	CAMERON, William	2380	CARSTEN, Hans
2277	CAMM, James	6730	CARTER, Albert William
2731	CAMPBELL, Alex William	4173	CARTER, Aubrey William
2791	CAMPBELL, Colin Knox	7489	CARTER, Charles Horsman St. John
7487	CAMPBELL, Charles Paul		
1642	CAMPBELL, Duncan	Capt	CARTER, Ernest Kenneth
4465	CAMPBELL, Henry Ernest	2123	CARTER, Harry Alexander
2678	CAMPBELL, James	Major	CARTER, Hubert Reginald
3016	CAMPBELL, James	7211	CARTER, John Arthur

252 HISTORY OF THE 15th BATTALION

No.	Name	No.	Name
1260	CARTER, Lavington Lewis	Lieut	CHATAWAY, Thomas Percival
2053	CARTER, Reginald Harry	3583	CHATWIN, William Raymond
4758	CARTER, Samuel	2669	CHEERS, Richard Henry
117	CARTER, Stanley Richard	5784	CHEESEMAN, Herbert Maitland
3170	CARVEL, Richard	6953	CHERRY, Arthur
3037	CASE, Horace Joseph	2118	CHICK, Francis Richard
6477	CASE, Reginald George	1166	CHILDS, Thomas Noel
4760	CASEY, John Thomas	1904	CHIMES, George Henry
Lieut	CASEY, Leo George	562	CHIPPENDALE, Robert
4	CASH, Osmond Cedric	7826	CHISHOLM, Albert Joseph Wilson
735	CASH, William Charles		
4469	CASS, Denis Sidney	6474	CHRISTENSEN, Andrew
1730	CASS, Emmett Waldo	6485	CHRISTENSEN, Paul Daniel
555	CASTLE, George Ernest	1728	CHRISTENSEN, Tennesse
1927	CASTLE, William	5995	CHRISTENSEN, William
118	CASTLESMITH, Rupert	6237	CHRISTIAN, Henry Clyne
731	CASTLEY, Albert	1471	CHRISTIANSEN, Axel
2565	CASTREE, John Henry	1470	CHRISTIANSEN, James
2345	CATON, Lyman	2733	CHRISTISON, William
2120	CAVANOUGH, Edward William	1930	CHURCHILL, John Richard
5356	CAVANAGH, Robert	6732	CLANAHAN, Andrew
538	CAVANOUGH, George	2348	CLANCY, Patrick Edward
2668	CAVE, Arthur	1311A	CLAPTON, Frederick James
2788	CAVE, Ernest	273	CLARK, Albert
727	CAVE, Francis Horace	3017	CLARK, Alexander
3018	CAVE, Harold	1605	CLARK, Archibald
119	CAWLEY, Frank Reginald	6733	CLARK, Archibald Kennedy
3261	CAWLEY, Frederick	6215	CLARK, Frank Edmund
271	CAWSEY, George	423	CLARK, Henry James
4275	CEDERGREEN, Victor Charles	6734	CLARK, Henry Samuel
4028	CHAFFEY, Basil Leslie	1307	CLARK, John
4363	CHALK, Ernest Tasman	4765	CLARK, John
4762	CHAMBERLAIN, Frederick Harold	424	CLARK, John
		6471	CLARK, John
1729	CHAMBERLIN, Sam John	1731	CLARK, Reginald George
1923	CHAMBERS, Thomas	5358	CLARK, Stanley Augustus
6731	CHAMBERS, Thomas Francis	6735	CLARK, Thomas
3270	CHAMPION, Percy William	1414	CLARK, Victor
6483	CHANDLER, Ernest	4761	CLARK, Walter Samuel Thomas
2539	CHANDLER, George James	3707	CLARK, William Constant
2566	CHANDLER, Harold Mitchell	5995	CLARKE, Alfred George
3025	CHAPLAIN, Archibald Scotland	6475	CLARKE, Ardys Daniel
		883	CLARKE, Cyril
2637	CHAPMAN, Albert Humphrey	884	CLARKE, Francis Andrew
2712	CHAPMAN, George	5588	CLARKE, Francis Burke
1167	CHAPMAN, John	7346	CLARKE, Joseph
2713	CHAPMAN, William Morrison	1015	CLARKE, Langley Edward
7221	CHAPPEL, Frederick Henry	5579	CLARKE, Norman Lester Spence
3719	CHAPPELL, William		
3015	CHARLES, William	6239	CLARKE, Sydney
881	CHARLTON, George	1604	CLARKE, William Edward
1929	CHARLTON, Maurice	4365	CLARKSON, Laurence Charles George
272	CHARLTON, Thomas Leonard		
3257	CHARNOCH, Thomas John	1724	CLARKSON, Thomas Wilfred
1474	CHARTERS, Joshua	3013	CLAXTON, Walter William
7689	CHASE, Henry Stanley	6746	CLAYTON, Ernest
3708	CHASELING, Stanley Gordon	3021	CLEAR, Leonard Albert

HISTORY OF THE 15th BATTALION

No.	Name	No.	Name
2056	CLEARY, Errol Vincent	5787	COLLINS, Henry John
6476	CLEARY, John Patrick	121	COLLINS, John Huntley
430	CLEARY, Richard Henry	3615A	COLLINS, Sydney
78	CLEAT, John	5062	COLLINS, Thomas Norman Hay
2503	CLEAVER, Arthur Ernest	2955	COLLINSON, Fred
885	CLEGG, Leslie	275	COLQUHOUN, Harold Robert
2057	CLEMENTS, Richard	1168	COLTHEART, Sydney John
1165	CLEMENTS, Roy Charles	1914	COLVILLE, George Edwin
3639	CLENCH, Alfred	1308	COLVILLE, William
2125	CLIFFORD, Vincent Thomas	6737	COLWILL, Charles
2846	CLIFT, Harold Digby	6234	COMAN, John Thomas
6955	CLINCH, James	6472	COMOLLATTI, Abondio
1406	CLOUGH, Leopold	7790	COMOLLATTI, Samuel George
3715	CLOUTIER, Le Andre Michon	2954	CONACHER, Percy Robert
2346	COAD, Leslie Joseph	1316A	CONAGHAN, Edward
274	COATES, Paul Tate	3263	CONDON, Arthur
1312	COATES, William	6631	CONDON, Cornelius Joseph
1472	COBBE, Henry Clermont	7784	CONDON, Thomas Joseph
557	COBBETT, Allan Lewis	3910	CONDON, Thomas Reader
2946	COBBETT, William James	1734	CONDONEY, George Anthony
1697	COBLEY, Charles	1024	CONLEY, Cyril John
4767	COCHRANE, James Wilson	4470	CONLEY, John
5373	COCKERILL, Albert	6952	CONNOLLY, Patrick Gerald
6232	COE, Walter James	426	CONNOR, Bernard
1816	COFFEY, Ernest Ivey Robinson	1035	CONNOR, Charles Stewart
		1021	CONNOR, John Vincent
3713	COFFEY, Robert Tough	2734	CONNORS, Oscar Thomas
583	COFFIN, Carl Douglas	1025	CONOLAN, Bernard
7091	COGHLAN, Percy Denis	3584	CONRADES, Frank
7223	COLDWELL, George Watson	2126	CONROY, Arthur Clive
2351	COLE, Ernest Hamilton	3712	CONROY, William
6736	COLE, Sydney Joseph	5349	CONSTABLE, Stephen Cheesman
1173	COLE, Sydney Rowland		
35	COLE, William	6738	CONSTANTINE, Peter
5974	COLE, William John Eric	1310	COOGAN, Andrew Joseph
3714	COLEFAX, Bazil Hope	1309	COOGAN, Thomas Patrick
120	COLEMAN, Francis	4149	COOK, Charles Godfrey
3478	COLEMAN, Frank Bernard	4770	COOK, Harold
1735	COLEMAN, James George	1014	COOK, John William
1312A	COLEMAN, Myles	Lieut	COOK, Maurice Alfred
5350	COLEMAN, Patrick	2737	COOK, Percy
5366	COLEMAN, William Arthur	3022	COOKE, Albert Edward
6238	COLEMAN, William Thomas	425	COOKE, Herbert William
3711	COLES, Frederick James	429	COOKE, Oliver
6954	COLES, Percy James	2568	COOKE, Percy Goude
2979	COLLEDGE, Albert Edward	6860	COOKE, William Ernest
4469	COLLIER, Frederick	3586	COOLEY, Albert Ernest
Lieut	COLLIER, James Douglas Archer	2055	COOLEY, Frederick
		7693A	COOLEY, Harry
Lieut	COLLIN, Leslie Norman	2054	COOLEY, Horace
366	COLLINGS, Mervyn Dave	1023	COOLEY, Tasman Pressland
5589	COLLINGWOOD, Ralph Percival	1924	COOLING, Henry William
		5968	COOMBE, Albert Roy
2399	COLLINS, Alexander Morgan	3182	COOMBE, Alfred Cyril
3020	COLLINS, Alfred	1016	COOMBE, Bernard Raymond
3585	COLLINS, Francis Stanley	6236	COOMBE, Melbourne Sydney
2278	COLLINS, Garnet	1019	COOMBE, Victor Ronald

No.	Name	No.	Name
6230	COOMBER, Harry Smith	2636	CRAIG, James Richardson
Capt	COOMBS, Walter William	1413	CRAIG, Thomas Johnson
6871	COOPER, Alfred Charles	4764	CRAKER, James
5663	COOPER, Arthur Sydney	6478	CRAMB, Sydney Lloyd
5360	COOPER, George	5	CRANE, Frederick William
3114	COOPER, Harold Herbert	2788	CRANE, James Albert
734	COOPER, Henry Harold	733	CRAVEN, Jack
6872	COOPER, John William	123	CRAWFORD, James
6739	COOPER, Joseph	7632	CRAWFORD, Mervyn Alexander
7768	COOPER, Thomas Percival		
Capt	COOPER, Walter Jackson	2730	CRAWFORD, Robert Abraham
7806A	COPE, Alfred James	1922	CRAWFORD, William
732	COPELAND, Frank Morton	5666	CRAZE, Arthur
Lieut	CORBETT, Ernest	1311	CREGAN, John
2733	CORBETT, Leslie	3264	CREIGHTON, Harold Melville
1931	CORBY, Emmet Arthur	5655	CREITH, James
1606	CORBY, Eugene Joseph	7694	CRESSWELL, Arthur Clyde
2728	CORDELL, George Raymond	729	CRESSWELL, Sydney
4763	CORDEROY, Douglas Keith	5070	CRISP, Leonard
4757	CORDERY, Noel Leon	2716	CRISP, William Arthur
7697	CORNISH, Harry Steele	1859	CROFT, Edward
2853	CORR, John	7210	CROFT, Edward William Thomas
Lt/Col	CORRIGAN, John Joseph		
Major	CORSER, Cyril Frederick	7218	CROFT, Herbert Henry
1825	COSTA, Edward	3705	CROKE, Arthur
1313A	COSTELLO, Mortimer	427	CROKER, Alexander John
2119	COSTELLO, William	Hon/Lieut	CROMPTON, William Henry
879	COTT, Reginald	2144A	CRONIN, Edward Denis
5665	COTTAM, Ernest John	3470	CRONIN, John Michael
7638	COUGHLAN, Edward	7695	CRONIN, Peter Joseph
5658	COUGHLIN, Patrick	4471	CRONK, Edwin
7692A	COULSON, Edmund	3266	CRONK, George Henry
1022	COULSON, Henry Frederick	3588	CROOK, William Henry
2124	COULTAS, George Herbert	5998	CROSBIE, Edgar
5368	COULTHARD, John	124	CROSBY, David
1172	COUNSEL, Wilfred John	5667	CROSS, Alfred
7225	COUPER, Andrew	2823	CROSS, Charles
3648	COURBARRON, Frederick Hamilton	5999	CROSS, Herbert
		125	CROSS, James
122	COURBARRON, James Edward	6743	CROSS, John William
7684	COURT, Renfrew Heathcote	4477	CROSSAN, William
730	CORTNEY, James Edward	4282	CROSSAN, James
816	COUSENS, Stanley Clifford	7820	CROSSMAN, George Leslie
Lieut	COUTTS, Allan	3269	CROSTHWAITE, George Jubilee
3138A	COWDEROY, Norman Wheatley	2122	CROUCH, Jonathan Charles
		Lieut	CROW, Alfred William Filby Goddard
880	COWELL, Arthur Alexander		
4768	COWPER, John	7695A	CROWLE, Athol George
7220	COWPER, Percy Garland	7614	CROWLEY, Patrick
2732	COX, Andrew Francis	2431	CROWTHER, Cecil Rankin
1644	COX, Frank	2571	CROWTHER, George
5375	COX, George William	582	CROWTHER, Travice
1643	COX, Herbert James	5355	CRUMMY, William James
7802A	COX, Leslie Stuart	3181	CUBITT, Colin Stanley Garfield
7217	CRADDOCK, Lance Edgell		
Hon/Major	CRAIG, Frederick William	2729	CUDDY, Alfred Reuben William
5352	CRAIG, George		

HISTORY OF THE 15th BATTALION 255

No.	Name	No.	Name
728	CUGLEY, John Walter	279	DARKER, Robert Henry
364	CULLEN, James	2013	DARLING, William
1725	CULLEN, James	6247	DARLINGTON, Joseph
1733	CULLEN, James	1313	DARRAGH, Charles
1013	CULLEN, Wallace	128	DAUTEL, Alfred
276	CULLIMORE, Edward Maurice	4780	DAVEY, Charles Albert
7857	CUMISKEY, James Joseph	2283	DAVEY, Richard
584	CUMMING, James	129	DAVEY, Thomas
5659	CUMMING, John Percy	1964	DAVID, Arthur Julius
Capt	CUMMINGS, Eric Douglas	6486	DAVID, Thomas Jackson
7479A	CUMMINGS, Frederick Joseph	1741	DAVIDGE, Alfred James
6482	CUMMINGS, Thomas Joseph	5560	DAVIDSON, Charles
Capt	CUMMINS, William	4403	DAVIDSON, John Roden
2907	CUNNINGHAM, Walter Herbert	4490	DAVIDSON, Joseph
		6490	DAVIE, George William Leaper
7212	CURLEY, William Lisle	2240	DAVIES, Benjamin Clifford
6951	CURNOW, Thomas Arnold	5386	DAVIES, David John
2556	CURRIE, Duncan	586	DAVIES, Harry
4755	CURRIE, Patrick	Capt	DAVIES, Henry Charles
5547	CURTIS, Frederick James	3589	DAVIES, James Henry
585	CURTIS, Harold	4792	DAVIES, Joshua
5359	CURTIS, Reginald	1317A	DAVIES, Morgan David
3721	CUSACK, Harold John Charles	409	DAVIES, Owen Mellion
6240	CUSHWAY, Frank	454	DAVIES, Ross
6216	CUTHBERTSON, Philip	6901	DAVIES, Sydney Lewis
7615	CUTTLER, Charles Edward	278	DAVIES, Thomas
1315	CUTTS, Frederick William	4481	DAVIS, Albert Harry
6245	DABELSTEIN, Albert Ernest	6242	DAVIS, Albert Joseph
6249	DABELSTEIN, Arthur	36	DAVIS, Benjamin Charles
3591	DADSON, James Edward	7226	DAVIS, Frederick
737	DAEMEN, Alfred	3126	DAVIS, Harold
6747	DAGG, George Stewart	4404	DAVIS, James
2575	DALEY, James	2128	DAVIS, John Henry
5670	DALEY, James William	4772	DAVIS, Leslie
739	DALEY, Victor	740	DAVIS, Percy
4775	DALLOWAY, Arthur	1645	DAVIS, Richard
5384	DALTON, Norman Charles	2129	DAVIS, Roland Herbert
2574	DALY, James	622	DAVIS, Sydney Phillip
3590	DALY, John	2662	DAVIS, Victor Frederick
2285	DALY, John Edward Joseph	1318A	DAVIS, William Richard Frederick
3281	DALY, Mark		
1936	DALZIEL, Henry	6492	DAVISON, Herbert George
Lieut	DANAHER, James	Lieut	DAVY, Cyril
741	DANIEL, Claude Arthur	1266	DAWES, Harold Ernest
6244	DANIEL, Francis	7844	DAWES, Thomas James Baden
1316	DANIEL, Leonard Lewis	1608	DAWSON, Jack McKay
550	DANIEL, Norman Wesley	6488	DAWSON, Justin Fox
3279	DANIELS, Alexander Edward	7349	DAWSON, Thomas
126	DANN, Frank	4781	DAY, Alfred
127	DANN, Thomas	1738	DAY, Alfred Ernest
2711	DARBY, Kenneth Herbert	1705	DAY, Charles
6	DARBY, William Pigott	3274	DAY, Francis Nathaniel
1479	DARCY, Edward Columbus	6001	DAY, Robert Alexander
Capt	D'ARCY, Michael Joseph	3593	DEACON, Amos Samuel
3284	DARE, Ernest Wilfred	1176	DEACON, Frederick Robert
2504	DARE, Harold Norman Charles	2281	DEACON, John Douglas
2523	DARE, John Ely Everstley	1174	DEACON, Joseph Herbert

HISTORY OF THE 15th BATTALION

No.	Name
79	DEAKIN, Alec Bertram
7227	DEAN, Alexander James
1470	DEAN, Joseph
7814	DEANE, Thomas
4289	DEARDS, Henry Frederick Leon Howard
3725	DEATON, Hercules Thomas
3624	DEAVILLE, Arthur
3027	DEBNAM, George Henry
5387	De CHASTEL, Leo
7081	DECKER, Eric Paul
1934	DEEPROSE, William
1478	DEGOUMOIS, Arnold Emile
6495	DEIGNAN, Leslie Reuben
3728	DELANEY, Michael Joseph
1415	DELANEY, Richard Patrick
6248	DELLA-BOSCA, William George Henry
2127	DEMPSEY, James
7230	DEMPSEY, Patrick
6966	DEMPSTER, John Dalziel
6220	DENDLE, William
587	DENEHEY, Phillip James George
6003	DENHAM, Edward
6004	DENHAM, John
2279	DENNIS, Arthur Reginald
1737	DENSLOW, Edward
1319A	DENT, Gordon Thomas
1607	DENT, Richard
7702	DENT, Stanley Gordon
1932	DENTON, Charles
3277	DENYER, Charles Frederick
2839	DENYER, Thomas James
1940	DERRICK, John Scott
2576	DESBOIS, Hugh Godfrey
1480	DESPLACE, Adam Stanley
4779	DEVANNY, Henry Bruce
1935	DEVERS, Charles John
2186	DEVERS, Richard
3272	DEVIN, Jack
3273	DEVLIN, William John
2897	DEVRIES, George Henry
1416	DEWAR, Douglas
2676	DE WARREN, Joseph James
7470	DE WELDON, Alexander Burnside
6491	DEWES, Harold
2738	DICK, James
2685	DICKINSON, Ernest
Major	DICKINSON, George Frederick
T/Capt	DICKSON, Herbert
4294	DICKSON, Joseph
Lieut	DICKSON, Norman
2824	DIGNAN, James
588	DILLON, Henry
3280	DIMAIO, Giuseppo

No.	Name
1320B	DIMMICK, Stanley
4494	DINGLE, John Henry
3594	DINHAM, William
1709	DINNING, Herbert Lester
2577	DINSEY, Robert Samuel
2735	DIPROSE, Dyer Albert
4860	DIXON, Alexander
3913	DIXON, John
2734	DIXON, John Arthur
1314	DIXON, Joseph
4778	DIXON, Thomas
Lieut	DODD, George Collingwood
3726	DODKIN, Arthur
6965	DOE, William Henry Christopher
2058	DOGGETT, John
738	DOHERTY, Francis Thomas
Capt	DOMENEY, William Lamuel Edward
6005	DONAGHY, John Hugh
7683	DONAHEE, Herbert Bede
5385	DONALD, George
1177	DONALD, Harold Francis
3932	DONALD, Harold John Kennedy
5377	DONALD, Jack
3730	DONALD, Robert
	DONALDSON, Alexander (Served As)
105	BARRATT, Maurice
2687	DONIGER, Samuel
7852	DONNELLY, Martin Thornton
1673	DONNELLY, Thomas
6967	DONNELLY, Vincent
1175	DONOHOE, William Henry
2059	DONOVAN, Percival William
6250	DOOLAN, Richard James
1317	DOOLEY, James Keith
2740	DOPSON, Abraham Patrick
681	DORAN, John James
2739	DORMAN, Felix James
2671	DORROUGH, Raymond Harold
6751	DOUDS, John Patrick
1027	DOUGHERTY, Alexander
6752	DOUGHERTY, Dudley
2530	DOUGHERTY, Mottram Heywood
Lieut	DOUGLAS, Archibald
5083	DOUGLAS, George
4493	DOUGLAS, John Robert
7698	DOUGLAS, Peter
4040	DOUGLAS, Thomas Victor
589	DOUGLAS, William Arthur
1919	DOVE, Arthur
4287	DOVER, Percy
6964	DOWD, Michael
7228	DOWEY, Samuel Welsh

No.	Name	No.	Name
2282	DOWLING, Edward Allan	863	DWYER, Thomas Vincent
3729	DOWLING, Walter Boyce	2354	DYER, Colin
6754	DOWLING, William Henry	3735	DYER, Frederick Arthur
6755	DOWLING, William Joseph	5380	DYER, Percy Alfred
661	DOWN, Edward	1178	EADY, Albert James
3798	DOWNEY, Richard James	2434	EAREA, James Thomas
4773	DOWNEY, William Clarence	2858	EARL, William Henry
5383	DOWNEY, William Joseph	6761	EARLY, Henry John
6487	DOWSE, Charles Edward	5672	EARY, George Ernest
4489	DOYLE, James	5389	EASEY, George Albert
1739	DOYLE, Patrick James	1485	EASTMENT, Walter
7500	DOYLE, Rexford James Edwin	6762	EATON, Charles Sydney
1938	DRAKE, Arthur	Lieut	EATHER, Richmond Cornwallis
6006	DRAKE, Theodore Augustus		
Capt	DRANE, Colin Cooper	Capt	EATHER, William Francis
6963	DRAPER, Leonard	7625	EAVES, John Charles
6591	DRAY, William George	744	EDELSTEN, Henry
1028	DRISCOLL, Darcy Wilmot	7839	EDGAR, Samuel John
2352	DRISCOLL, Frederick Thomas	1878	EDGECOCK, Alfred
1861	DRIVER, Walter Douglas	6252	EDMONDS, Harold
3732	DRUMMOND, Peter	1907	EDMONDSON, Edward Thornton
3276	DRURY, Frederick		
Lieut	DRYBROUGH, James Legat	889	EDNEY, Thomas
1318	DUBOIS, Fernand George Jules Marie	5812	EDWARDS, Albert Edward
		4495	EDWARDS, Alfred David
3722	DUCE, Edward	1319	EDWARDS, Arthur
3724	DUCHESNE, George Victor	6969	EDWARDS, Edward James
6758	DUCK, Albert	1261	EDWARDS, Ernest Ellis
3727	DUCKERING, Philip Elmhirst	130	EDWARDS, Ernest Irving
2280	DUFF, Sydney John	2580	EDWARDS, Henry Joseph
680	DUFFY, Richard	1179	EDWARDS, Herbert Francis
1669	DUFFY, Roger Bede	1937	EDWARDS, Hugh Richard
6899	DUGGAN, John	3286	EDWARDS, James Leonard
590	DUGGAN, Percy Clarence	1417	EDWARDS, John
4035	DUGGAN, Thomas Joseph	1609	EDWARDS, John Alfred
3595	DUGMORE, William	5392	EDWARDS, John Max
3278	DUMISKI, Otto Ernest	6009	EDWARDS, Stanley George
3723	DUNBAR, Allen Sinclair	281	EDWARDS, William
1477	DUNCAN, Alfred	4496	EELES, Walter
432	DUNCAN, James Ramsay	2928	EGAN, Daniel
1315	DUNCAN, John James	6251	EGAN, John
6007	DUNLOP, Andy	2983	EGAN, Michael James
1933	DUNMORE, Thomas Frederick		EGAN, Stephen Ambrose (Served As)
6864	DUNN, Ernest		
1690	DUNNING, Harold Ivo	2305	YOUNG, James
433	DUNSDON, Richard George	434	EGERTON, Jack George
5081	DUNSTAN, Ethlyn Cyril	5790	EGGAR, Edgar Leonard
Capt	DUNWORTH, David	Lieut	EIBEL, Henry Alfred
6759	DUPLOCK, Charles Edward	2357	EIG, Leslie Joseph
3281	DURDIN, Alexander	3289	EKBLAD, Nils Petter
4774	DURHAM, David	887	ELBRA, Claudius Powers
886	DURHAM, Thomas Charles	2132	ELDER, John Henderson
3271	DURRINGTON, Richard	1881	ELDRIDGE, Walter
3025	DWYER, Dominic	6010	ELFORD, Francis Granville
6860A	DWYER, James	6497	ELLEM, Vyvian Eric
3026	DWYER, John	888	ELLEN, David Harold
Lieut	DWYER, John James	131	ELLERY, Thomas Henry

No.	Name	No.	Name
1713	ELLINGHAM, John	3106	EWING, James Murchie
2356	ELLIAS, George	4503	FAGAN, Walter
742	ELLIOT, Alfred	6013	FAGG, John Alfred
2359	ELLIOT, Robert Tentress	6500	FAHEY, John Bartholomew
6496	ELLIOTT, Arthur Robert	2063	FAHEY, Joseph
4403	ELLIOTT, George	2062	FAHEY, Victor
3737	ELLIOTT, John Muir	2360	FAHY, Gerald
5673	ELLIOTT, John William	80	FAIRBAIRN, David
7082	ELLIOTT, Richard George	1035	FAIRMAN, George Ernest
2109	ELLIOTT, Victor Albert Paul	891	FALCONER, David
2061	ELLIOTT, William Henry	3746	FALLON, Andrew
6011	ELLIOTT, William Walter	4787	FALLON, John
1529	ELLIS, Bernard Hughes	405	FALLON, Stephen
2743	ELLIS, Frank Clifford	3308	FALLOWS, Herbert
1443	ELLIS, Hector Alfred	2362	FALLS, Walter Ernest
6254	ELLIS, James Jack	7235	FARLEY, Richard Stanislaus
Lieut	ELLIS, William Thomas	1039	FARNHAM, Leslie
280	ELSTOB, Robert Leonard	2744	FARQUHARSON, Alexander
3736	ELVERY, Henry Percival	3299	FARR, Arthur Thomas
2361	EMERSON, Charles Telford	3107	FARRELL, John
3288	EMERSON, Joseph Shield	Lieut	FARRELLY, Edward Patrick
2847	EMERY, John	7623	FARRINGTON, William Hancock
6012	EMERY, Percival George		
6255	ENGLAND, Harold Lewis	7	FARRY, James Alexander
4783	ENGLAND, Thomas George	3293	FAULKNER, Ernest Bennett
Lieut	ENGLERT, Harcourt Justin	7804	FAUX, William John
6972	ENGLISH, James Joseph	4371	FEBEY, David
7079	ENGLISH, William Andrew	4372	FEBEY, Frederick James
1486	ENSLOW, Edward	1180	FEBEY, Henry Walter
4370	ENSLOW, Edward	785	FEDRICK, William Henry
	EPTHORP, Reginald James (Served As)	4785	FEETAM, John William
		7509	FEENEY, Francis
497	SULLIVAN, Joseph	6501	FEENEY, John
2284	ERICSON, Alfred	7233	FELL, Thomas Arthur
7815	ERLANDSON, Eric	2135	FELLOWS, Benjamin James
7231	ESLER, John	Lieut	FENTON, Arthur Benjamin
2505	ETCHELL, Ernest James Herbert	1034	FENTON, Arthur Wallace
		2854	FENTON, George Samuel
7837	ETTERIDGE, Ruben	3665	FERDINAND, Charles
1031	EUSTACE, Harold Alfred	3741	FERGUS, Zeglar Hugh
1032	EUSTACE, John Montague	6766	FERGUSON, Bannerman Allen
683	EVA, Osward Francis St. David	1648	FERGUSON, David Bowie
1483	EVANS, Arthur Richard	6014	FERGUSON, Henry George
1482	EVANS, Aubrey Charles	5087	FERGUSON, Robert
5388	EVANS, Charles	709	FERGUSON, Robert William
3482	EVANS, Charles Clarence Albert	2581	FETTES, William Fyffe
		3290	FEW, Frederick George
6971	EVANS, David John	Lieut	FEWSTER, George Edward
3596	EVANS, Edward John	3291	FEWTRELL, George James
1030	EVANS, Frank Hubert	1865	FIELD, William Alfred
4161	EVANS, Gilbert Tidyman	3115	FIELDING, Harold Ernest
1484	EVANS, John	747	FIELDING, John Howard
5394	EVANS, Llewellyn	3745	FIENBERG, Leonard Maurice
592	EVANS, Stanley Prince	7232	FILL, William Boydon
4392	EVERDING, Burnett Albert	3739	FINGER, Norman Lionel
7504	EVERETT, Alfred Bertram	6767	FINIMORE, David Victor
6765	EVES, Joseph John	7508	FINLAYSON, Frank Japp

HISTORY OF THE 15th BATTALION

No.	Name	No.	Name
1151	FINN, George Frederick	2647	FORMAN, George
Capt	FISH, Walter William Page	7709	FORREST, Arthur
132	FISHER, Frank Francis	136	FORREST, Andrew Archibald
133	FISHER, Frederick George	3046	FORREST, Archibald James
134	FISHER, Henry Norman		FORRESTER, George John
4039	FISHER, Leslie George		(Served As)
1322A	FISHER, Vivian Williams	4238	MESURE, George John
3292	FISHER, William Archibald	1489	FORRESTER, William Henry
593	FITCHETT, George		Goldstraw
1944	FITTOCK, Edwin Rowlings	291	FORSTER, Albert Henry
4788	FITZGERALD, Cecil	3294	FORSTER, Ralph
1862	FITZGERALD, Emmett	2363	FORWARD, William Henry
5582	FITZGERALD, John	892	FOSTER, Edwin Charles
3485	FITZGERALD, Maurice	2134	FOSTER, Frederick Francis
2136	FITZGERALD, Thomas Joseph	282	FOSTER, Henry Albert
7236	FITZGERALD, William Thomas	1321	FOSTER, James Harry
1496	FITZHERBERT, Charles Edward	1745	FOSTER, John York
6260	FITZPATRICK, Edward George	7630	FOSTER, Kenneth John Henry
1418	FITZROY, Frederick	4374	FOSTER, Oakleigh Hawthorn
3109A	FITZSIMMONS, Francis Leo		Riggs
2241	FIVEASH, Herbert Edward	Lieut	FOSTER, Reginald William
6782	FLANAGAN, Daniel Mickel	3740	FOSTER, Samuel
1877	FLANAGAN, Francis	6257	FOWERAKER, John
3110	FLANAGAN, Martin Lawrence	2670	FOWLER, Charles William
890	FLANAGAN, William Thomas		Henry
594	FLEET, Francis John	7706	FOWLER, Frank
7346	FLEGG, Sydney Frank	3597	FOWLER, George Hopetoun
5398	FLEMING, Archibald	137	FOWLER, Wilbraham Lee
2835	FLEMING, Percy James	2065	FOX, Edward
3318	FLEMING, William Thomas	3173	FOX, Hugh
1380	FLEMING, Albert Victor	595	FOX, Roy
435	FLETCHER, Joseph	4498	FOX, William George
5577	FLETCHER, Merlin Dove	2066	FRA, Argentine
7707	FLEWELL-SMITH, Bernard	2708	FRAMPTON, Harold James
1647	FLIGHT, William	2137	FRANCIS, David Thomas
5399	FLINT, William	Lieut	FRANCIS, Eric
2064	FLOOD, Daniel	Capt	FRANCIS, Joseph
5396	FOGARTY, Cecil Norman	2677	FRANCIS, Norman
6262	FOGARTY, Frederick Thomas	2956	FRANCIS, Percy Sydney
Lieut	FOGARTY, Neville Richmond	7153	FRANCIS, William Douglas
7351	FOGG, Archibald Vincent	1036	FRANKCOMBE, Vernon Egbert
10	FOLEY, Archibald Thomas	1323A	FRANKLIN, Alfred Richard
11	FOLEY, Joseph Vincent	2550	FRANKLIN, John Frederick
1180	FOLEY, Percy Joseph	3744	FRASER, Arthur
135	FOOT, Henry Daintree	2217	FRASER, Bromley Campbell
2088	FORBES, Archibald Albert		Cadogan
2736	FORD, Arnold David	1488	FRASER, Henry Bromley
4784	FORD, Curtis		Cadogan
8	FORD, Ernest	4406	FRASER, James
190	FORD, Ernest	Lieut	FRASER, James Hugh William
6261	FORD, George Douglas	745	FRASER, John
1487	FORD, Harold John	4499	FRASER, John
4789	FORD, James	6556	FRASER, John Henry
6015	FORD, James Horn	1324A	FRASER, John Robert
3309	FORD, John Reginald	6615	FRASER, Malcolm John
3296	FORD, Robert	6017	FRASER, William George
3298	FORD, William	1669	FRAWLEY, Leslie Thomas

HISTORY OF THE 15th BATTALION

No.	Name	No.	Name
1945	FREDRICKSON, William	2856	GARVEY, Richard Oliver
3300	FREEMAN, Charles Henry	4797	GATES, Thomas
Lieut	FREEMAN, Douglas Stephen	3311	GATLEY, Francis Ernest
6768	FREEMAN, Edgar Cecil	2365	GAULD, Harry Rutland
4298	FREEMAN, John Edgar	6560A	GAULT, Joseph
1038	FREEMAN, Henry William Dew	711	GEARING, James
2/Lieut	FRENCH, Charles Granville	2706	GEARY, Osmond Richard Dudley
6499	FRENCH, Christopher Edward		
1646	FRENCH, Harold Dale	7816A	GEATER, Harry
3029	FRENCH, Herbert	1610	GELLIE, Harry Norman
3598	FRESHNEY, Charles Ernest	4311	GEMMELL, William
437	FRETWELL, John William	653A	GENDERS, Hugh Clyde
3743	FROHMULLER, Thomas	1325A	GENFORD, Benjamin
5676	FROST, Albert Anthony	4802	GEORGE, Edwin
5792	FROST, George	597	GEORGE, Ernest
6502	FROST, Percy Southwell	1749	GEORGE, Richard
1381	FROST, William	7090	GERARD, William Marshall
6258	FROSTROP, Patrick John	3754	GERRARD, William Charles
7771	FROY, Archibald Samuel	6018	GESLER, John Rae
1744	FRY, Ernest David	1382	GIBBONS, Arthur James
1943	FRY, John George	2958	GIBBONS, William
2988	FRY, Percy Oscar	6267	GIBSON, Colgan Stewart
5791	FUDGE, Edgar	1949	GIBSON, Frederick William
746	FUHRMAN, Norman	3032	GIBSON, James
205A	FULLER, David Henry	Lieut	GIBSON, Peter
2898	FULLER, Robert	3747	GIBSON, Thomas
6749	FULTON, William	2738	GIBSON, William Albert
6874	FUNNELL, Benjamin	2959	GIBSON, William James
2863	FURMAN, Henry Garfield	3819	GIGGINS, Archibald Roland
7239	GADSBY, Arthur Leslie	2366	GIGGINS, Thomas Charles
3051	GAFFEL, George Henry	1383	GILBERT, George Raymond
3751	GAGE, William Bramwell	1492	GILBERT, Harold Aubrey
138	GAILLARD, Lucien	6504	GILBERT, Herbert Maidment
1041	GALE, Frederick George	7241	GILES, Francis James
2430	GALL, Alexander Ward	4792	GILES, Roy William
5405	GALL, Frederick	286	GILL, Arthur Livingstone
3306	GALLAGHER, Albert Ernest	598	GILL, Henry Albert
2747A	GALLAGHER, Herbert	5407	GILL, John James
6769	GALLAGHER, Herbert Peter	5680	GILL, Thomas Henry
2669	GALLOWAY, John	438	GILL, Thomas Richard
38	GAMBLE, William Fitzpatrick	287	GILL, William James
4376	GARDAM, Harold Leon	2740	GILLARD, Solomon John
7354	GARDE, William Ievers	1326A	GILLESPIE, Robert
1868	GARDENER, Leslie	5402	GILLESPIE, William
7710A	GARDINER, Walter Henry	2/Lieut	GILLIES, David Martin
2745	GARDNER, Alfred James	1494	GILLIGAN, Francis Abraham
7240	GARDNER, Stephen Henry	1043	GILLIGAN, James
1691	GARDNER, William Elliott	1493	GILLIGAN, John
7475	GARDNER, William Henry	4790	GILLIGAN, Richard
2138	GARGET, Edward	2139	GILLINGHAM, Leslie William
3308	GARLICK, Richard	1718	GILLOT, Robert Leslie Richard
283	GARNER, Arthur Frederick	6129	GILMORE, Francis John
596	GARRATT, John Clarence	3307	GILMOUR, David Stewart
1040	GARRETT, Melville Roy	2364	GILSON, George Herbert
4803	GARTNER, Henry	6976	GILVEAR, Thomas
7712	GARTON, George William	3753	GIRDLER, Richard Radley
7711	GARTON, Richard James	1726	GIVENS, Alexander

HISTORY OF THE 15th BATTALION

No.	Name	No.	Name
Capt	GLASGOW, Robert	7715	GRAHAM, Carl Herbert Herman
7238	GLEESON, Michael		
2737	GLENDENNING, Clarence	1495	GRAHAM, Dickson David Ballantine
5818	GLINDON, John Edward		
599	GLITHRO, Arthur	351	GRAHAM, Edgar Richard
1182	GLOVER, Alfred Percy	2558	GRAHAM, George Clark
139	GLOVER, Walter Nestor	6C21	GRAHAM, James
4791	GLOVER, Walter Winford	1947	GRAHAM, Percy
2314	GNATZ, John Henry	2587	GRAINGER, William Paterson
2232	GODDARD, Owen	6777	GRANT, Garden
4619	GODDING, Roy William	895	GRANT, Jack
439	GODEBYE, Alfred Eugene	2140	GRANT, James Stevenson
3748	GODFREY, Charles	Lieut	GRANT, John
441	GODFREY, James William	3157	GRANT, Malcolm Fraser
6978	GOLDEN, George	142	GRANT, Patrick
7479	GOLDEN, James	1611	GRANT, Robert John
6977	GOLDEN, Lewes	4795	GRAY, Charles
140	GOLDRING, Gordon	143	GRAY, Christopher
Lieut	GONINON, Wesley	2/Lieut	GRAY, Michael Harcourt
1746	GOOD, James	1328A	GRAY, Robert Grogan
Capt	GOOD, John Anderson	1327A	GRAY, Robert Thomas
7788A	GOODALL, Reginald George	2068	GRAY, Walter
7480	GOODALL, Stanley	5773	GREASLEY, Arthur George
1817	GOODE, Lynton	3302	GREAVES, Charles William
3304	GOODFELLOW, George Graham	2957	GREEN, Charles Montieth
3749	GOODGER, Mainard Lancaster	6022	GREEN, Charles William
365	GOODING, Arthur George	1705	GREEN, Edgar
552	GOODLETT, Clifford	2368	GREEN, Frederick Charles
2748	GOODWIN, Edward	3315	GREEN, George Henry
601	GOODWIN, George	6503	GREEN, Harry
2739	GOODYER, Basil	4799	GREEN, John Herbert
1420	GOOK, George Edward	7350	GREEN, Thomas Herbert
6975	GORDON, Alexander	4902	GREEN, William
1419	GORDON, Hugh Henry	4776	GREENBERG, Isaac
600	GORDON, John	4828	GREENE, Ernest
4794	GORDON, John James	4798	GREENSILL, Walter Joseph
1183	GORDON, Louis Clive	7702	GREENWOOD, Amos
6265	GORDON, Norman Victor	3479	GREENWOOD, Arthur Louis
7481	GORDON, Robert Shepherd	Lieut	GREENWOOD, James Esrick
141	GORDON, William	7581	GREGORY, Hubert Hardy
5683	GORDON, William George	6776	GREGORY, Joseph
894	GORDYN, William Henry	2142	GREHOFF, Parfeny
1491	GORE, James Henry	3752	GRESHAM, George Munro
1490	GORE, Stanley Frederick	6266	GREY, Henry Stephens
2831	GORMAN, Peter	3305	GREY, Patrick
6019	GORMAN, Thomas Michael	1748	GRIFFIN, Claude Edward
5403	GORST, William Harold	2832	GRIFFIN, John
5401	GORTON, Frederick Leathes	3057	GRIFFIN, Roy Harold
4801	GOSMAN, Frederick Charles	7682	GRIFFIN, Thomas Gerald
Capt	GOSS, Cecil Spencer	442	GRIFFIN, William
3312	GOUGH, Edward	378	GRIFFITH, Henry Heath
440	GOUGH, Harold	3303	GRIFFITHS, Arthur Anderson
629	GOUGH, William John	3750	GRIFFITHS, John Kendall
12	GOWER, George Ernest	1322	GRIFFITHS, Norman Smith
1946	GOWER, Wilfred Rotherham	2067	GRIFFITHS, Rex Thorley
6020	GRACE, John Joseph	1421	GRIGG, Albert John
1818	GRAHAM, Andrew	285	GRIMES, Roland McMillan

HISTORY OF THE 15th BATTALION

No.	Name	No.	Name
2439	GRIMMER, William David	1330A	HAMILTON, James George
551	GRIMSEY, George Stephen	6274	HAMILTON, Joseph Edward
4889	GRISBROOK, Leonard	5694	HAMILTON, Leslie John
5564	GROGAN, Oliver Francis	1750	HAMILTON, Robert
144	GROOM, Frederick George	6389	HAMILTON, Sydney
1941	GROOM, Valentine Patrick	3037	HAMILTON, Thomas
3033	GROVES, Ernest Edwin	2686	HAMILTON, William
5678	GRUMMITT, William Henry	2754	HAMILTON, William
2811	GUBBINS, William	5424	HAMILTON, William Samuel
2707A	GUDGE, James Henry	13	HAMMANS, John Leonard
1612	GUERIN, Patrick Clarence	3766	HAMMATT, William Milton
502	GUILFOYLE, William Lake	1325	HAMMOND, Arthur Cyril
3310	GULLETT, Henry	3096	HAMMOND, Arthur James
671	GUNTON, Peter Thomas	2373	HAMMOND, Charles Ackroyd
7483	GUTHRIE, James	3334	HAMMOND, Edward Henry
1649	GUTHRIE, Norman Bruce	1651	HAMMOND, Robert Elijah
3035	GUY, James Cavan	7248	HAMMOND, Walter
1747	GUY, Robert Henry	3163	HAMPE, Rudolph Henry
37	GWYNNE, William David	6987	HANCOX, George
2374	HAAPANEN, Toivo	6779	HANDFORD, George
	HAAPANIEMI, Hugo Edmund (Served as)	1157	HANIGAN, Cecil Herbert
		145	HANLEY, Frederick Alexander
6706	ASPLUND, Hugo	2590	HANLON, Frank
2145	HACKETT, John Canham	902	HANMAN, Eric Francis
289	HACKETT, Thomas James	1951	HANN, Thomas James
2146	HACKETT, William Thomas	2149	HANNANT, Frederic
4813	HACKWOOD, Albert Edward	1844	HANSEN, Albert Edward
6023	HADDOW, Herbert James	2814	HANSEN, Arthur Delhlef
7721A	HAGEVALE, John Sevirin	555	HANSEN, Arthur Harold
443	HAGUE, Sydney Harold	6275	HANSEN, Ernest
907	HAHN, Ernest Francis	7703	HANSEN, Harold Anton
1734	HAINS, Malcolm	290	HANSEN, Henry
5430	HAIRS, Frances Walter	1950	HANSEN, Herbert Walter
3317	HALL, Ernest John Bradford	3140	HANSEN, Jack
3599	HALL, George Joseph Oakcliffe	3755	HANSEN, Lawrence
1731A	HALL, James Alexander	2788	HANSEN, Rasmus Martin
6992	HALL, James Augustus Octavius	6131	HANSEN, Sydney Matthew
		1737	HANSEN, Trevor Lorimor
7724	HALL, John Edward	5416	HANSEN, William Jesse
7244	HALL, Lindsay Gordon	5112	HANSHAW, Frank Layton
2451	HALL, Thomas Henry	5689	HANSON, Archibald Charles
7484	HALL, Wilfred Edward	158	HANSON, Richard Stephen
1732	HALLETT, George Henry	904	HARDAKER, William John Francis
2508	HALLETT, Harry Locke		
1696	HALLORAN, George Edgar	2369	HARDEN, James
3321	HALSEY, George Alfred	7848	HARDIN, Leslie Harold
1323	HAMBLIN, Ernest	1045	HARDING, George Ernest
6282	HAMILL, Roy	6981	HARDING, Theophilus George
3765	HAMILTON, Archibald Lloyd	1615	HARDMAN, Roy
5695	HAMILTON, Benjamin Burnett	3188	HARDSTAFF, Hazel Charles
2147	HAMILTON, Charles Frederick	146	HARE, Andrew
1446	HAMILTON, Charles Robert	147	HARE, Bertram
6778	HAMILTON, Donald Bruce	2961	HARE, Henry John
4314	HAMILTON, Frank Sidney Thalia	2749	HARGRAVE, Alexander
		905	HARGRAVE, Hugh
6514	HAMILTON, Hugh	2/Lieut	HARKINS, Thomas Patrick
1422	HAMILTON, James	291	HARLAND, Walter

HISTORY OF THE 15th BATTALION 263

No.	Name	No.	Name
4378	HARMAN, Augustine Thomas	2234	HATRICK, Robert Ellis
	HARMENING, Frederick	2752	HATTE, William
	William (Served as)	5108	HATTON, Ernest George
5412	HATTON, Frederick	6592	HAUENSCHILD, John Henry
7720A	HARP, Herman Henry	6025	HAUPT, Percy Alfred
1196	HARPER, Athol Thomas	2436	HAVERS, George James
4819	HARPER, Bertie	901	HAWKES, George John
1195	HARPER, David James	1952	HAWKES, James
6505	HARPER, Edwin James	2143	HAWKINS, Roy
3224	HARPER, Gordon	292	HAWKINS, Samuel
5108	HARPER, John Alexander	5411	HAWKINS, William Douglas
297	HARPER, Roland Henry	854	HAWKINS, William Frank
7791	HARPER, Walter Augustus	3774	HAWLEY, James Vincent
7681	HARPHAM, Francis Ratcliffe	5691	HAWORTH, Elijah
1751	HARRAP, Thomas William	7245	HAWTHORNE, Stuart
1329A	HARREX, Albert	3332	HAWTHORNE, William Francis
5414	HARRINGTON, Thomas	6026	HAY, Clarence Norman Edward
4817	HARRIS, Albert Victor	1189	HAYDEN, Arthur Vernon
1708	HARRIS, Alfred Victor	2820	HAYDON, John Paul
1049	HARRIS, George Albert	3187	HAYDON, Laurence Charles
7340	HARRIS, James	1324	HAYES, Herbert Richard
7344	HARRIS, Robert Harold	1953	HAYES, Joseph Alphonsus
2838	HARRIS, William	2069	HAYES, Joseph Charles
3759	HARRIS, William James	5688	HAYES, William John
603	HARRIS, William Locke	4808	HAYMAN, Ernest Thomas
5692	HARRISON, Frederick	2591	HAYS, George
6280	HARRISON, Henry Ernest	1739	HAYWARD, James William
1048	HARRISON, James Tasman	3036	HAZELTON, Stanley
5434	HARRISON, John	3063A	HEALEY, William Augustus
1199	HARRISON, Neville Mackersey	685	HEALY, Larry
4171	HARRISON, Robert Wood	4515	HEALY, Robert Rolf
3600	HARRISON, Vivian	4514	HEARD, Ernest George
899	HARRISON, William	1423	HEATH, Walter
86	HARRISON, William Edmund	748	HEATHCOTE, Frederick Merton
Capt	HARRY, Samuel William	1044	HEAWOOD, Edward Oscar
1652	HARRY, Victor Clarence	1754	HEENAN, John
	Curnow	Capt	HEFFER, Thomas Baker
7704	HARSLETT, John Richard	7246	HERRERNAN, Patrick Joseph
2916A	HART, George Charles	6630	HEGARTY, Francis
148	HARTIGAN, Philip Stanley	2376	HEHIR, Thomas
5697	HARTLEY, George William	2960	HEHIR, William John
2502	HARTLEY, William George	5693	HEILBROWN, Carswell
1865	HARTNETT, Arnold James		Alexander
121	HARVEY, Arthur	7723A	HEIRDSFIELD, Charles
1187	HARVEY, Athol Kingston		Frederick
5120	HARVEY, Christian William	2375	HELLICAR, Valentine Arthur
7243	HARVEY, Frederick Alfred	5687	HELMORE, Douglas William
4512	HARVEY, George		Ernest
5422	HARVEY, Richard	3185	HEMPHILL, Jeffrey
7718	HARVEY, William Crosbie	4815	HEMPSALL, James George
3634	HARVEY, William John	1613	HENDERSON, Alfred
6780	HARVIE, Harry	5432	HENDERSON, Donald Ewan
3322	HASSALL, Rowland James		Stewart
1404	HASTINGS, Frederick John	604	HENDERSON, George
6991	HASZ, William John	1500	HENDERSON, James
2689	HATCHMAN, Forbes James	445	HENDERSON, James Watson
3325	HATHAWAY, Leonard George	3601	HENDERSON, John

No.	Name	No.	Name
5431	HENDERSON, John	6031	HILL, David
3316	HENDERSON, Leonard Matthew	2594	HILL, Ernest Henry
6983	HENDERSON, Samuel	7531	HILL, George Arthur
554	HENDERSON, Thomas Kay	6032	HILL, Gilbert Frank
7705	HENDERSON, Walter Boon	1755	HILL, Henry
6782	HENDRY, James Ross	2753	HILL, James Robbie
1850	HENDRY, William	Major	HILL, John
4809	HENDY, Clifford Henry	1423A	HILL, John Thomas
6506	HENRY, Andrew Dow	3044	HILL, Leonard
6507	HENRY, James Buchanan	Lieut	HILL, Samuel John
715A	HENRY, John	4517	HILL, Thomas Aspel
446	HENRY, John Williaim	3039	HILL, William
1194	HENRY, Norman	3772	HILLAN, James
6982	HENZELL, Thomas Carlisle	1863	HILLIER, Louis
3326	HERBERTSON, Norman Ernest	3186	HILLS, Charles
7719A	HERMAN, Charles Albert	1192	HILLS, Clifford John
6511	HERMAN, Frank	1650	HILLS, Joseph Norman
Lieut	HERON, Gilbert Septimus	4051	HILLS, Percy
5565	HERON, Leslie Lionel	2370	HILTON, Thomas
1185	HERON, Walter Francis	1614	HINCHMORE, Arthur
2435	HERRIDGE, Arthur	1498	HIND, Stanley Arthur
3138	HERROD, Harry	4806	HINDMARSH, Edwin
2190	HERRON, George Knight	1186	HINDS, James
575	HESSEY, Bernard	4804	HINDS, Leonard Michael
6027	HESTER, Alfred	Lieut	HINES, Walter John
3768	HETHERINGTON, Hayslip Fairfax	Lieut	HINMAN, Arthur Gurr
		1864	HINTON, Vernon Huon
149	HETHERINGTON, John	6033	HIPATHITE, William
447	HEWITT, Frederick Charles	6783	HIRON, Francis Henry
6985	HEWITT, Victor Henry	6784	HIRON, Percy Augustus
6271	HICHENS, Walter Richard Howell	1050	HIRST, Percy Charles
		3762	HIRST, William
293	HICKERTON, Harry	3333	HISCOCK, Guy
4315	HICKEY, James Martin	4816	HOAR, Mark Reginald
6627	HICKEY, James Patrick	3101	HOARE, Frederick Percy
3327	HICKEY, John Morris	452	HOBBS, Henry George
6980	HICKEY, John Patrick	3320	HOBSON, Eric Scott
1402	HICKEY, Reginald James Thomas	3318	HOBSON, James Allan
		Lieut	HOCKER, Leonard Arthur
1753	HICKEY, Richard William	3764	HOCKING, Joseph Francis
6510	HICKEY, William Martin	6369	HOCKING, William Samuel
76	HICKLING, John Robert	298	HODGE, James D'Orset
6028	HICKS, John Leslie	2447	HODGE, John James
6979	HICKS, Leslie	3635	HODGE, Joshua Edward
3760	HICKS, Thomas Joseph Arthur	4521	HODGE, Leonard
7808	HIGGINS, Daniel	1994	HODGE, William James
4820	HIGGINS, Francis	3803	HODGE, William John
6029	HIGGINS, John	2144	HODGES, Lewis George
6030	HIGGINS, Thomas	632	HODGETTS, Mervyn
294	HIGSON, William Clarence	5794	HODGINS, Richard John
2371	HILDEBRAND, George Walter	1956	HODGKINSON, Arthur Herbert
3637	HILDER, Alfred Robert	6993	HODGKINSON, William Thomas
2291	HILDER, Arden Arthur Harold		
2290	HILDER, Basil Richard	1104	HODGMAN, Douglas Allan
1748	HILGENDORF, Hubert John Henry	750	HODSDON, Charles Harold
		6786	HODSON, William
453	HILL, Bert	1336	HOEY, Cyril Ashley

HISTORY OF THE 15th BATTALION

No.	Name	No.	Name
4814	HOEY, Henry	2510	HORTON, Frederick Norwood
1744	HOFFMANN, Henry Edward	605	HOSKIN, Frederick William
5969	HOGAN, John Joseph	3038	HOSKINS, William Vidall
2998	HOGAN, Matthew Thomas	4811	HOULDSWORTH, Henry
6036	HOGAN, Michael	5228	HOURIGAN, Joseph
3045	HOGAN, Patrick	2827	HOURIGAN, Robert Edward
6037	HOGAN, Patrick Joseph	5428	HOUSEGO, Thomas Henry
751	HOGBEN, William	2512	HOW, Neil
Lieut	HOHNEN, Frederick Henry	2509	HOW, Ralph
4888A	HOLCROFT, Irvine Edgar	2070	HOWARD, Charles
6989	HOLDEN, Herbert	1188	HOWARD, Earl Stephen
2433	HOLDEN, Walter	2151	HOWARD, Edward
3486	HOLDWAY, Walter Adrian	6508	HOWARD, John
1706	HOLLAMBY, Charles	2962	HOWARD, John Stephen
4575	HOLLAMBY, Walter Ernest	2963	HOWARD, Sidney
3757	HOLLAND, Albert Roy	4818	HOWARTH, George
1334A	HOLLAND, Cecil Walter	5418	HOWE, Albert
5774	HOLLAND, Thomas Edward	608	HOWELL, Charles William
3328	HOLLEY, Bertie	3132	HOWES, Ernest Sidney
900	HOLLIDAY, John Henry	3773	HOWIE, Hugh McLay
6990	HOLLINDALE, Douglas James	6988	HOWIE, Matthew Philip
1616	HOLLINGSWORTH, Allen	151	HOWITZ, Maxwell
898	HOLLINGSWORTH, Thomas Henry Montague	5433	HOWLETT, Daniel John
		6270	HOWLETT, John
6509	HOLLIST, Benjamin Bromley	7706	HOWLEY, Patrick Joseph
2506	HOLLOWAY, Arthur William		HOWLEY, Roger Francis
3467	HOLLOWAY, Henry Bonsell		(Served as)
5684	HOLMES, Henry Francis	1986	O'CONNOR, Patrick
6035	HOLMES, James Thomas	3767	HOXEY, Leslie George
295	HOLMES, William Ewart	1499	HUDSON, Frederick Arthur
2289	HOLT, Harold John	152	HUDSON, Robert William
4316	HOLT, Joseph	1497	HUDSON, Vincent
6787	HOLTER, William Frederick	897	HUGHES, Harrison
5415	HOOD, Edward James	749	HUGHES, Henry George
6269	HOOKER, William Albert	2596	HUGHES, Murdoch
2343	HOOLAHAN, John Patrick	6984	HUGHES, Walter Evan
606	HOOPER, Andrew Alexander	1335A	HUGHES, William John
5832	HOOPER, Ben	4812	HULBERT, George Edwin
6863	HOOPER, Frederick William	7726	HULETT, John Bertram
3761	HOOPER, John Henry	6278	HULL, George Thomas
449	HOOPER, John Walls Bamford	4522	HULSEN, Alexander
215	HOOPER, William Ernest	3040	HUME, James
1193	HOPE, Edward Somerville	1954	HUMPHREY, Jesse
3308	HOPGOOD, Thomas John	1955	HUMPHREY, William
607	HOPKINS, Sydney	4821	HUMPHREYS, Edward
908	HOPKINS, William Hedley	2372	HUMPHREYS, Frank Matthews
6227	HOPTON, Henry	1911	HUNN, Arthur Herbert
3330	HORNE, Alfred William	6513	HUNT, Andrew Clarence
Capt	HORNE, Harry Clarence	1052	HUNT, George Albury
	HORNE, John	296	HUNT, Herbert Clive
	(Served as)	1051	HUNT, Tennyson Elwin
1332A	BRAYTHWAITE, Arthur Joseph	7242	HUNT, Walter
2184	HORNUNG, George Frederick	1197	HUNT, William
150	HORRIGAN, James Fitzgibbon	451	HUNTER, Robert Alexander
717	HORROBIN, Robert Abraham	3342	HUNTER, William Andrew
1047	HORTIN, Edley Cyril	450	HUNTER, William Henry
1190	HORTIN, Henry Pierce		

No.	Name	No.	Name
906	HURFORD, Harold Charles Arthur	3335	JACKSON, William
5420	HURFORD, Thomas Stanley Norman	4380	JACKSON, William
		3376	JACOB, Francis
		2965	JACOBS, Ernest Roy
6995	HURLEY, Jermiah	155	JACOBS, Henry
5696	HURLEY, Joseph Patrick King	1053	JACOBSEN, Charles Thomas
6124	HURRELL, George Henry	427	JACOBSON, Albert Edward
Lieut	HURRY, George	7712	JAGD, Hans Peter
2751	HURST, Albert Victor	3046	JAGGER, Herbert
7083	HURST, Frederick Henry	5436	JAGGS, William Charles
2/Lieut	HURST, James Abraham	3776	JAGO, George James
4179	HUSBAND, William John	2741	JAMES, Alick Thomas
1653	HUTCHINGS, Charles	1505	JAMES, David
2750	HUTCHINGS, Walter	15	JAMES, Evan Edward
4516	HUTCHINS, Francis John	300	JAMES, Frederick
4518	HUTCHINSON, Charles Wesley	2725	JAMES, George Henry
6279	HUTCHINSON, Francis	2760	JAMES, Hay Francis
609	HUTCHINSON, John Thomas	1995	JAMES, Henry
6788	HUTCHINSON, Thomas Athalbyn	910	JAMES, Noel
		301	JAMES, Patrick Vernon
2597	HUTCHISON, Thomas	518	JAMES, Wilfred Skelton
1867	HYATT, Selwyn Garnet	2379	JAMESON, Patrick Francis
153	HYDE, Charles Edward William	Lieut	JAMIESON, George
		2/Lieut	JAMIESON, John Hay
1198	HYLAND, Patrick	3337	JAMIESON, Robert Reginald
Capt	HYNES, John Thomas	Lieut	JAMIESON, Walter James
5429	HYSLOP, Ernest	4385	JAMISON, Vincent Stanley
610	IDDLES, John	6288	JAPPE, Severin Leslie
3604	ISLES, Gorden Henery	6791	JARMAN, Herbert William
2964	ILLINGWORTH, Percy Edward	4823	JARMAN, Richard Roy
2152	INCH, James Gibson	3775	JARETT, George Bellinger
299	INESON, Abraham	7251	JARRETT, Harry
5713	INGHAM, Allan	6516	JARRETT, Walter Thomas
3934	INGLIS, Malcolm Fergus	3777	JARVIS, Arthur Thomas
5698	INGRAM, Charles Thomas	3605	JAYNES, Walter Tasmania
7708	INGRAM, Gordon	3778	JEFFERSON, Elliott Silvester
Capt	INGRAM, John	7711	JEFFERSON, Frederick
6286	INNES, David Minto Bannerman	1501	JEFFERY, Percival Napier
562	INNIS, Athol Rupert	5703	JEFFERY, William John
752	INMAN, Robert	1506	JEFFREY, John
977	INTRUP, Charles Alfred Blackwood	3336	JEFFREY, William Stuart
		7817	JEFFRIES, Cecil Herbert
2695	IREDALE, Tom George Warneford	1503	JEFFRIES, Maurice Edward
		2242	JELLETT, Frederick
5435	IRISH, John Joseph	6515	JEMMETT, Frank John
2493	IRVINE, Laurence	156	JENKIN, Roy Vernon
4379	IRVING, William	2012	JENKINS, Albert Howell
217	IRWIN, Hamilton William	3339	JENKINS, Alfred Barrett
4321	IRWIN, John David	3116	JENKINS, Lewis
3771	ISGAR, John Inman	2705	JENKINS, Mordecai
2756	ISZLAUB, Percy Harold	6289	JENKINS, Neily
6789	JACK, John	1424	JENKINS, Rees
1286	JACKLIN, Abe	1502	JENKINS, Roy
1070	JACKMAN, Townley James	6792	JENKINS, William
6790	JACKSON, John	6793	JENKINSON, Arthur
5701	JACKSON, John Ina	2328	JENNINGS, Charles Henry
Lieut	JACKSON, Rupert Vaughan		

No.	Name	No.	Name
6794	JENNINGS, Francis William Henry	2038	JONES, Harold Moore
6997	JENSEN, Carl Frederick	4322	JONES, Henry
387	JENSEN, Hans Peter	6041	JONES, Henry Austin
2401	JENSEN, Joseph Norman	4535	JONES, Herbert Wynne
7709	JENSEN, Peter Christian	3119	JONES, James Percy
4534	JESSER, Joseph	1880	JONES, John
1868	JETSON, Ernest John	5972	JONES, John Henry
3118	JOHNS, Richard Norman	7710	JONES, Malcolm
	JOHNSON, Albert Leslie (Served As)	909	JONES, Norman Lyndon Cyril
		3461	JONES, Philip Alfred
330	NICHOLSON, James Norman	455	JONES, Thomas Leonard
1995	JOHNSON, Arthur	2156	JONES, William Draper
1202	JOHNSON, George Albert	1338B	JONES, William Thomas
1759	JOHNSON, Harry	1339A	JOPE, Robert Anderson
7796	JOHNSON, Henry Edward Victoria	2/Lieut	JOPLING, David Sunley
		1240	JORGENSEN, James Peter
3340	JOHNSON, James Alfred Roy	6287	JOSEPH, Alexander James
2599	JOHNSON, John Hilton	302	JOSH, Frank
5795	JOHNSON, Joseph Jaques	Lieut	JOUBERT, Sydney Herbert
389	JOHNSON, Norman Harold	6626	JOWETT, Albert Victor
1761	JOHNSON, Robert	2842	JOWETT, Arthur Norton
7252	JOHNSON, Thomas		JOYCE, John
6038	JOHNSON, Thomas Alfred		(Server As)
1958	JOHNSTON, Allan	1418A	BURNS, John
6795	JOHNSTON, Archibald William	3342	JOYCE, Stephen
Lt/Col	JOHNSTON, Charles Melbourne	1760	JUDGE, James Henry
6994	JOHNSTON, Claude Mervyn	4324	JULL, George
1340A	JOHNSTON, Cyril Allen	6614	JURD, Eric Richmond
7798	JOHNSTON, Francis Christopher	456	JURY, Richard
2224	JOHNSTON, Herbert Edward	4637	KAJEWSKI, George
7720	JOHNSTON, Herbert James	7858	KALINOWSKI, Joseph Patrick
2154	JOHNSTON, James Steel	1447	KALUCY, Frederick
1341A	JOHNSTON, John	4777	KANN, Burnett William
817	JOHNSTON, Leslie William	2411	KAUFFMAN, Matthew Oswald
1504	JOHNSTON, Lewis Leonard	1329	KAUFMANN, Cuthbert
2759	JOHNSTON, Norman	2327	KAVANAGH, Venner Frank
5821	JOHNSTON, Robert	3346	KAY, Walter Bradley
3117	JOHNSTON, Walter Richard	5442	KAYE, Harold Beardmore
6796	JOHNSTONE, Irving Robert	520	KEAIRNS, Victor Roy
15241	JOHNSTONE, Joseph Charles Ross	3782	KEALY, Patrick
		6766	KEAN, John
6998	JOHNSTONE, William	1327	KEANE, Thomas Lawrence
5575	JOLLY, Albert Edward	2603	KEARNEY, Gordon James
Lieut	JONES, Adolphus William Percy	2386	KEARNEY, William Arthur
		2292	KEARNS, Ernest Owen
2378	JONES, Arthur	2966	KEATING, Frederick William
4532	JONES, Arthur Ernest	2691	KEATING, Walter Robert
3120	JONES, Arthur Robert	2357A	KEECH, Thomas Ernest
456	JONES, Arthur William	1055	KEEFE, Robert Fleetwood
6039	JONES, Austin	6295	KEEP, Wesley Simmons
3338	JONES, Charles Julius	517	KEERS, Harold
157	JONES, David Cadwalader	46	KEIRLE, Albert
391	JONES, David Francis	3121A	KEITH, James Alfred
2757	JONES, Ernest Tate	1511	KELLEHER, John
2153	JONES, Frederick Harold	7818	KELLEY, Walter Edward
6042	JONES, Harold	3345	KELLY, Francis James
		1509	KELLY, George Henry

No.	Name	No.	Name
158	KELLY, Herbert	3784	KILGOUR, John
2416	KELLY, James	6518	KILMINSTER, Everett Gordon
3048	KELLY, John William	1205	KILPATRICK, Bertram William
6801	KELLY, Joseph Michael	5439	KILPATRICK, John Atherson
1959	KELLY, Joseph Patrick	585	KIM, William John
7729	KELLY, Patrick	2513	KIMBERLEY, John William
612	KELLY, Patrick Joseph	4327	KINCAID, Thomas Andrew Ronald
4540	KELLY, Percy Douglas		
2767R	KELLY, William	Capt	KING, Charles Henry
2384	KELSO, Arthur Lennard	1054	KING, Frank
1656	KELTIE, David	Capt	KING, George
7000	KEMP, Charles	4332	KING, Gilbert Edward
2158	KEMP, William Joseph	7538	KING, George Frederick
1960	KEMPSON, Sydney Thomas	5705	KING, Henry Ernest
1344A	KENDALL, Ewart Henry	4824	KING, Leonard Charles
755	KENDALL, Kenneth William	3785	KING, Robert George
7823	KENEFAKE, Martin	1425	KING, Robert John
6520	KENNA, Michael Peter	6999	KING, Samuel Edward
3349	KENNEALLY, Alexander	3386	KING, Walter George
4826	KENNEALLY, Rody	2763	KINGSTON, Joseph
4450	KENNEALLY, William	3329	KINGSTON, Norman Walter
457	KENNEDY, Alexander	710	KIRBY, Edward Ashton
Lt/Col	KENNEDY, Basil Carlyle	5440	KIRBY, James
4381	KENNEDY, Cyril James	3130	KIRCHOFF, Ernest Musgrave
6291	KENNEDY, Daniel	3177	KIRK, John
1961	KENNEDY, Jock	3129	KIRK, Thomas Graham
3122	KENNEDY, John	4536	KIRKEGAARD, Albert Clemen
1753	KENNEDY, Patrick	802	KIRKHAM, George Thomas
2626	KENNEDY, William Gilchrist	2703	KIRKLAND, Henry Albert
1204	KENNEDY, Walter Scott	3047	KITCHEN, Percy James
2535	KENNY, Hugh James	1962	KITCHENHAM, John Henry
3324	KENNY, James Alexander Charles	4539	KITCHER, William Henry
		2704	KITCHING, Frederick
2385	KENT, Herbert	1346A	KITSON, Albert
Lieut	KENT, Hugh Leslie	1113	KLAUKE, Gustav
2227	KENYON, Arthur Leslie	3347	KLEVE, William Henreich
Capt	KENYON, William Duncan	2514	KLINE, John William
2764	KEOGH, William	6294	KLUGE, Granville Victor
Lieut	KEOGH, William Henry	3348	KLUVER, Albert
1654	KEPPLER, Thomas George	305	KNICKEL, John Fred
303	KER, Frank Innes	2193	KNIGHT, Herbert James
3344	KERLEY, Henry John	159	KNIGHT, James Taylor
5706	KERR, Alfred James	6045	KNIGHT, James Thomas
7539	KERR, Robert William	6132	KNIGHT, Reginald
1345A	KERRIDGE, Robert	459	KNIGHT, William
6800	KERRIGAN, George	2093	KNIGHT, William Joseph
1510	KERRIGAN, Robert	611	KNIPE, Rupert Charles
6043	KERSHAW, Frank	1869	KNOWLES, Harold Chester
3606	KERSLAKE, Richard Harwood	634	KNOWLES, Thomas
Lieut	KESSEL, Harry	2/Lieut	KOCH, Franz Richard
304	KETTLEWELL, Albert Lawrence	Capt	KOCH, Harold Reginald
7253	KETTLEY, Frederick William	1508	KOLSTER, William Thomas
6297	KEVIN, William Spencer	1762	KOZAKOFF, Alexis
7753	KEYS, Charles Albert	7730	KREIGHER, Frederick George
1657	KIDD, John Alexander	6292	KRISTOFERSEN, Hans
6296	KIDNER, Herbert James	6290	KRUGER, Lawrence Victor
754	KIDNER, James Merson		

HISTORY OF THE 15th BATTALION

No.	Name	No.	Name
	KUJALA, Antti (Served As)	6862	LAUCHLAND, Andrew Veitch
1424A	LIND, Thomas	2768	LAUDER, Sidney James
Lieut	KUNKLER, Allan Richmond	7008	LAUDER, William
3786	KUSCH, Albert George	3797	LAURENCE, Ernest
1507	KYDD, George	1387	LAURIE, Bertram
	KYLE, John Browne (Served As)	3787	LAURIE, Walter
		5714	LAVERY, Robert
7671	BELL, James	4836	LAW, Frederick Alexander
2217	KYLE, Charles Samuel	7715	LAW, John
3352	LACEY, Ebenezer James	4056	LAWER, Joseph
Lieut	LACK, Herbert Robert Henry	1659	LAWLER, Archibald
463	LAFFAN, Charles George William	1060	LAWLER, Charles Edward
		1389	LAWLER, Richard James
1386	LAHEY, Thomas John	3361	LAWRENCE, Harold Henry
1347A	LAHIFF, Alfred James	4835	LAWRENCE, Henry
2606	LAIDLAW, William	464	LAWRENCE, John
1971	LAING, Arthur Brown	5059	LAWRIE, Charles John
2071	LAIRD, James	6046	LAWS, Fred Ruxton
6304	LAKE, Charles Norris	3333	LAWS, Robert Eland
6388	LAKE, William	1968	LAWSON, Edward
16	LAMB, Thomas	3026	LAWSON, Felix Spencer
914	LAMBERT, Gilbert Henry	4542	LAWSON, William Ernest
2161	LAMBERT, Mark	5444	LAWTON, Arthur Charles
1870	LAMBERT, Rene George	7259	LAXTON, Edward James
3614	LAMBERT, Roy Harold	1512	LAY, Claude Clifford
3607	LAMBERT, William Thomas	1209	LAYCOCK, Samuel
1965	LAMBERTON, John Andrew	1765	LAYTON, William
307	LAMBOURN, Frederick George	2928A	LEADBETTER, Thomas Elliott
1333	LAMBOURN, Reginald	3609	LEE, Frederick George
2160	LAMONT, Donald William	3177	LEE, James
2663	LAMONT, William Edmond	18	LEE, John Patrick
2164	LAMPAN, William George	3088	LEE, Patrick
916	LAMY, Harry	913	LEE, Rufus Augustine Richmond
2690	LANCASHIRE, Samuel Paul	2766	LEECE, Leonard Barton
3793	LAND, Henry Walter	1966	LEEDING, Walter George
2/Lieut	LANDY, Patrick	5445	LEGGATT, Richard
4333	LANE, Alfred Charles	4829	LEGOOD, Charles Ernest Wilson
7257	LANE, Alick Falloon	308	LEHFELDT, William Robert
Lieut	LANE, Frederick William	1514	LEIPER, Thomas
1763	LANE, Gilbert William	2/Lieut	LEITCH, Alfred Edward George
2607	LANE, Henry Alfred	7003	LEITCH, Edward
1754	LANE, Horace Arthur Herd	7006	LEITCH, James
7258	LANE, Robert Allan	Capt/Chap	LE-MAITRE, Edward
Capt	LANGBORNE, Arthur Lewis	1061	LENDERS, Lawrence Colville Francis
1097	LANGDON, Alfred Ralph		
613	LANGHORN, John Lewis	3788	LENIHAN, Harry Randolph
2825	LANGMAN, Herbert	614	LENNAN, Ernest Albury
6802	LANGSTON, Frank	1658	LENNANE, John
5452	LAPRAIK, David Devon	5446	LENNON, Vincent Roy
2835	LARACY, Thomas Joseph	2367	LENNON, Walter
3790	LARDER, Thomas William	2162	LENNOX, John James
3354	LARSEN, George	160	LENTON, James Henry
1348A	LARSEN, William	756	LEONARD, Norman Albert
6303	LARSON, Neiles Julius	3355	LERGESSNER, Walter Henry
3353	LATCHAM, Frank Harold	Capt	LESLIE, Francis Alwyn
6217	LATHAM, Harold Stewart	2388	LESLIE, Herbert Percy

No.	Name	No.	Name
1349A	LESLIE, James	1655	LONERGAN, James
1916	LESTER, Norman	6302	LONERGAN, William Augustis Michael
1513	LETORD, Louis George		
5709	LETTE, James Claude	1332	LONG, Edward Douglas
2980	LETTS, Edward	3792	LONG, Henry Walter
462	LEVINE, Michael	4832	LONG, Victor William
6906	LEWIS, Albert	3318	LONGTON, Eric York
466	LEWIS, George Matthew	7092	LONGWILL, Frederick William Raymond
1972	LEWIS, Walter Clement		
1745	LILBURNE, Edmund Percival	2230	LOPATEN, Vladimir
615	LIND, Robert Houston	17	LORD, George
912	LINDEMAN, Veitch Park	1331	LORD, Reginald William
7505	LINDLEY, Joseph	1262	LORD, Robert Stanley
1350A	LINDSAY, David George	6049	LORENZEN, Peter
1764	LINDSAY, George	5448	LOVE, Alexander
3049	LINDSAY, Gordon	5576	LOVE, Alexander
1701	LINDSAY, Henry	3608	LOVE, Charles Edward
3789	LINDSAY, Herbert Arthur	7007	LOVE, James
4546	LINDSAY, James Douglas	Capt	LOVEDAY, Arthur Cecil
2390	LINDSAY, John	7004	LOVEDAY, Ross
4839	LINDSAY, Michael	1210	LOVELESS, William John
6521	LINDSAY, Robert Mackay	7714	LOW, Arthur Ediom
1874	LING, Oswald	6050	LOW, George Alexander
1760	LINNARD, Ernest Arthur	6805	LOW, Peter
2163	LINNETT, Hubert Frederick	3675	LOWE, Eric George
6300	LINTER, Arthur Bryne	525	LOWE, Frank
3610	LINTON, Joseph Edward	5449	LOWE, Frederick
7005	LIPP, George John	3611	LOWE, Henry James
3139	LISLE, Edward Alexander	7718	LOWE, William Henry
Lieut	LISLE, Percy Albert	3795	LOWRY, Thomas Munro
1681	LISLE, William Richardson	7002	LOWRY, William Ernest
7716	LITHGOW, David Lansell	7009	LUCAS, Albert Edward
6047	LITTLE, Charles Henry	618	LUCAS, Archie
2/Lieut	LITTLE, Edwin Maurice	161	LUCAS, Guy Edgar
1564	LITTLE, George	4434	LUDBY, Harry
	LITTLE, Henry (Served As)	617	LUDLOW, Edgar Frederick
		1352A	LUKEY, Edgar Joseph
753	JACKSON, Alfred	310	LULHAM, Cecil Allen
1334	LITTLE, Norman Henry	5711	LUPTON, Alexander Patrick
Lieut	LIVINGSTONE, Francis Neil	Capt	LUTHER, John Guy Fitzmaurice
2930	LOBBAN, George		
7719	LOCARNINI, Herbert	Lieut	LUTHRELL, Guy Weston
1351A	LOCHHEAD, John Tucker	Capt	LUXMOORE, Coryman Henry
6298	LOCK, Percy Harold	6299	LUXON, William Francis
3796	LOCKHART, Edward	911	LUXTON, Richard Allan
1211	LOCKLEY, Charles Albert	Lieut	LUXTON, Robert Joseph
1208	LOCKWOOD, Sergia Wesley	3613	LYALL, Alexander George
4837	LOEWE, Sigismund	1059	LYALL, William Charles
1766	LOFT, John	4830	LYDEMENT, Harold James
915	LOFTS, Albert	2769	LYDEMENT, Walter George
2387	LOGAN, James A.	311	LYDFORD, Joseph
Lieut	LOGAN, Michael Joseph	7255	LYNCH, Gilbert Douglas
1515	LOGAN, Ronald Thomas	7822	LYNCH, James
7717	LOGUE, Robert Charles	7507	LYNCH, John James
7594	LOMAS, Rowland Frank Eugene	1660	LYNCH, Mason
		2742	LYNCH, Michael William
3791	LOMAX, Thomas	1206	LYNCH, Percy Ambrose

No.	Name	No.	Name
2/Lieut	LYON, Charles Herbert Scott	1983	MANSFIELD, John William
162	LYON, Frederick Gilbert	7088	MANSON, Alfred Victor
2465	LYONS, Arthur Michael Joseph	2296	MANSON, Charles Frankland
7256	LYONS, James	3815	MANSON, Gilbert
1207A	LYONS, John Lyall	316	MANT, Charles Henry Richardson
4544	LYONS, William John	7261	MANTTAN, Albert Gentener
1618	MACE, Charles Tasman	920	MARA, Ernest
687	MACKIE, Herbert Clarence Fitzroy	622	MARDEL, Frank Charles
		1062	MARK, Edward Leslie
7737	MACKIE, Peter McBride	1218	MARKHAM, Horace
4864	MACOUN, Robert Prince McCann	2397	MARKHAM, Montgomery
		3487	MARLOW, Joseph
3468	MADDEN, James Joseph	2681	MARPOLE, Richard James
3986	MADDEN, John MacDonald	2673	MARSDEN, Henry
3379	MADDEN, William John	1984	MARSH, Aubrey
3483	MADGE, Maitland	2839	MARSH, Louis John
621	MADIGAN, Thomas	163	MARSHALL, Alan
5715	MADSEN, George	626	MARSHALL, Albert Edward
Lieut	MAEGRAITH, Hugh Gilmore	Capt	MARSHALL, Albert Morris
2412	MAGILL, James	465	MARSHALL, Alexander
5822	MAGUIRE, William Murray	7263	MARSHALL, Archibald Douglas
1356B	MAHAFFEY, Robert		
1517	MAHER, Charles Leo	1723	MARSHALL, Frederick Theodore
392	MAHER, James Joseph		
1357A	MAHER, James Thomas	6054	MARSHALL, James Fleming
7736	MAHER, John	6528	MARSHALL, John William
3184	MAHER, Leslie	6573	MARSHALL, Thomas James
1619	MAHER, Michael	3375	MARSHALL, William
2072	MAHONEY, William	7014	MARSHALL, William James
1072	MAINE, Clarence William	3189	MARSHALL, William Silby Joseph
1073	MAINE, Henry Charles		
2293	MAINWARING, George Allen	2166	MARSTELLA, Thomas William
7509	MAKINGS, Frederick George	6531	MARTENS, Francis
1354A	MALCOLM, James Ronald	1336	MARTIN, Arnold
4655	MALONE, Arthur	164	MARTIN, Edgar Rupert
2437	MALONE, Joseph	759	MARTIN, Ernest Ross
3916	MALONE, Joseph Patrick	2074	MARTIN, George Alfred
6806	MALONE, Thomas	6133	MARTIN, Jack
6053	MALONEY, Norman Henry	1769	MARTIN, John James
2075	MALONEY, William Bernard	1979	MARTIN, John William
1520	MALOY, William Michael Gregory	1359A	MARTIN, Richard
		2236	MARTIN, Thomas
7264	MALPAS, James	7015	MARTIN, Thomas Gladstone
7021	MANDERSON, George Yorkson	3813	MARTIN, William
1881	MANEFIELD, John	317	MARTIN, William George
314	MANGAN, Michael	2469	MARTINDALE, John
	MANI, Peter (Served As)	3811	MARTINSON, August
		7262	MARTYN, Harry Thomas
2952	MAINEY, Percy	2/Lieut	MARTYR, Frederick
3368	MANN, Charles John	6814	MASKREY, Walter
3488	MANNING, John	165	MASON, Reginald Harry
865	MANNING, William George	4854	MASSIE, Ernest Edward
2776	MANSBRIDGE, Arthur Edward	762	MASSON, Joseph
1066	MANSFIELD, Albert Douglas	Lieut	MASTERSON, George Frederick
315	MANSFIELD, Arthur		
6314	MANSFIELD, Hugh	919	MATHERS, Chapman

HISTORY OF THE 15th BATTALION

No.	Name
2295	MATHERS, Donald Andrew
2178	MATHERS, Thomas James
3817	MATHESON, Louis
1214	MATHESON, Neil
1070	MATHESON, William Thomas
6311	MATHEWSON, Samuel George
Capt	MATTHEWS, Basil Garland
7177	MATTHEWS, James Frederick
1067	MATTHEWS, Leonard Oscar
3369	MATTHEWS, Thomas Franz
6315	MAUDSLEY, William Josiah
166	MAUNDER, Charles
1063	MAWER, Pleasant
3489	MAWBY, George
3347	MAXWELL, James Hamilton
318	MAY, Herbert Norman
4580	MAY, Sydney
6218	MAYFIELD, Frank Walton
2294	MAYNARD, Edward Lewis
6457	MAYOSS, George Edward
1427	MAYWOOD, Ernest
1426	MAYWOOD, William
167	MAZLIN, Leslie Wright
168	MAZLIN, Norman Henry
2347	MEADE, John
6312	MEADE, Patrick James
1775	MEARNS, Malcolm Livingstone
5453	MEDHURST, Norman Oscar
7022	MEECH, Robert
7027	MEEHAN, James Patrick
2168	MEILING, Rasmus Frederick
1772	MELDRUM, Peter
319	MELEDINE, Louis
705	MELIA, Edward
7780	MELLOR, Frank William
1361A	MELZER, Albert Cecil
6059	MENG, Frank Andrew
5726	MENZIES, Hector Bennett
Lieut	MERRELL, Frederick John
421	MESKELL, Ernest Edward
7019	METCALFE, Charles Edward
761	METCALFE, William Stephenson
5971	MEW, William Stanley
7270	MICHELI, Charles Harry Julius
730	MIDDLETON, William Maxwell
169	MIGHELL, Norman Rupert
6529	MIGNOT, John Charles
928	MIHELL, Walter Collyer
1217	MILBOURNE, Jack Drake
1873	MILES, George
624	MILES, George Ambrose
4382	MILES, Thomas Francis
760	MILFORD, Henry
6526	MILHAM, Jack
623	MILL, James Henderson
408	MILLAR, Henry Robert
23	MILLARD, George Ernest Ryan
	MILLARD, John (Served As)
7783A	SNOW, John
3812	MILLEDGE, Alfred Henry
1065	MILLEN, Charles John
40	MILLER, Adam
1363A	MILLER, David
7515	MILLER, Francis Macdonald
1874	MILLER, Frederick Roy
2910	MILLER, Gustavas Thompson
2693	MILLER, Henry
3378	MILLER, Henry Ernest
6525	MILLER, Herbert William
3058	MILLER, James Reid
1527	MILLER, John Marshall
2507	MILLER, Robert
1777	MILLER, Robert Cameron
7742	MILLER, William Allan
1212	MILLHOUSE, Horace
3370	MILLICAN, Edwin Charles
7516	MILLROY, Joseph
5462	MILLS, Joseph Wheatley
2781	MILLS, Major Eli
170	MILLS, Thomas James
1871	MILLS, William Thomas
1815	MILNE, George
1364	MILNE, James
1365	MILNE, William
7735	MILNER, Harold Townsend
320	MINORS, William
758	MINTER, Henry
2381	MISKIN, Harold
Capt	MISSINGHAM, William Stanley
Capt	MITCHELL, Albert
1335	MITCHELL, Clifford Gordon
7265	MITCHELL, Evan William
2615	MITCHELL, Frederick Oliver
1982	MITCHELL, Harley Leslie
2775	MITCHELL, Joseph
4383	MITCHELL, Robert Gordon Melville
5457	MITCHELL, Sydney
7266	MITCHELL, William
7553	MITZSCHKE, Frederick William
322	MOESER, John Francis
2616	MOFFAT, Frederick
3371	MOHLE, Ernest Adam
7011	MOIR, William Russell
1064	MOLES, Edward
7807	MOLLER, William Alexander
1621	MOLLINEAUX, Bertie
1340	MOLLISON, James Murray
4858	MOLONEY, John
Lieut	MOLPHY, James John

No.	Name	No.	Name
6060	MONAGHAN, William Patrick	6310	MORRIS, Edward Terrence
4847	MONEY, Albert William	5570	MORRIS, George
2396	MONRO, Alexander Colville	3190	MORRIS, James Walter
6061	MONSON, Peter	918	MORRIS, Lambert Rudge
5798	MONTGOMERY, James Henry Carlisle	5461	MORRIS, Montague
		2947	MORRIS, Obey
2684	MONTGOMERY, John McNeill	7800	MORRIS, Stuart Knill
		1625	MORRISBY, Percy Frank
1042	MONTGOMERY, Robert	2773	MORRISON, James
2617	MONTGOMERY, Robert McEachran	1376	MORRISON, Roderick Evan
		5569	MORRISSEY, Albert
1162	MONTGOMERY, Wallace Douglas	7268	MORROW, Leslie Oswald
		7267	MORROW, Stanley
1366	MONTGOMERY, William	1367A	MORSHEAD, Herbert Dillon Edward
4562	MOODIE, Hugh		
6530	MOODY, Arthur Edmond	7851	MORTON, George Samuel Gray
1981	MOODY, Charles Edward		
4866	MOORE, Alexander Leslie	1866	MORTON, William
5718	MOORE, Arthur James	7836	MORTON, William
Lieut	MOORE, Basil Raymond	2685	MOSES, William
4843	MOORE, Cedric Charles	2/Lieut	MOSS, Albert Henry
3128	MOORE, Francis James	7020	MOSS, Amos James Henry
725	MOORE, Gordon John	6532	MOSS, Norman Phillips Harman
1876	MOORE, George Roland		
3373	MOORE, Harold Thomas	471	MOTT, Edward
171	MOORE, Henry	6527	MOUNFIELD, Harold
7517	MOORE, Norman Charles	2618	MOUNTAIN, Charles Henry
Lieut	MOORE, Rex Lorenzo	1528	MOYNEHAN, William Daniel
5052	MOORE, Stanley Herbert	Lieut	MUDGE, Francis Robert
2972	MOORE, Thomas Francis	7846	MUIR, Colville Currie
3054	MOORE, Thomas McAdam	6810	MUIRHEAD, Hawthorn
1069	MOORE, Wilfred Anthony	7794	MULHOLLAND, Edwin
1771	MOORE, William	7778	MULLALY, John
1773	MOORE, William Mark	2612	MULLAN, Justin Stanley
Capt	MORAN, Francis	2844	MULLEN, Samuel Davis
323	MORAN, Jack Llewellyn Grace	3050	MULLIGAN, Herbert
		6308	MULLINS, Joseph
4564	MORAN, Stephen	6309	MULLINS, Thomas William
3878	MORE, Orrock Mackay	6307	MULLINS, William
Capt	MORGAN, Albert Edward	624	MULRENAN, Arthur Reginald
2306	MORGAN, Daniel	2076	MULRENNAN, James
324	MORGAN, David Ewart	6313	MULRONEY, Matthew James
Lieut	MORGAN, Frederick William	1369A	MULVIE, Peter
6305	MORGAN, Harry	7738	MULVIHILL, Timothy Lawrence
3372	MORGAN, Herbert James		
625	MORGAN, James Hartley	2779	MUNCASTER, Rusland James Ferguson
6807	MORGAN, Robert John		
5464	MORGAN, Samuel Edward	7269	MUNDELL, Gordon Hooper
2694	MORISON, Alfred Peter	Major	MUNDELL, William Twynam
1116	MORLEY, Alexander	2424	MUNDY, Leslie
1531	MORLEY, Frederick John	1368A	MUNDY, Walter
6813	MORLEY, Ralph Ratcliffe	4845	MUNRO, Hugh
1872	MORLING, John Williams	7557	MUNRO, Hugo
1620	MORONEY, Michael	757	MUNRO, John Thomas
4861	MORONEY, Michael Edward	2967	MUNTING, Robert Frederick
1774	MORPHETT, Robert Ernest	1525	MURDEN, Robert Raymond
970	MORREY, Arthur	1715	MURDOCH, George Alexander

HISTORY OF THE 15th BATTALION

No.	Name
930	MURDOCH, James Archibald
Capt	MURDOCH, William
2915	MURISON, William Stewart
2664	MURPHY, Claude Arthur
6867	MURPHY, David Alexander
2399	MURPHY, Eric
3363	MURPHY, Francis Edward
2620	MURPHY, Frank William
2210	MURPHY, James
3399	MURPHY, James
6811	MURPHY, James Vincent Ernest
5468	MURPHY, John
1339	MURPHY, Patrick Vincent
2621	MURPHY, Robert George
6524	MURPHY, Thomas
6523	MURPHY, Victor Lionel
2123	MURRAY, Allan
2743	MURRAY, Dennis George
1522	MURRAY, James Pratt
21	MURRAY, James Keith
7734	MURRAY, Murdoch Ross
6062	MURRAY, Robert Burrell
1673	MURRAY, Robert Henry
1722	MURRAY, Walter Lawrence
1622	MURRAY, William Arrol
6063	MURRAY, William Page
4855	MURRELL, William
5458	MURRY, Charles Edward
5456	MURTAGH, Michael
173	MUSGRAVE, Aubury Ernest
3816	MUSSON, Jack
3906	MYERS, Charles Edward
4404A	MYERS, Joseph Stephen
174	MYLES, Harry Jackson
1516	MACAULAY, Adam
4060	MACFARLANE, Bruce
6051	MACFARLANE, George William
313	MACKAY, Archie Graham
706	MACKAY, William
1978	MACKAY, William
6821	MACLELLAN, Richard Alexander
5151	McALISTER, Colin
4851	McALISTER, Daniel Michael
1341	MacALLISTER, Charles
6816	McANALLY, Robert Joseph
922	McANDREW, Alexander
975	McANDREW, Henry Brown
924	McANDREW, Roy Millar
1526	McANDREW, Walter George
1360A	McARA, James Monteith
2968	McARTHUR, Colin
2515	McARTHUR, George William
3387	McARTHUR, James

No.	Name
3386	McARTHUR, John Frank Muller
2778	MacARTHUR, Kenneth Hugh
2609	McARTHUR, Thomas Archibald
6817	McARTHUR, William
3806	McATEE, John
1071	McAULEY, Lindsay Gordon
1362A	McAULEY, Michael Francis
6818	McAULIFFE, John Augustine
1823	McAUSLAN, John Sanderson
1973	McBRATNEY, Thomas
7801	McBRYDE, James Gordon
1974	McCABE, Francis
2391	McCABE, John
3393	McCALL, John
5719	McCALLUM, Robert Alexander Theodore Jacob
2771	McCALLUM, Robert James
1524	McCANN, Frederick
7754	McCANN, Harry
921	McCANN, Henry
3388	McCARTHY, Charles George
4796	McCARTHY, Daniel James
925	McCARTHY, James
7272	McCARTHY, James Paul
470	McCLYMONT, William Hugh
5823	McCORMACK, Malachy James
7809	McCORMICK, David
2014	McCORMICK, Patrick
2/Lieut	McCORMICK, Thomas Michael
3799	McCONAUGHY, Alfred
628	McCONNACHIE, George
853	McCONNACHIE, James
894	McCONNELL, John David Duncan
1390	McCONNELL, Louis Isherwood
326	McCONNELL, Quintin Edward
3915	McCONNELL, Thomas
Lieut	McCOY, Percival
6320	McCREADIE, John
1428	McCRIMMON, Stanley George
3396	McCULKIN, Percy
2715	McCULKIN, Thomas Cecil
1354	McCULLOCH, Ernest Arthur
5723	McCULLOCH, George Wallace
3380	McCULLOCH, Stewart Malcolm
5472	McCULLOUGH, Gerald
2696	McCULLOUGH, William Henry
3616	McDERMOTT, Joseph Patrick
3804	McDERMOTT, Michael Harold
1690	McDONALD, Alexander
6322	McDONALD, Alexander Archibald
5725	MacDONALD, Colin Duncan
7260	MacDONALD, Eric Shepherd

HISTORY OF THE 15th BATTALION

No.	Name	No.	Name
1770	McDONALD, Frederick John	6607	McILROY, Gabriel
7274	MacDONALD, Hector John	3391	McINERNEY, John
1781	McDONALD, Hugh Rennie	2231	McINTOSH, Adam Carmicael
1617	McDONALD, James Fairbairn	3398	McINTOSH, Alexander
2177	McDONALD, James Gordon	467	McINTOSH, Anderson
1519	McDONALD, James Joseph	3107	McINTOSH, Hubert John Charles
312	MacDONALD, John		
3997	McDONALD, John	Capt	McINTOSH, Robert Bruce
1337	MacDONALD, Kenneth	7721	McINTYRE, Donald
3134	McDONALD, Maurice Thomas	7856A	McINTYRE, Dugald
6130	McDONALD, Neil	926	McINTYRE, John Andrew
708	MacDONALD, Robert	5724	McINTYRE, Richard Walls
7273	McDONALD, Roderick	3136	McILWRAITH, James Thomas
175	McDONALD, Samuel Joseph	7276	McIVOR, James Bernard
5716	McDONNELL, Victor Peter	177	McKAIN, John James Norman
2165	McDONOUGH, George	328	McKAIN, Walter Bernard
1353A	MacDOUGALL, Donald	7280	McKARVEY, Michael
176	McDOUGALL, Robert	2356A	McKAVANAGH, Charles William
5253	McDOUGALL, Samuel Gordon		
4061	McDOUGALL, Stanley Robert	764	McKAY, Alexander George
1623	McDOWALL, John	619	McKAY, Donald
2395	McDOWELL, John	Lieut	MacKAY, Keith Hope
5086	McELLIGOTT, William	1763	McKAY, Roland Robert
1391	McEWAN, Tasman	765	McKAY, Thomas Albury
4853	McEWAN, William	4865	McKECHNIE, Neil
2611	McFARLANE, Arthur	7853	McKEE, Thomas Joseph
7845A	McFARLANE, James Alexander	7016	McKEEVER, Ernest
		1662	McKELLAR Claude Arthur
4113	McFARLANE, Leslie	1661	McKENDRICK, Robert James Mott
630	McGAFFIN, Robert John		
3801	McGAGHAN, John Joseph	1523	McKENNA, Henry Francis
7279	McGAHN, Joseph	1430	McKENZIE, Alexander
767	McGARRY, William James Herbert	650	McKENZIE, Alexander Forrest
		7685	McKENZIE, Charles Niel
640	McGAW, Thomas	631	McKENZIE, George
Hon/Capt	McGHIE, Malcolm John	327	McKENZIE, Hector
Lieut	McGHIE, Norman	857	McKENZIE, James
466	McGILLIVERY, Angus Robert	2170	McKENZIE, John
2770	McGILLICUDDY, Thomas	3381	McKENZIE, John
6056	McGILVERY, Morton	3908	McKENZIE, John Edward
7275	McGILVERY, Ronald	7024	MacKENZIE, Reginald Boyd
6321	McGIMPSEY, David	620	MacKENZIE, Walter Ray
3191	McGINLEY, Walter	7018	McKENZIE, William Archibald
1880A	McGINNITY, Michael	6318	McKIERNAN, Jack Murray
7632	McGOULRICK, John Leo	329	McKILLOP, Duncan
2392	McGOVERN, Patrick	82	McKILLOP, John
6820	McGRATH, Frank	3060	McKILLOP, Neil
7026	McGRATH, James Charles Patrick	3805	McKINLEY, Charles
		3327	McKINLEY, William
709A	McGRATH, Patrick John	4863	McKINNA, Charles Stafford
6621	McGREGOR, David Edward	5476	McKOY, Herbert
5478	McGREGOR, Henry John	2618	McLACHLAN, Arthur Hector
2077	McGREGOR, James	7278	McLADY, William George
2167	McGREGOR, Lewis Cameron	3389	McLAREN, Alexander Falkender
2612	McGUIRE, Robert Theodore		
5471	McHENRY, William	1055	McLAREN, Peter Donald
1428	McHUGO, William Henry	632	McLAREN, Samuel

K

HISTORY OF THE 15th BATTALION

No.	Name
633	McLAREN, William
3103	McLATCHEY, Francis Ritchie
3382	McLAY, James Archibald
1975	McLEAN, Alexander
2850	McLEAN, Donald
7277	McLEAN, George William Rodgers
1521	McLEAN, James
2394	McLEAN, John Douglas
5728	McLEAN, John Murdoch
923	McLEAN, Joseph Ronald
2175	McLEAN, Niel John
3052	McLEAN, Walter
2398	McLEISH, Alexander
3800	McLENNAN, Alexander
6055	McLENNAN, Ernest Stephen
1779	McLENNAN, James
927	McLENNAN, Roderick George
7526	McLEOD, Alexander John
4856	McLEOD, Archibald Angus
629	McLEOD, Donald
2440	McLEOD, Donald
469	McLEOD, John
769	McLEOD, Kenneth Hugh
768	McLEOD, Ronald
2777	McLEOD, Wallace Hugh Bruce
4850	McLOUGHLIN, Patrick
7578	McMANUS, James
22	McMANUS, Lawrence Percival
2073	McMASTER, John
2393	McMATH, Arthur Alexander
1518	McMILLAN, Donald
7012	McMINN, Hugh William
7281	McMINN, William James
3807	McMURTRY, William
635	McNAE, William Charteris
3383	McNAMARA, Joseph Francis
814	McNAMARA, Michael Brown
6537	McNAUGHTON, Alexander
5470	McNEE, Kenneth
770	McNEILL, James Stephen
4109	McNICHOL, Robert
3392	McPAUL, Charles Ernest
766	McPHEE, John William
5480	McPHERSON, Alexander
4857	McPHERSON, Dougald Arthur
5481	McPHERSON, Ernest
1429	McPHERSON, George Alexander
2744	McPHERSON, Percy James
1624	McPHERSON, William
1778	McPHERSON, William
1355A	McQUAID, John
4862	McQUILLEN, Edward
468	McQUEEN, Kenneth
7723	McQUEEN, William John

No.	Name
Lieut	MacROBERTS, Andrew Hamilton
Lt/Col	McSHARRY, Terence Patrick
921	McSKINIMING, William
7744	McWADE, Allen George
1652	McWALTERS, Peter Hannah
233	McWILLIAM, John Taylor
7567	NANCE, Henry James
1370A	NASH, Charles Ernest
7850	NASH, George Henry
1872	NASH, Patrick
4869	NASON, Percy William
7750	NASSAU, Harold
6601	NATION, Isaac
2782	NAVINE, Francis
1373A	NAYLOR, Percy
7029	NEALE, Edwin William
3062	NEDWICH, Francis George
2811	NEEDHAM, William Harold
3112	NEEDS, George Henry
1780	NEELAND, Robert
2516	NEIGHBOUR, Roy
2702	NEILL, Ernest
934	NELSON, Alfred
933	NELSON, Alfred James
1222	NELSON, Gordon Ernest
Lieut	NELSON, Joseph William
3402	NESTER, Christopher
7030	NETHERCOTE, John Dagleish
4867	NEUCOM, Frank
3821	NEVILLE, William Patrick
Lieut	NEVIN, Archibald Reinmuth
4567	NEW, Arthur Henry
2181	NEW, Leonard George
932	NEWALL, George Lawrence
3063	NEWBERY, Charles Alfred
6065	NEWBIGGING, William
3120	NEWELL, Albert Edward
931	NEWELL, Henry Lewis.
Lieut	NEWLAND, Bernard Charles
1219	NEWMAN, Ernest Walter
7773	NEWMAN, George Nelson
4868	NEWPORT, Samuel Percy
3400	NEWTON, Arthur Leslie
3401	NEWTON, George Oakey
3404	NEWTON, Vivian Richard Claude
1221	NIBBS, Wilfred John
1533	NICHOLAS, Herbert James
3617	NICHOLLS, Alec Edward
98	NICHOLLS, Arthur Daniel
4569	NICHOLLS, Ernest Alfred
1432	NICHOLLS, Frederick
4181	NICHOLLS, Richard John
935	NICHOLLS, Roy Elgin
Capt	NICHOLLS, William Harold
7568	NICHOLLS, William Henry

No.	Name	No.	Name
1220	NICHOLS, Herbert	4871	O'BRIEN, Harold Edwin
Lieut	NICHOLSON, Allen Ferguson	473	O'BRIEN, Michael James
636	NICHOLSON, Harold Oswald	Capt	O'BRIEN, Nicholas
6822	NICHOLSON, James	472	O'BRIEN, Richard
7746	NICOL, Daniel Wyllie	5490	O'BRIEN, Richard
7835	NICOLL, Andrew David	180	O'BRIEN, Robert Charles
6823	NIELSEN, Robert John Clarence	1985	O'BRIEN, Thomas
		6328	O'BRIEN, Thomas
6324	NIELSON, Niels	4352	O'BRIEN, Vincent John
5734	NIELSON, Stanley	3618	O'BRINE, Michael
7612	NILLE, Arthur Leo	7285	O'BRYAN, Martin Owens
3822	NILON, Kevin Thomas Joseph	474	O'CALLAGHAN, Michael
1371A	NILSSON, Albert Edward John	1761	O'CONNOR, Albert Barry
6066	NINEHAM, Raymond Lambert	4872	O'CONNOR, Daniel
178	NINNES, William Robert	1783	O'CONNOR, Francis Edward
7806	NIZETTE, Victor Emanuel	Lieut	O'CONNOR, George Victor
5583	NOAKES, William Thornhill	7810	O'CONNOR, Gregory Luke
4384	NOBES, Guildford Charles	936	O'CONNOR, John Joseph
6533	NOBLE, Alexander Angus	773	O'CONNOR, Patrick
6534	NOBLE, William Thomas	2624	O'CONNOR, William Dunne
2078	NOLAN, William	7284	O'DONNELL, Andrew Daniel
1948	NOLL, Albert Walter	1535	O'DONNELL, Francis Cornelius
4349	NORBERY, Stephen William	7725	O'DONNELL, James
7028	NORDSTROM, John Wilhelm	7785	O'DONNELL, John Victor
1366	NORMAN, Alfred Einar	4870	O'DONOGHUE, Joseph
5660	NORMAN, Erling	7724	O'DONOGHUE, Thomas Augustine
1013	NORMAN, Ernest		
1532	NORMAN, Gilbert Harry	7031	O'DONOGHUE, Vincent
6068	NORMAN, Robert Morton	2445	O'DOWD, Conway Joseph
2353	NORRIS, George Norman	1374A	ODY, William
97	NORRIS, William Edward	7034	OEHLMAN, Cyril Francis Leigh
Hon/Major	NORTH, Francis Roger	7613	OGLE, George Patrick
Lieut	NORTHOVER, Cecil Ernest	3917	O'GORMAN, David Sylvester
7282	NORTHOVER, Frederick	3918	O'GORMAN, Patrick Joseph
1372A	NORTON, Arthur	181	O'HANLON, Edward James
73	NORTON, Frank	Lieut	OHLSON, Peter Rudolph Adolph Gosta
	NORTON, John (Served as)		
5782	BURTON, Frederick John	2701	O'KEEFE, Sidney Charles
5082	NORTON, Percy	4890	OLD, Cyril James
6824	NOUD, Arthur Edward	1433	OLDFIELD, Farrer Richmond
4194	NOWELL, Frank	5485	O'LEARY, John Daniel
3823	NOYES, Richard Samuel	1534	OLIVEIRA, Walter
7751	NUGENT, Herbert Cecil	6827	OLIVER, Arthur Alfred
1791	NUGENT, John Joseph	1987	OLIVER, Harold Athelstan
7849	NURCOMBE, Cyril	754	OLIVER, Norman Osker
179	NYSTROM, John Ernest	4873	OLIVER, Thomas
2849	OAKES, William Montague	2571A	OLIVER, William
6825	OATES, Eric Edwin	694	OLLEY, Joseph Daniel
7331	OATES, George John Clive	475	O'LOUGHLIN, Michael
7327	OATES, Robert	1782	O'LOUGHLIN, Patrick John
4385	O'BRIEN, Bernard James	3171	O'LOUGHLIN, Thomas
6033	O'BRIEN, Charles Edward	102	OLSEN, Robert William
	O'BRIEN, David Richard Smith (Served as)	1434	OLSSON, Harold Victor
		6542	O'MARA, Mathew
2520	RYAN, Patrick	6544	O'NEILL, Peter Aloysius
7287	O'BRIEN, George Patrick	1875	ONIONS, Albert Carl
		101	ORCHARD, David William

No.	Name	No.	Name
6543	ORCHARD, Richard Hiram	7342	PARKER, Keith Stanley
2621	ORD, Percy Marstin	2183	PARKER, Louis
6541	O'REILLY, Eugene Peter	2404	PARKER, Richard
2227	O'REILLY, Patrick	1376A	PARKER, Robert James
5491	ORMISTON, Harry Edward	1876	PARKER, Rupert Yamand
2402	O'ROURKE, Joseph Patrick	4877	PARKER, Theophilus Stanley
7286	O'ROURKE, Thomas Herbert	3620	PARKER, William Gordon
2826	ORR, Hugh	774	PARKES, David
637	ORR, Joseph	638	PARKINSON, Gordon Wynne
2855	OSBORNE, Arthur Charles	4881	PARKINSON, Robert
4807	OSBORNE, Harold	2841	PARKINSON, William Henry
7612	ORBORNE, Reginald Frederick	103	PARRISH, Oliver James Wesley
3407	O'SHEA, Joseph	2517	PARRY, James Stephen
6327	O'SHEA, Michael	Lieut	PARRY, William
3826	O'SULLIVAN, James	2286	PARSONS, Athol Joseph
6123	O'SULLIVAN, James George	3490	PARSONS, Bertrid John
3131	O'SULLIVAN, Timothy	6330	PARSONS, Edgar
5149	O'TOOLE, Sylvester Francis	Lieut	PARSONS, Frederick Ernest
7032	OTTAWAY, Reginald	3195	PARSONS, Henry James
2625	OTTERBRIDGE, Herbert Stanley	1787	PARSONS, John William
2785	OUTERBRIDGE, Edward Stephen	2518	PARSONS, Norman Henry
6120	OWEN, Charles Henry	1786	PARSONS, Thomas Edward
24	OWEN, David Griffiths	15074	PARSONS, William Gerald Roy
6326	OWENS, James	775	PATERSON, Francis Milton
2297	OWENS, Leslie John	1377A	PATERSON, John
772	OWENS, Robert Thomas	2970	PATMORE, Jack
771	OXENHAM, Leo John	7289	PATON, Harold Femister
4386	PAGE, Darcy	2298	PATTEN, Alexander Roy
3069	PAGE, Frederick William	2403	PATTEN, Sydney Joseph
1344	PAGE, James Alexander	2222	PATTERSON, Alexander Smith
Lieut	PAGE, Leo Joseph	2223	PATTERSON, James Kerr
6332	PAGE, Stephen Edwin	3067	PATTERSON, Michael
182	PAGET, Salisbury Howard	6828	PATTERSON, William Walter
6331	PAIN, Francis	6384	PATTISON, Charles Squires
6069	PALFREY, Charles William	332	PAUL, Alexander Paterson
1228	PALMER, Charles Frederick	335	PAYNE, Alfred George
1348	PALMER, Clyde Vivian	6828	PAYNE, Charles Jacob Haynes
1227	PALMER, Edwin Samuel	6333	PAYNE, Edmund George
7296	PALMER, Frederick	4885	PAYNE, George Arthur
7760	PALMER, James	2408	PAYNE, Richard
4303	PALMER, James William	109	PAYTON, Stephen
1789	PALMER, Richard Gordon Hayes	1378A	PEACH, John
		940	PEACHEY, Frederick Abraham William Cleave
1963	PALMER, Thomas Edward		
2079	PAMPLIN, Auburn Tasman	7824	PEACOCK, Ernest Charles
5742	PANNELL, Eric James	1077	PEARCE, Jim
4886	PARCELL, Victor	2184	PEARCE, Richard Henry
7300	PARDON, Edward John	5744	PEARL, Benjamin
3409	PARFITT, Frank	4875	PEARMINE, Ulric James
639	PARISH, Charles Norton	1346	PEARS, Ernest Harry
476	PARKER, Albert	1345	PEARS, Frederick
2930A	PARKER, Alexander	3193	PEARSON, Claude William
1375A	PARKER, Alfred	1790	PEARSON, Harold
2674	PARKER, George	6071	PEAT, William
4810	PARKER, Gordon Raymond	3831	PECK, Leslie Gordon
4887	PARKER, James Albert	Lieut	PEDERSON, Algie Morèton
6335	PARKER, John	201	PEDWELL, Walter Henry

HISTORY OF THE 15th BATTALION 279

No.	Name	No.	Name
1720	PEELE, Wesley William	7292	PEUT, Peter Jacob Christopher
5738	PEGG, George Charles	3416	PEZET, Leslie Robert
425	PELHAM, William	333	PFEIFER, Alfred Edward
6072	PELIN, Sidney James	6386	PHELPS, Herbert
6329	PELISSIER, Arthur Henry	1379	PHIBBS, Alfred
3828	PENDALL, Frederick	1115	PHILLIPS, Albert
5495	PENDALL, William	477	PHILLIPS, Albert Joseph
2299	PENDREY, James Arthur	3413	PHILLIPS, Arthur Claude
939	PENE, Norman	7589	PHILLIPS, Edward James
1076	PENFOLD, William Johston	7604	PHILLIPS, Jack Aaron
110	PENGELLY, Arthur Knight	1380A	PHILLIPS, James Hamilton
1419A	PENGILLEY, William James	2143	PHILLIPS, Joseph William
938	PENN, Charles Arthur	6546/334	PHILLIPS, Thomas James
6548	PENN, John William		Phillips
5779	PENNING, George Andrew William	7329	PHILLIPS, William Harcourt
		7297	PHILP, Robert James
1347	PENNINGTON, Harold	5496	PHIPPS, Edward Cecil
4577	PENNINGTON, William Robert	6547	PHISTER, George
7336	PENO, John	6551	PHISTER, Robert Morrison
2265	PENNY, Francis Robert	2405	PICKEN, William Eric
4882	PENNY, Henry John	6075	PICKERING, David Edward
1791	PERCIVAL, Walter Samuel	7727	PICKERING, Richard Henry
3192	PERCY, Clement	4904	PICKERING, Thomas Joseph
7756	PERCY, Henry Raynor	1536	PICOT, Frank
7757	PERFECT, Arthur	6549	PIDCOCK, Thomas Edwin
3207	PERHAM, George William	4411	PIERCE, Alan James
639	PERKINS, Clarence Norbert Clyde	1394	PIERCE, Jack
		581	PIERSON, Albert Edward
16472	PERKINS, Cyril Cecil	107	PILKINGTON, Harold
6811	PERKINS, Francis Arthur	7843	PINION, Stanley
1988	PERKINS, Sydney	106	PINKERTON, George Charles
1356	PERKINS, Sydney Alexander	1989	PINKERTON, Robert
183	PERKINS, William Taylor	6830	PIOCH, Henry Alfred Charles
Lieut	PERKS, George Herbert	1877	PITCHFORD, John Edwin Wallace
776	PERRETT, Francis Evan		
2827	PERRIE, Thomas	7754A	PITMAN, Charles Leslie
	PERRY, Alfred James (Served as)	3196	PITT, Charles Clarence
		6831	PITT, Richard
2382	KING, Harry	6832	PITTS, William Arthur
942	PERRY, George Joseph	7298	PLACE, Christie James
6336	PERRY, John	3197	PLAISTER, Eric Roy
3833	PERRY, Thomas	Capt	PLANE, Alfred Agnew
6073	PERRY, Thomas Alexander	1740	PLANT, Henry Homer
2481	PERRY, Walter	3121	PLATT, Benjamin Merchant
6128	PERSHOUSE, Albert Henry	Lieut	PLATT, Francis Joseph
1225	PESCIO, Lacey Antonio	3382	PLATT, Thomas George
7761A	PETERS, James	7793	PLUMB, John Joel
937	PETERSEN, Charles Godfrey	1663	PLUMLEY, Charles Edward
184	PETERSEN, Christen Knutzon	7759	PLUMMER, Arthur Frederick
4874	PETERSEN, Samuel	6553	PLUNKETT, Gerald James
1537	PETERSEN, Thomas Frederick	4579	POEPPEL, George Augustus
1538	PETERSON, Grahame King Page	2745	POLDEN, Donald George
		7633	POLLARD, Charles
7726	PETERSON, Peter	941	POLLEY, Harry
3068	PETRIE, Herbert	5092	POLLEY, Marshall John Gordon
4884	PETTIFORD, George William	7291	POLLOCK, Walter
2407	PETTS, Arthur	3191	POMFRET, Victor

HISTORY OF THE 15th BATTALION

No.	Name	No.	Name
6076	PONTING, Arthur William	2/Lieut	PROCTOR, James Thomas Gordon
1627	POOLE, Gordon Alfred		
7345	POON, Hunter Robert George	7802	PROCTOR, Richard
3411	POPE, John	2700	PROCTOR, Roy Douglas
7821	POPE, John James	2406	PROTHEROE, Sydney David
3072	POPE, Walter James	3623	PROUSE, Charles Arthur
1990	POPLAVSKI, George	4883	PRYOR, Joseph Henry
3621	PORCH, Laurence Richard	1382A	PSHEVOLODSKEY, Marian
7290	PORTER, Alan Ernest	7036	PUCKERING, William Alfred
478	PORTER, Sidney Nathaniel	726	PULLEN, Charles
Capt	PORTER, Simon Fahey	3625	PULLEN, Christopher Charles
5581	PORTLEY, James	3217	PULLEN, Jenkin William
7295	POSCHELK, Edward Ernest	4876	PULLEN, William Toft
108	POTTER, George	5571	PUNZELL, John Joseph
1785	POTTER, Wallace	1784	PURCELL, Charles
6596	POTTS, David Cunningham	7813	PURCELL, Tommy
7756	POULSEN, Ernest Herbert	3832	PURCHASE, Richard George
3198	POVEY, Arthur John	7294	PURNELL, William
Capt	POWELL, Arthur Hunter	4387	PURTON, Harold Robert
1224	POWELL, Ernest	7037	PURVIS, Robert Alfred
2486	POWELL, John William	6552	PUTNAM, Edward Watson
3622	POWELL, William Francis	1349	QUAYLE, F.ederick William
701	POWELL, William John	111	QUINLAN, James
5824	POWER, Benjamin	7576	QUINN, Albert Joseph
3066	POWER, Charles Norman	481	QUINN, Charles
4880	POWER, Percival James	6337	QUINN, Henry Grattan
Major/Chpln	POWER, Thomas Stanislaus	Major	QUINN, Hugh
1788	POWER, William O'Sullivan	7301	QUINN, Patrick Francis
1381A	PRAIN, William Charles	1350	QUINNELL, John Henry
7332	PRATT, George Harry	2409	QUIRK, John
6545	PREECE, George Eugene	3838	RABNOTT, Thomas Arthur
1226	PRESCOTT, William George	6833	RACKHAM, Wilby
7616	PRESHO, Joseph Lawson	1728	RADBURN, Ambrose
7334	PRESTON, Bertram	1235	RADFORD, Arthur
6077	PRESTON, Henry Ernest	2893	RADFORD, Edward
2819	PRESTON, Percy Leopold	Lieut	RAE, John McIntyre
4067	PRETTY, Charles	4590	RAE, Joseph
2081	PRICE, Charles Edward	3490	RAFF, Kenneth
5740	PRICE, Charles Jackson	1384A	RAHILL, Edmond
5825	PRICE, David	7849	RAIL, William
5741	PRICE, Frederick John	7043	RAINE, Robert Burdett
Lieut	PRICE, James Henry Norman	7538	RALEIGH, James Taylor
5162	PRICE, Morris	482	RALLING, Ernest George William
1967	PRICE, Percy Pierce		
2786	PRIESTLY, Norman	5503	RALPH, Frederick Edward
2701	PRINCE, George Edward	6874	RALPH, William Ernest
4879	PRINGLE, Frederick James	2789	RALSTON, Malachy Norton
4878	PRINGLE, James Percival	3079	RAMSAY, James Mark
2969	PRITCHARD, Allan Patrick	2300	RAMSAY, Lawrence
2746	PRITCHARD, James Henry Langton	42	RAMSDEN, William Ernest
		6560	RAMSEY, Alfred Yarnell Garfield
6334	PROBERT, Kenneth William		
	PROBETS, Arthur (Served as)	947.	RAND, Alfred
		6078	RAND, Ernest James
1540	ROGERS, John	336	RANKIN, David
7038	PROCTOR, Daniel	2749	RANKIN, Joseph William
480	PROCTOR, George	6379	RANKINE, Andrew

No.	Name	No.	Name
7854	RANSON, John	1820	REYNOLDS, Robert Gordon
4892	RAPER, Robert Bernard	43	REYNOLDS, Samuel
337	RAPKINS, Eric Harold	1386A	REYNOLDS, Walter
6079	RASMUSSEN, Neils Peter	1114	REX, Percy Hugh
1793	RATCLIFF, Frederick William	7770	RHODES, William Charles
1665	RATTRAY, Lawrence Wilfred	7341	RICE, Samuel Thomas Lewis
1666	RAVENOR, Herbert	5504	RICE, William Thomas
6080	RAWLINS, Percy Charles Francis Owen	1630	RICHARDS, Harold Graham
		5505	RICHARDS, James
6081	RAY, Harry Moreton	3075	RICHARDS, John
1629	RAY, Stanley Lyell	5806	RICHARDS, John
483	RAYMENT, Joseph Claude	Capt	RICHARDS, Samuel Alexander
186	RAYMENT, Sydney Thomas	2190	RICHARDS, Theophilus
2820	RAYMOND, Victor Claude	7046	RICHARDS, William Henry
729	RAYNER, George Albert	485	RICHARDSON, Arthur
1232	READING, Leslie James	1879	RICHARDSON, Edward
2490	REARDON, Albert John	2790	RICHARDSON, Edward
3627	REASON, Joseph	3429	RICHARDSON, Forrest
6082	REASTON, Joseph	944	RICHARDSON, George Thomas
3839	REDDIE, Charles	Major	RICHARDSON, John Foulkes
5584	REDFEARN, Percival	1955	RICHARDSON, Peter Stanley
3125	REDMOND, John Edward	26	RICHES, Cecil Lewis
7781	REDWOOD, George Edwin	4825	RICHMAN, Leslie
1805	REED, Colin Oliver	4413	RICHMOND, Leslie Amiger
85	REED, Hugh James	4414	RICHMOND, Rupert
5266	REED, Walter James	3422	RICHMOND, William Thomas
4624	REES, Owen	6083	RICKARDS, Geoffrey Glennie
1996	REES, Vernon Evan	1899A	RICKETTS, James Christopher
6554	REESE, Arthur Bernard	3074	RICKETTS, William Ernest
3082	REESE, George Edward	6556	RIELLY, James
4894	REEVE, Charles James	6557	RIELLY, Thomas
3078	REEVES, Arthur Henry	6555	RIELLY, William Henry
7768	REEVES, James William	1364	RIGBY, Curtis Edwin
3084	REEVES, William Henry Church	1078	RIGBY, William Thomas
		1667	RIGGS, Arthur Charles
7728	REGAN, Charles	3080	RIGLEN, Henry Thomas
3841	REGAN, Daniel	1231	RILAT, Lionel
4827	REGAZZOLI, John Eugene	1233	RILEY, Arthur
1353	REID, Edmond	3836	RILEY, Arthur Fred Albert
2411	REID, George Crowe	7772	RILEY, Arthur Harold
668	REID, John Donald	5748	RILEY, Jack William
6818	REID, Oswald Morris	2358	RILEY, Terence
338	REID, Ralph	1880	RILEY, Walter Robert
4412	REID, Ronald Armstrong	6084	RILEY, William Henry
187	REIDY, Peter	7787	RINDBERG, Andreas
7825	REINHARDT, Ulrich Frederick Charles	3423	RIORDEN, Charles Esmond
		1900B	RITCHIE, Robert Charles Fryer
2747	REINMUTH, Harold Claude	2828	ROACH, Albert James
484	RENFREW, Robert Houston	7730	ROACHE, William Albert
3837	REOCH, Ronald	3081	ROBB, Arthur Oliver
1395	REUBENICHT, Robert	1354	ROBERTS, Arthur Wilson
4891	REUTER, Henry Christian	6835	ROBERTS, Edward
3419	REUTER, Jacob	5966	ROBERTS, George
4391	REVELL, Charles Richard	1355	ROBERTS, John Alfred
1079	REVELL, Louis Edgar Raymond	1522	ROBERTS, John Barwise
943	REYNOLDS, Bernard		
2372	REYNOLDS, Martin Mary		

HISTORY OF THE 15th BATTALION

No.	Name	No.	Name
2683	ROBERTS, Walter Charles Llewellyn		ROOTS, Archibald (Served As)
1081	ROBERTS, William Eric	2235	BAKER, George
2331	ROBERTS, William Henry	6387	ROOTS, David Daniel
3199	ROBERTSON, Charles James	945	ROOTS, Gilbert
188	ROBERTSON, David	1543	ROOTSEY, Sydney Joseph
3086	ROBERTSON, James Allen	Lieut	ROSE, Duncan Clark
6613	ROBERTSON, John	1083	ROSE, Lawrence Tasman
2188	ROBERTSON, Robert Mackenzie	340	ROSE, Walter Kenneth
Lieut	Robertson, Thomas	3844	ROSS, Alexander Clow
7303	ROBERTSON, Valentine William	4795	ROSS, Charles Chadwick
		2287	ROSS, Colin Leslie Frazer
3835	ROBERTSON, William McDonald	2410	ROSS, Frank
		1351	ROSS, George Archibald
7304	ROBINS, Clifford	119	ROSS, Harold
Lieut	ROBINSON, Andrew	5103	ROSS, Harold James
4070	ROBINSON, Arthur	1389A	ROSS, John Atkinson
7041	ROBINSON, Arthur Edmund	1388A	ROSS, John Randolph
946	ROBINSON, Arthur John	1325	ROSS, Peter John
7042	ROBINSON, Edward Blackett	778	ROSS, William
2355	ROBINSON, Eric Stuart	6558	ROSSI, James
Lieut	ROBINSON, Ernest	640	ROSSINGTON, George Matthew
7861	ROBINSON, Fred		
3592	ROBINSON, Frederick Charles	3420	ROSSITER, Oscar
3629	ROBINSON, Hugh Hay	6085	ROTHMAN, Alexander Martin
1997	ROBINSON, James	4367	ROUGHLEY, John Haughton
7044	ROBINSON, James Kevin	4895	ROW, Reginald Ronald
642	ROBINSON, Norman	643	ROWAN, John
7580	ROBINSON, Percy	3425	ROWE, Edward Stanford
1542	ROBINSON, Richard	118	ROWE, William John Thomas
7764	ROBINSON, Victor John	6372	ROWELL, William Bell
339	ROBSON, Frederick	3077	ROWEN, Peter
1628	ROBSON, Thomas Keith Macleod	3920	ROWLES, Albert Edward
		1020	ROWLES, Charles
1664	ROCHLIFFE, Wilfred Rubin	2837	ROWLEY, Frank
4389	ROCK, Henry Charles	1792	ROY, William
2748	RODEN, Percy Henry	7759	ROYAL, Horace
780	RODGERS, Thomas Terrance	6559	RUB, Edward Joseph
7767	ROFF, Sydney Edgar	3427	RUBENACH, Thomas James
5750	ROGERS, George	1395	RUBENICHT, Robert
1375	ROGERS, George Sandilands	3229	RUEGGER, Walter
2788	ROGERS, George William	1539	RUFFLEY, William
7763	ROGERS, James Maxwell	1881	RUMNEY, Eric
1234	ROGERS, John Alexander	1390A	RUSH, Cecil
3366	ROGERS, Thomas George	4390	RUSH, Frederick Robert
5501	ROGERS, Walter John	4291	RUSH, John
972	ROGERSON, Roy Drummond	7811	RUSH, John Thomas
123	ROLFE, Alexander	3834	RUSH, Olly Carl
1950	ROLLASON, Herbert Henry	861	RUSHFORTH, Norman Mervyn
25	ROLLESTON, Hugh Charles	117	RUSSELL, Alfred
7786	ROLLOND, Edward John	6836	RUSSELL, Charles Frederick
1435	ROMILLY, Whitfield Lucian	3840	RUSSELL, Francis John
7045	RONALD, William	3366	RUSSELL, Herbert
6340	RONLUND, Arthur Nicholas	116	RUSSELL, James
7766	ROONEY, James	641	RUSSELL, Sydney John
1230	ROOTES, William Henry	1080	RUSSELL, William
		1541	RYAN, Benjamin

No.	Name	No.	Name
813	RYAN, Casimar Edric Pennefather	644	SAXON, Ernest
		7774A	SAYER, Walter David
3877	RYAN, Colin	3853	SCATENI, Frank
4844	RYAN, Eric Francis	1801	SCHAFER, Albert Edward
6342	RYAN, Forbes Denis	7733	SCHEIBEL, Tage Kielland
6343	RYAN, Hugh	7544	SCHLUMPF, Albert
2412	RYAN, James	189	SCHNEIDER, John Berthold
6086	RYAN, James Joseph Patrick	787	SCHOFIELD, Norman Charles
779	RYAN, John Joseph	786	SCHOFIELD, Reginald George Hornby
2634	RYAN, John Patrick		
2413	RYAN, Leo	3090	SCHOLEFIELD, Arthur George
	RYAN, Michael Francis (Served As)	7608	SCHULZ, Herman Edward
		6568	SCHWARTZ, Albert Frederick
1530	McKINLEY, Joseph	2527	SCOTNEY, Albert
7859	RYAN, Reginald Joseph Andrew	949	SCOTT, Albert Stanley
		1391A	SCOTT, Arthur
1794	RYAN, Thomas Francis	3847	SCOTT, Arthur
4831	RYAN, Victor William	3201	SCOTT, Cecil
1229	RYAN, William Daniel	3633	SCOTT, Douglas
4587	RYAN, William Joseph	486	SCOTT, Douglas Henry
Lieut	RYAN, William Patrick	2679	SCOTT, Frederick
114	RYNNE, John Michael	1420A	SCOTT, George
2498	SALMON, Herbert William	6838	SCOTT, Hugh
1796	SALMON, William Thomas	7541	SCOTT, James
791	SALMONI, Frederick Stanley	7057	SCOTT, John James
3848	SALOTTI, Dominica George	1392A	SCOTT, Leith Hay
6565	SALSBURY, Robert Emilius-Paynter	2195	SCOTT, Peter
		2750	SCOTT, Robert
1951	SALTZER, Ludie Emil Alexander	7305	SCOTT, Thomas
		1544	SCOTT, Walter
1800	SAMMON, Patrick Joseph	Capt	SCOTT, Walter
Major	SAMPSON, Burford	7543	SCOTT, William
1086	SAMPSON, Charles Edward	6608	SCOTT, William Rufus Bruce
2505	SAMPSON, Cyril Claude	793	SCOULLER, John Gordon
3630	SAMPSON, Samuel	7338	SCOVELL, Albert Jackson
1093	SAMPSON, William Aaron	1998	SCRASE, George James
3858	SANDEESON, George	1802	SCULLY, Jeremiah
3432	SANDER, Gustav	1798	SEAGER, Frederick
7548	SANDERS, Arthur Carew	28	SEAR, Alfred
1555	SANDERS, Charles Herbert	1240	SEARLE, Edward George
4415	SANDLES, Ivan John	3851	SECCOMBE, Roland
3435	SANKEY, William Peter	712	SECCOMBE, Walter Thomas
953	SANNE, Sydney Arthur Melville	2519	SEDGMAN, Walter Spencer
		1745	SEE, William
1357	SANT, George Albert Harold	1546	SELLARS, Albert John
6837	SARGEANT, Charles	2/Lieut	SELLARS, Ernest George
7059	SARGOOD, John Christopher	Lieut	SELLARS, Reginald Arthur
645	SAUNDERS, Frank Walter	5585	SELLS, John Richard
7761	SAUNDERS, George William	6352	SENDON, Edward
3631	SAUNDERS, Gordon Henry Joseph	4043	SENIOR, Frederick William Bay
6567	SAUNDERS, Herbert John	2424	SERVICE, Albert Cecil
1915	SAUNDERS, William Arthur	1549	SETON, Thomas
1084	SAUNDERS, William Harold	1359	SEWELL, John Thomas
5801	SAVAGE, John	2194	SEXTON, Alfred John
499	SAVILLE, Julian Harry	948	SEXTON, John
1558	SAWYER, John William	6351	SEXTON, William Bradshaw

J

No.	Name	No.	Name
7309	SEYMOUR, Frederick Robert	2522	SHIELDS, Clarence
487	SEYMOUR, James	954	SHIELLS, Leslie John
1245	SHACKCLOTH, Frederick Henry	7058	SHIELS, Charles Warren
		4393	SHIPP, Duncan
2840	SHACKLETON, Richard	4911	SHIRER, William
4407	SHANAHAN, Jeremiah	4906	SHORLEY, Clide Leslie
6840	SHANKS, David	2404	SHORT, Cecil Patrick
7545	SHANKS, Frederick	2243	SHORT, Harry
5514	SHANNON, James	2/Lieut	SHRUBB, Alfred Boniface
1977	SHANNON, Tasman William John	3862	SIBLEY, James William
		3438	SIDDINS, Charles Hewitt
1085	SHARMAN, Norton John Randolph	781	SIDDONS, Charles Augustine
		863	SIDNEY, Ernest Cecil
1089	SHARP, Reuben Henry	7825	SIGSTON, Charles Henry
1182	SHARP, Walter John	192	SIGVART Charles
488	SHAW, Albert Edward	4897	SILLETT, Cecil Vivian
1358	SHAW, Alexander James	7777	SILVER, John Alexander
Lieut	SHAW, Bernard Joseph	125	SILVESTER, Albert William
4905	SHAW, Darcy Richard Nottingham	1818	SIMCOCK, Albert Victor
		Lieut	SIME, Andrew Ramsey
4907	SHAW, Frank Albert Percy	2389	SIMMERS, William
1246	SHAW, Henry	7764	SIMMONDS, Wilfred Mylchreest
489	SHAW, James		
6088	SHAW, James	3088	SIMMS, Andrew
1091	SHAW, John	3845	SIMMS, William
1548	SHAW, Sidney Wigmore	Lieut	SIMON, Eric Wilson
3091	SHAW, Thomas	5316	SIMON, Ivan Nonnet
1557	SHAW, William Edward	951	SIMONS, Leslie John
7049	SHAWYER, Charles Hugh	6098	SIMONSEN, Charles Reginald
3570	SHEA, Vernon Reginald	7549	SIMONSEN, John Morton
6564	SHEARER, James	1906	SIMPSON, John
7047	SHEARER, James Hutchison	3923	SIMPSON, Oliver Robert
1797	SHEARER, Samuel Augustus	788	SIMPSON, Peter
1273	SHEARGOLD, John Francis	1556	SIMS, Albert Tom
1243	SHEARING, Herbert Harold	950	SIMS, James William
4600	SHEEDY, Sylvester James Joseph	1550	SIMS, William
		1373	SINCLAIR, Arthur Leslie
515	SHEEHAN, Patrick	7776	SINCLAIR, Arthur Smith
7314	SHEEHAN, William Frederick Francis Alexander David	2762	SINCLAIR, James
		2438	SINCLAIR, Robert
7308	SHEEHY, Alexander	6841	SINCLAIR, Robert
Lieut	SHELLEY, Walter Albert	1953	SINFIELD, Jack David
1088	SHELTON, Harold William	1241	SING, George
7779	SHEPHERD, Arthur		SJOSTROM, Frank August (Served As)
6849	SHEPHERD, Francis		
1999	SHERATON, Richard William	2211	WELSH, Frank August
191	SHERIDAN, Charles	84	SKIMMING, John Campbell
4899	SHERIFF, John	650	SKINNER, Andrew
3434	SHERLOCK, Alexander Neil	3471	SKUSE, James William
3924	SHERMAN, Percy Edward	654	SLACK, Joseph
2301	SHERRIN, Allan Edward	7587	SLADE, Arthur Edwin
1237	SHERRIN, Michael	1553	SLADE, Henry Arthur
5587	SHERWIN, Percy William	3485	SLADEN, Alfred James
5802	SHERWIN, Reynold	2799	SLADEN, Thomas
3027A	SHETLAND, John Lewis	7786	SLATER, Edmund Joseph
86	SHEVELLING, James Walter	4395	SLATTER, Reginald Arthur
646	SHIELDS, Charles	4833	SLATTERY, John

HISTORY OF THE 15th BATTALION 285

No.	Name	No.	Name
2655	SLATYER, Raymond Walter	6092	SMITH, Herbert
6091	SLEIGHT, Robert	343	SMITH, Herbert Cleveland
6090	SLEIGHT, Thomas	1320	SMITH, Hugh Maurice
Lieut	SLOAN, Beresford Terence	341	SMITH, James
1448	SLOAN, John	952	SMITH, James
7551	SLOAN, John	3433	SMITH, James Dawson
3857	SLOCOMB, Frank Thomas	3441	SMITH, James Sinclair
2196	SMAGIN, Gregory	1397A	SMITH, John
796	SMALE, Albany	4371	SMITH, John
797	SMALE, Alfred John	649	SMITH, John Alexander
3849	SMALL, William	792	SMITH, John Carlisle Alvin
5807	SMALLBONE, Herbert Lawrence	4593	SMITH, John Edward
		1236	SMITH, John Henry
7827	SMART, Edward Darius	2204	SMITH, John Inglis
1863A	SMEDLEY, Stanley	45	SMITH, Joseph
136	SMITH, Albert	5752	SMITH, Keith Hodson
1248	SMITH, Albert Montague	5070	SMITH, Leonard John
1803	SMITH, Alfred	934	SMITH, Leslie
3172	SMITH, Alfred	6619	SMITH, Percival
7763	SMITH, Andrew Daniells	1632	SMITH, Peter
Lieut	SMITH, Arthur Blackburn	2638	SMITH, Philip Lanclot
2936	SMITH, Arthur David	667	SMITH, Richard Joseph
1631	SMITH, Arthur James	5833	SMITH, Robert Ernest
3493	SMITH, Arthur James	3581	SMITH, Sidney Goodwin
1436	SMITH, Beith	4898	SMITH, Stewart Allen
3632	SMITH, Bert	1397	SMITH, Tasman Henry Hamilton
193	SMITH, Charles Albert Percy		
1395A	SMITH, Charles Burston	Lieut	SMITH, Thomas James
491	SMITH, David Augustus	2006	SMITH, Victor Patrick
648	SMITH, Duncan Archibald Sinclair	87	SMITH, Walter Edward
		2202	SMITH, William Francis
647	SMITH, Edward	783	SMITH, William James
7056	SMITH, Ernest Edward	2415	SMITH-SCARGILL, John
7089	SMITH, Everett Wallace Pinchin	88	SMOOTHY, George
		794	SMYTH, Cyril Bishop
7355	SMITH, Evrod	Capt	SNARTT, Cecil Edwin
4097	SMITH, Forbes Strachan	2201	SNELHAM, Arthur
7048	SMITH, Frank Raymond	956	SNELL, Francis William
492	SMITH, Frederick	Lt/Col	SNOWDEN, Robert Eccles
6842	SMITH, Frederick Whitehead	5510	SNOWDON, Thomas
1396A	SMITH, George	7734	SONDERGELD, John Hubert
2637	SMITH, George	2001	SOONING, James Albert
790	SMITH, Gordon	3436	SOPPA, William
Capt	SMITH, Gordon Arthur Friend	2198	SORENSEN, James Yates
4746	SMITH, Gordon Roy	5515	SOUTHWORTH, Thomas
7055	SMITH, Gordon Vincent	7805	SPANNING, Charles
2/Lieut	SMITH, Harold George	344	SPARKES, William Percival
3850	SMITH, Harry	Lieut	SPARKS, Joseph Edward
1799	SMITH, Harry Harold	7312	SPEAR, William Thomas
2680	SMITH, Harry Hugh	7783	SPEAS, Charles Robert
5509	SMITH, Henry	2795	SPEERING, Hugh Corneil
3093	SMITH, Henry James	795	SPEIRS, William Joseph
789	SMITH, Henry Leighton Lewis	1398A	SPELLACY, Frank
2003	SMITH, Henry Lewis	3846	SPENCER, Archibald Dunlop
4396	SMITH, Henry Richard	7583	SPENCER, Ernest William
1360	SMITH, Herbert	1672	SPENCER, Frederick Norman Joseph
2203	SMITH, Herbert		

HISTORY OF THE 15th BATTALION

No.	Name	No.	Name
Lieut	SPENCER, William James	4910	STEVENSON, Walter
7781	SPICELEY, Arthur George	27	STEVENSON, William Fyffe
6566	SPIEGEL, Jack	7782	STEWART, Bruce
2801	SPIERS, James	7828	STEWART, Charles Edward
2083	SPILLANE, Daniel John	3860	STEWART, Frank
2417	SPILSBURY, Herbert Leslie	6562	STEWART, Frederick Miller
5804	SPINAZE, Anthony	7826	STEWART, Hersee John
7315	SPINKS, Frederick	15263	STEWART, Horace
2639	SPODE, Eric Copeland	494	STEWART, Hugh
7595	SPODE, Maurice Middlemore	2640	STEWART, James Thomas
493	SPRITCH, Thomas Arthur	5751	STEWART, John
3864	SPROWELL, Ernest	3869	STEWART, Robert John
1551	SPRY, Samuel	1402A	STEWART, William
345	SPRY, Stanley Richard	7779	STEWART, William John
4364	SQUIRE, Roley	3444	STEWART, William Joseph
651	STACEY, Frederick	4370	STIBBARDS, Fred
7313	STACEY, George Henry	2243	STICK, John
961	STACEY, Robert Ernest	5755	STICKLEY, Frederick Charles
2792	STAFFORD, James McLean	1980	STILL, Vivian Roy
3870	STALEY, Percival Robert	3141	STIRLING, James Leslie
1263	STANLEY, Arthur Clarence	7307	STITZ, Gordon
971	STANLEY, John	Lieut	STITZ, Harold Frederick
195	STANLEY, Robert Henry	6844	ST. LEDGER, Francis
3097	STANSFIELD, Charles Joseph	3868	STOCKDALE, Arthur Phillips
1087	STANTON, Archibald Job	3855	STOCKS, Francis Robert
3442	STANTON, Wallace John	3437	STOCKS, William John
7054	STAPLETON, Albert	1795	STOKER, John David
4901	STAPLETON, John Thomas	3863	STOKES, William Charles
1244	STEEL, Gordon Malcolm	2525	STOKES, William Joseph
348	STEELE, James	6846	STOLTENBERG, Hans Asmus
6096	STEEMSON, Thomas William	1554	STONE, Allen
7774	STEER, Herbert Ashley	2945	STONE, Ernest
1247	STEIN, Alfred James	4903	STONE, George
7593	STEMBRIDGE, Albert	7799	STONE, James
196	STENHOUSE, Charles Stuart	Lieut	STONE, Walter Herbert
1399A	STENSON, William Patrick	6563	STONE, William Thomas
1838	STEPHEN, Virginius Hamilton	6561	STONEBRIDGE, Alfred
3373	STEPHENS, Harry Montague Richard	7610	STORER, Fred
		2288	STOREY, Albert Forrester
Lieut	STEPHENS, Robert Edgar	3600	STOREY, Arthur Robert
858	STEPHENS, Thomas	198	STOREY, Frank
1400A	STEVENSON, Adam	199	STOREY, Frederick
7787	STEPHENSON, Arthur	Capt	STORMOUTH, Stewart Lyle
Lieut	STEPHENSON, Frederick	653	STORR, Harold Francis
2791	STEPHENSON, George Francis	7552	STORY, Lewis Ford
7310	STEPHENSON, John	Lieut	STOTT, Philip Schofield
7819	STEPHENSON, Leslie	6345	STOUT, Harry
3854	STEPHENSON, William Woblas	6381	STOUT, Victor Harold
5116	STERNE, William John	2796	STOWARD, Alfred Percy
2414	STEVEN, Alexander	1833	STOYER, William John
1361	STEVENS, Charles	347	ST. PIERRE, Herbert James
2851	STEVENS, Frank	Lieut	STRANGMAN-TAYLOR, Richard
1244	STEVENS, James		
4347	STEVENS, James	1239	STROCHNETTER, William Henry
7053	STEVENS, Murdock		
1362	STEVENS, Robert John	1668	STRONACH, William
1882	STEVENSON, Charles	6380	STRONG, Albert Joseph

HISTORY OF THE 15th BATTALION

No.	Name	No.	Name
2798	STUART, John	655	SWIFT, James Hammond
495	STUART, John Charles	1404A	SWINDELLS, George Henry
2641	STUART, John Simpson	1242	SYLVESTER, John Thomas
3092	STUART, Percy Seymour	656	SYVERSEN, Charles
1401A	STUART, William Alexander Barring	703	TAAFE, William James
		1885	TAGG, Thomas
6571	STUART-RUSSELL, Aubrey Beverley	1670	TAIT, Lawrence
		2418	TALBOT, Edward Vernon.
26077	STUBBS, Thomas Victor	6573	TALBOT, John Duncan Campbell
6848	STUDT, Alfred Henry		
5827	STUNDEN, Jesse	500	TALL, Alexander
496	STUPART, George Campbell	2804	TANCRED, John
7773	STUTTARD, William	587	TANNER, Sydney Arthur
3447	STYLES, Denis Patrick	5518	TANSLEY, Percy
	SUCKLING, Robert (Served As)	1633	TANSLEY, Richard
		644	TARGETT, Richard Henry
508	VINCENT, Robert	3098	TARRANT, Cecil William
1090	STRACHAN, Charles	2643	TASKER, Thomas William
2200	STRACHAN, Frederick	469	TATTON, Michael John
5803	STRANG, William	Lieut	TAYLOR, Benjamin
4369	SULLIVAN, Francis Patrick	1829	TAYLOR, Charles Frank
3095	SULLIVAN, Frank	501	TAYLOR, Denis Charles
2500	SULLIVAN, James	799	TAYLOR, Ernest Archibald
1821	SULLIVAN, Joseph	1405A	TAYLOR, Ernest Arthur
1018	SULLIVAN, Thomas Patrick	1406A	TAYLOR, Gilbert
3094	SULLIVAN, William	Lieut	TAYLOR, Harry
2793	SUMMERFIELD, William Jefferson	351	TAYLOR, Henry Christopher
		3876	TAYLOR, Henry Joseph
692	SUMMERS, Andrew	957	TAYLOR, Henry Joseph Thomas
5800	SUNDBERG, Robert		
6166	SUTHERLAND, Hector Laurence	674	TAYLOR, Herbert
		5126	TAYLOR, James
1374	SUTHERLAND, Percy Robert	6575	TAYLOR, John Thomas Henry
1552	SUTTON, David George	7317	TAYLOR, Joseph
3087	SUTTON, John Charles	202	TAYLOR, Joseph Richardson
200	SUTTON, Oscar Oswald	Lieut	TAYLOR, Laurence John Walter
3861	SUTTON, Phillip Henry		
1559	SUTTON, William Henry	3448	TAYLOR, Maurice
Lieut	SVENSEN, Nikolai Theodore	2006	TAYLOR, Robert Stanley
201	SWAIN, Frederick Cecil	3100	TAYLOR, Stanley William
2/Lieut	SWAIN, Roy Vivian	852	TEALE, John
825	SWAINSTON, Ernest Allan	1203	TEMPLE, Clarence William.
1422A	SWALLOW, Herbert	5762	TEMPLEMAN, William Henry Sidney
Lieut	SWAN, George Leslie		
7436	SWAN, Harold Webster	5757	TEMPLETON, Samuel Shaw
3439	SWANSTON, John	Capt	TERRY, Eric Arthur
1449	SWEENEY, Cornelius James	1096	TERRY, William Garrard
350	SWEENEY, Edward Daniel	7853	THACKER, William Charles
6346	SWEENEY, George	7554	THACKRAY, James Reginald
498	SWEENEY, James	1672	THICKINS, William
1403A	SWEENY, Patrick Vincent	7555	THIELE, George
3036	SWEET, Bertie Joseph	7063	THOM, James Willoughby
7311	SWEET, Frank Lacey	4913	THOMAS, Alfred
137	SWENSSON, Alfred Gustav Adolph	7788B	THOMAS, Charles Llewelyn
		4916	THOMAS, Claude
7353	SWEPSON, George	1847	THOMAS, Ernest Norman
7306	SWIFT, Harold Danby	5573	THOMAS, Frank

HISTORY OF THE 15th BATTALION

No.	Name	No.	Name
3450	THOMAS, George Samuel James	1908	TOLL, Frederick Vivian
7735	THOMAS, Harold James	5760	TOLSTOI, Andre
4397	THOMAS, Henry	1807	TOMLIN, James William
1442	THOMAS, John Edward	7334	TOMLINSON, Harold
353	THOMAS, Norman Bailey	3879	TOMLINSON, John Sewell
2802	THOMAS, Owen William	4912	TOMLINSON, Theodore
6099	THOMAS, William Henry	2096	TONNING, Alfred Ernest
1805	THOMLINSON, Alfred	7331A	TOOHEY, Cecil
4802	THOMPSON, Alfred Richard	4919	TOOLEY, William
2302	THOMPSON, Byron John	559	TOOMEY, James
2805	THOMPSON, David James Patrick	1094	TOOP, Robert Daniel
		764	TORBITT, Windsor
5520	THOMPSON, Ernest Vyvyan	2848	TORMEY, Daniel
5519	THOMPSON, George	7065	TORPEY, Henry Vincent
4914	THOMPSON, George Henry	6101	TOTTEN, Robert Joseph
3871	THOMPSON, Harry	1267	TOWERS, William
7062	THOMPSON, James	7736	TOWERTON, Daniel
657	THOMPSON, James Cowie	4917	TOWNLEY, George
4915	THOMPSON, James Henry	2205	TOWNSEND, Benjamin
3102	THOMPSON, John	7152	TOWNSEND, Edward
89	THOMPSON, Osmond	503	TOWNSEND, Leslie
3875	THOMPSON, Thomas	3874	TOWNSEND, Thomas
1098	THOMPSON, William	5200	TOWNSON, John Jenkins
206	THOMSON, Albert James	4252	TOZER, Henry John
1834	THOMSON, Charles Wyville	2644	TRACKSON, Bertie
7064	THOMSON, James	354	TRAISE, Jack Herbert
2420	THOMSON, John Steel	1184	TRAPPES, Marcus Byrnand
6850	THORLEY, Edward James	6875	TREBILCO, Herbert John
4607	THORNE, Herbert Thomas	2525	TREEBY, Frederick
203	THORNHILL, Amos	704	TREHERNE, James Carter
2233	THOROUGHGOOD, John Alfred	6355	TRENERY, Percy
		3101	TRETHOWAN, William
Lieut	THORP, Garnet Alfred	1804	TREVENA, Harold Larlee
2421	THORPE, Allan	1363	TREVETT, Arthur Cecil
1560	THORPE, Leonard George	2751	TREWEEK, Albert James
7786A	THRESHER, Walter Charles	504	TREWEEK, Edward
725	THUMPKINS, Percival Albert	1671	TRICKETT, Russell
6851	THURLBECK, Peter	1191	TRIFFETT, Gordon Tasman
1673	THURLEY, Edward Harold	4084	TRIFFITT, Ambrose Joseph
3926	THWAITES, George	2971	TROON, Benjamin Alexander
5756	TIBBETT, Frederick George	2972	TROON, John James
6599	TIBBEY, George Thomas	5772	TROTT, Stanford Richard Boys
204	TICKNER, Mervin Ray	4376	TROUSDELL, Henry James
502	TIGHE, Alfred	3872	TROW, Pryce
3449	TIGHE, Arthur Sommerville	1561	TROYAHN, William John
Capt/Chap	TIGHE, Patrick F.	6852	TRUDGIAN, Lionel Robert
2005	TILBURY, Clive William	2526	TRULL, William Albert
6814	TILL, Harold Richard	3384	TRUNDLE, Henry James
205	TILLEY, Edward William Rankin	2350	TRUNDLE, Victor Charles
1707	TILLIDGE, Henry William	6853	TRUSCOTT, Frederick John
2717	TIMBS, Ernest James	7557	TUCKER, Arthur
2752	TIMOTHY, Norman Morris	5417	TUCKER, Ernest Clifford
1249	TIPPETT, Albert Ernest Arthur	1364	TUCKER, Reginald
5761	TIPPETT, George Henry	1365	TUDOR, Daniel Thomas
4918	TJABERINGS, Wilhelmus Antoon	7848A	TULLOCH, Robert Andrew
		2529	TUNKIN, Robert Hallett
Capt	TOFT, Percy John Gilbert	2377	TUNSTEAD, William James

No.	Name	No.	Name
7816	TURNBULL, Hugh Edward	3602	WADE, William James
1421A	TURNER, Austin	2530	WAGNER, Frederick Percy
2974	TURNER, Edgar Charles	6585	WAGSTAFF, Sydney
3873	TURNER, George Carlton	6628	WAINWRIGHT, Hugh
3603	TURNER, George Wilson	6102	WAINWRIGHT, Thomas David
2973	TURNER, Leslie James	1408A	WAITE, Samuel
4398	TURNER, Oscar Henry	5764	WALDIE, James Denholm
2419	TURNER, Thomas	1823	WALDOCK, Alfred Henry
1545	TURNOCK, Joseph Arnold	6104	WALDOCK, Eric Alex
3880	TUSKER, Albert	2756	WALES, David Thomas
6100	TUTIN, James Leslie Russell	4071	WALKER, Alving George
1806	TUTTY, William	2214	WALKER, Benjamin
798	TWEEDALE, Arthur Norman	2808	WALKER, Charles Robert Alexander
6574	TWIDALE, Frederick George		
2477R	TYE, Ernest William	2815	WALKER, Henry Herbert Robert
2169	TYLER, George William		
1437	TYNAN, Joseph	4934	WALKER, John
2422	TYNAN, Patrick Joseph	3898	WALKER, John Kenneth Radcliffe
3123	TYRRELL, James Leslie		
5758	TYSON, Lionel George Robert	Lieut	WALKER, Keeran Frederick
7789	TYSON-DONELEY, James	4933	WALL, Daniel
7066	UNDERWOOD, Percy Alexande	6105	WALL, Edward Joseph
5973	UNDY, William James Anderson	1854A	WALL, Keith John
		4922	WALLACE, George Herbert
958	UPSON, Herbert	4834	WALLACE, Sydney Henry
5525	UREN, Joseph Richard	1809	WALLACE, William James George
2423	URQUHART, Finlay		
Lieut	URQUHART, George	6582	WALLACE, William John
5524	URQUHART, William	1840	WALLER, Frederick George
3135	USHER, James	5532	WALSH, James
1634	VALENTINE, Sydney Harold	Major	WALSH, John Francis
3105	VALLINS, Herbert	3897	WALSH, Joseph Norman
2807	VANDERWOLF, Harry	7797	WALSH, Patrick John
2806	VANES, William	1992	WALSH, Thomas
6577	VARCIN, Marcel Firmin	659	WALSH, William
3137	VARY, Robert John	3112	WALSH, William
6578	VAUBELL, Frederick Gladstone	2702	WALTERS, Henry Bernard
90	VAUGHAN, Alfred Lewis	6939	WARBEY, Albert Eugene
7833	VAUGHAN, Arthur Moore	522A	WARBRICK, Thomas
507	VEAGE, Charles Lewis	1438	WARD, Ben Cedric
4920	VERRYCK-FLEETWOOD, Anthony Louis	6866	WARD, Charles Powers
		2/Lieut	WARD, Geoffrey
1566	VERTIGAN, John William	356	WARD, George Henry
3882	VICKERS, Alfred Joseph	4399	WARD, James Henry
7788	VICKERY, Fred	2274	WARD, Tom
2/Lieut	VIDGEN, Jack Grahame	5765	WARE, George
1407A	VILE, Henry Worthy	Lieut	WAREHAM, Edward Graham
3104	VILES, Keith McLean	2645	WARNEMINDE, Leonard David
3451	VINE, Phillip	3473	WARNER, Albert
1398	VINEN, Harold	4270	WARNER, Thomas Henry
1099	VINEY, Adye Roy	3144	WARR, Harry
1839	VIRGIN, Roy Leslie Hezakiha	5967	WARRELL, Charlie
4609	VOGLER, John George	966	WARREN, Arthur Edwin
2208	VOLKOFF, John	3636	WARREN, Charles William
2303	VON BIBRA, Elbert, Louis	1841	WARREN, Edwin John
Lieut	VOSS, Eric Houlton	3885	WARREN, James Edward
2206	VOWLES, George	2213	WARREN, John

HISTORY OF THE 15th BATTALION

No.	Name	No.	Name
3714	WARREN, Stanley	7321	WEBBER, Albert Edgar
4400	WARREN, Victor Reginald	2381	WEBBER, John Alfred Lund
1303	WATERFIELD, David	1735	WEBBER, William Arnold
2646	WATERS, Edward Mathew	1409A	WEBSTER, Charles
5533	WATERS, George Reid	2516	WEBSTER, Henry
4379	WATERS, George Young	2212	WEDLOCK, Henry Francis
2425	WATERS, James Edward	4927	WEEDON, Thomas
Lieut	WATERS, Leslie John	7074	WEEDON, Walter James Furney
1106	WATERS, Percival		
723	WATES, Robert	2975	WEEKS, John Clarence
3458	WATKINS, Charles Frederick	360	WEEL, Albert
2675	WATKINS, George	6861	WEICKS, Hugo Edward Otto
2753	WATKINS, Thomas James	1993	WEILER, Albert
964	WATKINSON, Arthur Vernon	1824	WEIR, Duncan Archibald
7739	WATKINSON, Hugh William	3889	WELCH, Albert
1117	WATLING, Alfred	6851	WELCH, Stephen Wilson
1255	WATLING, Arthur	1372	WELLARD, James Ernest
2528	WATLING, Edward	2754	WELLARD, Leslie William
3454	WATSON, Alexander Norman	4931	WELLER, William Charles
92	WATSON, Alfred	4309	WELLS, George Martin
7791A	WATSON, Arthur Nunnick	965	WELLS, Ralph
2647	WATSON, Edgar Charles	1366	WELLS, Roy
6584	WATSON, Edmund	1091	WELSH, Clarence James
30	WATSON, Fred	1257	WELSH, George
1991	WATSON, George Grainger	802	WEMYSS, Oswald Stewart
6108	WATSON, Gerald Edward	4925	WENHAM, Bert Edward
3462	WATSON, James Joseph	Lieut	WERTHEIMER, Arnold Talbot
Capt	WATSON, John Malcolm	2976	WEST, Alfred Ernest
207	WATSON, Keith	805	WEST, Charles Edward Lionel
660	WATSON, Richard	3405	WEST, Ernest Harold
5540	WATSON, Samuel Nelson	210	WEST, Harold
2429	WATSON, Thomas	6359	WEST, Oscar Stanwell
2019	WATSON, Thomas Forsythe	1258	WEST, Percy John
1812	WATSON, William David	357	WEST, Walter Henry
2426	WATSON, William Theo	3204	WEST, Wilmot Ernest
1400	WATT, David	211	WESTAWAY, George
1822	WATTERS, William Henry	6595	WESTAWAY, Percival Harold
7326	WATTERSON, Percy Gordon	7347	WESTERMAN, James Gray
Capt	WATTS, Frank Reginald	334	WESTERN, Leslie John
358	WATTS, Frederick	851	WESTON, George Edward
208	WATTS, George	212	WESTON, Thomas
359	WATTS, George Ernest	514	WETHERALL, Walter Bert
961	WATTS, Walter	1976	WETHERBY, Lucian Porter
959	WAUGH, Sydney Musgrave	4932	WETTENHALL, Reginald
2809	WAUGH, William Richard	29	WETTON, Charles Alfred
2013	WAYGOOD, Henry William	5844	WHALLEY, Hubert James
3389	WAYMAN, Samuel Neville	1104	WHEATLEY, Percy Alfred
7319	WEBB, Charles Alfred	7841	WHEELDON, Errol Ray
3106	WEBB, Edward Marsh	2011	WHEELER, James Corrie
2816	WEBB, Frederick George	1105	WHELAN, John Joseph
2978	WEBB, Frederick William	3902	WHELAN, Vincent Henry
6362	WEBB, John Alexander	804	WHIFFIN, Charles
6109	WEBB, Joseph Bowen	658	WHILDE, Richard Clive
531	WEBB, Leslie George	3134	WHIP, Albert James
7828	WEBB, Stephen	1808	WHIPPS, Frederick
692A	WEBB, William	2697	WHIPPS, Stanley
807	WEBB, William James	4615	WHITAKER, Albert Edward

No.	Name	No.	Name
7356	WHITE, Arthur Edward	6588	WILLIAMS, Henry George
1252	WHITE, Charles Henry	661	WILLIAMS, Herbert Francis
2340	WHITE, Daniel	Lieut	WILLIAMS, Herbert Mouat
2216	WHITE, Frederick James	1810	WILLIAMS, Herbert Stanley
663	WHITE, George James	3460	WILLIAMS, Hugh
3245	WHITE, George Crossley	2186	WILLIAMS, James Albert
513	WHITE, John Irwin	742A	WILLIAMS, James Andrew
511	WHITE, Joseph Benjamin	808	WILLIAMS, John
1845	WHITE, Lionel Pearce	1407	WILLIAMS, John
801	WHITE, Robert Henry	1444	WILLIAMS, John
3455	WHITE, Thomas Henry	510	WILLIAMS, John Edward
6857	WHITE, William	2430	WILLIAMS, Kelsey Norman
2209	WHITE, William Forsyth	1367	WILLIAMS, Percy
1368	WHITEHEAD, Thomas	2304	WILLIAMS, Sydney Leonard
2/Lieut	WHITEHOUSE, Norman Clyde	553	WILLIAMS, Thomas
974	WHITELEY, George Patrick	1439	WILLIAMS, Thomas Alfred
361	WHITING, David	7609	WILLIAMS, Walter Benjamin
3452	WHITING, Ernest William		WILLIAMS, William Cecil
3205	WHITING, James Joseph		(Served As)
2977	WHITING, John Charles	5538	WILLIAMS, George
4929	WHITMAN, Thomas	7566	WILLIAMS, William Henry
1111	WHITNEY, Allan Claude	6111	WILLIAMSON, Albert
6364	WHITTAM, John	Capt	WILLIAMSON, George McKay
3248	WHITTRED, George William	7794A	WILLIAMSON, Henry Alex
1886	WHYMAN, Bertram Robert	Lieut	WILLIS, Jock William
967	WHYTE, William James	3456	WILLIS, John William
2649	WICKHAM, Gilbert	6587	WILLIS, Richard Henry
2086	WICKINS, Vernon John	Capt	WILLIS, William Organ
6110	WICKS, Charles Rowland	2931	WILLOUGHBY, Arthur Edward
6360	WICKS, Thomas Ernest	2416	WILLOUGHBY, Frank
803	WIDDON, Albert Edward	782	WILSON, Albert
7067	WILDE, Harry	4923	WILSON, Alfred
3173	WILES, Frederick Clive	1412A	WILSON, Arthur
6361	WILEY, William	2698	WILSON, Frederick David Gilmore
1410A	WILKIE, Richard Begbie		
Lieut	WILKINS, George Henry	2813	WILSON, Frederick Sylvester
2428	WILKINS, Herbert Claude	5097	WILSON, George
3486	WILKINSON, Eugene Blake	7845	WILSON, Gerald Gordon
3255	WILKINSON, John	1903	WILSON, Harry
7737	WILKINSON, Peter James	7789	WILSON, Henry
6367	WILLETT, William Harold	3929A	WILSON, James Barnes
3108	WILLIAMS, Albert Sydney	Capt	WILSON, James Henry
1885	WILLIAMS, Charles Edward	3459	WILSON, John Turner
1108	WILLIAMS, Charles Henry Ernest	7738	WILSON, John William
		3929	WILSON, Joseph
1110	WILLIAMS, Clarence Oscar	1253	WILSON, Luke John
1411A	WILLIAMS, Clifford	662	WILSON, Robert Victor
724	WILLIAMS, David	3180	WILSON, Roy
6112	WILLIAMS, David	6356	WILSON, Walter
362	WILLIAMS, David Ennett	1370	WILSON, William
Capt	WILLIAMS, Edward Oliver	3628	WILSON, William
1884	WILLIAMS, Eric Archibald	2085	WILSON, William James
6858	WILLIAMS, Evan Vincent	3110	WILTON, Harry
7068	WILLIAMS, Frederick George	3111	WINDON, Benjamin Edward
1814	WILLIAMS, George	2531	WING, Robert George
1562	WILLIAMS, George Allan	7070	WINKLEMAN, Albert Ernest
1264	WILLIAMS, Gordon	7323	WINKS, Natal Gregory

No.	Name	No.	Name
3206	WINTER, Philip Eric	5775	WORTLEY, Frank Arthur
7322	WINTER, William Alexander	6373	WRIGHT, Alexander
7610	WINTER, Woodley	4930	WRIGHT, Bertie Trantie William
2755	WINTERS, Alfred James		
6876	WINTZLOFF, Frederick	1251	WRIGHT, Cecil
4401	WISE, Cyril Bertram	960	WRIGHT, Claude Elijah
7830	WITHERS, Albert Leonard	6586	WRIGHT, Erric Vivian Lyle
5767	WITHERS, Walter Matthias James	1811	WRIGHT, George
91	WITHERWICK, Charles	1857	WRIGHT, Harold Percy Yonge
1103	WITTISON, William	Lieut	WRIGHT, Phillip Henry
7862	WIXTED, Thomas Michael	1254	WRIGHT, Robert James
664	WOOD, Charles	1413A	WRIGHT, Samuel James
978	WOOD, Charles	1440	WRIGHT, Sydney
2812	WOOD, Frederick Feathersone	7325	WRIGHT, Thomas
665	WOOD, Percy Victor	7069	WRIGHT, William Charles Cecil
6623	WOOD, Thomas Dugald		
2007	WOODBRIDGE, John Michael Paul	1107	WYLES, James Henry
		1414A	WYLIE, James
2000	WOODBRIDGE, Patrick Benjamin	1101	WYLIE, Randolph Monteith
		2427	WYNN, Percy Austin
2008	WOODBRIDGE, William Isaac	962	WYNNE, Alfred Thomas
2009	WOODBURN, John	800	WYNNE, William Henry
5143	WOODFORTH, Eric Gilston		
2367	WOODHAM, Frank	92	YAPP, Alfred
3133	WOODHEAD, Charles Frederick	215	YATES, John Edward
5534	WOODHOUSE, James	1113	YATES, Rhoderick George
7597	WOODLAND, Charles	216	YELLS, Cyril Alfred
7076	WOODRUFF, Thomas	7087	YORK, Kirby
1102	WOODS, Ambrose Augustine	2/Lieut	YOUDEN, Frederick Charles
4921	WOODS, Cecil Norman	2916	YOUNG, Arthur Andrew
4935	WOODS, Donald Charles	543	YOUNG, Charles
7338A	WOODS, John Henry	5770	YOUNG, Charles Harley
4936	WOODS, Robert Henry	1636	YOUNG, Edward
811	WOODS, Thomas Augustine	6213	YOUNG, George Clement
7073	WOODS, Wallace Edgar	7568A	YOUNG, Harold Leslie
4926	WOODWARD, Charles	1416A	YOUNG, James
6579	WOODWARD, Ernest Frederick	6119	YOUNG, Joseph Henry
1112	WOODWARD, Walter	3124	YOUNG, Leslie William
1029	WOOLDRIDGE, William John	6118	YOUNG, William
4276	WOOLFENDEN, John	1441	YOUNGS, Harry
666	WOOLSEY, George Robert	519	YUILL, Alexander
6116	WOOSTER, Bertram George	4846	YULE, John Irving
1369	WOOTTON, Frank William		
7606	WOOTTON, William	3464	ZIMMERMAN, Robert Bertie
7832	WORTHINGTON, George Herbert	7856	ZIGENBINE, Thomas
		5541	ZILLFLEISCH, William Carl

SUPPLEMENTARY ROLL

No.	Name	No.	Name
52983	BROWN, Robert	52995	MESURE, Peter George Albert
50618	DANDON, James William	53050	MURRAY, Maurice Allan
50616	DAVEY, John Charles	50677	McCABE, Edward Alexander Joseph
52999	DERRINGTON, John Arthur		
50623	DICKSON, John David	50729	NOYLES, Clarence Robert
53119	KEENAN, Daniel	57897	O'NEILL, Vincent Erin
50652	KERR, Robert	53074	PATERSON, Frederick Woolnough
50755	KING, Vincent Louis		
Lieut	LANE, James	53084	PEDERSEN, Francis George
50664	LOVEDAY, Vincent Charles	50686	PRICKETT, Thomas Walter
53045	LUKE, Archibald	53124	SISLEY, Francis Andrew
50659	LYNCH, Thomas Phillip	Lieut	SMITH, Hubert John Cawardine
50673	MARNANE, William St. John		
50665	MELLOR, William Oaklands	53114	WILSON, Geoffrey Leaf

◊   ◊   ◊   ◊

HONOURS and AWARDS

to

Members of the 15th Battalion

Australian Imperial Forces

War 1914-1918

HONOURS and AWARDS

Victoria Cross.
No. 1936 — H. Dalziel.

Companion of the Order of the Bath (C.B.).
T/Brigadier General J. H. Cannan.

Companion of the Order of St. Michael and St. George (C.M.G.).
T/Brig. General J. H. Cannan (While attached to 11th Bde. Hqrs.).
Lieut-Col. T. P. McSharry.

Distinguished Service Order (D.S.O.).
T/Brig.-General J. H. Cannan (While attached to 11th Bde. Hqrs.).
Lieut-Col. T. P. McSharry.
Lieut-Col. J. J. Corrigan.
Lieut.-Col. C. M. Johnston (While attached to 4th Bde. Hqrs.).
Major A. H. Powell.
Major Burford Sampson.
Major G. F. Dickinson (While attached to 14th Bde. Hqrs.).
QM/H/Major F. W. Craig.
Capt. R. Glasgow.
Capt. J. T. Hynes.
Capt. H. M. Brettingham-Moore.

Bar to Distinguished Service Order.
Lieut-Colonel T. P. McSharry.
Lieut-Colonel J. J. Corrigan.

Member of the Order of the British Empire (M.B.E.).
Capt. G. King.
Lieut. C. Davy.

Military Cross (M.C.).

Lieut-Colonel T. P. McSharry.
Major J. Hill.
Hon. Major F. R. North (46th Bn).
Capt. B. S. Atkinson.
Capt. E. M. Bradley.
Capt. E. K. Carter.
Capt. W. L. E. Domeney.
Capt. C. C. Drane.
Capt. D. Dunworth.
Capt. R. Glasgow.
Capt. C. S. Goss.
Capt. L. J. Hunter
  (A.A.M.C. Attached).
Capt. W. D. Kenyon.
Capt. H. R. Koch.
Capt. R. B. McIntosh.
Capt. S. V. O'Regan
  (A.A.M.C. Attached).
Capt. S. F. Porter.
Capt. P. J. G. Toft.
Lieut. J. H. W. Fraser.
Lieut. W. Goninon.
Lieut. J. E. Greenwood.
2/Lieut. S. H. Joubert.
Lieut. H. R. H. Lack.
Lieut. H. G. Maegraith.
Lieut. C. E. Northover.
Lieut. J. McI. Rae.
Lieut. F. Stephenson.
Lieut. G. H. Wilkins.

Bar to Military Cross.

Hon. Major F. R. North (46th Bn). Capt. P. J. G. Toft.

Distinguished Conduct Medal (D.C.M.).

Capt.	J. Craven.	601	G. Goodwin.
Capt.	W. Murdoch.	518	W. S. James.
Lieut.	A. W. P. Jones.	1208	S. W. Lockwood.
1410	R. Barrett.	1357	J. T. Maher.
878	C. E. Beadon.	5151	C. McAlister.
3258	H. Carr.	5473	P. McCoy.
119	F. R. Cawley.	2674	G. Parker.
1310	A. J. Coogan.	1800	P. J. Sammon.
94	E. Corbett.	5514	J. Shannon.
6001	R. A. Day.	650	A. Skinner.
744	H. Edelsten.	1374	P. R. Sutherland.
4495	A. D. Edwards.	204	R. Tickner.
594	F. J. Fleet.	5538	G. Williams.
3749	M. Goodger.	213	A. Wright.

Military Medal (M.M.).

2552	D. J. Alcorn.	6222	A. E. Burton.
1001	H. Alexander.	3233	W. J. Byrne.
565	S. Allkin.	3706	C. S. K. Cameron.
4732	L. P. Ardill.	7215	E. H. Carlyle.
5049	F. S. Baker.	1415	I. R. Carroll.
4753	H. K. Baker.	2564	J. Carroll.
2556	F. E. Barnes.	3261	F. Cawley.
4449	W. F. Barry.	1307	J. Clark.
3250	K. C. Bassett.	6476	J. P. Cleary.
3688	F. W. Baunach.	430	R. H. Cleary.
4359	A. G. Belbin.	6737	C. Colwill.
4744	A. E. Blackmur.	6472	A. Comollatti.
971	N. H. Bowers.	6952	P. G. Connolly.
3692	W. P. N. Boyce.	2568	P. G. Cooke.
3245	A. Broadfoot.	7210	E. W. T. Croft.
576	H. J. Browne.	3470	J. M. Cronin.
6462	W. M. Burns.	277	A. W. F. G. Crow.

HISTORY OF THE 15th BATTALION 299

2907	W. H. Cunningham.	1356	R. Mahaffy.
6245	A. E. Dabelstein.	2681	R. J. Marpole.
6001	R. A. Day.	3817	L. Matheson.
2127	J. Dempsey.	4580	S. May.
1607	R. Dent.	Lieut.	F. J. Merrell.
2577	R. S. Dinsey.	1064	E. Moles.
1317	J. K. Dooley.	2684	J. McN. Montgomery.
4773	W. C. Downey.	2617	R. McE. Montgomery.
6758	A. Duck.	Lieut.	R. L. Moore.
5389	G. A. Easey.	6305	H. Morgan.
1485	W. Eastment.	625	J. H. Morgan.
5790	E. L. Eggar.	970	A. Morrey.
2361	C. T. Emerson.	2424	L. Mundy.
2505	E. J. H. Etchell.	5473	P. McCoy.
1032	J. M. Eustace.	1880A	M. McGinnity.
591	H. Evans.	1428	W. H. McHugo.
3299	A. T. Farr.	5724	R. W. McIntyre.
2835	P. J. Fleming.	2170	J. McKenzie.
7707	B. Flewell-Smith.	3382	J. A. McLay.
2708	H. J. Frampton.	2398	A. McLeish.
4406	J. Fraser.	43850	B. J. O'Brien.
4803	H. Gartner.	3131	T. O'Sullivan.
5402	W. Gillespie.	7300	E. J. Pardon.
2364	G. H. Gilson.	2674	G. Parker.
4619	R. W. Godding.	2222	A. S. Patterson.
3748	C. Godfrey.	940	F. A. W. C. Peachey.
440	H. Gough.	1720	W. W. Peele.
Lieut.	J. Grant.	6073	T. A. Perry.
1611	R. J. Grant.	7292	P. J. C. Peut.
5424	W. S. Hamilton.	108	G. Potter.
3755	L. Hansen.	1788	W. O'S. Power.
7808	D. Higgins.	4878	J. P. Pringle.
1192	C. J. Hills.	480	G. Proctor.
1050	P. C. Hirst.	2700	R. D. Proctor.
2998	M. T. Hogan.	7037	R. A. Purvis.
2433	W. Holden.	6552	E. W. Putnam.
3467	H. B. Holloway.	Lieut.	J. McI. Rae.
4316	J. Holt.	4892	R. B. Raper.
2070	C. Howard.	6080	P. C. Rawlins.
6278	G. T. Hull.	3422	W. T. Richmond.
451	R. A. Hunter.	3080	H. T. Riglen.
Capt.	J. T. Hynes.	7787a	A. Rindberg.
217	H. W. Irwin.	7861	F. Robinson.
3335	W. Jackson.	3229	W. Ruegger.
Lieut.	G. P. Jamieson.	Lieut.	W. P. Ryan.
2691	W. R. Keating.	1800	P. J. Sammon.
3606	R. H. Kerslake.	1240	E. G. Searle.
3329	N. W. Kingston.	5514	J. Shannon.
6045	J. T. Knight.	Lieut.	B. J. Shaw.
611	R. C. Knipe.	7047	J. H. Shearer.
Lieut.	A. R. Kunkler.	3438	C. H. Siddins.
6217	H. S. Latham.	1393	E. W. Simon.
6862	A. V. Lauchland.	650	A. Skinner.
3177	J. Lee.	654	J. Slack.
18	J. P. Lee.	Lieut.	B. T. Sloan.
1655	J. Lonergan.	Lieut.	R. Strangman-Taylor.
3483	M. Madge.	1847	E. N. Thomas.

M

Capt.	P. J. G. Toft.	2697	S. Whipps.
4912	T. Tomlinson.	3255	J. Wilkinson.
2419	T. Turner.	1110	C. O. Williams.
2753	T. J. Watkins.	6858	E. V. Williams.
1812	W. D. Watson.	662	R. V. Wilson.
358	F. Watts.	1102	A. A. Woods.
961	W. T. Watts.	4930	B. T. W. Wright.

Bar to Military Medal.

4732	L. P. Ardill.	4316	J. Holt.
4744	A. E. Blackmur.	1655	J. Lonergan.
2568	P. G. Cooke.	Lieut.	R. L. Moore.
6001	R. A. Day.	1880A	M. McGinnity.
1607	R. Dent.	2398	A. McLeish.
1032	J. M. Eustace.	1720	W. W. Peete.
3748	C. Godfrey.	4878	J. P. Pringle.
3755	L. Hansen.	1393	E. W. Simon.
3467	H. B. Holloway.	Lieut.	R. Strangman-Taylor.

Meritorious Service Medal (M.S.M.).

1305	C. H. Baker.	3274	F. N. Day.
859	H. J. Bowers.	5288	J. Hourigan.
271	G. Cawsey.	4546	J. D. Lindsay.
2716	W. A. Crisp.	392	J. J. Maher.
		4397	H. Thomas.

Mentioned in Despatches (M.I.D.).

T/Brigadier General J. H. Cannan (5 times).		859	H. J. Bowers.
Lieut-Colonel T. P. McSharry (4 times).		Capt.	H. M. Brettingham-Moore.
Lieut-Colonel J. J. Corrigan (Twice).		Capt.	J. C. Browne.
QM/H/Major F. W. Craig (Twice).		418	E. Bryans.
		94	E. Corbett.
Lieut-Colonel C. M. Johnston (3 times).		Capt.	J. Craven.
		Lieut.	C. Davy.
Hon. Major F. R. North (47 Bn.).		744	H. Edelsten.
Major	G. F. Dickinson (Twice) (While attached to 14th Bde. Hqrs.).	711	H. A. Eibel.
		2505	E. J. H. Etchell.
		2835	P. J. Fleming.
		1041	F. G. Gale.
Major	A. H. Powell (Twice).	Capt.	R. Glasgow.
Chaplain	T. S. Power.	6777	G. Grant.
Lieut.	J. McI Rae.	1652	V. C. C. Harry.
Major	B. Sampson.	715	J. Henry.
654	J. Slack.	Major	J. Hill.
5515	T. Southworth.	3767	L. Hoxey.
651	F. Stacey.	Capt.	L. J. Hunter.
587	S. A. Tanner.	5420	T. S. N. Hurford.
Capt.	E. A. Terry.	Capt.	J. T. Hynes.
Lieut.	G. Urquhart.	517	W. S. James.
213	A. Wright.	2/Lieut	S. H. Joubert.
Capt.	B. S. Atkinson.	705	L. Melia.
2556	F. E. Barnes.	Capt.	F. Moran.
1410	R. Barrett.	Major	W. T. Mundell.
3575	W. Beaumont.	Lieut.	P. R. A. G. Ohlson.
		Capt.	S. V. O'Regan.

Congratulatory.

6383	E. P. Barton.		4858	J. Moloney.
2636	J. R. Craig.		5458	C. E. Murray.
6981	T. G. Harding.		6062	R. B. Murray.
6510	W. M. Hickey.		3816	J. Musson.
2217	C. S. Kyle.		5724	R. W. McIntyre.
6531	F. Martens.			

Gallantry.

4882   H. J. Penny.   26077   T. V. Stubbs.

Honourable Mention.

119   F. R. Cawley.   1357   J. T. Maher.

FOREIGN DECORATIONS.
Croix de Guerre.

T/Brigadier General J. H. Cannan.   2379   P. F. Jameson.
609   J. T. Hutchinson.   1390   C. Rush.

Medaille Militaire.
594   F. J. Fleet.

Serbian Silver Medal.
662   R. V. Wilson.

Cross of Kara George. Serbian 2nd Class (With Swords).
Capt.   J. T. Hynes.

Russian Order of St. Stanislas 3rd Class (With Swords).
Major G. F. Dickinson (while attached to 14th Bde. Hqrs.).

Summary of Honours and Awards.

V.C.	1	D.C.M.	28
C.B.	1	M.M.	162
C.M.G.	2	Bar to M.M.	18
D.S.O.	11	M.S.M.	9
Bar to D.S.O.	2	Congratulatory	11
M.B.E.	2	Gallantry	2
		Hon. Mention	2
M.C.	28	M.I.D.	64
Bar to M.C.	2	Foreign	8

DECEASED ROLL

of

Members of the 15th Battalion

Australian Imperial Forces

War 1914-1918

DECEASED ROLL

Reg. No.	Name.	Cause of Death.	Place of Death.	Date.
1155	ABEL, A. E.	K.I.A.	Gallipoli	9/ 5/1915
402	ADAM, C. R.	D.O.W.	Gallipoli	5/ 5/1915
2496	ADAMS, H.	K.I.A.	France	9/ 8/1916
31	ADAMS, J. H.	K.I.A.	Gallipoli	8/ 8/1915
253	ADAMS, S. J.	K.I.A.	Gallipoli	8/ 8/1915
870	AGUTTER, F.	D.O.I.	At Sea	27/ 1/1915
1637	AHERNE, R. P.	Drowned	England	23/ 9/1917
3677	ALCOCK, F. C.	K.I.A.	France	28/ 8/1916
564	ALEXANDER, T.	K.I.A.	Gallipoli	9-10/ 5/1915
5259	ALFRED, F.	K.I.A.	Belgium	26/ 9/1917
869	ALLAN, J.	K.I.A.	Gallipoli	9-10/ 5/1915
7681A	ALLASON, S. E.	K.I.A.	France	4/ 7/1918
1002	ALLOM, O. B.	K.I.A.	Gallipoli	7/ 8/1915
5810	ALSBURY, D. A.	K.I.A.	France	1/ 2/1917
2102	ANDERSON, B. J.	D.O.W.	France	16/ 6/1917
566	ANDERSON, F. A.	K.I.A.	Gallipoli	18/ 5/1915
5975	ANDERSON, H. D.	K.I.A.	France	28/ 1/1917
2/Lieut	ANDERSON, K. H.	K.I.A.	Gallipoli	9/ 5/1915
254	ANDERSON, W. H.	Accid. Killed	Egypt	31/12/1915
713	ANDERSON, W.	K.I.A.	Gallipoli	28/ 4/1915
251	ANDREW, W.	K.I.A.	Gallipoli	27/ 4/1915
6461	ANDREWS, A. C.	D.O.I.	Germany	16/12/1918
3034	ANDREWS, D. L.	K.I.A.	France	9/ 8/1916
6931	ANSTIS, C. C.	K.I.A.	Belgium	14/ 8/1917
Lieut	ARMSTRONG, F. L.	K.I.A.	Gallipoli	10/ 5/1915
Lieut	ARMSTRONG, H. P.	K.I.A.	Gallipoli	10/ 5/1915
5817	ARNEY, R. W.	D.O.I.	England	3/ 3/1919
2/Lieut	ARNOLD, R. I.	K.I.A.	France	8/ 8/1916
1377	ARNOT, J. A.	D.O.W.	Alexandria	4/ 7/1915
103	ASHFORD, L. J.	D.O.W.	Gallipoli	10/ 5/1915
1151	ATKINSON, T. C.	D.O.W.	At Sea	2/ 5/1915
1710	AUBIN, A. L.	K.I.A.	Gallipoli	8/ 8/1915
1702	AUCHTERLONIE, B. I.	K.I.A.	Gallipoli	8/ 8/1915
1469	AUSTIN, G.	K.I.A.	Gallipoli	9/ 5/1915
867	AVERY, H. McL.	K.I.A.	Gallipoli	8/ 8/1915
2860	AVERY, N. L.	K.I.A.	France	28/ 3/1918
1153	AYERS, W. B.	K.I.A.	Gallipoli	9/ 5/1915
4731	AYLING, E. T.	D.O.W.	France	3/ 2/1917
3234	BACH, P.	K.I.A.	France	7/ 8/1916
406	BACK, H. S.	K.I.A.	Gallipoli	8/ 8/1915
7444	BAGSTER, W. H.	D.O.W.	France	10/ 4/1918
2889	BAILES, H. P.	K.I.A.	France	3/ 8/1918
6947	BAILEY, A. L.	D.O.W.	Belgium	10/ 7/1917
	BAILEY, J.	D.O.I.	Brisbane, Q'ld.	16/ 9/1916
255	BAILEY, M. J.	K.I.A.	Gallipoli	8/ 8/1915
367	BAKER, A. A.	K.I.A.	Gallipoli	29/ 5/1915
338	BAKER, B. H.	D.O.W.	France	4/ 7/1918
7744	BAKER, C. J.	D.O.W.	France	13/ 8/1918
4741	BAKER, E. C.	K.I.A.	France	11/ 4/1917
408	BAKER, F.	K.I.A.	Gallipoli	20/ 5/1915
3574	BAKER, G. A.	K.I.A.	France	11/ 4/1917
7206	BAKER, T. J.	K.I.A.	France	28/ 3/1918
1164	BAKER, T. V.	K.I.A.	Gallipoli	8/ 8/1915
1716	BAKER, W. E.	K.I.A.	Gallipoli	8/ 8/1915
409	BALLARD, A.	D.O.W.	At Sea	1/ 6/1915

HISTORY OF THE 15th BATTALION

Reg. No.	Name.	Cause of Death.	Place of Death.	Date.
726	BAMBERY, G. S.	K.I.A.	Gallipoli	26/ 4/1915
725	BAMBERY, T. R.	K.I A.	Gallipoli	27/ 4/1915
2432	BANKS, W. J.	D.O.W.	France	4/ 7/1918
5332	BARDON, P. J.	D.O.W.	France	12/ 8/1916
3626	BARNARD, W. H.	K.I.A.	France	21/ 1/1918
3573	BARNES, C. A.	D.O.I.	Caulfield, Vic.	14/ 6/1919
2/Lieut	BARNES, F. E.	K.I.A.	France	11/ 4/1917
1715	BARNES, H.	K.I.A.	France	7/ 8/1916
256	BARNES, W.	K.I.A.	Gallipoli	18/ 5/1915
569	BARR, A.	K.J.A.	Gallipoli	8/ 8/1915
3703	BARRATT. S. V.	D.O.W.	France	11/ 8/1916
5033	BARRIE, J.	D.O.W.	France	7/ 7/1917
6944	BARROW, E. W.	K.I.A.	Belgium	27/ 9/1917
2557	BARROW, G. C.	K.I.A.	France	6/ 8/1916
33	BARTLEM, F. J.	D.O.W.	Gallipoli	29/ 5/1915
2341	BASING, W. H.	D.O.W.	France	6/ 7/1918
6226	BATTERSBY, W. J.	K.I.A.	France	11/ 4/1917
1720	BAXTER, J. P.	K.I.A.	Gallipoli	8/ 8/1915
1308	BAXTER, N	K.I.A.	Gallipoli	26/ 4/1915
6946	BEACOM, J. C.	K.I.A.	France	13/ 8/1918
874	BEACON, J. A.	K.I.A.	France	10/ 8/1916
1004	BEARD, E. F.	K.I.A.	Gallipoli	9-10/ 5/1915
	BECK, L. P.	D.O.I.	Maryborough, Qld.	20/ 4/1916
4738	BEHAN, E.	K.I.A.	France	7/ 4/1917
4733	BELCHER, W.	K.I.A.	France	11/ 4/1917
6713	BELL, H.	K.I.A.	France	18/ 8/1917
2271	BELL, R. T.	K.I.A.	Gallipoli	7/ 8/1915
6961	BENNETT, L. E.	K.I.A.	Belgium	28/ 9/1917
106	BENNETT, L. S.	K.I.A.	Gallipoli	9-10/ 5/1915
4257	BENNION, E. E.	K.I.A.	Belgium	11/ 7/1917
1405	BENSON, F. McL.	K.I.A.	France	11/ 4/1917
261	BENSON, S. E. W	K.I.A.	Gallipoli	10/ 5/1915
411	BENTZON, S. M.	K.I.A.	Gallipoli	26/ 4/1915
3687	BERGIN, P.	K.I.A.	France	8/ 8/1916
1675	BERKINGSHAW, W. E.	D.O.I.	France	16/12/1916
107	BERRY, J.	K.I.A.	Gallipoli	8/ 8/1915
4360	BESIER, E. F.	K.I.A.	Belgium	11/ 7/1917
4358	BETHEL, W. M.	K.I.A.	France	7/ 8/1916
405	BEVERLEY, T.	K.I.A.	Gallipoli	30/ 4/1915
1467	BIDDLE, A. E.	K.I.A.	Gallipoli	10/ 5/1915
7813	BIRKE, H. O.	Accid. Inj.	France	25/ 9/1918
2106	BLACKLOCK, H. J.	K.I.A.	Gallipoli	8/ 8/1915
1917	BLACKMORE, F. S.	K.I.A.	Gallipoli	8/ 8/1915
1309	BLAIR, W.	K.I.A.	Gallipoli	26/ 4/1915
3578	BLAKE, A. C.	D.O.W.	France	8/ 8/1916
724	BLAKE, F.	K.I.A.	Gallipoli	8/ 8/1915
1714	BLANDFORD, L. C.	K.I.A.	Gallipoli	8/ 8/1915
7197	BLUNDELL, H. E.	K.I.A.	France	9/ 6/1918
6960	BLUNT, J. J.	D.O.W.	France	7/ 7/1917
34	BOGIE, R. D.	K.I.A.	Gallipoli	29/ 5/1915
6950	BOGUE, W.	K.I.A.	Belgium	17/10/1917
5985	BOLCK, R.	K.I.A.	France	4/ 7/1918
5986	BOLGER, P. J.	K.I.A.	France	11/ 4/1917
260	BOLTON, W.	K.I.A.	Gallipoli	18/ 5/1915
4736	BOND, D. A.	K.I.A.	France	19/12/1916
4026	BONDING, J J.	D.O.W.	France	20/ 5/1918
6718	BONNEFIN F. A. A.	D.O I.	United Kingdom	4/ 8/1917
1905	BOOKER, H. F.	K.I.A.	Gallipoli	8/ 8/1915

HISTORY OF THE 15th BATTALION 307

Reg. No.	Name.	Cause of Death.	Place of Death.	Date.
6962	BOOTH, J. O. A.	K.I.A.	Belgium	4/ 7/1917
4747	BOSEL, C. F.	D.O.W.	France	26/10/1916
723	BOSTON, P. W.	K.I.A.	Gallipoli	10/ 5/1915
1310	BOURKE, D. C.	D.O.W.	Alexandria	2/ 5/1915
110	BOURKE, E. W.	D.O.W.	At Sea	30/ 5/1915
1457	BOURNE, H.	K.I.A.	France	11/ 4/1917
4735	BOURNE, O. G.	K.I.A.	France	11/ 4/1917
1463	BOWERMAN, G.	K.I.A.	Gallipoli	17/ 5/1915
2727	BOWRING, A.	D.O.W.	France	4/ 7/1918
12	BOYD, R.	D.O.W.	France	9/ 4/1917
4362	BRAMICH, S. S.	K.I.A.	Belgium	28/ 9/1917
1688	BRATCHFORD, A. J.	K.I.A.	France	11/ 4/1917
5647	BRAY, W.	K.I.A.	France	11/ 4/1917
577	BRENNAN, W.	K.I.A.	Gallipoli	18/ 5/1915
5990	BREWER, W. J.	K.I.A.	France	29/ 3/1918
1920	BRICE, J. W.	K.I.A.	Gallipoli	8/ 8/1915
2110	BRIGGS, J.	K.I.A.	Gallipoli	8/ 8/1915
7692	BRIMBLECOMBE, I. H.	D.O.W.	France	5/ 8/1918
264	BROADBENT, H. O.	D.O.W.	Randwick, N.S.W.	27/11/1915
2113	BRODEY, W. J.	K.I.A.	Gallipoli	22/ 8/1915
7199	BROMFIELD, J. M.	K.I.A.	France	4/ 7/1918
6967	BROOKE, A. B.	D.O.I.	Brisbane, Q'ld.	21/ 1/1917
5820	BROOKS, A.	K.I.A.	France	1/ 2/1917
2/Lieut	BROOKS, W. A.	D.O.I.	Egypt	2/ 3/1916
265	BROOME, G. G.	K.I.A.	Gallipoli	18/ 5/1915
413	BROOME, H. S. F.	D.O.W.	At Sea	30/ 4/1915
2692	BROSTROM, J.	K.I.A.	France	8/ 8/1916
32	BROUGHTON, T. R. R.	K.I.A.	Gallipoli	29/ 5/1915
1305	BROWN, A. B.	K.I.A.	Gallipoli	8/ 8/1915
872	BROWN, A. D.	K.I.A.	Gallipoli	30/ 4/1915
1302	BROWN, C. R.	D.O.I.	Egypt	24/ 2/1915
1641	BROWN, D.	K.I.A.	Gallipoli	9/ 8/1915
1918	BROWN, D. S.	K.I.A.	Gallipoli	27/ 8/1915
2275	BROWN, H.	K.I.A.	France	8/ 8/1918
1159	BROWN, H. B.	K.I.A.	Gallipoli	2/ 5/1915
717	BROWN, J.	K.I.A.	Gallipoli	9/ 5/1915
1259	BROWN, O.	K.I.A.	Gallipoli	30/ 4/1915
3265	BROWN, P.	K.I.A.	France	7/ 6/1918
7688A	BROWN, R. V.	D.O.W.	France	24/ 9/1918
6722	BROWN, W. R.	D.O.I.	At Sea	5/ 12/1916
575	BROWN, W. W.	K.I.A.	France	27/ 8/1916
1379	BROWNE, G.	D.O.W.	At Sea	13/ 8/1915
578	BRUCE, F. A.	D.O.W.	France	8/ 8/1916
1902	BRUCE, G. H.	K.I.A.	Gallipoli	8/ 8/1915
2560	BRUCE, H.	K.I.A.	France	1/ 2/1917
1602	BRUCE, W.	D.O.W.	Gallipoli	9/ 8/1915
7201	BRUNTON, A. N.	K.I.A.	Belgium	9/ 8/1917
1911	BUCHANAN, D. S.	K.I.A.	Gallipoli	27/ 8/1915
1910	BUCHANAN, L. A.	D.O.W.	France	29/ 8/1916
718	BUCKLEY, D.	K.I.A.	Gallipoli	26/ 4/1915
3	BULL, T. H.	D.O.W.	Gallipoli	29/ 5/1915
5993	BUNTER, W. F.	K.I.A.	France	11/ 4/1917
579	BURDEKIN, J. V.	K.I.A.	Gallipoli	8/ 8/1915
2117	BURGIN, H. G.	K.I.A.	France	22/ 4/1918
1719	BURKE, C.	D.O.I.	At Sea	2/ 8/1915
7747	BURKE, M. J. J.	D.O.I.	France	5/ 7/1918
4742	BURNE, C. R.	K.I.A.	France	11/ 4/1917
1845A	BURNS, J. J.	K.I.A.	France	8/ 8/1916

HISTORY OF THE 15th BATTALION

Reg. No.	Name.	Cause of Death.	Place of Death.	Date.
719	BURNS, W. H.	D.O.W.	Gallipoli	2/ 5/1915
2115	BURRIDGE, A. D.	K.I.A.	Gallipoli	7/ 8/1915
1011	BURSLEM, C. H.	K.I.A.	France	8/ 8/1916
7687	BUSIKO, J. W.	D.O.W.	France	2/ 5/1918
5342	BUTLER, E. C.	D.O.W.	Brisbane, Q'ld.	5/ 11/1920
1445	BUTLER, E. H.	K.I.A.	Gallipoli	26/ 4/1915
2561	BUTLER, G. G.	K.I.A.	France	7/ 8/1916
76	BUTTERFIELD, E.	D.O.W.	At Sea	4/ 5/1915
1071	BUXTON, J. C.	D.O.W.	France	20/12/1916
417	BYRNE, H. F.	K.I.A.	Gallipoli	9/ 5/1915
115	BYRNE, H. H.	D.O.W.	At Sea	6/ 5/1915
116	BYRNE, J.	K.I.A.	Gallipoli	27/ 4/1915
1008	BYRON, J.	K.I.A.	Gallipoli	8/ 8/1915
270	CAIRNS, W. B.	D.O.W.	Gallipoli	7/ 5/1915
6957	CALDWELL, R. R.	K.I.A.	France	13/ 6/1918
1314	CALLUM, W. F.	K.I.A.	Belgium	17/10/1916
4272	CALNAN, C.	D.O.I.	England	20/11/1918
5369	CAMERON, J. K.	P.O.W.	Germany	3/ 5/1917
1925	CAMERON, W.	K.I.A.	Gallipoli	8/ 8/1915
2277	CAMM, J.	K.I.A.	Gallipoli	8/ 8/1915
3016	CAMPBELL, J.	Accid. Killed	Egypt	9/11/1915
5786	CAMPBELL, W.	K.I.A.	France	11/ 4/1917
Capt	CANNAN, D. H.	K.I.A.	Gallipoli	8/ 8/1915
7636	CARBERRY, M. J.	K.I.A.	France	9/ 6/1918
6473	CAREY, J.	D.O.I.	Germany	14/ 8/1917
866	CAREY, T. J.	K.I.A.	Gallipoli	9-10/ 5/1915
421	CARLETON, N. E.	D.O.I.	At Sea	24/ 1/1915
1858	CARLSEN, A.	D.O.W.	Gallipoli	8/ 8/1915
269	CARNOCHAN, A.	D.O.W.	Lemnos	10/ 8/1915
422	CARRINGTON, J.	K.I.A.	Gallipoli	9/ 5/1915
732	CARROLL, J. T.	K.I.A.	Gallipoli	8/ 8/1915
6730	CARTER, A. W.	D.O.W.	France	2/10/1917
3170	CARVEL, R.	K.I.A.	France	6/ 8/1916
735	CASH, W. C.	K.I.A.	Gallipoli	9/ 5/1915
118A	CASTLESMITH, R.	K.I.A.	France	11/ 4/1917
2565	CASTREE, J. H.	K.I.A.	France	1/ 9/1916
2788	CAVE, E.	K.I.A.	France	11/ 4/1917
4762	CHAMBERLAIN, F. H.	P.O.W.	Germany	14/ 4/1917
1923	CHAMBERS, T.	K.I.A.	Gallipoli	8/ 8/1915
6731	CHAMBERS, T. F.	K.I.A.	Belgium	26/ 9/1917
6483	CHANDLER, E.	D.O.W.	Belgium	10/ 7/1917
1167	CHAPMAN, J.	K.I.A.	Gallipoli	9-10/ 5/1915
3257	CHARNOCK, T. J.	K.I.A.	France	27/ 8/1916
3583	CHATWIN, W. R.	K.I.A.	France	31/12/1916
6953	CHERRY, A.	D.O.W.	France	6/ 6/1918
1904	CHIMES, G. H.	K.I.A.	Gallipoli	8/ 8/1915
	CHING, W. F.	D.O.I.	Brisbane, Qld.	2/ 9/1915
5995	CHRISTENSEN, W.	D.O.W.	France	8/ 7/1918
6237	CHRISTIAN, H. C.	K.I.A.	France	11/ 4/1917
1471	CHRISTIANSEN, A.	C.N.S.	Gallipoli	/ 8/1916
273	CLARKE, A.	K.I.A.	Gallipoli	10/ 5/1915
6215	CLARK, F. E.	K.I.A.	France	1/ 2/1917
424	CLARK, J.	K.I.A.	Gallipoli	8/ 8/1915
6471	CLARK, J.	D.O.W.	Belgium	26/ 9/1917
1414	CLARK, V.	K.I.A.	Gallipoli	8/ 8/1915
4761	CLARK, W. S. T.	K.I.A.	France	1/ 2/1917
883	CLARKE, C.	K.I.A.	Gallipoli	30/ 4/1915
884	CLARKE, F. A.	K.I.A.	Gallipoli	17/ 8/1915

HISTORY OF THE 15th BATTALION 309

Reg. No.	Name.	Cause of Death.	Place of Death.	Date.
1604	CLARKE, W. E.	K.I.A.	Gallipoli	9/ 8/1915
4365	CLARKSON, L. C. G.	K.I.A.	Belgium	16/ 8/1917
3013	CLAXTON, W. W.	K.I.A.	France	9/ 8/1916
2056	CLEARY, E. V.	K.I.A.	Gallipoli	7/ 8/1915
6476	CLEARY, J. P.	D.O.W.	France	5/ 4/1918
885	CLEGG, L.	D.O.I.	Egypt	9/ 3/1915
3639	CLENCH, A.	K.I.A.	France	6/ 8/1916
2125	CLIFFORD, V. T.	D.O.W.	Alexandria	22/ 8/1915
6955	CLINCH, J.	D.O.C.	London	15/ 7/1919
2346	COAD, L. J.	D.O.I.	France	7/12/1916
1472	COBBE, H. C.	K.I.A.	Gallipoli	8/ 8/1915
557	COBBETT, A. L.	K.I.A.	France	4/ 7/1918
1816	COFFEY, E. I. R.	K.I.A.	Gallipoli	8/ 8/1915
583	COFFIN, C. D.	K.I.A.	Gallipoli	26/ 4/1915
2351	COLE, E. H.	K.I.A.	France	11/ 4/1917
6736	COLE, S. J.	D.O.W.	Belgium	1/ 7/1917
1735	COLEMAN, J. G.	K.I.A.	Gallipoli	8/8/1915
Lieut	COLLIN, L. N.	K.I.A.	Gallipoli	9/ 5/1915
366	COLLINGS, M. D.	K.I.A.	Gallipoli	3/ 5/1915
5589	COLLINGWOOD, R. P.	K.I.A.	France	9/ 8/1916
5787	COLLINS, H. J.	K.I.A.	France	1/ 2/1917
275	COLQUHOUN, H. R.	K.I.A.	Gallipoli	27/ 8/1915
5349	CONSTABLE, S. C.	D.O.W.	France	21/ 3/1918
1309A	COOGAN, T. P.	K.I.A.	Gallipoli	8/ 8/1915
1014	COOK, J. W.	K.I.A.	Gallipoli	8/ 8/1915
425	COOKE, H. W.	K.I.A.	Gallipoli	30/ 4/1915
2055	COOLEY, F. J.	K.I.A.	Gallipoli	7/ 8/1915
5968	COOMBE, A. R.	D.O.I.	At Sea	6/10/1916
1019	COOMBE, V. R.	D.O.W.	London	29/ 9/1915
5360	COOPER, G.	K.I.A.	Belgium	28/ 9/1917
3114	COOPER, H. H.	K.I.A.	France	1/ 2/1917
1606	CORBY, E. J.	K.I.A.	Gallipoli	9/ 5/1915
1825	COSTA, E.	K.I.A.	Gallipoli	8/ 8/1915
879	COTT, R.	K.I.A.	Gallipoli	8/ 8/1915
5665	COTTAM, E. J.	K.I.A.	France	1/ 2/1917
7692A	COULSON, E.	D.O.W	France	9/ 7/1918
2124	COULTAS, G. H.	K.I.A.	France	25/ 9/1916
816	COUSINS, S. C.	K.I.A.	France	9/ 8/1916
1644	COX, F.	K.I.A.	Gallipoli	18/ 5/1915
1643	COX, H. J.	K.I.A.	Gallipoli	29/ 5/1915
7217	CRADOCK, L. E.	D.O.W.	France	4/ 7/1918
5352	CRAIG, G.	K.I.A.	France	8/ 8/1916
1413	CRAIG, T. J.	K.I.A.	Gallipoli	8/ 8/1915
729	CRESSWELL, S.	K.I.A.	Gallipoli	8/ 8/1915
7210	CROFT, E. W. T.	K.I.A.	France	8/ 8/1918
3705	CROKE, A.	K.I.A.	France	27/ 8/1916
427	CROKER, A. J.	K.I.A.	Gallipoli	1/ 5/1915
4471	CRONK, E.	P.O.W.	France	28/ 8/1917
7614	CROWLEY, P.	D.O.W.	France	5/ 7/1918
2571	CROWTHER, G.	D.O.W.	France	24/ 9/1916
582	CROWTHER, T.	D.O.W.	Germany	
1733	CULLEN, J.	D.O.W.	At Sea	10/ 8/1915
5547	CURTIS, F. J.	D.O.W.	France	25/ 8/1916
5359	CURTIS, R.	K.I.A.	Belgium	3/10/1916
737	DAEMEN, A.	K.I.A.	Gallipoli	9/ 5/1915
5384	DALTON, N. C.	D.O.W.	France	9/ 8/1916
2285	DALY, J. E. J.	D.O.W.	At Sea	30/ 8/1915
741	DANIEL, C. A.	K.I.A.	Gallipoli	3/ 5/1915

HISTORY OF THE 15th BATTALION

Reg. No.	Name.	Cause of Death.	Place of Death.	Date.
126	DANN, F.	K.I.A.	France	9/ 8/1916
279	DARKER, R. H.	D.O.I.	England	24/10/1918
6486	DAVID, T. J.	K.I.A.	France	11/ 4/1917
1741	DAVIDGE, A. J.	K.I.A.	Gallipoli	8/ 8/1915
6490	DAVIE, G. W. L.	D.O.W.	Belgium	9/ 7/1917
2240	DAVIES, B. C.	D.O.W.	France	19/ 9/1918
4481	DAVIS, A. H.	K.I.A.	France	28/ 8/1916
7226	DAVIS, F.	K.I.A.	Belgium	16/10/1917
2128	DAVIS, J. H.	K.I.A.	Gallipoli	8/ 8/1915
1645	DAVIS, R.	K.I.A.	Gallipoli	9/ 5/1915
2129	DAVIS, R. H.	K.I.A.	Gallipoli	8/ 8/1915
6492	DAVISON, H. G.	K.I.A.	Belgium	17/10/1917
7844	DAWES, T. J. B.	K.I.A.	France	4/ 7/1918
1608	DAWSON, J. McK.	D.O.W.	Alexandria	16/ 5/1915
1738	DAY, A. E.	K.I.A.	Gallipoli	8/ 8/1915
2281	DEACON, J. D.	D.O.W.	London	15/ 9/1915
79	DEAKIN, A. B.	K.I.A.	Gallipoli	18/ 8/1915
1740	DEAN, J.	K.I.A.	Gallipoli	8/ 8/1915
4289	DEARDS, H. F. L. H.	K.I.A.	Belgium	18/ 8/1917
5387	DE CHASTEL, L.	K.I.A.	France	9/ 8/1916
1934	DEEPROSE, W.	K.I.A.	Gallipoli	8/ 8/1915
7230	DEMPSEY, P.	D.O.W.	Belgium	16/10/1917
1737	DENSLOW, E.	K.I.A.	Gallipoli	8/ 8/1915
2839	DENYER, T. J.	D.O.W.	France	7/ 7/1917
1940	DERRICK, J. S.	K.I.A.	Gallipoli	8/ 8/1915
4779	DEVANNY, H. B.	D.O.I.	France	17/12/1916
1416A	DEWAR, D.	K.I.A.	Gallipoli	8/ 8/1915
7470	DEWELDON, A. B.	D.O.W.	France	6/ 8/1918
6491	DEWES, H.	D.O.W.	France	17/ 9/1918
2738	DICK, J.	K.I.A.	Gallipoli	5/12/1915
4294	DICKSON, J.	D.O.W.	Belgium	27/ 8/1917
Lieut	DICKSON, N.	D.O.W.	At Sea	27/ 4/1915
4778	DIXON, T.	D.O.W.	France	27/ 3/1918
1177	DONALD, H. F.	K.I.A.	Gallipoli	7/ 8/1915
3932	DONALD, H. J.	K.I.A.	France	11/ 4/1917
6967	DONNELLY, V.	K.I.A.	France	18/ 9/1918
1175	DONOHOE, W. H.	K.I.A.	Gallipoli	29/ 5/1915
6751	DOUDS, J. P.	D.O.W.	Belgium	14/10/1917
4493	DOUGLAS, J. R.	K.I.A.	France	9/ 8/1916
2282	DOWLING, E. A.	K.I.A.	Gallipoli	9/ 8/1915
4773	DOWNEY, W. C.	D.O.W.	England	23/ 9/1918
5383	DOWNEY, W. J.	K.I.A.	France	8/ 8/1916
4489	DOYLE, J.	K.I.A.	France	28/ 8/1916
6963	DRAPER, L.	K.I.A.	France	18/ 9/1918
6591	DRAY, W. G.	D.O.W.	Belgium	15/ 8/1917
2352	DRISCOLL, F. T.	D.O.W.	Belgium	15/ 8/1917
1318	DUBOIS, E. G. J. M.	K.I.A.	Gallipoli	8/ 8/1915
2280	DUFF, S. J.	K.I.A.	Gallipoli	7/ 8/1915
1315	DUNCAN, J. J.	K.I.A.	Gallipoli	7/ 8/1915
453	DUNSDON, R. G.	K.I.A.	Gallipoli	30/ 4/1915
5380	DYER, P. A.	K.I.A.	France	27/ 8/1916
744	EDELSTEN, H.	D.O.W.	France	30/ 8/1916
6252	EDMONDS, H.	D.O.W.	Belgium	13/ 6/1917
889	EDNEY, T.	D.O.I.	Lemnos	4/ 5/1915
1319	EDWARDS, A.	D.O.W.	At Sea	10/ 9/1915
130	EDWARDS, E. I.	K.I.A.	Gallipoli	3/ 5/1915
6969	EDWARDS, E. J.	D.O.I.	At Sea	9/ 1/1917
1179	EDWARDS, H. F.	K.I.A.	France	8/ 8/1916

HISTORY OF THE 15th BATTALION 311

Reg. No.	Name.	Cause of Death.	Place of Death.	Date.
5392	EDWARDS, J. M.	K.I.A.	France	8/ 8/1916
6009	EDWARDS, S. G.	K.I.A.	France	11/ 4/1917
4496	E'ELES, W.	D.O.I.	England	10/ 2/1919
	EGAN, S. A. (Served as)			
2305	YOUNG, J.	D.O.W.	France	9/ 8/1916
2/Lieut	EIBEL, H. A.	K.I.A.	France	11/ 4/1917
6010	ELFORD, F. G.	P.O.W.	Germany	29/ 4/1917
6497	ELLEM, V. E.	K.I.A.	France	30/ 3/1918
888	ELLEN, D. H.	K.I.A.	Gallipoli	1/ 5/1915
2359	ELLIOT, R. V.	K.I.A.	France	6/ 8/1916
6496	ELLIOTT, A. R.	D.O.W.	France	22/10/1917
7082	ELLIOTT, R. G.	K.I.A.	France	4/ 7/1918
2743	ELLIS, F. C.	D.O.W.	France	28/ 3/1918
280	ELSTOB, R. L.	K.I.A.	Gallipoli	9-10/ 5/1915
3736	ELVERY, H. P.	K.I.A.	France	8/ 8/1916
7079	ENGLISH, W. A.	K.I.A.	France	6/ 8/1918
	EPTHORP, R. J. (Served as)			
497	SULLIVAN, J.	K.I.A.	Gallipoli	1/ 5/1915
1031	EUSTACE, H. A.	D.O.W.	Alexandria	7/ 9/1915
1483	EVANS, A. R.	K.I.A.	France	11/ 4/1917
1030	EVANS, F. H.	K.I.A.	Gallipoli	4/ 8/1915
1484	EVANS, J.	K.I.A.	Gallipoli	4/ 5/1915
6500	FAHEY, J. B.	K.I.A.	France	11/ 4/1917
1039	FARNHAM, L.	K.I.A.	Gallipoli	30/ 4/1915
3299	FARR, A. T.	K.I.A.	France	1/ 2/1917
3293	FAULKNER, E. B.	K.I.A.	France	9/ 8/1916
4785	FEETAM, J. W.	D.O.W.	France	15/ 2/1917
5087	FERGUSON, R.	K.I.A.	Belgium	1/ 7/1917
709	FERGUSON, R. W.	K.I.A.	Gallipoli	9-10/ 5/1915
Lieut	FEWSTER, G. E.	K.I.A.	France	4/ 7/1918
1865	FIELD, W. A.	K.I.A.	France	11/ 4/1917
747	FIELDING, J. H.	K.I.A.	Gallipoli	30/ 4/1915
7232	FILL, W. B.	D.O.I.	England	4/10/1917
6767	FINIMORE, D. V.	D.O.W.	France	28/ 3/1918
1151	FINN, G. F.	K.I.A.	France	11/ 4/1917
132	FISHER, F. F.	D.O.I.	Egypt	5/ 8/1915
1322	FISHER, V. W.	D.O.W.	Gallipoli	7/ 8/1915
3292	FISHER, W. A.	K.I.A.	France	4/ 7/1918
5582	FITZGERALD, J.	K.I.A.	France	11/ 4/1917
2136	FITZGERALD, T. J.	D.O.W.	At Sea	30/ 8/1915
1496	FITZHERBERT, C. E.	K.I.A.	Gallipoli	4/ 5/1915
5399	FLINT, W.	D.O.W.	Belgium	18/10/1916
6262	FOGARTY, F. T.	K.I.A.	France	11/ 4/1917
135	FOOT, H. D.	K.I.A.	Gallipoli	1/ 5/1915
8	FORD, E.	K.I.A.	Gallipoli	2/ 5/1915
4789	FORD, J.	K.I.A.	France	27/ 3/1918
136	FORREST, A. A.	K.I.A.	France	11/ 4/1917
3046	FORREST, A. J.	K.I.A.	France	1/ 2/1917
291	FORSTER, A. H.	D.O.W.	France	30/ 3/1918
1321	FOSTER, J. H.	K.I.A.	Gallipoli	14/ 5/1915
Lieut	FOSTER, R. W.	K.I.A.	Gallipoli	8/ 8/1915
137	FOWLER, W. L.	K.I.A.	Belgium	27/ 9/1917
2137	FRANCIS, D. T.	K.I.A.	Gallipoli	8/ 8/1915
1036	FRANKCOMBE, V. E.	K.I.A.	Gallipoli	13/ 5/1915
2217	FRASER, B. C. C.	K.I.A.	Gallipoli	8/ 8/1915
745	FRASER, J.	K.I.A.	Gallipoli	9-10/ 5/1915

HISTORY OF THE 15th BATTALION

Reg. No.	Name.	Cause of Death.	Place of Death.	Date.
4499	FRASER, J.	K.I.A.	France	9/ 8/1916
Lieut	FRASER, J. H. W.	K.I.A.	France	4/ 7/1918
1324	FRASER, J. R.	D.O.W.	Malta	10/ 6/1915
6615	FRASER, M. J.	K.I.A.	Belgium	10/ 7/1917
6017	FRASER, W. G.	K.I.A.	France	11/ 4/1917
Lieut	FREEMAN, D. S.	K.I.A.	Gallipoli	3/ 5/1915
6258	FROSTROP, P. J.	K.I.A.	France	13/ 8/1918
1943	FRY, J. G.	D.O.W.	Gallipoli	22/ 8/1915
5791	FUDGE, E.	D.O.W.	France	27/ 2/1918
746	FUHRMAN, N.	K.I.A.	France	11/ 4/1917
3751	GAGE, W. B.	K.I.A.	France	9/ 8/1916
138	GAILLARD, L.	K.I.A.	Gallipoli	10/ 5/1915
5405	GALL, F.	D.O.W.	France	4/ 7/1918
6769	GALLAGHER, H. P.	D.O.W.	Belgium	26/ 9/1917
1868	GARDENER, L.	K.I.A.	France	9/ 8/1916
2138	GARGET, E.	K.I.A.	Gallipoli	8/ 8/1915
596	GARRATT, J. C.	K.I.A.	Gallipoli	9-10/ 5/1915
4803	GARTNER, H.	D.O.W.	Belgium	26/ 9/1917
4797	GATES, T.	K.I.A.	Belgium	15/10/1917
4311	GEMMELL, W.	K.I.A.	Belgium	8/ 7/1917
4802	GEORGE, E.	K.I.A.	Belgium	15/10/1916
1749	GEORGE, R.	K.I.A.	Gallipoli	8/ 8/1915
1949	GIBSON, F. W.	K.I.A.	Gallipoli	8/ 8/1915
Lieut	GIBSON, P.	K.I.A.	Gallipoli	8/ 8/1915
1383	GILBERT, G. R.	D.O.W.	France	21/ 2/1917
6504	GILBERT, H. M.	D.O.W.	Belgium	16/10/1917
598	GILL, H. A.	K.I.A.	Gallipoli	8/ 8/1915
5407	GILL, J. J.	K.I.A.	France	9/ 8/1916
438	GILL, T. R.	K.I.A.	Gallipoli	10/ 5/1915
1326	GILLESPIE, R.	K.I.A.	Gallipoli	4/ 5/1915
2/Lieut	GILLIES, D. M.	K.I.A.	Gallipoli	7/ 8/1915
1493	GILLIGAN, J.	K.I.A.	France	1/ 2/1917
599	GLITHRO, A.	K.I.A.	Gallipoli	8/ 8/1915
1182	GLOVER, A. P.	K.I.A.	Gallipoli	9/ 8/1915
139	GLOVER, W. N.	D.O.I.	Egypt	12/12/1915
140	GOLDRING, G.	K.I.A.	Gallipoli	8/ 8/1915
1746	GOOD, J.	K.I.A.	France	11/ 4/1917
1817	GOODE, L.	K.I.A.	Gallipoli	7/ 8/1915
3304	GOODFELLOW, G. G.	K.I.A.	France	1/ 2/1917
6975	GORDON, A.	D.O.W.	France	6/ 7/1918
1183	GORDON, L. C.	K.I.A.	Gallipoli	18/ 5/1915
6265	GORDON, N. V.	Accid. Killed	France	17/11/1917
5683	GORDON W. G.	K.I.A.	France	1/ 2/1917
6019	GORMAN, T. M.	D.O.I.	England	14/ 3 1917
4801	GOSMAN, F. C.	D.O.W.	France	10/ 7/1918
1946	GOWER, W. R.	K.I.A.	Gallipoli	8/ 8/1915
	GRAHAM, A.	D.O.I.	Enoggera, Q'ld.	1/ 5/1917
1947	GRAHAM, P.	K.I.A.	Gallipoli	8/ 8/1915
2/Lieut	GRANT, J.	D.O.W.	France	23/ 5/1918
1611	GRANT, R. J.	D.O.W.	France	5/ 7/1918
1328	GRAY, R.	D.O.W.	Alexandria	14/ 5/1915
6022	GREEN, C. W.	D.O.I.	Ayr, Q'ld.	18/ 1/1920
1705	GREEN, E.	D.O.I.	Turkey	10/10/1918
6776	GREGORY, J.	D.O.W.	Belgium	13/ 6/1917
442	GRIFFIN, W.	K.I.A.	Gallipoli	10/ 5/1915
144	GROOM, F. G.	K.I.A.	Gallipoli	9-10/ 5/1915
602	GUILFOYLE, W. L.	D.O.W.	At Sea	22/ 5/1915
3310	GULLETT, H.	D.O.W.	France	15/ 8/1916

HISTORY OF THE 15th BATTALION

Reg. No.	Name.	Cause of Death.	Place of Death.	Date.
1649	GUTHRIE, N. B.	K.I.A.	Gallipoli	29/ 5/1915
	HAAPANIEMI, H. E. (Served as)			
6706	ASPLUND, H.	D.O.W.	France	15/10/1917
7721	HAGEVOLE, J. S.	D.O.W.	France	13/ 8/1918
907	HAHN, E. F.	D.O.I.	England	25/ 6/1915
1731A	HALL, J. A.	K.I.A.	France	8/ 8/1918
6514	HAMILTON, H.	D.O.W.	France	20/8/1918
1422	HAMILTON, J.	K.I.A.	Gallipoli	8/ 8/1915
1157	HANIGAN, C. H.	K.I.A.	Gallipoli	3/ 5/1915
1951	HANN, T. J.	P.O.W.	Germany	11/ 7/1918
2149	HANNANT, F.	K.I.A.	Gallipoli	8/ 8/1915
290	HANSEN, H.	D.O.W.	At Sea	10/ 8/1915
1950	HANSEN, H. W.	K.I.A.	Gallipoli	8/ 8/1915
2788	HANSEN, R. M.	K.I.A.	Belgium	17/10/1917
5112	HANSHAW, F. L.	D.O.I.	France	20/ 7/1918
1045	HARDING, G. E.	K.I.A.	Gallipoli	9/ 8/1915
1615	HARDMAN, R.	D.O.W.	At Sea	5/ 5/1915
4378	HARMAN, A. T.	K.I.A.	Belgium	16/10/1917
	HARMENING, F. W. (Served as)			
5412	HATTON, F.	K.I.A.	France	11/ 4/1917
7720A	HARP, H. H.	K.I.A.	France	13/ 8/1918
1195	HARPER, D. J.	K.I.A.	Gallipoli	9-10/ 5/1915
3324	HARPER, G.	D.O.W.	France	14/ 8/1916
1329	HARREX, A.	D.O.I.	At Sea	29/12/1915
603	HARRIS, W. L.	K.I.A.	Gallipoli	8/ 8/1915
5692	HARRISON, F.	P.O.W.	Germany	21/ 8/1917
5434	HARRISON, J.	K.I.A.	France	18/ 9/1918
1199	HARRISON, N. McK.	D.O.I.	Lemnos	16/10/1915
899	HARRISON, W.	K.I.A.	Gallipoli	8/ 8/1915
Capt	HARRY, S. W.	K.I.A.	Gallipoli	10/ 5/1915
148	HARTIGAN, P. S.	D.O.W.	Alexandria	20/ 5/1915
5697	HARTLEY, G. W.	D.O.W.	France	23/ 6/1917
1187	HARVEY, A. K.	D.O.W.	France	3/ 9/1916
4512	HARVEY, G.	K.I.A.	France	11/ 4/1917
1404	HASTINGS, F. J.	K.I.A.	Gallipoli	27/ 7/1915
6991	HASZ, W. J.	D.O.I.	Durban	11/ 1/1917
2234	HATRICK, R. E.	K.I.A.	Gallipoli	8/ 8/1915
2436	HAVERS, G. J.	K.I.A.	France	26/ 1/1917
901	HAWKES, G. J.	K.I.A.	Gallipoli	8/ 8/1915
5411	HAWKINS, W. D.	K.I.A.	France	1/ 2/1917
854	HAWKINS, W. F.	K.I.A.	Gallipoli	7/ 8/1915
6026	HAY, C. N. E.	D.O.W.	France	29/ 4/1917
1324	HAYES, H. R.	D.O.W.	Gallipoli	27/ 8/1915
	HEAD, H.	D.O.I.	Brisbane. Q'ld.	16/11/1914
1044	HEWOOD, E. O.	K.I.A.	France	8/ 8/1916
604	HENDERSON, G.	D.O.W.	Gallipoli	29/ 5/1915
3601	HENDERSON, J.	D.O.W.	France	9/ 8/1916
5565	HERON, L. L.	K.I.A.	France	7/ 8/1916
2435	HERRIDGE, A.	K.I.A.	Belgium	29/ 6/1917
3138	HERROD, H.	K.I.A.	France	8/ 8/1916
6027	HESTER, A.	K.I.A.	Belgium	10/ 7/1917
447	HEWITT, F. C.	K.I.A.	Gallipoli	7/ 8/1915
6029	HIGGINS, J.	K.I.A.	Belgium	25/ 9/1917
294	HIGSON, W. C.	K.I.A.	Gallipoli	8/ 8/1915
2290	HILDER, B. R.	K.I.A.	Gallipoli	8/ 8/1915
1423	HILL, J. T.	K.I.A.	Gallipoli	8/ 8/1915

HISTORY OF THE 15th BATTALION

Reg. No.	Name.	Cause of Death.	Place of Death.	Date.
4806	HINDMARSH, E.	K.I.A.	France	11/ 4/1917
1186	HINDS, J.	K.I.A.	Gallipoli	7/ 8/1915
Lieut	HINES, W. J.	D.O.W.	France	6/ 8/1918
Lieut	HINMAN, A. G.	D.O.W.	Gallipoli	10/ 5/1915
6033	HIPATHITE, W.	D.O.W.	Belgium	30/ 6/1917
4816	HOAR, M. R.	D.O.W.	France	7/ 8/1916
3101	HOARE, F. P.	K.I.A.	France	7/ 8/1916
452	HOBBS, H. G.	D.O.W.	Gallipoli	15/ 5/1915
3320	HOBSON, E. S.	D.O.W.	France	11/ 6/1917
3318	HOBSON, J. A.	K.I.A.	France	9/ 8/1916
3764	HOCKING, J. F.	P.O.W.	Germany	
298	HODGE, J. D. O.	D.O.W.	Gallipoli	28/ 5/1915
3635	HODGE, J. E.	K.I.A.	France	8/ 8/1916
2447	HODGE, J. J.	D.O.W.	Belgium	16/10/1917
4521	HODGE, L.	D.O.W.	France	6/ 8/1916
2144	HODGES, L. G.	P.O.W.	Turkey	24/ 8/1915
632	HODGETTS, M.	P.O.W.	Germany	6/ 5/1917
1956	HODGKINSON, A. H.	K.I.A.	Gallipoli	8/ 8/1915
750	HODSDON, C. H.	D.O.W.	Turkey	21/ 1/1916
6786	HODSON, W.	D.O.W.	Belgium	3/10/1917
4814	HOEY, H.	K.I.A.	France	18/ 9/1918
6036	HOGAN, M.	D.O.W.	France	12/ 4/1917
2998	HOGAN, M. T.	D.O.W.	France	18/ 9/1918
751	HOGBEN, W.	D.O.W.	Gallipoli	17/ 8/1915
1706	HOLLAMBY, C.	K.I.A.	France	4/ 7/1918
4575	HOLLAMBY, W. E.	K.I.A.	France	8/ 8/1916
5774	HOLLAND, T. E.	K.I.A.	France	14/ 6/1918
3328	HOLLEY, B.	K.I.A.	France	11/ 4/1917
898	HOLLINGWORTH, T. H. M.	K.I.A.	Gallipoli	20/ 5/1915
5684	HOLMES, H. F.	K.I.A.	France	11/ 4/1917
4316	HOLT, J.	K.I.A.	France	18/ 9/1918
6787	HOLTER, W. F.	K.I.A.	Belgium	28/ 9/1917
606	HOOPER, A. A.	K.I.A.	Gallipoli	29/ 5/1915
1193	HOPE, E. S.	D.O.W.	At Sea	9/ 5/1915
6277	HOPTON, H.	K.I.A.	France	4/ 7/1918
605	HOSKIN, F. W.	D.O.W.	Alexandria	21/ 5/1915
5418	HOWE, A.	K.I.A.	Belgium	27/ 9/1917
3773	HOWIE, H. McL.	D.O.W.	France	18/ 6/1917
151	HOWITZ, M.	K.I.A.	Gallipoli	7/ 8/1915
6270	HOWLETT, J.	K.I.A.	France	11/ 4/1917
1499	HUDSON, F. A.	K.I.A.	Gallipoli	25/ 8/1915
1497	HUDSON, V.	D.O.W.	At Sea	7/ 5/1915
897	HUGHES, H.	K.I.A.	Gallipoli	8/ 8/1915
1335	HUGHES, W. J.	K.I.A.	Gallipoli	3/ 5/1915
1954	HUMPHREY, J.	K.I.A.	Gallipoli	8/ 8/1915
4821	HUMPHREYS, E.	K.I.A.	France	4/ 7/1918
1191	HUNN, A. H.	K.I.A.	France	9/ 8/1916
1052	HUNT, G. A.	D.O.W.	At Sea	6/ 5/1915
5696	HURLEY, J. P. K.	K.I.A.	France	11/ 4/1917
6124	HURRELL, G. H.	K.I.A.	France	30/ 1/1917
Lieut	HURRY, G.	K.I.A.	Belgium	18/10/1917
2152	INCH, J. G.	K.I.A.	France	11/ 4/1917
6286	INNES, D. M. B.	K.I.A.	France	1/ 2/1917
4321	IRWIN, J. D.	D.O.I.	Fremantle, W. A.	4/ 5/1919
155	JACOBS, H.	K.I.A.	Gallipoli	8/ 8/1915
1053	JACOBSEN, C. T.	D.O.I.	At Sea	14/ 1/1917
3046	JAGGER, H.	K.I.A.	France	18/ 9/1918
3776	JAGO, G. J.	D.O.W.	France	10/ 8/1916

HISTORY OF THE 15th BATTALION 315

Reg. No.	Name.	Cause of Death.	Place of Death.	Date.
1505	JAMES, D.	K.I.A.	Gallipoli	8/ 8/1915
300	JAMES, F.	D.O.W.	Belgium	15/10/1916
1506	JEFFREY, J.	K.I.A.	Gallipoli	8/ 8/1915
2242	JELLETT, F.	K.I.A.	Gallipoli	8/ 8/1915
156	JENKIN, R. V.	D.O.I.	Egypt	30/11/1915
2012	JENKINS, A. H.	D.O.I.	Turkey	16/ 1/1916
1502	JENKINS, R.	K.I.A.	Gallipoli	8/ 8/1915
6794	JENNINGS, F. W. H.	K.I.A.	France	18/ 9/1918
1868	JETSON, E. J.	K.I.A.	Gallipoli	9/ 8/1915
3118	JOHNS, R. N.	K.I.A.	France	9/ 8/1916
1995	JOHNSON, A.	K.I.A.	Gallipoli	8/ 8/1915
1340	JOHNSON, C. A.	D.O.W.	Gallipoli	14/ 7/1915
1202	JOHNSON, G. A.	D.O.W.	At Sea	24/ 5/1915
1761	JOHNSON, R.	K.I.A.	France	9/ 8/1916
1958	JOHNSTON, A.	K.I.A.	Gallipoli	8/ 8/1915
6795	JOHNSTON, A. W.	K.I.A.	Belgium	17/10/1917
1341	JOHNSTON, J.	K.I.A.	Gallipoli	7/ 5/1915
817	JOHNSTON, L. W.	K.I.A.	Gallipoli	8/ 8/1915
2759	JOHNSTON, N.	D.O.I.	Mudros	14/11/1915
5821	JOHNSTON, R.	D.O.W.	Belgium	18/ 8/1917
6796	JOHNSTONE, I. R.	K.I.A.	Belgium	27/ 9/1917
5575	JOLLY, A. E.	P.O.W.	Germany	21/ 4/1917
4532	JONES, A. E.	K.I.A.	France	8/ 8/1916
Lieut	JONES, A. W. P.	K.I.A.	Belgium	24/ 9/1917
2153	JONES, F. H.	K.I.A.	Gallipoli	8/ 8/1915
455	JONES, T. L.	K.I.A.	Gallipoli	3/ 5/1915
2156	JONES, W. D.	P.O.W.	Turkey	31/ 1/1917
302	JOSH, F.	K.I.A.	Gallipoli	10/ 5/1915
Lieut	JOUBERT, S. H.	D.O.W.	Belgium	29/ 9/1917
	JOYCE, J. (Served as)			
1418	BURNS, J.	K.I.A.	France	11/ 4/1917
1329	KAUFMAN, C.	K.I.A.	Gallipoli	1/ 5/1915
3346	KAY, W. B.	K.I.A.	France	9/ 8/1916
5442	KAYE, H. B.	D.O.W.	France	31/ 8/1916
520	KEAIRNS, V. R.	D.O.W.	At Sea	4/ 5/1915
517	KEERS, H.	K.I.A.	Gallipoli	8/ 8/1915
7818	KELLEY, W. E.	D.O.W.	France	17/ 9/1918
158	KELLY, H.	K.I.A.	Gallipoli	8/ 8/1915
1959	KELLY, J. P.	P.O.W.	Turkey	26/ 8/1915
612	KELLY, P. J.	K.I.A.	Gallipoli	8/ 8/1915
1960	KEMPSON, S. T.	K.I.A.	Gallipoli	8/ 8/1915
1344	KENDALL, E. H.	K.I.A.	France	9/ 8/1916
1961	KENNEDY, J.	K.I.A.	Gallipoli	8/ 8/1915
2227	KENYON, A. L.	K.I.A.	Gallipoli	8/ 8/1915
1345	KERRIDGE, R.	K.I.A.	Gallipoli	3/ 5/1915
1510	KERRIGAN, R.	P.O.W.	Turkey	
Lieut	KESSELL, H.	D.O.W.	Egypt	3/ 7/1915
754	KIDNER, J. M.	D.O.W.	Gallipoli	4/ 5/1915
3784	KILGOUR, J.	K.I.A.	France	27/ 8/1916
1054	KING, F.	K.I.A.	Gallipoli	2/ 5/1915
4824	KING, L. C.	D.O.W.	Germany	
6999	KING, S. E.	D.O.W.	Belgium	16/ 8/1917
710	KIRBY, E. A.	K.I.A.	Gallipoli	2/ 5/1915
5440	KIRBY, J.	K.I.A.	France	9/ 8/1916
4539	KITCHER, W. H.	K.I.A.	France	10/ 6/1917
159	KNIGHT, J. T.	D.O.W.	Gallipoli	7/ 8/1915
6290	KRUGER, L. V.	K.I.A.	Belgium	11/ 7/1917
1507	KYDD, G.	K.I.A.	Gallipoli	14/ 5/1915

HISTORY OF THE 15th BATTALION

Reg. No.	Name.	Cause of Death.	Place of Death.	Date.
1386	LAHEY, T. J.	D.O.I.	Malta	23/ 8/1915
6304	LAKE, C. N.	P.O.W.	France	9/ 2/1917
6388	LAKE, W.	K.I.A.	France	11/ 4/1917
914	LAMBERT, G. H.	D.O.W.	Belgium	16/ 6/1917
2161	LAMBERT, M.	K.I.A.	France	8/ 8/1916
1870	LAMBERT, R. G.	K.I.A.	France	8/ 8/1916
1965	LAMBERTON, J. A.	D.O.W.	France	26/ 8/1916
307	LAMBOURN, F. G.	K.I.A.	Gallipoli	28/ 5/1915
2164	LAMPAN, W. G.	K.I.A.	Gallipoli	8/ 8/1915
3354	LARSEN, G.	D.O.W.	France	9/ 8/1916
1387	LAURIE, B.	K.I.A.	Gallipoli	30/ 4/1915
3787	LAURIE, W.	D.O.W.	France	28/ 3/1918
4056	LAWER, J.	K.I.A.	Belgium	24/ 9/1917
1389	LAWLER, R. J.	K.I.A.	Gallipoli	9/ 8/1915
4835	LAWRENCE, H.	D.O.W.	Belgium	1/ 3/1918
3361	LAWRENCE, H. H.	D.O.W.	France	14/ 8/1918
5059	LAWRIE, C. J.	K.I.A.	France	11/ 4/1917
3333	LAWS, R. E.	K.I.A.	France	4/ 7/1918
2766	LEECE, L. B.	D.O.W.	France	29/ 8/1916
1966	LEEDING, W. G.	K.I.A.	France	28/ 3/1918
308	LEHFELDT, W. R.	K.I.A.	Gallipoli	8/ 8/1915
614	LENNARN, E. A.	P.O.W.	Germany	12/ 2/1917
2367	LENNON, W.	K.I.A.	Belgium	27/ 9/1917
160	LENTON, J. H.	K.I.A.	Gallipoli	8/ 8/1915
Capt	LESLIE, F. A.	K.I.A.	France	11/ 4/1917
462	LEVINE, M.	K.I.A.	Gallipoli	29/ 5/1915
615	LIND, R. H.	K.I.A.	Gallipoli	8/ 8/1915
1424	LIND, T.	K.I.A.	Gallipoli	26/ 4/1915
1350	LINDSAY, D. G.	K.I.A.	Gallipoli	8/ 8/1915
3789	LINDSAY, H. A.	K.I.A.	France	4/ 7/1918
6300	LINTER, A. B.	K.I.A.	France	11/4/1917
1681	LISLE, W. R.	D.O.W.	France	27/ 3/1918
6047	LITTLE, C. H.	K.I.A.	Belgium	18/ 8/1917
4837	LOEWE, S.	D.O.W.	France	9/ 7/1918
1766	LOFT, J.	K.I.A.	Gallipoli	8/ 8/1915
2387	LOGAN, J.	D.O.W.	France	3/ 2/1917
7594A	LOMAS, R. F. E.	D.O.W.	France	29/ 3/1918
1262	LORD, R. S.	K.I.A.	Gallipoli	8/ 8/1915
1331	LORD, R. W.	K.I.A.	Gallipoli	3/ 5/1915
7004	LOVEDAY, R.	D.O.I.	England	22/ 2/1917
7714	LOW, A. E.	D.O.I.	England	12/10/1918
6050	LOW, G. A.	D.O.I.	At Sea	29/ 1/1918
310	LULHAM, C. A.	K.I.A.	France	9/8/1916
5711	LUPTON, A. P.	D.O.I.	Germany	15/10/1918
Capt	LUTHER, J. F. G.	K.I.A.	Gallipoli	25/ 8/1915
2/Lieut	LUXTON, R. J.	K.I.A.	France	11/ 4/1917
4830	LYDEMENT, H. J.	K.I.A.	France	7/ 4/1917
2/Lieut	LYON, C. H. S.	D.O.W.	Belgium	27/ 9/1917
4544	LYONS, W. J.	K.I.A.	France	8/ 8/1916
2412	MAGILL, J.	K.I.A.	Belgium	17/10/1917
5822	MAGUIRE, W. M.	D.O.I.	England	8/12/1916
1517	MAHER, C. L.	K.I.A.	Gallipoli	26/ 4/1915
1072	MAINE, C. W.	D.O.W.	At Sea	27/ 5/1915
6053	MALONEY, N. H.	D.O.W.	Belgium	9/ 8/1917
3368	MANN, C. J.	K.I.A.	France	26/ 1/1917
865	MANNING, W. G.	D.O.W.	Egypt	24/ 6/1915
1066	MANSFIELD, A. D.	K.I.A.	Gallipoli	18/ 5/1915
6314	MANSFIELD, H.	D.O.W.	France	18/ 9/1918

HISTORY OF THE 15th BATTALION 317

Reg. No.	Name.	Cause of Death.	Place of Death.	Date.
1983	MANSFIELD, J. W.	K.I.A.	Gallipoli	8/ 8/1915
7088	MANSON, A. V.	K.I.A.	France	11/ 4/1917
1062	MARK, E. L.	K.I.A.	France	11/ 4/1917
1218	MARKHAM, H.	K.I.A.	Gallipoli	9/ 8/1915
1984	MARSH, A.	D.O.W.	France	7/ 4/1917
163	MARSHAL, A.	D.O.I.	Malta	23/ 7/1915
2166	MARSTELLA, T. W.	K.I.A.	Gallipoli	9/ 8/1915
164	MARTIN, E. R.	D.O.W.	At Sea	30/ 4/1915
759	MARTIN, E. R.	K.I.A.	Gallipoli	24/ 5/1915
2074	MARTIN, G. A.	D.O.W.	Gallipoli	8/ 8/1915
1769	MARTIN, J. J.	K.I.A.	Gallipoli	21/ 8/1915
2/Lieut	MARTYR, F.	K.I.A.	France	8/ 8/1916
4854	MASSIE, E. E.	D.O.I.	France	17/10/1918
762	MASSON, J.	D.O.W.	Gibraltar	20/ 5/1915
919	MATHERS, C.	D.O.I.	Asia Minor	
2178	MATHERS, T. J.	K.I.A.	Gallipoli	8/ 8/1915
1214	MATHESON, N.	K.I.A.	Gallipoli	29/ 5/1915
1070	MATHESON, W. T.	K.I.A.	Gallipoli	3/ 5/1915
318	MAY, H. N.	K.I.A.	Gallipoli	9-10/ 5/1915
6218	MAYFIELD, F. W.	K.I.A.	France	11/ 4/1917
2294	MAYNARD, E. L.	K.I.A.	Gallipoli	8/ 8/1915
167	MAZLIN, L. W.	K.I.A.	Gallipoli	30/ 4/1915
168	MAZLIN, N. H.	K.I.A.	Gallipoli	8/ 8/1915
1775	MEARNS, M. L.	K.I.A.	Gallipoli	8/ 8/1915
319	MELEDINE, L.	K.I.A.	Gallipoli	9-10/ 5/1915
705	MELIA, E.	K.I.A.	Gallipoli	2/ 5/1915
1217	MILBOURNE, J. D.	K.I.A.	Gallipoli	3/ 5/1915
624	MILES, G. A.	K.I.A.	Gallipoli	26/ 4/1915
1065	MILLEN, C. J.	K.I.A.	Gallipoli	8/ 8/1915
1363A	MILLER, D.	K.I.A.	Gallipoli	8/ 8/1915
1527	MILLER, J. M.	D.O.W.	At Sea	4/ 5/1915
2507	MILLER, R.	K.I.A.	France	8/ 8/1916
1212	MILLHOUSE, H.	K.I.A.	Gallipoli	9/ 8/1915
1364	MILNE, J.	D.O.W.	At Sea	18/ 7/1915
320	MINORS, W.	K.I.A.	Gallipoli	4/ 5/1915
758	MINTER, H.	D.O.W.	Gallipoli	11/ 8/1915
4383	MITCHELL, R. G.	D.O.W.	Belgium	10/10/1916
5457	MITCHELL, S.	K.I.A.	France	8/ 8/1916
7266	MITCHELL, W.	K.I.A.	Belgium	17/10/1917
1162	MONTGOMERY, W. D.	K.I.A.	Gallipoli	18/ 5/1915
6530	MOODY, A. E.	K.I.A.	France	10/ 6/1918
1981	MOODY, C. E.	D.O.W.	Gallipoli	9/ 8/1915
4866	MOORE, A. L.	P.O.W.	Germany	11/ 2/1917
Capt	MORAN, F.	D.O.W.	At Sea	20/ 8/1915
2306	MORGAN, D.	K.I.A.	Gallipoli	9/ 8/1915
1531	MORLEY, F. J.	K.I.A.	France	11/ 4/1917
4861	MORONEY, M. E.	K.I.A.	France	11/ 4/1917
1774	MORPHETT, R. E.	K.I.A.	Gallipoli	8/ 8/1915
6310	MORRIS, E. T.	K.I.A.	France	11/ 4/1917
5570	MORRIS, G.	K.I.A.	France	28/ 8/1916
5461	MORRIS, M.	D.O.W.	France	8/ 8/1916
1625	MORRISBY, P. F.	K.I.A.	Gallipoli	8/ 5/1915
1376	MORRISON, R. E.	K.I.A.	Gallipoli	8/ 8/1915
1367	MORSHEAD, H. D. E.	K.I.A.	Gallipoli	9-10/ 5/1915
6809	MORTON, J.	D.O.I.	England	19/ 2/1917
Lieut	MOSS, A. H.	D.O.W.	France	19/ 6/1918
1528	MOYNIHAN, W. D.	K.I.A.	Gallipoli	10/ 5/1915

HISTORY OF THE 15th BATTALION

Reg. No.	Name.	Cause of Death.	Place of Death.	Date.
7846	MUIR, C. C.	K.I.A.	France	19/ 5/1918
7794	MULHOLLAND, E.	K.I.A.	France	7/ 7/1918
2612	MULLAN, J. S.	K.I.A.	France	6/ 8/1918
6308	MULLINS, J.	K.I.A.	France	22/ 6/1918
6309	MULLINS, T. W.	K.I.A.	France	11/ 4/1917
1369	MULVIE, P.	K.I.A.	France	1/ 2/1917
Major	MUNDELL, W. T.	D.O.W.	Belgium	19/ 8/1917
757	MUNRO, J. T.	K.I.A.	France	11/ 4/1917
1525	MURDEN, R. R.	K.I.A.	Gallipoli	1/ 5/1915
1715	MURDOCH, G. A.	K.I.A.	France	8/ 8/1916
6867	MURPHY, D. A.	K.I.A.	Belgium	26/ 9/1917
5468	MURPHY, J.	K.I.A.	France	8/ 8/1916
6523	MURPHY, V. L.	K.I.A.	France	28/ 3/1918
1522	MURRAY, J. P.	K.I.A.	France	8/ 8/1916
7734	MURRAY, M. R.	K.I.A.	France	18/ 9/1918
1673	MURRAY, R. H.	P.O.W.	Germany	13/ 4/1917
4855	MURRELL, W.	D.O.W.	France	30/ 1/1917
5456	MURTAGH, M.	K.I.A.	France	11/ 4/1917
1341	McALLISTER, C.	K.I.A.	Gallipoli	27/ 8/1915
975	McANDREW, H. B.	D.O.W.	At Sea	21/ 5/1915
1360	McARA, J. M.	K.I.A.	Gallipoli	8/ 8/1915
3806	McATEE, J.	P.O.W.	Germany	
1362	McAULEY, M. F.	C.N.S.	Gallipoli	7/1915
7801	McBRYDE, J. G.	D.O.W.	France	4/ 7/1918
1974	McCABE, F.	K.I.A.	Gallipoli	8/ 8/1915
1524	McCANN, F.	D.O.W.	France	9/ 6/1918
925	McCARTHY, J.	K.I.A.	Gallipoli	9-10/ 5/1915
628	McCONNACHIE, G.	D.O.I.	Egypt	16/ 1/1916
853	McCONNACHIE, J.	K.I.A.	Gallipoli	26/ 4/1915
3915	McCONNELL, T.	K.I.A.	France	8/ 8/1916
7809	McCORMICK, D.	K.I.A.	France	8/ 8/1918
2014	McCORMICK, P.	D.O.W.	Gallipoli	22/ 8/1915
6320	McCREADIE, J.	D.O.W.	Belgium	10/ 7/1917
1428	McCRIMMON, S. G.	K.I.A.	Gallipoli	9/ 5/1915
708	MacDONALD, R.	K.I.A.	Gallipo'i	9-10/ 5/1915
5716	McDONNELL, V. P.	K.I.A.	Belgium	27/ 9/1917
1353	MacDOUGALL, D.	K.I.A.	Gallipoli	8/ 8/1915
630	McGAFFIN, R. J.	K.I.A.	Gallipoli	8/ 8/1915
3191	McGINLEY, W.	K.I.A.	France	11/ 4/1917
2392	McGOVERN, P.	K.I.A.	France	8/ 8/1916
7026	McGRATH, J. C. P.	D.O.I.	England	2/ 3/1917
6621	McGREGOR, D. E.	D.O.I.	England	23/ 1/1917
5478	McGREGOR, H. J.	K.I.A.	France	1/ 2/1917
5471	McHENRY, W.	K.I.A.	France	6/ 8/1916
6607	McILROY, G.	D.O.I.	England	19/ 2/1917
467	McINTOSH, A.	D.O.W.	Malta	19/ 8/1915
2231	McINTOSH, A. C.	K.I.A.	Gallipoli	8/ 8/1915
313	MacKAY, A. G.	K.I.A.	Gallipoli	9-10/ 5/1915
857	McKENZIE, J.	K.I.A.	Gallipoli	26/ 4/1915
7018	McKENZIE, W. A.	K.I.A.	France	4/ 7/1918
620	McKENZIE, W. R.	D.O.W.	France	12/ 8/1916
6318	McKIERNAN, J. M.	K.I.A.	France	4/ 7/1918
3327	McKINLEY, W.	D.O.I.	England	16/ 1/1919
1975	McLEAN, A.	K.I.A.	Gallipoli	27/ 8/1915
2394	McLEAN, J. D.	K.I.A.	France	1/ 2/1917
5728	McLEAN, J. M.	D.O.W.	France	6/ 4/1917
1779	McLENNAN, J.	K.I.A.	Gallipoli	8/ 8/1915

HISTORY OF THE 15th BATTALION

Reg. No.	Name.	Cause of Death.	Place of Death.	Date.
927	McLENNAN, R. G.	K.I.A.	Gallipoli	10/ 5/1915
469	McLEOD, J.	D.O.I.	England	16/ 6/1915
769	McLEOD, K. H.	K.I.A.	Gallipoli	3/ 5/1915
768	McLEOD, R.	D.O.I.	Mudros	10/ 7/1915
4850	McLOUGHLIN, P.	K.I.A.	France	11/ 4/1917
7578	McMANUS, J.	K.I.A.	France	4/ 8/1918
2073	McMASTER, J.	K.I.A.	Belgium	28/ 9/1917
635	McNAE, W. C.	K.I.A.	Gallipoli	6/ 5/1915
4109	McNICHOL, R.	D.O.W.	France	16/ 6/1918
1624	McPHERSON, W.	D.O.W.	At Sea	11/ 5/1915
1778	McPHERSON, W.	K.I.A.	Gallipoli	8/ 8/1915
1355	McQUAID, J.	K.I.A.	Gallipoli	8/ 8/1915
Lt/Col	McSHARRY, T. P.	D.O.W.	France	6/ 8/1918
7744	McWADE, A. G.	D.O.W.	France	11/ 8/1918
7850	NASH, G. H.	D.O.W.	France	4/ 7/1918
1780	NEELAND, R.	K.I.A.	France	6/ 8/1916
934	NELSON, A.	P.O.W.	Asia Minor	28/11/1916
1222	NELSON, G. E.	K.I.A.	Gallipoli	3/ 5/1915
Lieut	NELSON, J. W.	D.O.W.	Belgium	26/ 9/1917
7030	NETHERCOTE, J. D.	D.O.W.	France	7/ 7/1918
Lieut	NEVIN, A. R.	K.I.A.	Belgium	23/ 9/1916
4567	NEW, A. H.	K.I.A.	France	4/ 7/1918
2181	NEW, L. G.	Accid. Inj.	Turkey	7/ 5/1916
932	NEWALL, G. L.	D.O.W.	At Sea	29/ 4/1915
931	NEWELL, H. L.	K.I.A.	Gallipoli	9/ 5/1915
1219	NEWMAN, E. W.	K.I.A.	Gallipoli	2/ 5/1915
1221	NIBBS, W. J.	D.O.W.	Alexandria	8/ 5/1915
935	NICHOLLS, R. E.	K.I.A.	Gallipoli	9-10/ 5/1915
4181	NICHOLLS, R. J.	D.O.I.	France	23/12/1916
Capt	NICHOLLS, W. H.	K.I.A.	France	26/ 1/1917
5583	NOAKES, W. T.	K.I.A.	France	26/ 1/1917
4384	NOBES, G. C.	K.I.A.	France	21/12/1916
1366	NORMAN, A. E.	D.O.W.	Belgium	29/ 9/1917
7282	NORTHOVER, F.	K.I.A.	Belgium	27/ 9/1917
7327	OATES, R.	K.I.A.	France	4/ 7/1918
4385	O'BRIEN, B. J.	D.O.W.	France	29/ 3/1918
474	O'CALLAGHAN, M.	K.I.A.	Gallipoli	8/ 8/1915
936	O'CONNER, J. J.	D.O.W.	Alexandria	1/ 6/1915
1986	O'CONNER, P.	D.O.W.	At Sea	13/ 8/1915
7284	O'DONNELL, A. D.	D.O.W.	Belgium	22/10/1917
1374	ODY, W.	K.I.A.	Gallipoli	9/ 8/1915
	OGDEN, A. R.	Accid. Inj.	Melbourne, Vic.	22/12/1914
2701	O'KEEFFE, S. C.	K.I.A.	France	9/ 8/1916
754	OLIVER, N. O.	K.I.A.	France	11/ 4/1917
4873	OLIVER, T.	D.O.W.	Germany	4/ 2/1917
1782	O'LOUGHLIN, P. J.	K.I.A.	Gallipoli	8/ 8/1915
6542	O'MARA, M.	K.I.A.	Belgium	15/10/1917
6544	O'NEILL, P. A.	D.O.W.	Belgium	20/ 8/1917
101	ORCHARD, D. W.	D.O.W.	France	28/ 3/1918
637	ORR, J.	K.I.A.	Gallipoli	3/ 5/1915
6123	O'SULLIVAN, J. G.	K.I.A.	France	6/ 7/1918
2297	OWENS, L. J.	K.I.A.	Gallipoli	9/ 8/1915
1344	PAGE, J. A.	K.I.A.	France	5/ 8/1916
6069	PALFREY, C. W.	K.I.A.	France	11/ 4/1917
1228	PALMER, C. F.	K.I.A.	Gallipoli	25/ 8/1915
1227	PALMER, E. S.	K.I.A.	Gallipoli	8/ 8/1915
4303	PALMER, W. J.	P.O.W.	Germany	13/ 4/1917

HISTORY OF THE 15th BATTALION

Reg. No.	Name.	Cause of Death.	Place of Death.	Date.
4886	PARCELL, V.	K.I.A.	France	1/ 2/1917
1375	PARKER, A.	D.O.W.	France	18/ 8/1916
4887	PARKER, J. A.	K.I.A.	France	11/ 4/1917
2183	PARKER, L.	D.O.W.	Gallipoli	8/ 8/1915
1876	PARKER, R. G.	K.I.A.	Gallipoli	7/1915
4877	PARKER, T. S.	K.I.A.	France	1/ 2/1917
3620	PARKER, W. G.	D.O.W.	England	9/ 4/1918
774	PARKES, D.	K.I.A.	Gallipoli	9/ 5/1915
638	PARKINSON, G. W.	K.I.A.	Gallipoli	30/ 4/1915
775	PATERSON, F. M.	K.I.A.	Gallipoli	14/ 5/1915
2222	PATTERSON, A. S.	K.I.A.	France	27/ 8/1916
6829	PAYNE, C. J. H.	D.O.W.	France	23/ 4/1918
4885	PAYNE, G. A.	D.O.I.	France	9/11/1918
7824	PEACOCK, E. C.	K.I.A.	France	5/ 7/1918
2184	PEARCE, R. H.	K.I.A.	Gallipoli	27/ 8/1915
6071	PEAT, W.	K.I.A.	France	1/ 2/1917
3831	PECK, L. G.	K.I.A.	France	9/ 8/1916
6072	PELIN, S. J.	K.I.A.	France	1/ 2/1917
6329	PELISSIER, A. H.	K.I.A.	France	4/ 7/1918
5495	PENDALL, W.	D.O.I.	France	15/ 2/1919
2299	PENDREY, J. A.	D.O.W.	France	8/ 9/1916
938	PENN, C. A.	K.I.A.	France	4/ 7/1918
939	PENN, N.	D.O.W.	At Sea	.27/ 5/1915
4577	PENNINGTON, W. R.	D.O.W.	England	24/ 8/1916
2265	PENNY, F. R.	D.O.W.	France	5/ 7/1918
4882	PENNY, H. J.	K.I.A.	France	1/ 2/1917
7336	PENO, J. A.	K.I.A.	Belgium	14/ 8/1917
639	PERKINS, C. N. C.	D.O.W.	At Sea	5/ 5/1915
183	PERKINS, W. T.	K.I.A.	Gallipoli	30/ 4/1915
776	PERRETT, F. E.	K.I.A.	Gallipoli	3/ 5/1915
6336	PERRY, J.	D.O.W.	Germany	19/ 6/1917
3833	PERRY, T.	K.I.A.	France	1/ 9/1916
4874	PETERSEN, S.	K.I.A.	France	11/ 4/1917
1538	PETERSON, G. K. P.	D.O.W.	At Sea	12/ 5/1915
7292	PEUT, P.	D.O.W.	France	31/ 3/1918
1115	PHILLIPS, A.	K.I.A.	Gallipoli	3/ 5/1915
1380A	PHILLIPS, J. H.	K.I.A.	Gallipoli	9/ 5/1915
6551	PHISTER, R. M.	D.O.W.	Belgium	27/ 9/1917
4904	PICKERING, T. J.	K.I.A.	Belgium	17/10/1917
1536	PICOT, F.	D.O.W.	Alexandria	8/ 6/1915
1394	PIERCE, J.	K.I.A.	Gallipoli	9/ 8/1915
7843	PINION, S.	K.I.A.	France	4/ 7/1918
106	PINKERTON, G. C.	D.O.W.	France	6/ 7/1918
Lieut	PLATT, F. J.	K.I.A.	Gallipoli	8/ 8/1915
1663	PLUMLEY, C. E.	K.I.A.	Gallipoli	5/ 7/1915
4579	POEPPEL, G.	P.O.W.	Germany	2/ 2/1917
941	POLLEY, H.	D.O.W.	At Sea	28/ 8/1915
6076	PONTING, A. W.	K.I.A.	France	1/ 2/1917
1627	POOLE, G. A.	D.O.W.	At Sea	7/ 5/1915
1990	POPLAVSKI, G.	Accid. Inj.	Brisbane, Q'ld.	19/ 6/1916
Capt	PORTER, S. F.	D.O.W.	England	25/11/1918
478	PORTER, S. N.	K.I.A.	Gallipoli	9/ 8/1915
5581	PORTLEY, J.	K.I.A.	France	8/ 8/1916
1381A	PRAIN, W. C.	K.I.A.	Gallipoli	9/ 5/1915
7616	PRESHO, J. L.	K.I.A.	France	18/ 8/1918
2081	PRICE, C. E.	K.I.A.	Gallipoli	8/ 8/1915
5162	PRICE, M.	K.I.A.	France	10/ 6/1918

HISTORY OF THE 15th BATTALION

Reg. No.	Name.	Cause of Death.	Place of Death.	Date.
6334	PROBERT, K. W.	D.O.W.	France	25/ 9/1918
	PROBETS, A. (Served as)			
1540	ROGERS, J.	K.I.A.	Gallipoli	8/ 8/1915
2/Lieut	PROCTOR, J. T. G.	K.I.A.	France	11/ 4/1917
2700	PROCTOR, R. D.	K.I.A.	France	1/ 2/1917
1382	PSHEVOLODSKEY, M.	K.I.A.	Gallipoli	9-10/ 5/1915
4876	PULLEN, W. T.	K.I.A.	France	28/ 8/1916
5571	PUNZELL, J. J.	K.I.A.	France	11/ 4/1917
1784	PURCELL, C.	K.I.A.	France	6/ 8/1916
7813	PURCELL, T.	D.O.W.	France	19/ 9/1918
481	QUINN, C.	K.I.A.	Gallipoli	8/ 8/1915
Major	QUINN, H.	K.I.A.	Gallipoli	29/ 5/1915
7301	QUINN, P. F.	K.I.A.	Belgium	16/ 8/1917
3838	RABNOTT, T. A.	K.I.A.	France	4/ 7/1916
1235	RADFORD, A.	D.O.W.	At Sea	8/ 5/1915
6078	RAND, E. J.	K.I.A.	France	22/ 6/1918
336	RANKIN, D.	K.I.A.	Gallipoli	7/ 8/1915
1666	RAVENOR, H.	K.I.A.	France	27/ 8/1916
1232	READING, L. J.	K.I.A.	Gallipoli	9/ 5/1915
3839	REDDIE, C.	D.O.W.	France	9/ 6/1918
5584	REDFEARN, P.	K.I.A.	France	8/ 8/1916
3125	REDMOND, J. E.	K.I.A.	France	11/ 4/1917
4624	REES, O.	D.O.W.	Belgium	30/ 9/1917
7728	REGAN, C.	K.I.A.	France	13/ 8/1918
4412	REID, R. A.	K.I.A.	France	8/ 8/1916
484	RENFREW, R. H.	K.I.A.	Gallipoli	9/ 8/1915
1395	REUBENICHT, R.	K.I.A.	Gallipoli	1/ 5/1915
3419	REUTER, J.	K.I.A.	Belgium	15/10/1916
1114	REX, P. H.	D.O.W.	At Sea	24/ 5/1915
943	REYNOLDS, B.	K.I.A.	France	28/ 8/1916
2372	REYNOLDS, M. M.	K.I.A.	Belgium	27/ 9/1917
485	RICHARDSON, A.	K.I.A.	Gallipoli	9/ 5/1915
2790	RICHARDSON, E.	K.I.A.	France	6/ 7/1916
3429	RICHARDSON, F.	K.I.A.	France	11/ 4/1917
944	RICHARDSON, G. T.	K.I.A.	Gallipoli	9-10/ 5/1915
7302	RIDGWAY, W.	D.O.I.	Sydney	7/ 2/1917
6557	REILLY, T.	K.I.A.	Belgium	10/ 7/1917
1078	RIGBY, W. T.	K.I.A.	Gallipoli	9/ 8/1915
1667	RIGGS, A. C.	D.O.W.	France	9/ 8/1916
1880	RILEY, W. R.	K.I.A.	At Sea	26/ 5/1915
1354	ROBERTS, A. W.	K.I.A.	France	9/ 8/1916
1355	ROBERTS, J. A.	K.I.A.	France	8/ 8/1916
188	ROBERTSON, D.	K.I.A.	Gallipoli	27/ 8/1915
Lieut	ROBERTSON, T.	K.I.A.	Gallipoli	27/ 4/1915
946	ROBINSON, A. J.	K.I.A.	Gallipoli	9/ 5/1915
1997	ROBINSON, J.	D.O.I.	Belgium	9/ 9/1917
339	ROBSON, F.	K.I.A.	Gallipoli	18/ 5/1915
1628	ROBSON, T. K. McL.	K.I.A.	Gallipoli	9/ 5/1915
4389	ROCK, H. C.	K.I.A.	France	8/ 8/1916
1375	ROGERS, G. S.	K.I.A.	Gallipoli	27/ 4/1915
1234	ROGERS, J. A.	K.I.A.	Gallipoli	9/ 8/1915
5501	ROGERS, W. J.	K.I.A.	Belgium	26/ 9/1916
7045	RONALD, W.	K.I.A.	France	28/ 3/1918
7766	ROONEY, J.	D.O.W.	France	29/ 6/1918
1230	ROOTES, W. H.	K.I.A.	Gallipoli	9-10/ 5/1915
1325	ROSS, P. J.	D.O.W.	At Sea	4/ 5/1915

322 HISTORY OF THE 15th BATTALION

Reg. No.	Name.	Cause of Death.	Place of Death.	Date.
778	ROSS, W.	K.I.A.	Gallipoli	26/ 4/1915
6558	ROSSI, J.	K.I.A.	Belgium	4/ 7/1917
640	ROSSINGTON, G. M.	K.I.A.	France	11/ 4/1917
643	ROWAN, J.	K.I.A.	Gallipoli	8/ 8/1915
118	ROWE, W. J. T.	K.I.A.	France	13/ 8/1918
1792	ROY, W.	K.I.A.	Gallipoli	8/ 8/1915
861	RUSHFORTH, N. M.	K.I.A.	Gallipoli	26/ 4/1915
1080	RUSSELL, W.	D.O.W.	Alexandria	23/ 8/1915
779	RYAN, J. J.	D.O.W.	Alexandria	1/ 5/1915
2634	RYAN, J. P.	K.I.A.	France	11/ 4/1917
	RYAN, M. F. (Served as)			
1530	McKINLEY, J.	K.I.A.	Gallipoli	8/ 8/1915
7859	RYAN, R. J. A.	K.I.A.	France	4/ 7/1918
791	SALMONI, F. S.	K.I.A.	Gallipoli	26/ 4/1915
1093	SAMPSON, W. A.	K.I.A.	Gallipoli	14/ 5/1915
3445	SAMPSON, W. E.	D.O.I.	Murwillumbah, N.S.W.	16/12/1915
3858	SANDEESON, G.	D.O.W.	France	8/ 8/1916
7059	SARGOOD, J. C.	K.I.A.	Belgium	15/ 8/1917
3853	SCATENI, F.	D.O.W.	France	5/ 9/1916
7544	SCHLUMPF, A.	K.I.A.	France	8/ 6/1918
787	SCHOFIELD, N. C.	K.I.A.	Gallipoli	27/ 4/1915
786	SCHOFIELD, R. G. H.	K.I.A.	Gallipoli	24/ 5/1915
949	SCOTT, A. S.	K.I.A.	Gallipoli	28/ 4/1915
3633	SCOTT, D.	K.I.A.	France	11/ 4/1917
486	SCOTT, D. H.	D.O.W.	Egypt	12/ 5/1915
6838	SCOTT, H.	K.I.A.	Belgium	16/10/1917
793	SCOULLER, J. G.	K.I.A.	Gallipoli	9-10/ 5/1915
3851	SECCOMBE, R.	K.I.A.	France	8/ 8/1916
712	SECCOMBE, W. T.	K.I.A.	Gallipoli	10/ 5/1915
2/Lieut	SELLARS, E. G.	K.I.A.	France	23/ 6/1918
1549	SETON, T.	K.I.A.	Gallipoli	8/ 8/1915
1359	SEWELL, J. T.	K.I.A.	Gallipoli	27/ 4/1915
487	SEYMOUR, J.	D.O.W.	At Sea	10/ 5/1915
1085	SHARMAN, N. J. R.	K.I.A.	Gallipoli	9/ 8/1915
Lieut	SHAW, B. J.	K.I.A.	France	8/ 8/1918
4905	SHAW, D.R.N.	K.I.A.	France	1/ 2/1917
4907	SHAW, F. A. P.	K.I.A.	France	5/ 4/1918
489	SHAW, J.	K.I.A.	Gallipoli	10/ 5/1915
1091	SHAW, J. G.	K.I.A.	Gallipoli	7/ 8/1915
1548	SHAW, S. W.	K.I.A.	Gallipoli	10/ 5/1915
1243	SHEARING, H. H.	K.I.A.	Gallipoli	9/ 5/1915
7314	SHEEHAN, W. F. F. A. D.	K.I.A.	Belgium	8/ 8/1917
1088	SHELTON, H. W.	D.O.W.	Constantinople	3/ 9/1915
191	SHERIDAN, C.	K.I.A.	Gallipoli	10/ 5/1915
3924	SHERMAN, P. E.	K.I.A.	France	9/ 8/1916
646	SHIELDS, C.	D.O.W.	Belgium	18-19/ 7/1917
954	SHIELLS, L. J.	D.O.W.	Egypt	12/ 5/1915
4911	SHIRER, W.	K.I.A.	France	1/ 2/1917
2/Lieut	SHRUBB, A. B.	K.I.A.	France	8/ 8/1916
863	SIDNEY, E. C.	K.I.A.	Gallipoli	6/ 5/1915
1818	SIMCOCK, A. V.	D.O.W.	France	11/ 4/1917
951	SIMONS, L. J.	D.O.W.	Gallipoli	24/ 5/1915
7549	SIMONSEN, J. M.	K.I.A.	France	10/ 6/1918
950	SIMS, J. W.	D.O.I.	Lemnos	24/ 7/1915
6841	SINCLAIR, R.	K.I.A.	Belgium	21/10/1917

HISTORY OF THE 15th BATTALION 323

Reg. No.	Name.	Cause of Death.	Place of Death.	Date.
	SJOSTROM, F. A. (Served as)			
2211	WELSH, F. A.	K.I.A.	Gallipoli	7/ 8/1915
84	SKIMMING, J. C.	K.I.A.	Gallipoli	3/ 5/1915
3471	SKUSE, J. W.	K.I.A.	France	7/ 8/1916
1553	SLADE, H. A.	K.I.A.	Gallipoli	5/ 5/1915
3485	SLADEN, A. J.	D.O.W.	France	19/ 9/1918
6090	SLEIGHT, T.	K.I.A.	France	11/ 4/1917
7551	SLOAN, J.	K.I.A.	France	28/ 3/1918
797	SMALE, A. J.	D.O.W.	At Sea	12/ 5/1915
3849	SMALL, W.	K.I.A.	France	9/ 8/1916
1863	SMEDLEY, S.	K.I.A.	France	11/ 4/1917
2936	SMITH, A. D.	K.I.A.	France	28/ 1/1918
1631	SMITH, A. J.	K.I.A.	Gallipoli	1/ 5/1915
1436	SMITH, B.	K.I.A.	Gallipoli	9-10/ 5/1915
1395	SMITH, C. B.	K.I.A.	France	1/ 2/1917
648	SMITH, D. A. S.	D.O.W.	France	11/ 8/1916
492	SMITH, F.	D.O.W.	Alexandria	9/ 5/1915
790	SMITH, G.	D.O.W.	France	18/ 9/1918
1396	SMITH, G.	K.I.A.	Gallipoli	29/ 5/1915
2203	SMITH, H.	K.I.A.	Gallipoli	7/ 8/1915
343	SMITH, H. C.	K.I.A.	Gallipoli	28/ 4/1915
2/Lieut	SMITH, H. G.	D.O.W.	At Sea	10/ 5/1915
2003	SMITH, H. L.	K.I.A.	Gallipoli	8/ 8/1915
952	SMITH, J.	K.I.A.	Gallipoli	9/ 5/1915
792	SMITH, J. C. A.	K.I.A.	Gallipoli	8/ 8/1915
2204	SMITH, J. I.	K.I.A.	Gallipoli	8/ 8/1915
1632	SMITH, P.	K.I.A.	Gallipoli	9/ 8/1915
5833	SMITH, R. E.	K.I.A.	France	1/ 2/1917
667	SMITH, R. J.	D.O.W.	At Sea	5/ 9/1915
4898	SMITH, S. A.	K.I.A.	France	11/ 4/1917
794	SMYTH, C. B.	K.I.A.	Gallipoli	9/ 5/1915
2201	SNELHAM, A.	K.I.A.	Gallipoli	8/ 8/1915
956	SNELL, F. W.	D.O.W.	At Sea	3/ 5/1915
2001	SOONING, J. A.	K.I.A.	Gallipoli	8/ 8/1915
2198	SORENSEN, J. Y.	K.I.A.	France	11/ 4/1917
1398	SPELLACY, F.	K.I.A.	Gallipoli	27/ 8/1915
Lieut	SPENCER, W. J.	K.I.A.	France	4/ 7/1918
2083	SPILLANE, D. J.	K.I.A.	Gallipoli	9/ 8/1915
493	SPRITCH, T. A.	K.I.A.	Gallipoli	6/ 5/1915
3864	SPROWELL, E.	K.I.A.	France	8/ 8/1916
4364	SQUIRE, R.	D.O.W.	Belgium	23/10/1917
1263	STANLEY, A. G.	K.I.A.	France	28/ 8/1916
1244	STEEL, G. M.	K.I.A.	France	7/ 8/1916
1247	STEIN, A. J.	D.O.W.	At Sea	3/ 5/1915
858	STEPHENS, T.	K.I.A.	Gallipoli	30/ 4/1915
2414	STEVEN, A.	K.I.A.	Belgium	6/ 7/1917
1400	STEVENSON, A.	K.I.A.	Gallipoli	14-15/ 5/1915
6562	STEWART, F. M.	K.I.A.	Belgium	27/ 9/1917
494	STEWART, H.	D.O.W.	At Sea	6/ 5/1915
2640	STEWART, J. T.	K.I.A.	France	11/ 4/1917
3869	STEWART, R. J.	D.O.W.	France	14/ 8/1916
3444	STEWART, W. J.	K.I.A.	France	11/ 4/1917
1980	STILL, V. R.	K.I.A.	Gallipoli	8/ 8/1915
1554	STONE, A.	K.I.A.	Gallipoli	27/ 8/1915
2288	STOREY, A. F.	D.O.I.	Alexandria	20/ 9/1915
198	STOREY, F.	K.I.A.	Gallipoli	26/ 4/1915

324　HISTORY OF THE 15th BATTALION

Reg. No.	Name.	Cause of Death.	Place of Death.	Date.
199	STOREY, F.	K.I.A.	Gallipoli	8/ 8/1915
2200	STRACHAN, F.	K.I.A.	Gallipoli	8/ 8/1915
1401	STUART, W. A. B.	K.I.A.	Gallipoli	3/ 5/1915
6571	STUART-RUSSELL, A. B.	D.O.W.	France	4/ 7/1918
7052	STUBBINGS, F.	D.O.I.	Windsor, Q'ld.	27/11/1916
496	STUPART, G. C.	K.I.A.	Gallipoli	1/ 5/1915
	SUCKKLING, R. (Served As)			
508	VINCENT, R.	K.I.A.	Gallipoli	9-10/ 5/1915
1821	SULLIVAN, J.	K.I.A.	Gallipoli	8/ 8/1915
692	SUMMERS, A.	D.O.W.	England	31/10/1918
1552	SUTTON, D. G.	K.I.A.	Gallipoli	29/ 5/1915
200	SUTTON, O. O.	K.I.A.	France	8/ 8/1916
201	SWAIN, F. C.	K.I.A.	Gallipoli	19-20/ 5/1915
1422A	SWALLOW, H.	K.I.A.	Gallipoli	8/ 8/1915
1449	SWEENEY, C. J.	K.I.A.	France	11/ 4/1917
6346	SWEENEY, G.	K.I.A.	France	11/ 4/1917
7311	SWEET, F. L.	K.I.A.	France	27/ 9/1917
7306	SWIFT, H. D.	K.I.A.	Belgium	28/ 8/1917
656	SYVERSEN, C.	K.I.A.	Gallipoli	8/ 8/1915
1670	TAIT, L.	K.I.A.	Gallipoli	14-15/ 5/1915
644	TARGETT, R. H.	K.I.A.	France	25/ 1/1917
501	TAYLOR, D. C.	K.I.A.	Gallipoli	1/ 5/1915
1405	TAYLOR, E. A.	K.I.A.	Gallipoli	5/ 5/1915
1406	TAYLOR, G.	K.I.A.	Gallipoli	8/ 8/1915
3876	TAYLOR, H. J	K.I.A.	France	1/ 2/1917
957	TAYLOR, H. J. T.	K.I.A.	Gallipoli	10/ 5/1915
7317	TAYLOR, J.	K.I.A.	France	28/ 3/1918
202	TAYLOR, J. R.	K.I.A.	Gallipoli	27/ 8/1915
2006	TAYLOR, R. S.	K.I.A.	Gallipoli	7/ 8/1915
852	TEALE, J.	K.I.A.	Gallipoli	29/ 5/1915
1203	TEMPLE, C. W	K.I.A.	Gallipoli	14-15/ 5/1915
5762	TEMPLEMAN, W. H. S.	D.O.I.	France	24/12/1916
1672	THICKENS, W.	K.I.A.	Gallipoli	8/ 8/1915
4916	THOMAS, C.	K.I.A.	France	8/ 8/1918
7788B	THOMAS, C. L.	K.I.A.	France	4/ 7/1918
3450	THOMAS, G. S.	K.I.A.	France	6/ 8/1916
6099	THOMAS, W. H.	K.I.A.	France	1/ 2/1917
5519	THOMPSON, G.	K.I.A.	France	8/ 8/1916
3102	THOMPSON, J.	K.I.A.	France	5/ 4/1918
3875	THOMPSON, T.	D.O.W.	France	9/ 8/1916
1098	THOMPSON, W.	K.I.A.	Gallipoli	10-14/ 5/1915
206	THOMSON, A. J.	D.O.W.	England	14/ 8/1916
7786A	THRESHER, W. C.	K.I.A.	France	8/ 8/1918
502	TIGHE, A.	D.O.W.	At Sea	10/ 8/1915
2005	TILBURY, C. W.	K.I.A.	Gallipoli	8/ 8/1915
1707	TILLIDGE, H. W.	K.I.A.	Gallipoli	7/ 8/1915
1249	TIPPETT, A. E. A.	K.I.A.	Gallipoli	3/ 5/1915
1908	TOLL, F. V.	K.I.A.	Gallipoli	8/ 8/1915
5760	TOLSTOI, A.	K.I.A.	France	11/ 4/1917
7331A	TOOHEY, C.	K.I.A.	France	8/ 8/1918
1094	TOOP, R. D.	D.O.W.	At Sea	31/ 5/1915
6101	TOTTEN, R. J.	D.O.W.	France	11/ 4/1917
4917	TOWNLEY, G.	D.O.I.	France	9/ 1/1917
354	TRAISE, J. H. McG.	K.I.A.	Gallipoli	29/ 5/1915
6975	TREBILCO, H. J.	K.I.A.	Belgium	3/ 7/1917
2525A	TREEBY, F.	K.I.A.	Belgium	27/ 9/1917

HISTORY OF THE 15th BATTALION 325

Reg. No.	Name.	Cause of Death.	Place of Death.	Date.
1363	TREVETT, A. C.	K.I.A.	Gallipoli	8/ 8/1915
1671	TRICKETT, R.	K.I.A.	Gallipoli	8/ 8/1915
1561	TROYAHAN, W. J.	K.I.A.	Gallipoli	8/ 8/1915
5417	TUCKER, E. C.	D.O.W.	France	18/ 8/1918
1365	TUDOR, D. T.	D.O.I.	Germany	14/ 6/1917
1421	TURNER, A.	K.I.A.	Gallipoli	7/ 8/1915
1545	TURNOCK, J. A.	K.I.A.	Gallipoli	10/ 5/1915
1437	TYNAN, J.	K.I.A.	Gallipoli	18/ 5/1915
2422	TYNAN, P. J.	K.I.A.	France	9/ 8/1916
5758	TYSON, L. G. R.	K.I.A.	Belgium	16/ 8/1917
958	UPSON, H.	D.O.W.	Malta	5/ 7/1915
2423	URQUHART, F.	K.I.A.	France	11/ 4/1917
6577	VARCIN, M. F.	D.O.W.	France	12/ 8/1918
6578	VAUBELL, F. G.	K.I.A.	Belgium	15/10/1917
507	VEAGE, C. L.	K.I.A.	Gallipoli	9/ 5/1915
1566	VERTIGAN, J. W.	K.I.A.	Gallipoli	9/ 8/1915
2/Lieut	VIDGEN, J. G.	K.I.A.	Gallipoli	8/ 8/1915
1839	VIRGIN, R. L. H.	D.O.W.	France	31/10/1916
4609	VOGLER, J. G.	K.I.A.	France	4/ 7/1918
2208	VOLKOFF, J.	K.I.A.	Gallipoli	8/ 8/1915
6628	WAINWRIGHT, H.	K.I.A.	Belgium	27/ 9/1917
1823	WALDOCK, A. H.	K.I.A.	Gallipoli	27/ 8/1915
6104	WALDOCK, E. A.	D.O.I.	France	2/ 7/1918
2756	WALES, D. T.	K.I.A.	France	8/ 8/1916
4071	WALKER, A. G.	P.O.W.	Germany	21/10/1917
Major	WALSH, J. F.	K.I.A.	Gallipoli	28/ 4/1915
1992	WALSH, T.	K.I.A.	Gallipoli	8/ 8/1915
4399	WARD, J. H.	K.I.A.	France	6/ 8/1918
5765	WARE, G.	K.I.A.	France	1/ 2/1917
Lieut	WAREHAM, E. G.	K.I.A.	Gallipoli	10/ 5/1915
2646	WATERS, E. M.	P.O.W.	Germany	16/ 2/1917
4379	WATERS, G. Y.	K.I.A.	Belgium	1/ 7/1917
Lieut	WATERS, L. J.	K.I.A.	Gallipoli	27/ 4/1915
1117	WATLING, A.	D.O.W.	Gallipoli	7/ 8/1915
1255	WATLING, A.	K.I.A.	Gallipoli	9/ 8/1915
92	WATSON, A.	K.I.A.	France	4/ 7/1918
2647	WATSON, E. C.	K.I.A.	France	9/ 8/1916
Capt	WATSON, J. M.	K.I.A.	France	11/ 4/1917
207	WATSON, K.	D.O.W.	At Sea	4/ 5/1915
660	WATSON, R.	D.O.W.	Alexandria	14/ 5/1915
7326	WATTERSON, P. G.	K.I.A.	France	4/ 7/1918
358	WATTS, F.	D.O.W.	France	18/ 9/1918
208	WATTS, G.	D.O.W.	Mudros	30/ 8/1915
359	WATTS, G. E.	K.I.A.	Gallipoli	9/ 5/1915
959	WAUGH, S. M.	D.O.W.	Alexandria	14/ 8/1915
2013	WAYGOOD, H. W.	K.I.A.	Gallipoli	27/ 8/1915
7321	WEBBER, A. E.	D.O.W.	Belgium	27/ 2/1918
4927	WEEDON, T.	P.O.W.	Germany	
360	WEEL, A.	D.O.W.	Alexandria	5/ 7/1915
1993	WEILER, A.	K.I.A.	Gallipoli	8/ 8/1915
1824	WEIR, D. A.	K.I.A.	Gallipoli	8/ 8/1915
4309	WELLS, G. M.	D.O.I.	At Sea	
802	WEMYSS, O. S.	K.I.A.	Gallipoli	29/ 4/1915
851	WESTON, G. E.	K.I.A.	Gallipoli	9-10/ 5/1915
514	WETHERALL, W. B.	K.I.A.	Gallipoli	9/ 5/1915
1976	WETHERBY, L. P.	K.I.A.	Gallipoli	7/ 8/1915
1104	WHEATLEY, P. A.	D.O.W.	At Sea	5/ 5/1915

HISTORY OF THE 15th BATTALION

Reg. No.	Name.	Cause of Death.	Place of Death.	Date.
7841	WHEELDON, E. R.	K.I.A.	France	5/ 7/1918
804	WHIFFEN, C.	K.I.A.	Gallipoli	8/ 8/1915
1808	WHIPPS, F.	K.I.A.	Gallipoli	8/ 8/1915
2216	WHITE, F. J.	K.I.A.	Gallipoli	8/ 8/1915
3455	WHITE, T. H.	K.I.A.	France	8/ 8/1916
2209	WHITE, W. F.	K.I.A.	Gallipoli	8/ 8/1915
2/Lieut	WHITEHOUSE, N. C.	K.I.A.	Belgium	16/ 8/1917
361	WHITING, D.	K.I.A.	Gallipoli	7/ 8/1915
3452	WHITING, E. W.	K.I.A.	France	27/ 8/1916
4929	WHITMAN, T.	D.O.W.	France	4/ 6/1918
1111	WHITNEY, A. C.	D.O.I.	Alexandria	18/ 6/1915
1886	WHYMAN, B. R.	K.I.A.	Gallipoli	29/ 5/1915
2086	WICKINS, V. J.	K.I.A.	Gallipoli	8/ 8/1915
803	WIDDON, A. E.	K.I.A.	Gallipoli	30/ 4/1915
6367	WILLETT, W. H.	K.I.A.	France	11/ 4/1917
1411	WILLIAMS, C.	K.I.A.	Belgium	15/10/1916
1108	WILLIAMS, C. H. E.	K.I.A.	Gallipoli	2/ 5/1915
6112	WILLIAMS, D.	K.I.A.	Belgium	17/10/1917
5538	WILLIAMS, G.	K.I.A.	France	13/ 8/1918
6588	WILLIAMS, H. G.	K.I.A.	France	4/ 7/1918
808	WILLIAMS, J.	K.I.A.	Gallipoli	8/ 8/1915
510	WILLIAMS, J. E.	K.I.A.	Gallipoli	8/ 8/1915
2304	WILLIAMS, S. L.	K.I.A.	Gallipoli	7/ 8/1915
553	WILLIAMS, T.	D.O.W.	At Sea	12/ 8/1915
1439	WILLIAMS, T. A.	K.I.A.	Gallipoli	1/ 5/1915
7794A	WILLIAMSON, H. A.	D.O.W.	France	2/ 5/1918
3456	WILLIS, J. W.	D.O.W.	France	10/ 8/1916
Capt	WILLIS, W. O.	K.I.A.	Gallipoli	3/ 5/1915
782A	WILSON, A.	K.I.A.	Belgium	11/ 7/1917
1903	WILSON, H.	D.O.W.	Alexandria	18/ 8/1915
7789A	WILSON, H.	K.I.A.	France	5/ 7/1918
3929A	WILSON, J. B.	K.I.A.	France	4/ 7/1918
3459	WILSON, J. T.	K.I.A.	France	8/ 8/1916
1253	WILSON, L. J.	D.O.W.	At Sea	6/ 8/1915
2085	WILSON, W. J.	K.I.A.	Gallipoli	7/ 8/1915
2531	WING, R. G.	K.I.A.	France	9/ 8/1916
4401	WISE, C. B.	K.I.A.	France	8/ 8/1916
7830	WITHERS, A. L.	D.O.I.	Panama Zone	25/11/1917
5767	WITHERS, W. M. J.	K.I.A.	France	11/ 4/1917
2007	WOODBRIDGE, J. M. P.	K.I.A.	Gallipoli	8/ 8/1915
2008	WOODBRIDGE, W. I.	D.O.W.	France	14/ 8/1916
4936	WOODS, R. H.	D.O.I.	France	4/ 2/1917
811	WOODS, T. A.	D.O.W.	Alexandria	1/ 6/1915
4926	WOODWARD, C.	K.I.A.	France	8/ 8/1916
6579	WOODWARD, E. F.	K.I.A.	Belgium	15/10/1917
1112	WOODWARD, W.	K.I.A.	Gallipoli	11/ 5/1915
1029	WOOLDRIDGE, W. J.	D.O.I.	Alexandria	10/ 4/1915
6116	WOOSTER, B. G.	D.O.W.	France	23/ 6/1918
1369	WOOTTON, F. W.	D.O.W.	At Sea	8/ 5/1915
7832	WORTHINGTON, G. H.	K.I.A.	France	4/ 7/1918
5775	WORTLEY, F. A.	K.I.A.	Belgium	27/ 9/1917
1440	WRIGHT, S.	K.I.A.	Gallipoli	7/ 8/1915
1413	WRIGHT, S. J.	K.I.A.	Gallipoli	8/ 8/1915
1107	WYLES, J. H.	D.O.I.	France	2/ 4/1918
215	YATES, J. E.	K.I.A.	France	11/ 4/1917
216	YELLS, C. A.	K.I.A.	France	11/ 4/1917
2/Lieut	YOUDEN, F. C.	K.I.A.	Gallipoli	8/ 8/1915

Reg. No.	Name.	Cause of Death.	Place of Death.	Date.
543	YOUNG, C.	K.I.A.	France	11/ 4/1917
1636	YOUNG, E.	K.I.A.	Gallipoli	9/ 8/1915
6213	YOUNG, G. C.	K.I.A.	France	1/ 2/1917
1416	YOUNG, J.	K.I.A.	Gallipoli	8/ 8/1915

EXPLANATORY NOTE.

K.I.A.—Killed In Action.
D.O.W.—Died Of Wounds.
D.O.I.—Died Of Illness.
C.N.S.—Cause Not Stated.
P.O.W.—Died Whilst Prisoner Of War, Cause Not Stated.
D.O.W.—Germany—Died Of Wounds Whilst Prisoner Of War.

Where the soldier served under an assumed name, he is shown under his correct name (Served As).

www.ingramcontent.com/pod-product-compliance
Lightning Source LLC
Chambersburg PA
CBHW031132160426
43193CB00008B/116